Our Latest Longest War

OUR LATEST LONGEST WAR

Losing Hearts and Minds in Afghanistan

Edited by

LIEUTENANT COLONEL AARON B. O'CONNELL, USMC

The University of Chicago Press
Chicago and London

The University of Chicago Press, Chicago 60637
The University of Chicago Press, Ltd., London

Published 2017
Printed in the United States of America

26 25 24 23 22 21 20 19 18 17   1 2 3 4 5

ISBN-13: 978-0-226-26565-0 (cloth)
ISBN-13: 978-0-226-26579-7 (e-book)
DOI: 10.7208/chicago/9780226265797.001.0001

Library of Congress Cataloging-in-Publication Data

Names: O'Connell, Aaron B., 1973–
Title: Our latest longest war : losing hearts and minds in Afghanistan / edited by Aaron B. O'Connell.
Description: Chicago ; London : The University of Chicago Press, 2017. | Includes bibliographical references.
Identifiers: LCCN 2016034770 | ISBN 9780226265650 (cloth : alk. paper) | ISBN 9780226265797 (e-book)
Subjects: LCSH: Afghan War, 2001–
Classification: LCC DS371.412.O95 2017 | DDC 958.104/7—dc23 LC record available at https://lccn.loc.gov/2016034770

⊗ This paper meets the requirements of ANSI/NISO Z39.48-1992 (Permanence of Paper).

Contents

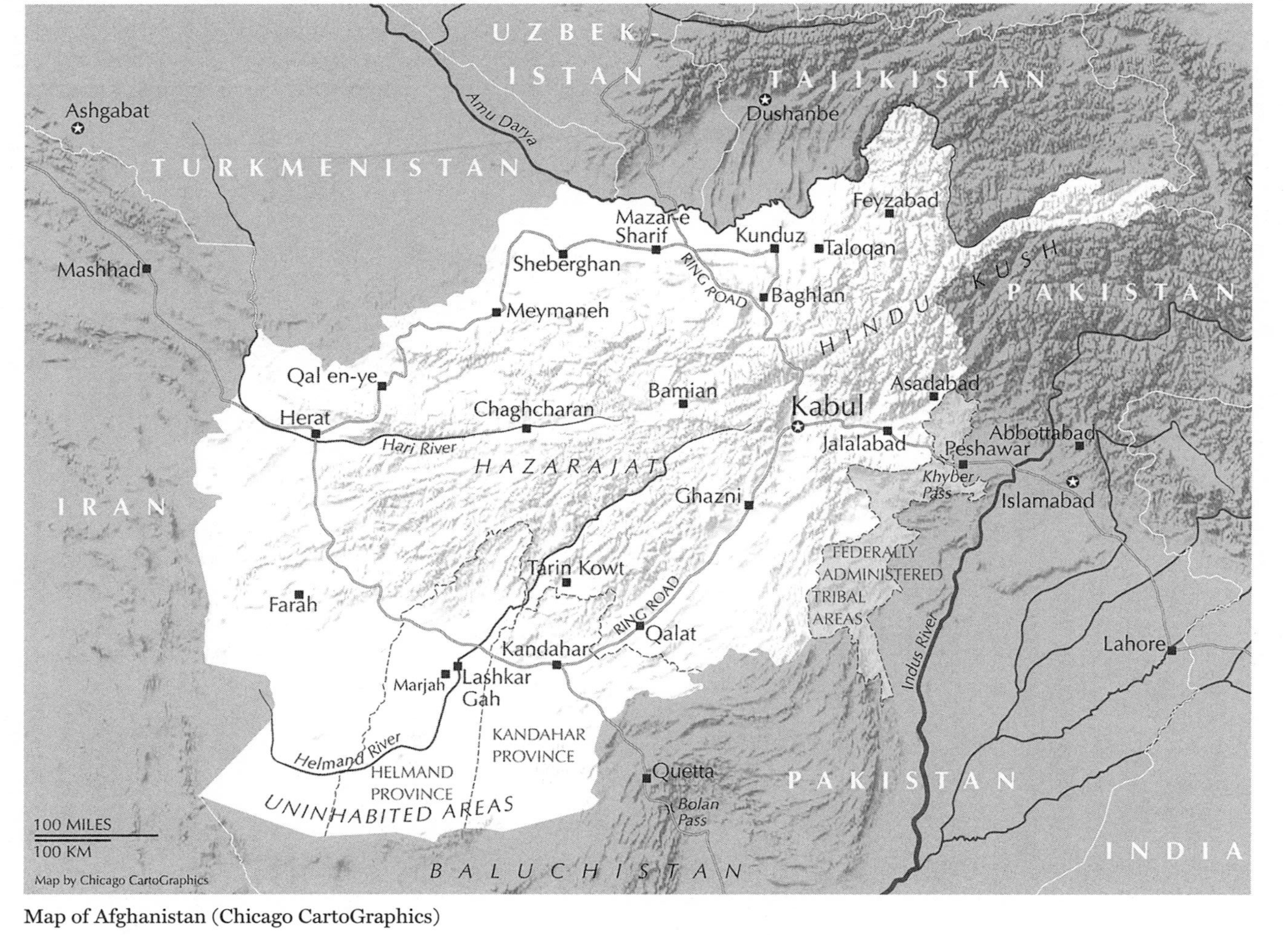

Map of Afghanistan (Chicago CartoGraphics)

INTRODUCTION

Moving Mountains

CULTURAL FRICTION IN THE AFGHANISTAN WAR

Lieutenant Colonel Aaron B. O'Connell, USMC

There is a saying about the Prophet that most Americans know, even if they know little about Islam: "If the mountain will not come to Mohammed, then Mohammed must go to the mountain."[1] This old adage—typically used to suggest that some things can't be changed, and that the wise person will bend to unmovable objects rather than repeatedly attempting the impossible—is a metaphor rich with relevance for America's latest longest war. For years, it seems, the United States and its partners strove to change things in Afghanistan that are as permanent and insurmountable as the ancient peaks that have determined so much of the country's history and culture. Despite massive advantages in resources and technology, the effort to move mountains in Afghanistan has not worked—both because of the nature of Afghan society and because the United States has its own seemingly permanent and insurmountable cultural qualities that condition how the US military operates abroad and for what purposes.

This volume is a critical appraisal of America's combat operations in Afghanistan, known in military circles as Operation Enduring Freedom, which began in October 2001 and ended in stalemate on

December 31, 2014.[2] It is also a book about institutions and culture, one that explores the organizations that fight America's wars, and the ideologies that empower and direct those institutions. The overarching thesis shared among the authors is that problems of culture were central to the war's outcomes. Specific choices by politicians and military leaders certainly shaped the course of the war—President Bush under-resourced the effort because of Iraq, and President Obama may have stayed too long or left too soon—but in the end, the most consistently important factor was the persistent cultural friction that pervaded interactions between Americans and Afghans and among coalition members. Despite three-quarters of a trillion dollars and 13 years of trying, America and its allies could not convince Afghan rulers to adopt Western norms of governance or rural Afghans to break fully with the Taliban insurgency. We argue that differing complexes of ideas about governments, states, democracy, freedom, religion, and the law were at the heart of that failure to persuade. These cultural obstacles became mountains in themselves that no president, general, or military force could dislodge or work around.

This book is also about the United States' role in the world, specifically America's pattern of using military force to promote its values overseas. Afghanistan is not the first time the United States has pledged to install democracy abroad or to protect foreign populations by winning their hearts and minds. Similar ideologies were at work in the Vietnam War, the Cold War, and earlier nation-building efforts in Haiti, Nicaragua, the Dominican Republic, and the Philippines. We argue that deep-running currents in American culture explain this pattern—currents that are unlikely to change direction anytime soon.

We expect this argument will generate some controversy. Using culture to explain the war's outcomes will probably be greeted with skepticism by those military historians who like to focus on more quantifiable factors: raw numbers of troops, trucks, days of supply, and provinces and districts lost or gained. But tracking the quantifiable factors in the Afghanistan War sheds little light, for the United States and its allies had clear advantages over the Taliban in all those categories. By 2011, over 100,000 American troops were in the country, and allies added another 40,000. That same year, the United States spent over $100 billion on combat operations at a rate of roughly $11 million per hour. Against an enemy that was armed primarily with rifles and homemade bombs, the United States deployed the most advanced technology ever used in war: remotely piloted reconnaissance aircraft, biometric retina scanners, helicopter gunships, and advanced software that mapped IEDs, tracked tribal affiliations, and gathered intelligence at the speed of light. The troops were the best trained, the best educated, and the best supplied of any that have ever fought in Afghanistan. None of these factors led to success or explain failure. Something else mattered more.[3]

Experts in culture—anthropologists in the social sciences and American studies scholars in the humanities, in particular—will likely be skeptical of our argument but for different reasons. Since the earliest days of their disciplines, those who study culture have struggled to reconcile their scholarly interests with the fact that governments want very much to use their expertise for military purposes. Some of anthropology's greatest luminaries have ended up on different sides of this debate: the father of American anthropology, Franz Boas, strongly opposed cooperation with the military; his students Margaret Mead and Ruth Benedict both participated in War Department programs during World War II, and Mead even worked for the OSS—the predecessor of the CIA.[4] A similar degree of collaboration with the US government existed in the field of American studies in the 1950s, but following the upheavals of the Vietnam War (which brought several revelations of university involvement in secret military programs), scholars in both disciplines turned decidedly away from cooperating with the military.[5] As a result, academics seeking to understand culture's effects in warfare are in something of a catch-22. If they have experience-based credibility in military affairs or work with those who do, they are often accused of militarizing academia; if they avoid the military, they lose access to the actual practitioners of warfare, who we believe have something useful to say on the topic.

The war in Afghanistan reignited this debate, particularly in regard to the Human Terrain Teams—a now-discontinued DOD program that put anthropologists on the battlefield, ostensibly to increase cultural awareness in military decision making. None of us had any involvement in that program nor are any of us anthropologists. Instead, we hold advanced degrees in a range of other academic disciplines: four of us are historians, two are political scientists, three are international relations scholars, and one has a background in the classics. We all served in Afghanistan in various roles: ambassador, rule of law advisor, infantry platoon commander, staff officer, Afghan police officer, and special assistant to the commander of the International Security Assistance Force. We are not bound together by a theoretical or methodological approach or even common backgrounds: Two of us are Marines, three are Army officers, three are Naval officers, one is from the Air Force, one is an Afghan, and two are civilians. Some of us are Republicans; some are Democrats; others are uninterested in political labels or unaffiliated with political parties. And while our various backgrounds lead us to different conclusions on a number of issues in this volume, we agree on two major points: the war has been less than fully successful, and an inability to turn lofty ideals into practical outcomes is a principal reason why.

It is likely that some readers outside academia will be uncomfortable with much of this book too, for in these essays, military veterans and still-serving officers question the conduct of the Afghanistan War and the assumptions that led to it and shaped its day-to-day prosecution. We ask, in a variety of ways, what good the billions spent did for the United States or for Afghanistan, and come up with strikingly little in the way of an answer. These are not easy topics for any American or Afghan to write about, particularly those who participated in the war. All of us are sensitive to the strong emotions both soldiers and civilians have on these issues, and we seek neither to provoke nor to offend. Our goal is simply to offer a fact-based accounting of the major events of the war and to generate debate about the assumptions and ideologies that led to those events.

Culture Wars and Turf Wars over Culture

When Americans speak of Afghanistan, the word "tribes" usually appears early in the conversation, but American society has tribes too, as does the US military. Indeed, in Afghanistan the various Special Operations Forces (SOF) were even referred to as the "SOF Tribes"—a term that highlighted their tight-knit nature and preoccupation with differentiating themselves from each other and from the conventional forces. Academics have their own scholarly tribes as well that draw boundaries based on method, subject, and pedigree. Even scholars of culture tend to come from two separate methodological communities, the social sciences and the humanities, which disagree perennially on how to study culture or even how to define it. These differences have hardened into turf wars inside the academy that flare up with regular and unhelpful skirmishes over terminology or ideology that are mostly irrelevant to all but the few in the fray.

Much like actual land disputes in Afghanistan, no academic discipline has an uncontested claim to culture's intellectual turf. Anthropologists usually name themselves as the first owners of the field, but literary scholars contest that homesteading claim. In fact, both disciplines started studying the subject at approximately the same time, but came at it from different directions and ended up staking claims in adjacent (and sometimes overlapping) conceptual spaces. Since the 1960s, the cultural turn in academia brought a number of new trespassers in—historians, political scientists, sociologists, economists, and international relations scholars—all of whom continue to debate approaches to culture to this day.[6] Because of these battles over original appropriation, too many scholars of culture devote their energies to policing boundaries rather than crossing them, and to arguing among themselves rather than speaking to lay audiences.

We take no sides on who should study culture, and we borrow from a variety of scholars and methods to make our arguments. All of us are admirers of the noted anthropologist and Afghan specialist Thomas Barfield, whose writings have done more than anything else to help senior policymakers and military officers understand Afghan culture.

If we have an implied definition of culture, it is something of disciplinary hybrid. In the pages that follow, we borrow from the work of a sociologist (Immanuel Wallerstein), a historian (Warren Susman), and a scholar of literature (Michael Denning) to describe culture as the stories individuals and groups tell themselves and others to understand themselves and the world around them.[7] Like other related terms ("worldview," "ideology," "habitus"), "culture" is a way to talk about the beliefs that have power in people's lives, whether they commit to them deliberately, borrow them from others, or repeat them uncritically simply because they have always been accepted in their communities as "common sense." Oftentimes it is this last category of ideas—the commonsense beliefs that everyone already knows—that have the most power in a community, because their wide acceptance often serves as proof of their accuracy, a substitute for truth. Such unexamined certainties function like an operating system on a computer or a phone—invisible to everyday users, but constantly shaping the lenses, screens, and texts that serve as windows into the world. And when incompatible operating systems are forced to interact, the result is usually friction: slower processing, a failure to connect, unanswered commands, and in the worst cases, a crash.

The terms "cultural friction" and "cultural obstacles" are important ones because they emphasize our central point that the problems in Afghanistan stem not from the cultures themselves but from the *interaction* of incompatible cultures—both within the Western coalition and between the Afghans and the Westerners. Friction only occurs when two objects collide; a boulder only becomes an obstacle when someone tries to climb over or smash through it. We do not think either American or Afghan culture is inherently right, wrong, or universally true, any more than a boulder is right or wrong or true. We are not interested in evaluating either society according to prescriptive moral formulas. Our argument here is simple and specific: American and Western ideals, as expressed by soldiers and civilians in the Afghan War, proved inappropriate for persuading the Afghan people to change their behaviors and narratives. What worked in theory encountered difficulties in practice. As a result, the American-led effort to stabilize Afghanistan through counterinsurgency has already failed or is on a path to failure. Few of us have any hope that a course correction is likely or possible in the future.

While the differences between Americans and Afghans were persistent and disruptive, they alone do not explain the outcomes of the war. There were also conflicts within the various departments, bureaus, and offices of the US government, and between the different elements of the International Security Assistance Force (ISAF)—the UN-authorized, NATO command that ran the war with military units and other support from 50 different countries. This too is one of our volume's major themes. Because these organizations' cultures of bureaucracy so dramatically inhibited pragmatic policy and action, we spend as much time—perhaps more—exploring the friction between various Western institutions as we do charting the mismatches between the American and Afghan peoples and their governments.

But if conflicting ideas were so central to America's failures in Afghanistan, why couldn't the various parties just change their narratives—adapt and overcome as the Marines like to say? This question misses the fact that there is an intimate link between culture and community.[8] People attach to beliefs not only because of their inherent accuracy but also because holding them marks them as members of a group, whether Pashtun or Tajik, Marine or Green Beret, New Englander or Southerner, historian or anthropologist, Republican or Democrat. Thus complex choices become even more so, as changing course places at risk the shared stories that give a community its cohesion, direction, and sense of purpose. This is particularly true with narratives that justify wars, and with books like this one that analyze and critique those narratives.

Western Modernity, Cold War Culture, and the Modern American Military

A first rule of warfare is to know one's enemy, his strengths and weaknesses, assets and liabilities. A second might be to know thyself: to frankly assess one's biases and assumptions and to evaluate their impact on both goals and tactics. In Afghanistan, the United States followed neither rule well. It did not understand the culture it was operating in, and it failed to appreciate how its own narratives and beliefs shaped action and generated friction. The result was a dramatic mismatch of means and ends that neither money nor technology nor the force of arms could overcome.

American culture shaped every aspect of the United States' involvement in the war: the decision to begin it, strategic end states, campaign plans, and individual tactical engagements. No one was free from culture's reach: it affected the policymakers in Washington, the troops in the field, and the American people who followed the war with varying degrees of interest and awareness. It was America's belief in its own special providence—a tradition stretching back to the 17th century—that led President George W. Bush not only to pursue al Qaeda in Afghanistan but also to insist that the country be remade into a democracy. It was the Cold War's culture of militarized foreign policy that made an unending and ubiquitous "war on terror" a seemingly reasonable response to the actions of several dozen people operating from Afghanistan and Germany and within the United States. And it was the modern American military's increasingly bureaucratic and technophilic style of warfighting that created regular friction with Afghans at the local and national levels. These three cultural habits brought the United States, its people, and its partners to an illogical and contradictory trio of conclusions: that a centrally run parliamentary democracy was a natural right for the Afghan people; that such a system was what they themselves wanted; and that even though it was natural and desired, it needed to be installed and defended with an occupying army of foreigners.

Each of these habits deserves explanation. How did they operate inside American society, and how do they help explain success or failure in the Afghanistan war?

The first habit concerns Western modernity and a specific American version of it known as American exceptionalism. Ever since Europeans first crossed the Atlantic, they and their American descendants have believed that their values are superior to all others and will, in time and with God's help, spread throughout the world to everyone's benefit. This prophetic, universalizing vision—which was Christian in its early iterations but developed secular analogues in the Enlightenment—has always contained a light side and a dark: the lofty rhetoric of civilization and liberation paired with military violence and race-based subjugation. The new institutions of the early modern era supported modernity's dialectic. Parliaments gave some citizens the ostensibly natural right of self-government and then denied the same right to women, slaves, and colonial subjects. Laboratories, factories, and universities produced both the evidence of reason's triumph and the tools for imposing it on others. Everywhere it spread, modernity brought with it the emblems of its contradictions: ships that carried both scientists and slaves; colonial governments that enriched the center by impoverishing the periphery; and, eventually, technologies that could connect the world or destroy it. The result was four centuries of European conquest enabled by the benevolent rhetoric of freedom and progress.[9]

Americans like to believe that their country kicked this habit—that what makes the United States exceptional is its embrace of modernity without the corruption of colonial conquest. But that story does not square with the facts.[10] New England Puritans spoke of an "errand into the wilderness"—a divine mission to establish a "city on a hill," perfect the world, and civilize its inhabitants—and then they massacred the Pequot, Narraganset, and Wampanoag tribes for being uncivilized.[11] The Founding Fathers railed against the injustice of colonialism, but then began their own century-long colonial project that reframed the conquest of the continent as civilization's blessing. Thomas Jefferson may have spoken of an "empire for liberty," and of governments "deriving their just powers from the consent of the governed," but he did so while advocating forced Indian removal and warning that "if ever we are constrained to lift the hatchet against any tribe, we will never lay it down till that tribe is exterminated."[12] This pattern of pairing emancipatory narratives with military domination continued all through the 19th century in the Mexican War, numerous Indian wars, and the Philippine-American War, which President McKinley later explained was done "to educate the Filipinos, and uplift and civilize and Christianize them."[13]

Twentieth-century presidents—both Democrats and Republicans—eventually distanced themselves from full-throated endorsements of Manifest Destiny and the White Man's Burden, but only after their predecessors seized a colony and over a dozen islands and territories in the Caribbean and the Pacific. Even after rejecting outright conquest, American presidents still retained the related assumption that the United States should use its military power to advance Enlightenment values overseas. Woodrow Wilson sent the Marines to occupy Haiti, the Dominican Republic, and Nicaragua in order to "teach the South American republics to elect good men," and fought World War I to make the world "safe for democracy."[14] Franklin D. Roosevelt justified World War II with similarly lofty rhetoric, and the eventual rehabilitations of Germany and Japan seemed to confirm that democracy could flower from seeds planted through military occupation. The Vietnam War caused a temporary loss of confidence—both in armed nation-building and in American exceptionalism more generally—but with Ronald Reagan's presidency, America returned to a providential vision of itself as a "shining city upon a hill" with a "rendezvous with destiny" to be "the last, best hope of man on earth."[15]

The Cold War only strengthened Americans' stories of their nation as democracy's guardian, giving its people and leaders a misplaced faith in the universality of American values. As President George H. W. Bush explained in 1989: "We know what works: Freedom works. We know what's right: Freedom is right. We know how to secure a more just and prosperous life for man on Earth: through free markets, free speech, free elections, and the exercise of free will unhampered by the state. For the first time in this century, for the first time in perhaps all history, man does not have to invent a system by which to live. We don't have to talk late into the night about which form of government is better."[16] The collapse of the Soviet Union provided the final proof: scholars began speaking of "the end of history"—a global consensus on the universal desirability of the West's political and economic systems.[17] Every American war fought since has been framed in one way or another as a defense of these Western values—values that shouldn't need defending if they were actually universal.

The war in Afghanistan was both a continuation of and departure from this historical pattern of remaking the world in America's image. The United States did not go to Afghanistan to colonize as it did in the American West (though that is an argument the Taliban have successfully promulgated among many distrustful Pashtuns); the original mission was to destroy al Qaeda and remove the Taliban from power. But that mission expanded into nation-building almost immediately precisely because of the pull of these expansionist values. With George W. Bush's Freedom Doctrine, parliamentary political systems and free market economics became "the non-negotiable demand of human dignity; the birthright of every person—in every civilization."[18] Elections became the proof of progress, even when they facilitated the rise of corrupt power brokers who undermined the legitimacy of the state. Experts spoke of "teaching" the Afghans democracy, as if they had no tradition of egalitarian, consultative decision making. So grounded in the faith that their objectives were benign and desired, American politicians, generals, and ordinary soldiers did far more talking than listening and tried to impose ruling systems on a people who have rejected foreign rule since the creation of the Afghan state.

If the narratives of American exceptionalism helped frame the mission in Afghanistan, a second habit of American culture—the militarization of foreign policy brought on by the Cold War—determined the tools and techniques for accomplishing it. This habit also has a long history. While the United States has never been reticent about using force to protect its interests, it only recently developed a truly global military infrastructure for influencing world affairs. In 1935, the United States had just 2 overseas bases on foreign soil. By the end of World War II, it had a network of 2,000 bases covering every continent on earth, including Antarctica, as well as the world's the largest navy and air force.[19] Successive presidents retained between 500 and 800 military bases overseas, and this enabled a pattern of augmenting diplomacy with military force—a pattern that is now a constant feature of American foreign policy. President Truman used military force roughly 5 times per year in his presidency; President Eisenhower did so 7 times per year; and President Kennedy, 13 times per year.[20] Following President Nixon's secret expansion of the Vietnam War into Laos and Cambodia (itself, an example of overreliance on military force that had tragic consequences for the Cambodian people), lawmakers passed the War Powers Resolution, which attempted to check the use of military power by requiring the president to notify Congress when placing troops in harm's way. Those reports show that presidents after Nixon conducted military operations overseas on 145 occasions between 1975 and 2010, not counting covert operations. There have been just two years after World War II when the United States conducted no overt overseas military operations: 1977 and 1979.

Many of these military operations were less than fully successful: Vietnam was the largest and still-lingering tragedy, but smaller military failures followed in Iran (1980), Lebanon (1982–1983), and Somalia (1993), to name but a few. Yet none of these experiences permanently dampened American enthusiasm for military adventurism—in fact, the number of overseas military operations increased after the Soviet Union's collapse. President William J. Clinton made nine separate "use of force" notifications to Congress in 1999—one more than President George W. Bush made in 2001.[21] The September 11 attacks and the ensuing Global War on Terrorism caused a massive expansion in the scope and scale of interventions, and by 2004, "combat-equipped forces" were conducting "anti-terror related activities" in eight countries (Afghanistan, Iraq, Georgia, Djibouti, Kenya, Ethiopia, Yemen, and Eritrea) and peacekeeping and security activities in Haiti, Bosnia and Herzegovina, and Kosovo.[22] By 2009, interventions had become so regular that President Barack Obama's reports to Congress stopped naming all the countries where military operations were occurring, stating instead that the United States had deployed "various combat-equipped forces to a number of locations in the Central, Pacific, European, Southern, and Africa Command areas of operation"—a blanket description that could conceivably include every country on earth except the United States.[23]

Our purpose here is not to condemn all American uses of force;

indeed, we would be very strange military officers if we did. In fact, in terms of large-scale conflict, most of us believe the rise of the American military has largely had a stabilizing effect on the international system —a belief reinforced by the fact that deaths through military conflict have declined precipitously since 1945.[24] But even though the globalization of American military power has helped decrease state-on-state conflict worldwide, it also has had unintended effects on American foreign policy in general and the war in Afghanistan in particular. Presidents respond to global events with the tools they have on hand. Since America's rise to superpower status after World War II, its military capabilities have steadily expanded to reach across the world, but the nonmilitary instruments of statecraft have been funded less generously and more haphazardly. For these and other reasons, the State Department was unable to provide the civilian surge President Obama called for in 2009, and the military had to step into roles even it thought inappropriate for soldiers to perform. The sheer mismatch of military to nonmilitary resources in the US government created a momentum of its own in policy discussions that left one of President Obama's closest advisors "stunned by the political power the military was exerting."[25] By 2010, nearly every field of endeavor in Afghanistan had become militarized: governance efforts, economic development, police training, and even rule of law and prison reform. Naturally, once in the hands of the military, those efforts took on military characteristics: a focus on rigid adherence to timelines and deadlines, distrust of nonmilitary interlocutors, impatience with consultations, and a desire to centralize decision making at the top. Thus, not only did the Americans fail to listen to the people they were there to help, but they also demanded action from them in ways appropriate within the US military, but less so outside it.

A final set of cultural factors concerns some shared habits of mind inside the various elements of the US Armed Forces. At first glance, the US military might seem to be the best subculture for interacting with the Pashtun tribes of Afghanistan: both have male-dominated, martial cultures where strength, physical courage, and personal honor are venerated. But that heroic stereotype of the American military is just one facet of its culture, one that is often overemphasized in films, politics, and combat memoirs. Less well known are a number of other traits that were far more foreign to the Afghans and that caused constant problems at the officer and senior advisor levels: layers of bureaucracy that inhibited effective decision making, a penchant for technology-driven solutions that alienated and angered the Afghans, and a heavy reliance on Taylorist specialization and quantitative metrics of progress. At lower levels, the military's dependence on visible markers of rank and authority made it difficult for Americans to read the power networks of Afghan society, and different cultures of violence made it hard for each side to use force in ways that the other understood. These characteristics created regular friction within the American military and between it and the society it was trying to transform.

Militaries have always relied on technology and bureaucracy to organize themselves and to fight, but since 1945, that reliance has grown decidedly more pronounced. The reasons for this are the very same factors that helped decrease state-on-state conflict after World War II: the rise of atomic weapons and the four-decade standoff between the United states and the Soviet Union. Fearing that a nuclear-armed Soviet Union would invade and conquer Western Europe, the United States built a permanent national security state and an enduring defense bureaucracy. Offices, directorates, and military commands proliferated as fast as the new Department of Defense's ample budgets would allow, and the nuclear age's technological requirements prompted a host of new engineering marvels: jet aircraft, satellites and rockets, peer-to-peer networked computers, and other high-tech information systems that sought to see through the fog of war and control the chaos of combat. A culture that had once relied on courage and personal charisma now turned increasingly toward science, engineering, and quantitative approaches to warfare. Information technology became even more important when automated data processing arrived in the 1950s, and modern computers' abilities to handle exponentially greater amounts of information generated more data and more bureaucracy: offices of statistical analysis, review boards, and quality control mechanisms. In the end, these developments pushed the armed services toward a style of warfare that privileged quantifiable metrics over human, emotional, and psychological factors.

These cultural changes made the US military much more prepared for a nuclear war that thankfully never happened, but they had adverse effects on its ability to fight counterinsurgencies, where technological and computational advantages are far less relevant. In 1960, the University of Chicago's Morris Janowitz was among the first to note a trend of "technological conservatism" in the military, where "military managers" had begun replacing leaders whose bona fides rested mostly in their social intelligence, leadership abilities, and personal courage.[26] In 1972, Ambassador Robert W. Komer's landmark study for RAND, *Bureaucracy Does Its Thing*, detailed how the US government's "business-as-usual" approach to Vietnam—an approach marred by specific "institutional constraints" and cultural frameworks—had "a significant adverse impact" on the war's prosecution.[27] In later years, historians Andrew Bacevich, Martin Van Creveld, Paul N. Edwards, James William Gibson, and others filled out the picture Komer had outlined, showing how overly complex bureaucracies, undue faith in statistics, and a tendency to overvalue technological solutions made the military ill-prepared in Vietnam.[28] They explained how General Westmoreland's Military Assistance Command, Vietnam (MACV) had to report to, or coordinate with, a host of new Cold War bureaucracies thousands of miles away—the National Security Council, the Office of the Secretary of Defense, the Joint Staff, and US Pacific Command—which made unified action a rare event. A desire to measure success on a war without fronts made body counts a principal measure of effectiveness—an approach that wholly misunderstood the drivers of the conflict and was counterproductive on the ground. Tech-heavy programs like Operation Igloo White, which spent almost $1 billion per year to emplace sensors along the Ho Chi Minh trail, had little effect on the overall course of the war. (And, much like body counts, the statistics eventually became inflated and meaningless: as a Senate report noted in 1971, the "truck kills claimed by the Air Force [in Igloo White] last year greatly exceeds the number of trucks believed by the Embassy to be in all of North Vietnam.")[29]

These problems would reoccur in Afghanistan in one way or another. The top layer of command in the war—ISAF—was a bureaucratic behemoth that had to report to even more entities than Westmoreland's MACV. The ISAF commander had two reporting chains—one to NATO and another through Central Command to the secretary of defense and the president—but he also had to meet regularly with representatives of the 15 non-NATO, non-US countries in the coalition. The commander also had to coordinate regularly with the United Nations Assistance Mission in Afghanistan (UNAMA) and the embassy in Kabul (which, by 2011, had four officers of ambassadorial rank all serving under Ambassador Eikenberry, who was himself in a power struggle with the special representative for Afghanistan and Pakistan—a position cobbled together largely by the force of will of Washington insider and Democratic Party heavyweight Richard Holbrooke). The ISAF staff had 19 general officers from various countries, some of whom lacked the security clearances to be involved in major decisions. Headquarters had separate computer systems for NATO and non-NATO traffic, and at lower levels, Marine units in Helmand Province had their own computer networks that often could not interface with the headquarters computers in Kabul.[30]

Problems with metrics added other difficulties. Perhaps because there was such difficulty communicating within the various commands and subcommands in ISAF, each produced its own assessments. By one count, over 40 different assessments of the war were being conducted in 2010, and information on significant activities (SIGACTS) was stored in 39 separate databases. A RAND study published in 2012 noted that more than a decade into the Afghanistan War, the metrics used were neither transparent nor credible nor balanced nor relevant.[31] In the final years of the war, there was still no agreement on which violence statistics to track: some organizations used security incidents, others relied on enemy-initiated attacks, and still others focused on complex and coordinated attacks. By 2015, the Department of Defense shifted its principal metric to "effective enemy-initiated attacks," an entirely new data set that made it impossible to make comparisons to previous years. The emphasis on body counts returned as well; as late as August 2015, the US commander in Afghanistan argued that the Afghan government was winning the war because Taliban losses were "three to four times" more than those of the Afghan military in 2014. (This statement obscured the fact that civilian casualties in 2014 were the highest of the entire war—hardly an indication of progress.)[32] Ryan Crocker, the US ambassador to Iraq and, later, Afghanistan, summarized the problem well: "Our whole notion [is] that we can somehow develop a mathematical model that includes concrete achievements, factor in a time frame and voilà. Iraq doesn't work that way and Afghanistan doesn't work that way."[33]

These problems with bureaucracy and metrics mostly affected commanders and senior staff officers. At more junior levels, the cultural friction between American soldiers and Afghans stemmed from different sources. The principal problem was Western soldiers' dependence on visible markers of authority. Inside most military cultures, rank communicates who is in charge, and command charts explain each organization's equities and reporting lines. None of that existed in the Pashtun villages of Afghanistan, and as a result, sergeants and lieutenants struggled to discern who was in charge and often got it wrong. Adding to this, junior leaders rarely understood how violence functions in Pashtun societies and thus either underreacted or overreacted when violence was required. Taken together, these habits of American military culture hindered the United States' ability to change Afghans' opinions about the relative merits of the Taliban and the central government in Kabul.

Conquest and Resistance: A Brief History of Warfare in Afghanistan

Just as centuries of history have shaped the boundaries of common sense in the United States, so too have a few repetitive experiences given Afghans a sense of their collective identities and a few nonnegotiable demands for their own dignity. Chief among these experiences has been a pattern of near-constant warfare that predates the Afghan state, a story in which the Pashtuns—Afghanistan's largest ethnic group—have always played a principal role. Geography matters too, and Afghanistan's mountains, which have both defined the country's boundaries and hardened its people, are important for understanding how they think, live, and fight. Finally, the Pashtuns' own exceptionalist narratives—a set of norms known colloquially as *Pashtunwali*—have their own internal rules and assumptions, which rarely matched up with those of the foreigners fighting in their mountains. These three interconnected factors made Afghanistan perhaps the worst possible testing ground for a Western democratic experiment conducted at the point of a gun.

The oldest and most permanent influence on Afghanistan has been its mountains, which do much to explain why it has been a highway of conquest for centuries.[34] The Indian subcontinent—present-day India, Pakistan, and Bangladesh—has long been of interest to invaders. For those coming from the West, the Hindu Kush and the Sulaiman mountain ranges present formidable obstacles. Two breaks in the highlands give passage to India and both are accessed from Afghanistan: the famed Khyber Pass near Jalalabad and the Bolan Pass southeast of Kandahar. A break in Afghanistan's northern highlands is one of the few that allow access to the Middle East from Eurasia, a route Genghis Khan slashed and burned through in the early 13th century. In the south, mountains give way to desert, which runs across the border with Pakistan's Baluchistan Province. Between the hills and the sand is a strip of fertile soil running across Helmand and Kandahar Provinces that the Pashtuns have used for centuries to grow grapes, pomegranates, cotton, and now, more than anything else, poppy. Because of the mountains, the desert, and the strategic land routes through them, Afghanistan's people have seen a steady pattern of invasion and conquest followed by eventual but inexorable expulsion of the foreigners since Alexander the Great invaded in 330 BC.

Mountains also do much to explain Afghan xenophobia, as well as the fractious relations between the country's many ethnicities, tribes, and subtribes. The hand-shaped Pamir range reaches into the center of the country, separating southern Pashtuns from northern Tajiks and Uzbeks, who have fought each other since time immemorial. The wrist of the hand, which covers northeastern Afghanistan, protects some of the fiercest and most isolated tribes in the world in Kunar and Nuristan Provinces—areas that resisted Islam until they were forcibly converted in the 19th century. The high mountains in the center of the country—the barren Hazarajat—protect and isolate the poorest and most abused of Afghanistan's ethnic minorities: the Shi'ite Hazara, who still bear the genealogical traces of the region's 13th-century Mongol conquerors.

There has been no real census of the population in years, but most ethnographers estimate that Afghanistan has roughly 30 million people, concentrated mostly in the south and east. The Pashtuns, the largest ethnicity, make up 40 percent of the population, followed closely by the Tajiks (30 percent). The Hazara of the central mountains are the third largest (15 percent), followed by the Uzbeks and Turkmen of the north and northwest (10 percent), the seminomadic Aimaq of the west and northwest (5 percent), and a smattering of other ethnicities: Parsiwans, Baluchs, and Afghan Arabs who usually speak Persian or Uzbek—not Arabic. As the largest group, the Pashtuns have always held pride of place in Afghan society, so much so that even today some speak of Afghanistan as Pashtunistan. But numbers can be misleading too, for Afghans are famed for breaking tribal alliances, choosing partnerships of convenience, and fighting with each other—a reputation proven by the fact that most of the leaders of both the American-backed Afghan government and the Taliban are Pashtuns.

There are between 10 and 15 million Pashtuns in Afghanistan and another 20 million in Pakistan. They break down into four major tribes that self-divide further into over 350 clans.[35] And while all of Afghanistan's Pashtuns still number less than half of the country's population, they are the most important group for understanding the conflict, because it is in many ways an intra-Pashtun civil war: the Ghilzai Pashtuns of the mountainous east provide the Taliban with most of their foot soldiers, and the Durrani Pashtuns of the south have almost always held the reins of power in Kabul and Kandahar. The story of these two tribes' constant fighting—which predates the Afghan state and continues today—lays bare the challenges of building a functional and peaceful Afghanistan.

The Durrani tribe has always been the more urban and politically successful of the two, but the Ghilzai tribe is larger, more rural, and, by most accounts, tougher. Throughout the 16th and 17th centuries, as Europeans were just beginning their conquest of the Americas, the Pashtun lands were divided between two competing powers: the Mughal Empire, which controlled Kabul, Kandahar, and points east; and the Persian Safavid Empire, which controlled western Afghanistan and modern-day Iran. For much of that period, the Ghilzais and Durranis sometimes collaborated, sometimes competed, but mostly enriched themselves through cooperation with the Persians. That pattern changed in 1709, when the Ghilzais revolted and defeated both the Persians and the Durranis.[36] The Durrani Pashtuns helped the Persians regain power in the 1730s, and a young, charismatic chief named Ahmad Shah became commander of the Persian king's bodyguards. When the Persian king was assassinated, Ahmad Shah robbed the coffers, assembled a cavalry force of 4,000 men, and returned to Kandahar. Along the way, a council of Pashtun elders elected him the paramount chief of the Durranis, and in 1747, the Afghan kingdom was born.[37]

Armed with men, money, and religious legitimacy, Ahmad Shah embarked on a two-decade campaign that gave him tenuous control over all of modern Afghanistan, Pakistan, and portions of India and Iran. His descendants quickly lost most of what he had gained. Challenges from relatives and nonblood rivals persisted through the end of the 18th century and were dealt with via the usual methods: imprisonment, exile, blinding, torture, and execution, sometimes by "progressive dismemberment."[38] The Ghilzais participated in a number of these rebellions against the Durranis but never succeeded in regaining their earlier dominance. With only a few brief exceptions, members of two Durrani clans—the Popalzais and the Barakzais—ruled Afghanistan until 1978.

One tribe holding the formal reins of power did not mean an end to warfare in Afghanistan, however, for the government's writ rarely extended outside the few urban centers or productive agricultural areas. Peace with rivals was typically bought through subsidies or temporarily gained through punitive expeditions. Nothing approaching a social contract between the urban rulers and the rural subjects existed, except perhaps for an oft-violated tacit agreement to leave each other alone.

This is a key difference between Afghanistan and the United States, something that is well understood by anthropologists like Thomas Barfield, but seemingly less so by those who sought to transform Afghanistan into a modern liberal state. For almost all of America's history, its people have viewed the government as a public institution. While some argue that local rules should trump national ones, and others protest the inequality inherent in the system, the vast majority of Americans still believe their government provides them services, of which safety is the most important. This narrative has broad legitimacy not only because it is mostly accurate, but also because the federal government has held a monopoly on the use of force in the United States since the Civil War. Challenges to that monopoly have emerged from time to time (Ku Klux Klan terrorism, race riots, and armed standoffs at Waco, Ruby Ridge, and elsewhere), but these movements have largely been disarmed and delegitimized. As a result, the state's writ is largely accepted, and most Americans operate within its guidelines, using nonviolent methods to petition their government and to seek redress of grievances.

Central Asia does not have anything like this century-long Western tradition of acquiescing to federal power. In Afghanistan, states have always been the private property of the rulers—not the people. Thus, for the 150 years before the US intervention, Afghans could count on only two things from their rulers: a demand for taxes *without* the provision of services, and, if they failed to pay, retributive violence until they did. Those close to the seats of power—typically Kabul's elites and Durrani Pashtuns with tribal connections to the emir—sometimes found reasons to cooperate with the central government, but this never approached a Rousseauian social contract between rulers and ruled. Because of this history, the majority of Afghans are more distrustful of state power than even the most hard-line of American libertarians, and as afraid of the police as African Americans in the Jim Crow South.

Afghans' tradition of resisting federal authority would have made any effort to democratize the country difficult, but the added history of foreign military intervention in the region made that project all but impossible from the outset. This is another key difference between Americans and Afghans that shapes how each sees the world. In America, the European colonizers became the federal government, which then expanded its reach and authority steadily across the continent. The last time a foreign army invaded the United States was in the War of 1812. Afghans, on the other hand, suffered through three British invasions and a decade-long Soviet occupation. In all four conflicts, the Afghans eventually ejected the invaders. This history has given Afghans both confidence and patience in their military operations, which proved valuable assets for opposing the American democratic experiment in their land.

The history of these earlier conflicts explains much about how Afghans have viewed this latest war in their country. The First Anglo-Afghan War began in 1838, when the British suspected that the Afghan emir, a Durrani Pashtun named Dost Mohammed, had grown too friendly with the encroaching Russian Empire and needed replacing. The British invaded from India with 20,000 troops, bought off the Ghilzai clans along their march, and occupied Kandahar. Dost Mohammed fled, and the British replaced him with another Durrani—Shah Shuja, the aging grandson of Ahmad Shah Durrani. But the military victory did not ensure peace, and over the ensuing two years, British spending in Kabul unbalanced the economy and the soldiers' carousing offended the conservative Muslim population. In the end, it was the Ghilzais who broke first after the British halted the subsidy payments that had enabled the initial invasion. Afghans of all stripes—Pashtuns, Uzbeks, Tajiks, and others—joined forces to eject the foreigners. Under constant attack in Kabul, the British brokered a deal for safe passage back to India, but the Ghilzais tergiversated and massacred all but one of them as they approached the Khyber Pass. Once returned to the throne, Dost Mohammed conquered the very Ghilzais who had enabled his return, whom he only subdued after six separate insurrections. For the next 30 years, Dost Mohammed conquered and reconquered northern and western Afghanistan and fought off several fratricidal challenges from his own Durrani relatives.[39]

The Second Anglo-Afghan War followed a pattern similar to the first. When the Afghan emir refused to accept a British diplomatic mission in Kabul in 1878, the British invaded again. They quickly seized Kandahar and forced the Afghans to accept their terms, but defeating the Afghans militarily did not secure a lasting peace. As with the First Anglo-Afghan War, a dispute over subsidy payments was the spark that ignited the powder. When the new British diplomatic staff arrived in Kabul, they found themselves facing angry Afghan troops whose salaries had been cut. British troops fired on the assembled crowd and the city erupted into violence. A mob stormed the British mission and killed all therein, which prompted Britain to unleash a punitive campaign that would turn the few remaining moderate Afghans away from cooperation with the invaders. "Every Afghan brought to death I shall regard as one scoundrel the less in a nest of scoundrelism," British General Frederick Roberts wrote. "Anyone found in arms should be killed on the spot like vermin."[40] Soon thereafter, the Durrani emir abdicated, General Roberts declared martial law, and thousands of Afghans (mostly Ghilzais urged on by a charismatic mullah known as the "Perfume of the Universe") rose up once again to eject the Christian invaders. After an initial Afghan victory in the Battle of Maiwand, British firepower eventually won the day, and the British departed Afghanistan in 1881, leaving a new Durrani on the throne: the Iron Emir, Abdur Rahman Khan, whom they endowed with a healthy subsidy to keep Afghanistan firmly in the British orbit.[41]

Even after the British departure, tribal conflict persisted, both within the Pashtun tribes and between Pashtuns and Afghanistan's other ethnicities. By most accounts, Rahman was the most successful in quelling rebellion, and he built that success on British money, religious authority, and sheer brutality. Like his predecessors, his initial position was tenuous, as his own Durrani kinsmen assembled an army to defeat him as soon as he assumed the throne. In response, Rahman diverted British money and weapons to the Ghilzai Pashtuns to defeat his challengers, and then put down a separate Ghilzai revolt that followed. When mullahs protested his rule, he proclaimed himself divine, took over the religious institutions, and insisted that he alone had the right to call a jihad. Using that religious authority, he declared an anti-Shia campaign against the Hazara, mobilized the Ghilzai to win it, and then enslaved thousands of the losers. In the 1890s, he conquered the last remaining animistic regions of the northeast, turning Kafiristan (Land of the Infidels) into Nuristan (Land of Light). To break the power of the Ghilzais, he forcibly migrated some 10,000 to the northern Tajik lands of Kunduz and Baglan Provinces—areas that still suffer from ethnic conflict and Taliban violence as a result. He centralized the state's institutions, required exams for government officials, reformed the legal system, created a modern cabinet, and raised an army, which he used to stamp out over 40 tribal revolts in his 20-year reign. Multifaceted in his approach, he sometimes bought off rivals, other times took their children as hostages, employed a vast network of spies, orchestrated arranged marriages, and, when needed, executed rivals and razed villages to the ground. By his own account, he killed more than 100,000 of his own people. And yet while Rahman had as close to a monopoly on the use of force as Afghanistan has ever seen, even he never truly controlled the rural regions. He created the modern Afghan state, but his direct control of its inhabitants never extended far beyond Kabul.[42]

The Iron Emir's descendants had similar problems balancing urban and rural factions, but they lacked Rahman's savvy and eventually paid heavy prices. With the conservative religious elites temporarily disempowered by Rahman's rule, urban reformers gained strength and argued for greater attention to modern ideas, science, and engagement with the outside world. Rahman's son tolerated the urbanites for a time, but his successor, Amanullah, tilted heavily toward them in the name of reform. He started, and lost, the short-lived Third Anglo-Afghan War, and then instituted a series of progressive laws to bring Afghanistan into the modern world. He established a constitution, a government budget, new taxes, and a secular legal code, and abolished domestic slavery, all of which prompted the Ghilzais to revolt yet again. After putting down the rebellion and executing its leaders, Amanullah departed on a year-long tour of the world. Upon his return, in a new Rolls-Royce no less, he demanded a minimum age for marriage, coeducational schools, and the abolishment of the *purdah*—the wearing of the veil. Rural conservative tribes in the east revolted and their rebellion turned into a broader civil war. In 1929, Amanullah fled in his Rolls-Royce, which, in a telling irony, got stuck in the snow. The West's most advanced technology, it seems, could not overcome Afghanistan's harsh environment.

The 50 years that followed Amanullah's reign were perhaps the closest thing to peace Afghanistan has known in its history. A new Durrani family—the Barakzai Musahiban brothers—took power and elevated to the throne 19-year-old Zahir Shah, who ruled in name while his brothers governed in practice. They first placated the rural and religious conservatives by reinstating the veil, reducing land taxes, and exempting the most powerful tribes from military conscription. As urban reform movements grew in power in later years, the Musahibans acceded to incremental social change, mostly only in Kabul, but also increased taxation on the urban economy and brought the first modern corporations to Kabul. Once the Cold War began, they courted both the Americans and the Soviets for development and military aid. With the economy buoyed by both dollars and rubles, Afghanistan's rulers seemed to have found a working governing model: salutary neglect with the mostly rural religious conservatives, incremental progressive reform in the urban centers, and a steady appeal to outsiders for the resources the state was too weak to extract from its own people.[43]

What followed was an era of relative calm, and in the 1960s, Westerners could visit even the most rural areas of Afghanistan without fear for their safety. The peace was only temporary, however, and,

Figure I.1 Kabul in the 1960s. Development aid from both the United States and the Soviet Union allowed for social progress in Kabul without taxing and angering the deeply religious and conservative rural areas. (Zh. Angelov / Getty Images)

like the Iron Emir's reign, was largely dependent on the foreign aid that made up two-thirds of government revenues by the mid-1970s.[44] Challenges now came from modernists and religious conservatives in Kabul as well as from rural Ghilzais, and the Musahiban regime responded with arrests and authoritarian measures. In 1973, the king's own cousin, Mohammed Daúd, overthrew him in a bloodless coup and reverted to the harsh methods of an earlier era, arresting or exiling hard-line religious figures like Burhanuddin Rabbani and Gulbaddin Hekmatyar. Soviet aid empowered socialist reformers in the capital, and a strong communist party, the PDPA, became the principal vehicle for advancing the urban progressives' agenda. Even here, however, tribal affiliations did not disappear: one faction of the PDPA—the Khalqis—was Ghilzai-dominated, radical in its objectives, and, in good Soviet fashion, opposed to all religion, including Islam. The Khalqis' rivals, the Parchamists, had better and stronger relations with the Musahiban rulers, wanted incremental change, and were comfortable making concessions to the conservative religious elite. Led by Hafizullah Amin, the more extreme Khalqis pushed the communist party into open conflict with itself, and in 1978, the

Khalqis overthrew Daúd. For the first time in Afghanistan's modern history, a Ghilzai held the reins of power in Kabul.

Once in office, Hafizullah Amin overreached almost immediately, and his lack of moderation would lead directly to the Soviet invasion a year later. First, he muscled out his rivals within the party, and then attempted almost all the progressive reforms that Amanullah had failed to enact a generation earlier, with predictable results. As resistance grew throughout the country (including, of course, among many of his own fellow Ghilzais), Amin arrested thousands, purged dissenters from the party, destroyed villages, and executed challengers from prominent religious families. Even though Amin was a communist ideologue, and ran the very communist party the Soviets had supported, the Brezhnev regime concluded that it could not allow such chaos on the Soviet Union's southern border. In December 1979, the Soviets invaded.

The brutality of the 10-year Soviet occupation of Afghanistan is already well known; what is more important here is how American actions in that war helped empower the religious extremists that would eventually destabilize Afghanistan. Eager to repay the Soviets for their support of the communists in the Vietnam War, the United States began channeling covert military aid through Pakistan to the groups that were the most committed to bringing down the communists, namely, the Islamists. Gulbaddin Hekmatyar's Ghilzai-dominated Hezb-i-Islami was the best organized of the groups, and significant aid flowed to it, as well as to another Ghilzai militia under Yunis Khalis. Tajik Islamists, led by Burhanuddin Rabbani and Ahmed Shah Massoud, also proved effective fighters. Foreigners came too. Encouraged by Pakistan, who incentivized the jihad with American dollars and US-bought weapons, some 35,000 Muslim radicals from 43 states traveled to Afghanistan to fight the Soviet infidels between 1982 and 1992.[45] Among them was a wealthy young Saudi, Osama bin Ladin, who was almost killed on several occasions, mostly because of his own basic military incompetence.[46]

In the years following the Soviet expulsion, the various Mujahideen groups descended into internecine conflict. Forces that were once united in their hatred of the infidel foreigners now fell back on older enmities: Tajiks and Uzbeks versus Pashtuns in some cases, and Pashtuns versus Pashtuns in others. By 1993, with Pakistan supporting Hekmatyar's Pashtuns and India backing the Tajik forces of Rabbani and Massoud, the Afghan Civil War settled into a seemingly intractable stalemate. In early 1994, however, a new Pashtun group, also dominated by Ghilzai foot soldiers and led by a one eyed-cleric named Mullah Omar, became Pakistan's newest proxy. Aided by Pakistani arms and Saudi money, the Taliban recruited 20,000 Pakistani Pashtun fighters in just six months and defeated most of the remaining Mujahideen forces. By the end of 1996, Kabul had fallen and only Massoud's and Rabbani's forces (whom the Americans would later christen the Northern Alliance) remained unconquered.[47]

When the Taliban took power, they immediately forged a partnership with Osama bin Ladin's al Qaeda (literally, "the base"), which by this point had shifted its focus from the Soviet Union to the United States. Angry over American support for Israel and over US military bases in Saudi Arabia, Bin Ladin dreamed of igniting a global war that would both eject the "crusaders" and topple pro-American regimes throughout the Muslim world. His plan was well conceived. Drawing on his own experience with the Soviets, and mindful of the US failure in Vietnam, Bin Ladin predicted that even the most powerful military would struggle against an insurgency, particularly in the harsh terrain of Afghanistan. A long costly war would weaken the United States financially and sap American morale. Muslims the world over—even moderate Muslims—would have to choose: either side with the infidel invaders or join the global struggle to defeat them. To lure the Americans in, all that was necessary was a spectacular attack that would force America's hand. Bombings throughout the 1990s—the Yemen hotel bombings in 1992, the first World Trade Center in 1993, the US embassies in Kenya and Tanzania in 1998—and the attack on the USS *Cole* in 2000 produced only US cruise missile strikes and tough talk, but with the September 11 attacks of 2001, Bin Ladin got almost exactly what he wanted. When the Taliban refused to turn over al Qaeda (for reasons logical to any Pashtun, but less so to the Americans), the United States invaded Afghanistan and toppled the government within weeks. Bin Ladin escaped into hiding in Pakistan, where he remained until Navy SEALs killed him in Abbottabad in 2011.[48]

Decisions concerning the use of military force are almost always controversial, but in most of the world, even in most Muslim countries, the decisions to attack al Qaeda and to topple the Taliban were not. Nor did the follow-on decisions by the United States and United Nations to rebuild Afghanistan produce the global awakening Bin Ladin hoped for; he would have to wait for the 2003 invasion of Iraq for that dream to come true. But when America's Afghan mission began to falter, it did so along three enduring fault lines that have existed for centuries—fault lines that this abbreviated history of Afghanistan has attempted to expose.

The first is the intra-Pashtun tribal divide between the Ghilzais and the Durranis. From 2002 to 2014, Kabul was run by Hamid Karzai, a Popalzai Durrani—the very clan of the first ruler of Afghanistan, Ahmed Shah Durrani. Even after being ousted from power, the Taliban remained dominated by Ghilzais. With three centuries of Ghilzai-Durrani feuds as prologue, it should have surprised no one when the Afghans continued to follow a similar script as the Americans attempted to build Afghanistan anew.

The second fault line divides urban and rural Afghans, specifically in regard to the role and utility of the government in Afghan society. Since statehood, some Afghans in the urban areas have supported (or at least acquiesced to) the central government, because it usually gave them something: security in the city or access to the rulers' patronage networks. Rural Afghans, on the other hand, have had only occasional interaction with the Kabul government, usually when it demanded payment or punished rebellion. Thus, the Westerners' narrative of states as providers of services and protectors of basic rights was occasionally well received in the urban areas but rarely outside them, where the Taliban consistently found their strongest support.

Adding to the tribal and geographic fault lines is a cultural divide that has separated Afghans from non-Afghans for centuries. The single strongest narrative in Afghan culture concerns the duty to resist outside interference and to defend Islam, and so, naturally, many Afghans understood a NATO intervention composed mostly of Westerners (read: Christians) in a similar light. The Americans' calls for democracy may have stemmed from good motivations, but they sounded nearly identical to earlier occupations and reform movements, which offended religious conservatives and, when accompanied by soldiers, frightened everyone. These three historical trends began long before the US invasion, and persisted long after—indeed, for most Afghans, they will likely continue for generations.

Pashtun Culture and Afghan Ways of Warfare

Different experiences were not the only obstacles to successful cooperation between Americans and Afghans; the Pashtuns' own entrenched ideas about honor, Islam, and democracy also led to enduring friction with the foreigners in their lands. And while less than half of the Afghan population is Pashtun, Pashtun resistance became a center of gravity in the war, because almost everywhere Pashtuns lived or came into contact with Afghanistan's other ethnicities, Taliban violence seemed to follow (see fig. I.2).

In 2008, two scholars of the Afghan War, Thomas H. Johnson and M. Chris Mason probed this overlap with a basic but crucial question: why has the Taliban's militant Islamism taken root so well in the Pashtun lands? Part of their answer was Pashtun culture, more specifically *Pashtunwali*—the social code of the Pashtuns. *Pashtunwali* is not a written legal code, but it carries the force of law nonetheless. It is a loose set of social expectations and customs, malleable at times, rigid at others, that melds local practice with Islam and provides centuries-old practices for resolving grievances and maintaining social equilibrium.[49] Essentially communal in its outlook, it both binds individuals together in collective responsibilities and protects personal autonomy in ways that even committed libertarians might find extreme. Because it has a high tolerance for violence, Westerners have often mistaken it for lawlessness, but the opposite is more accurate. For over 1,000

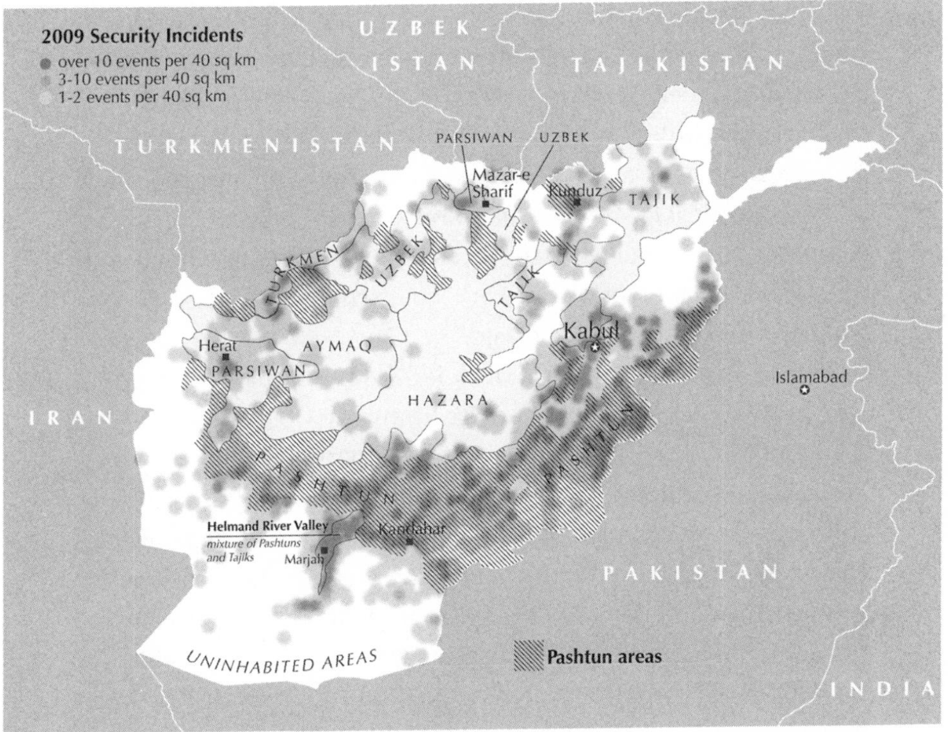

Figure I.2 Areas of Taliban influence, ca. 2009. The Taliban is a Pashtun movement that rejects the multiethnic coalition government in Kabul. As a result, most of Afghanistan's violence occurs in Pashtun areas and where Pashtuns and other ethnicities come into contact. (Chicago CartoGraphics)

years, *Pashtunwali* has provided a system of governance within the Pashtun tribes precisely by adjudicating when violence is acceptable and when it is not. Among its key elements are the primacy of honor (*nang*), an uncompromising sense of male personal autonomy, a non-negotiable requirement to resist outside interference, and the necessity of seeking revenge (*badal*) when honor has been affronted.

Nang, or honor, is the essential life resource for all adult Pashtun men—as important as water or food. It is not an abstract concept of using violence to protect one's reputation (a concept early Americans understood well—just ask Alexander Hamilton or Andrew Jackson); rather it is a man's "obligation to protect the inviolability of his person, his property, and his women."[50] For this reason, *nang* is inextricably connected to personal autonomy in a way that is best described as radical egalitarianism. No Pashtun man may tell another what to do. Even tribal leaders are at most "first among equals"—respected, but unable to give orders outside their immediate families. In fact, Pashtuns' focus on personal freedom explains many of the near-constant rebellions against fellow Pashtuns in Kabul and foreign invaders alike. As one Pashtun explained to the British in 1809, "We are content with discord, we are content with alarms, we are content with blood . . . we will never be content with a master."[51]

There are "masters" in Pashtun society, however, but only two types, and both govern when and how Pashtuns use violence. The first is the family patriarch. (For all the talk about personal freedom among Pashtuns, it is important to remember that none of this applies to women, who remain partially enslaved across much of Afghanistan.) Inside the immediate family, male elders can make decisions for younger men and demand loyalty from them. In fact, the communal nature of Pashtun life demands that all accept responsibility for the actions of other family members and take collective action when family members—male or female—have been wronged.

The second type of Pashtun master is Islam, or, more specifically, a credible mullah who makes the case that Islam has been affronted and requires defending. Thus, while the tribal khans cannot demand anything other than temporary obedience to a just military cause (and the men usually vote to select the militia leader), Pashtuns' resistance to coercion falls away when a mullah calls for jihad. Thus, as Johnson and Mason explain, "Pashtunwali creates a conservative dynamic in which large-scale warfare and social change take place only under religious leadership—such as that of the Taliban's Mullah Omar."[52]

Two other concepts—hospitality (*melmastia*) and revenge (*badal*)—impose other obligations on Pashtuns and provide direction to their day-to-day living. For all their focus on personal autonomy, Pashtuns will lose honor if they refuse to protect guests, and this binds them to whoever asks for hospitality, even their own enemies. This explains the Taliban's refusal to turn over al Qaeda in September

2001—something that the threat of an American invasion did nothing to change. *Badal,* which means both "revenge" and "exchange," is the primary mechanism for settling grievances in Pashtun society, and as with almost everything, it is first and foremost a process for restoring honor. Violence is a critical component of *badal*—the cycles of revenge killings, blood feuds, and honor killings of women make this fact undeniable—but it is not lawless. In fact, *Pashtunwali*'s process for addressing serious crimes is far older than any American law, and Pashtuns are inherently convinced of its basic superiority.

From this quick overview of *Pashtunwali,* it should be clear that Pashtun culture presents a number of obstacles to any foreign effort to target al Qaeda or the Taliban or to import even seemingly benevolent ideas like American democracy. First, just as Americans have notions of their own unique and superior culture, so do Pashtuns (in fact, Pashtun exceptionalism is much older and probably far stronger than the American version). Second, as far as Pashtun men are concerned, democracy is already alive and well in Pashtun society. Tribal decision making *has always* been rule by the people, complete with voting and debates, and it has existed in Afghanistan for thousands of years. While the system of *shuras* and *jirgas* excludes women, as far as the men are concerned, it needs none of the improvements offered by outsiders, and certainly not from outsiders who are not Muslims. Third, when the outsiders are soldiers with guns, they present a prima facie challenge to Pashtun honor, and when those soldiers then radio back to headquarters instead of making their own decisions, they show themselves to lack the basic autonomy and honor to merit respect. Finally, when violence leads to killing, *Pashtunwali* demands *badal,* and foreigners do not understand (nor would they be accepted into) the tribal councils that are the principal forum for resolving grievances nonviolently. The only tools left are violent ones, and there are no statutes of limitations. As one Pashtun proverb puts it, "I took my revenge after a hundred years, and I only regret that I acted in haste."[53] These were the mountains of Afghan culture that US policymakers tried to move for over a decade with little success.

From Counterterrorism to Counterinsurgency

Given these mismatches between US and Afghan history and culture, it should have been obvious that a wholesale transformation of Afghan society and politics was always a bridge too far. In fact, this *was* understood by some of President George W. Bush's closest advisors, and as a presidential candidate, Bush had explicitly denounced nation-building as an inappropriate role for the US military.[54] And yet just weeks after beginning a counterterrorism operation to destroy al Qaeda and overthrow the Taliban, the president formally committed the United States to a strategic partnership with Afghanistan that would "ensure security, stability and reconstruction for Afghanistan, and foster representative and accountable government for all Afghan women and men."[55] In 2004, the United States committed over $4 billion for these tasks, and in 2006, it signed on to the expansive Afghanistan Compact, which pledged support for almost every function a government undertakes: security, governance, rule of law, human rights, private sector development, education, health, agricultural and rural development, and counternarcotics, among others.[56] During those years, the Taliban slowly reinfiltrated from Pakistan, and by the end of George W. Bush's presidency, they had de facto control over large portions of southern and eastern Afghanistan.

When President Barack Obama took office in 2009, he revised the war goals downward, tripled the troop levels, and adopted a counterinsurgency strategy that militarized almost all the governance and development efforts in the country.[57] That strategy, known colloquially in military circles as the "Anaconda Strategy," was the war's strategic blueprint from 2009 until 2011. Thereafter, in ways similar to President Richard M. Nixon's Vietnamization program, the United States shifted to "transition"—drawing down forces and handing the war over to the Afghans. The combat mission ended in December 2014 and ISAF folded up its flag and departed. Since then, American assistance to Afghanistan has been largely financial with only a small contingent of troops still in the country for the purposes of training

Figure I.3 The "Anaconda" counterinsurgency strategy in Afghanistan. By protecting civilians from the Taliban and offering them jobs, governance, basic services, and rule of law, the military hoped to squeeze the life out of the insurgency, just as an anaconda suffocates its prey. (Department of Defense)

and advising Afghan forces and conducting the occasional counterterrorism operation.

The military likes to describe the Anaconda Strategy as "population-centric counterinsurgency," but it is really a blueprint for militarized nation-building. Its ideas were first developed as doctrine in *The U.S. Army/Marine Corps Counterinsurgency Field Manual,* and then field-tested in Iraq under the leadership of General David H. Petraeus, who had written his doctoral dissertation at Princeton University on the US Army and the Vietnam War. Inferring lessons from those conflicts, Petraeus's strategy in Afghanistan proceeded from the first principle that the insurgency's strength flowed from the civilians, who either were cowed by the Taliban or cooperated willingly out of frustration with the central government's incompetence and predatory behavior. Therefore, the keys to victory were twofold: protect the population and install a working social contract between the government and the governed. Basic safety and viable, legitimate, enduring state institutions would then squeeze the life out of the insurgency, much as a constrictor suffocates its prey.

The Anaconda Strategy was not only the overarching framework for counterinsurgency operations in Afghanistan; it also provides the structure of this book. Each of the chapters that follow focuses on one "muscle" in that snake—conventional operations, Special Forces operations, Afghan army and police training, reconstruction and development, governance and rule of law—and examines how cultural factors either enabled or hindered success on the ground from the initial invasion in October 2001 until the end of Operation Enduring Freedom in December 2014. Some chapters discuss culture explicitly (Washington culture, military culture, Pashtun culture, or Western culture); others give detailed accounts of how the cultural habits discussed in this introduction shaped decisions on the ground. All but one of the chapters argue that the military mission to stabilize Afghanistan through counterinsurgency has either failed (partially or totally) or is on the path to failure. We note that after 13 years of sustained combat operations, Afghanistan remains as violent and volatile as it ever was; indeed, in terms of civilian casualties, it is appreciably worse. While there have been major gains in health, and other advancements in education and development, the government suffers from intractable corruption and a crisis of legitimacy. Of course, there may still be some way for Afghanistan to emerge as a moderately functional and secure state, but from our vantage point, that outcome seems unlikely.

Chapter 1 begins in Washington, DC, where the war's major policy decisions occurred. The author is a seasoned veteran of US and Afghan politics: Ambassador Ronald E. Neumann, who served as the US ambassador to Afghanistan from 2005 to 2007 and later as deputy assistant secretary of state for Near Eastern affairs. Neumann takes as his subject the Washington culture of decision making and explains the factors that impeded coherent, rational policymaking over the course of the war. Drawing on the work of Robert W. Komer—who served in Vietnam at roughly the same time Neumann was an army infantry platoon commander there—the ambassador argues that many of the problems that plagued the war are explained by a dysfunctional bureaucracy, inattention to details, and a basic neglect of the Afghans' concerns.

Chapter 2 gives readers a basic military overview of the war, which will be useful for those who are unfamiliar with its major decisions and turning points. Army Lieutenant Colonel Colin Jackson, an associate professor of history and strategy at the Naval War College and the former executive officer to the ISAF deputy chief of staff for operations, argues that Operation Enduring Freedom has been a tragedy in five acts because the United States kept shifting its goals and neglected the urban and rural dynamics that are so deeply entrenched in Afghan society.

Chapters 3 and 4 focus on the effort to recruit, train, and field the Afghan army and police, collectively known as the Afghan National Security Forces (ANSF). The first analysis comes from Dr. Martin Loicano and Captain Craig C. Felker, USN, both of whom served on the staff of the NATO command that had overall responsibility for training the army and police. Loicano and Felker argue that despite constant lip service about the dangers of imposing Western values on a foreign culture, the troops of the NATO training mission did exactly that, with predictable results. Chapter 4 turns to police development in particular and offers the perspective of a former Afghan police officer, Captain Pashtoon Atif. In tracing the history of police forces in Afghanistan since the start of the 20th century, Captain Atif argues that the police have always taken on the character traits of the regimes supporting them—a fact that goes a long way in explaining why Afghans everywhere have always distrusted them.

Chapters 5 and 6 concern development and governance in Afghanistan. Both chapters acknowledge partial successes but conclude that neither endeavor yielded sustainable trust in, or respect for, the Karzai regime in Kabul. In chapter 5, Navy Lieutenant Commander Jamie Lynn De Coster, a former special assistant to General David H. Petraeus in Afghanistan, argues that temporary gains occurred in the areas of health, education, and infrastructure development, but that disorganization between competing international bodies and, later, an overall militarization of development in Afghanistan hindered reconstruction. Chapter 6, by two army officers—Colonel Abigail T. Linnington and Lieutenant Colonel Rebecca D. Patterson—comes to very similar conclusions about the efforts to install a working, sustainable rule of law regime in Afghanistan.

In chapter 7, Marine Corps Captain Aaron MacLean takes the most philosophical and theoretically nuanced approach to the war. Building on his classical education at St. John's College in Annapolis, Maryland, and Balliol College, Oxford, MacLean traces the hidden assumptions about states, governance, and sovereignty in Western societies, and argues that those assumptions blinded Western leaders to the reality of how questions of power are settled now—and have always been settled—in Afghanistan: with violence. Drawing on his own experiences as an infantry platoon commander in the 2010 Battle for Marjah, Maclean offers a deeply critical accounting of how the West's deep-seated idealism led it to expectations unmoored from reality.

Chapter 8 turns to Special Operations in Afghanistan and, more specifically, to the effort to train the community defense forces known as the Afghan Local Police (ALP). Navy Lieutenant Commander Daniel R. Green argues that more than any other group, the US Special Forces mastered the key components of Afghan culture and in so doing had perhaps the best model for how to win over Afghans and turn them permanently against the Taliban insurgency. While the ALP program that Green praises was never expanded to the scale needed to win the war—at its height, it accounted for just 8 percent of Afghanistan's security forces and had serious conduct problems despite intense vetting and mentorship—Green's argument that the Special Forces found ways to overcome the war's cultural hurdles is an important challenge to the basic thrust of most of the other contributors' arguments in the book.

Lieutenant Commander Green's and Captain Maclean's chapters also address another theoretical issue concerning counterinsurgency, albeit indirectly. Unlike in conventional military operations, which use violence to influence governments, in counterinsurgency the goal is to influence civilians—to convince them to adopt new narratives about the legitimacy of their rulers. It is fundamentally a cultural endeavor; as the *Counterinsurgency Field Manual* explains, with a phrase that all Vietnam War historians will recognize, the "decisive battle is for the people's minds."[58] In Afghanistan, this required Westerners to know Pashtun culture well enough to communicate effectively, build trust, and create a meeting of the minds between very different peoples under very dangerous circumstances. The military calls this "operationalizing culture"; its critics call it "weaponizing culture."[59] Regardless of the term one uses, the questions raised are important ones: In theory, can outsiders carrying guns learn a foreign culture well enough to win hearts and minds? In practice, did American soldiers move beyond their preconceived notions of Pashtun culture or the often-hidden assumptions and habits of their own societies? Lieutenant Commander Green's chapter suggests they did; Captain Maclean's chapter suggests they did not.

Chapter 9, covers *inteqal*, or "transition"—the three-year process of handing control of the war over to the Afghan government. The author, Air Force Lieutenant Colonel Benjamin F. Jones, served two tours in Afghanistan, first as an advisor in the Afghan air force and second as a member of the Strategic Transition Assistance Group—the very organization inside the ISAF headquarters that coordinated the turnover process. Like several other contributors, Jones argues that cultural habits endemic to the American way of war—incompatible bureaucracies, conflicting timelines, and an unwillingness to listen to the Afghans—caused constant friction and disorganization. The volume ends with a short conclusion that summarizes the major themes in the book, explores the parallels to the Vietnam War, and offers thoughts for future research.

CHAPTER ONE Washington Goes to War

Ambassador Ronald E. Neumann

We defined the necessary [policy actions in Vietnam] in terms totally counter to Diem's personality and the realities of the Vietnamese power structure and society.

—WILLIAM COLBY, director of Central Intelligence, 1973–1976

As a young infantry officer fighting in Vietnam in 1969, I saw Washington bureaucratic approaches that seemed to undermine our effectiveness on the battlefield. Junior military officers always think the politicians in Washington are disconnected from the ground truth, but over the years, I watched us endlessly fail to learn lessons that seemed clear to me. As Director Colby noted some years after the war, we regularly ignored the culture we encountered in Vietnam—a practice that helped explain failure in that war. The entire effort in Vietnam was also plagued by institutional constraints—poor institutional memory, myriad layers of bureaucracy, a total disconnect between policy and implementation, and a penchant for throwing money and resources at different problems.[1]

Now, decades later, having served as a deputy assistant secretary of state in Washington, a senior official in Iraq, and the US ambassador to Afghanistan in Kabul, I see even more clearly that many of these problems were not specific to the Vietnam War. There is a political culture in Washington—a set of habits, tendencies, and bureaucratic limitations—that affects the art of the possible in matters both domestic and foreign. Some of those constraints make sense of course; it is good to have checks and balances, but many of the habits that affect business as usual in DC do not serve the nation well in armed conflict. When Washington goes to war, it takes its culture with it, and in the 13-year-long war in Afghanistan, that culture quite simply got in the way. Even more troubling, despite failures in both Vietnam and Afghanistan, I see no compelling evidence that Washington is willing to change.

Pinning down a specific Washington "way of war" is difficult, because the US government is actually a collection of organizations and individuals, all with their own assumptions and institutional cultures. Some ways of thinking discussed below may be broadly found throughout American society, such as the disregard for considering how to implement policy. (Anecdotally, this may be as much a function of academic approaches to international relations as of Washington decision making.) Others are part of Washington's own "inside the beltway" culture. Some may be attributed to particular subtribes such as the military, aid workers, or diplomats. Whatever the attribution, there is no denying that there are discernable habits of behavior and thinking that are recurrent and observable, that affect decisions and outcomes (usually badly), and that rarely seem to be brought forth for examination and challenge.

Moreover, it is fair to say that these habits of mind had specific effects on the conduct and outcome of the war. Assumptions about avoiding nation-building, derived in part from the Balkans, led to serious underfunding and wasted opportunities. (In fact, nation-building has come into such bad repute that the Obama administration has denied it has such a policy even as it funds exactly such endeavors.) Development theory clashed with Afghanistan's developmental realities, leading to more waste and disorganization. Military devotion to different patterns of warfare impeded success in some instances and became actively counterproductive in others. Washington's fiscal practices caused other troubles, both when it withheld funds and when it dispersed them. Finally, a conspicuous habit of not listening to locals led to years of political bickering and mistrust between the Americans and the Afghans.

Not every assumption or bureaucratic difference should be grouped under the term "culture." People have personalities and institutions have rules; both of these facts shape actions and limit choices in explicit ways. What this chapter focuses on are the less obvious constraints—the behaviors and ideals, recurring over time, that were neither stated explicitly nor examined for validity. Together, they represent *implicit* rules and intellectual frameworks—things that may reasonably be called a part of a larger culture: a Washington way of war.

This chapter groups examples roughly into four sections. The first section describes the perennial problems—the ones that blossomed in the earliest stages of the war and have continued ever since. These are perhaps the decisions that caused the most damage to successful policy outcomes and are where lessons most need to be actually learned rather than simply observed. The second section covers assumptions particular to the early phase of the war, 2001 to 2005, when the insurgency began to gather force. The third section discusses 2005–2008, when issues of funding the war had major consequences on the ability to wage it. The last section discusses the Obama administration's shift to a counterinsurgency strategy and the worsening relations with President Karzai that characterized the final years of the war.

None of these categories are perfect. Some habits, such as the resistance to nation-building, were present in the early phases of the war—and have remained present—but appear to have very different intellectual sources. Resistance to nation-building is intertwined with problems of governance that are fundamental to the war but not part of the discussion of culture.[2] The last phase covers several years, and my descriptions may not sufficiently recognize changes in thinking within that period. Furthermore, the chapter does not deal with the strains occurring in Washington between the uniformed military and the White House and National Security Council staff of the Obama administration because they seem driven by personalities and differ from the type of civilian-military strains that have occurred in Afghanistan. Despite these limitations, the categories may yet help us understand the culture that Americans take to war.

The Perennials

From the earliest days of the Afghanistan War, a series of intellectual habits impeded success. The most important of these are inattention on the part of senior leaders to the details of implementing policy, a general ignorance or avoidance of how funding is managed, a penchant for short personnel tours, and an abiding inability to take into account the views and reactions of the foreigners with whom the US government had to cooperate. All of this was exacerbated by confused chains of command that made it hard to pin down exactly who had responsibility for key decisions.

One of the most prevalent characteristics among senior policymakers in Washington is a complete inattention to the details of implementing policy in Afghanistan. Even the most desirable policy goals are useless if they cannot be achieved; the hard work of governing requires matching goals to means—resources, influence, and sometimes military force. This is a core element of success in military operations and business alike, and yet it was sadly lacking in Washington throughout the war. Dov Zakheim, who served as the Defense Department's comptroller in the early years of the war, reflected that there "are many reasons why analysts, observers, and pundits of all kinds have paid less attention to these practicalities of implementation . . . despite the fact that they were the keys to success or failure in both Iraq and Afghanistan. Practicalities involve details, and details are not sexy."[3] The result is that practicalities are accorded very little status in senior policymaking.

This American habit of avoiding the details of policy is evident outside Afghanistan as well. In my time as an ambassador and as a deputy assistant secretary of state, I have never known implementation issues to be the focus of deputies or cabinet-level meetings. Nor do young diplomats-in-training seem to learn it in the classroom. When I taught a graduate class at George Washington University, I often asked students these questions: What policy choice do you seek? How will you implement it? How will you apply resources and mitigate or overcome opposition? Most students had strong ideas about the first question but had never dealt with the latter two. Obviously, not every professor or course ignores implementation, but this problem remains widespread nonetheless: when the American Academy of Diplomacy held a workshop on teaching diplomatic practice, nearly a dozen former ambassadors turned full-time professors cited policy execution issues as the ones students had the most difficulty with.[4] At the Washington level, it could also be that the type of foreign policy issues many political leaders have experienced in their careers have been essentially about policy. As a result, there is little in the life experience of most political leaders to help them understand complex, detailed issues of implementation stretching over multiple years.

Whatever the cause, implementation is not a focus of Washington policymakers in general, and this regularly inhibited success in Afghanistan. Below the level of the president, no agency, department, or institution could even agree on who was in charge of the war. Just within the Pentagon and the Joint Staff, a plethora of offices under different generals and assistant secretaries competed for direction of the war.[5] The commander of the International Security Assistance Force (ISAF) ran operations in Afghanistan, but had to answer at various times to the NATO leadership, the commander of US Central Command, the chairman of the Joint Chiefs of Staff, and members of the National Security Staff—not to mention the secretary of defense and the president. In the State Department, this problem of overlapping bureaucracies was similarly debilitating. The creation of the office of the special representative for Afghanistan and Pakistan (SRAP), first held by Richard Holbrooke, was an effort to circumvent bureaucratic layers and streamline the effort, but it failed. Holbrooke was frequently excluded from White House policy deliberations, and the power of his office faded dramatically when he died in 2010.[6]

Other senior leaders noticed this as well. DOD comptroller Zakheim fumed that the federal government's multiple committees with overlapping jurisdictions created an interagency culture that was antithetical to doing anything quickly.[7] Former secretary of defense Gates spends significant portions of his book about his time in office excoriating the military and civilian defense bureaucracy for slowness in providing sufficient drones and proper armored vehicles. Perhaps Gates is extreme in saying that "effectively waging war on our enemies . . . would also require successfully waging war on the Pentagon itself."[8] Yet while Gates was able to combine pressure and ad hoc procedures to solve immediate problems, neither he nor Holbrooke nor Zakheim were able to change the bureaucratic culture that caused the difficulties.

A key element of implementing a policy is funding it, and here, too, Washington's efforts were disjointed and at times counterproductive. Funding an American war involves two broad issues, one political and the other organizational. The political issue involves how much cost the public will be asked to bear, how those funds will be raised, whether by increasing taxes, issuing war bonds, or, in earlier days, asking ladies for their jewelry. Separate from those issues are the organizational ones: Who will control the funds? How will they be dispersed? And what limitations will be applied on how each entity can use its resources? These issues of implementation were badly mismanaged in Afghanistan, and bureaucratic turf wars were again part of the reason why. Even though State and DOD had the job of implementing the president's policies in the war, the two departments rarely coordinated efforts on funding. In fact, as DOD comptroller Zakheim notes, while he was designated as the single senior Pentagon person for funding the Afghan war, he did not learn until after he retired that the State Department had designated Richard Haass for a similar role for the State Department. Making things worse was the fact that until 2008 the White House's Office of Management and Budget (OMB) played a detailed and frequently micromanagerial role in the allocation of funds and the timing of their disbursement. Time and again, OMB chose to slow the utilization of funds already approved for the war. This added a separate and additional layer of bureaucracy to how Defense fought the war and how State managed diplomacy. These basic disagreements over who had authority over funding exacerbated the already-existing breakdown between policy choices and their implementation.[9]

Three additional perennial problems with implementation illustrate how immutable American habits are even when they continually impede success. One is personnel policies—and the short-tour policy in particular. A second lies in how the US military adjusted to a war for which it had not prepared, while a third concerns command arrangements.

In her study of successful UN operations, Lise Moraj Howard emphasizes the importance of building a "learning organization" that can draw on past experience to adapt to new challenges across multiple operations.[10] Unfortunately, US military and civilian assignment policies are directly antithetical to building such an organization. Initially, personnel in the American embassy in Kabul were rotated in for periods as short as 30 days.[11] The assumption seemed to be that tour length and continuity didn't matter. Even as tours lengthened to a year, many agencies continued to fill positions with short-tour rotating personnel. The loss in institutional knowledge and operational continuity is atrocious. In a country where effectiveness depends heavily on personal relationships and knowledge of multiple power bases outside formal government structures, the constant personnel churn is operationally costly and confusing to Afghans. As one example of many, within two months of my arrival in Afghanistan virtually all my section and agency heads were new. It is the same problem that led John Paul Vann to remark caustically of Vietnam, "We don't have twelve years' experience. We have one year's experience twelve times over."[12]

The situation was essentially the same for the military. Most tours in Afghanistan were nine months to one year, although there was a period beginning in 2007 when they were lengthened to 15 months.

However, this change was due to a troop shortage for rotations and not a deliberate effort to improve the learning culture of the force. Allied forces often had shorter tours, some as little as six months. One exception was in Special Forces units where the same teams rotated back and forth to the same area so that they were able to build up a great deal of local knowledge.[13]

Training and turnover processes also limited the continuity of knowledge and expertise. With its deeper personnel resources, the military has generally been able to do more advance training than the State Department, and in some cases arriving units took the time to learn about the area and people they would work with. This helped but did not solve the problem. For one thing, the turnover briefings rarely extend any further back in time past one predecessor's deployment. Anything before that was unknown, except, of course, to all the Afghans who had to live through it. Secondly, as General George Casey, former chief of staff of the Army, put it, there was an attitude prevalent throughout the ranks that "the war began when I got here." As Casey said, "Every time this happened, something big fell apart, and it happened on every major rotation of troops."[14] What's worse, these flawed policies are deeply ingrained in bureaucratic systems that are highly resistant to change despite direct and damaging effects on the conduct of the war.

One military effort to deal with the continuity problem was the Afghan Hands program, which gave officers and some civilians specialized language and culture training and then required them to serve two tours in Afghanistan with an Afghan-related job in the United States in between. The program, largely a concept of General Stanley McChrystal, had some limited success but was never well supported by the individual services. The institutional antipathy to letting war interrupt established personnel practices remained disturbingly high.[15] As Secretary of Defense Gates noted ironically, the military services seem to regard wars as "unwelcome military aberrations."[16]

The tour-length issue is a complex one, but the failure to get it right had deeply negative effects on the conduct of the war. Clearly, not everyone should stay forever in a difficult and dangerous environment, and personnel policies must take account of matters other than the conditions on the battlefield. But surely there should be room to adjust policies when a country is losing a war, and this never occurred in Afghanistan. Essential senior leaders needed to stay long enough to establish trust with their counterparts, to understand political power dynamics, and to learn from mistakes, but with only a few exceptions, this did not happen. In 37 years of diplomatic service in countries less complex than Afghanistan, I found that my effectiveness always went up in the second year of an assignment and that I was really hitting maximum effectiveness in the third year. Even among those in the most important positions, almost no one ever stayed in Afghanistan long enough for this to happen. The State Department has a strong resistance to forced personnel assignments, so it tackled the problem with increased incentives that attracted some volunteers and convinced others to extend their tours for a second year. Nonetheless, these were mere Band-Aids to a personnel system that needed major surgery. I have followed Afghanistan's politics with interest since 2005, and I remain continually struck (if not appalled) by the basic lack of political knowledge of the many civilian and military officers in positions of authority. Individuals are well aware of the problems, but as an institution, the US government seems unable to change. Toward the end of the war, ambassadors and commanding generals began staying longer but short tours remained the norm for almost everyone else.

Another persistent problem is the failure of Americans to listen to the people they are attempting to influence. An old joke notes that the problem with US foreign policy is that Americans make much of it without reference to foreigners. It is unfortunate because listening is at the heart of a diplomat's trade. Understanding the other side's view and forecasting reactions are essential to constructing effective policies and monitoring how one's own actions are interpreted. And yet in Washington, such understanding and area expertise seems little valued.

The problem is not a new one but it was particularly damaging in Afghanistan. One perennial example concerned President Karzai and his concern over civilian casualties. He began to express concern early on, particularly after US Special Forces were accused of bombing and strafing a wedding party in 2002 that resulted in extensive civilian deaths.[17] The issue of mounting civilian death tolls and recurring complaints festered for years until it became a major source of public conflict, resentment, and bitterness. While civilian casualties are inevitable in war, it took eight years and the arrival of General McChrystal to recognize that the issue could not be ignored. As one National Security Council staffer later admitted in the final year of the war, "We were dealing with civilian casualties in proclamations but not in policy."[18]

The lack of listening and the mounting civilian casualties were made far worse by the badly structured military chain of command. The Special Forces units that were responsible for most of the raids operated under a different chain of command than other units on the ground. Many raids were effective in capturing Taliban commanders, but the lack of coordination, mistakes in targeting (especially in the early days), and insensitivity to Afghan culture became major grievances within both local communities and the Afghan government.[19] As Secretary Gates later remarked, these "jury-rigged arrangements violated every principle of unity of command."[20]

It took eight years of war to consolidate the chain of command and to improve coordination regarding night raids. One consequence of this was that President Karzai developed a deep and debilitating distrust of the US government and military. From his perspective, there had to be a reason why the Americans continued to ignore serious problems and complaints, particularly after US officials promised action and then didn't deliver. The idea that a country as strong as the United States just couldn't be bothered to pay attention, or that personnel turnovers and chain-of-command problems inhibited communication and continuity, simply was not credible to him. This contributed to a worsening of political relations, although there were many other causes equally related to the lack of cultural understanding.

2001–2005: First Assumptions and Persistent Problems

Alongside the perennial problems, other, more specific assumptions governed decision making in the early phase of the Afghan campaign. In fairness, hindsight is always clearer. No one understood in 2001 that a robust insurgency would emerge by 2006. Nevertheless, Washington's mental frameworks are deeply resistant to change, and as a result, assumptions were taken as "givens" and not examined in depth. The first of these assumptions was a general and deeply felt resistance to nation-building in the highest levels of government, including the president, vice president, and secretary of defense. A second concerned how the Afghans and Americans would react to a multiyear war in Afghanistan. These, in turn, led to other assumptions about how long American forces should stay and what type of development work the United States should undertake. All of which led the United States toward short-term thinking that caused it to under-resource the war in Afghanistan. Later, once Washington tried to change course, the war in Iraq made it impossible to adapt quickly.

Even before September 11, the Bush administration had a well-developed antipathy to nation-building. Future national security advisor Condoleezza Rice authored an article during the campaign that made this explicit, and candidate George W. Bush left little doubt in the second presidential debate when he said, "I don't think our troops ought to be used for what's called nation-building."[21] Secretary of Defense Donald Rumsfeld viewed the Balkans as a vivid example of how the United States got bogged down in nation-building and was characteristically outspoken about its dangers. This attitude was well understood in the field.

This premise was reinforced by two other widely shared attitudes: that the UN was incapable of discharging major responsibilities for nation-building, and that the US military was a fighting force that should not get drawn into other tasks. The resistance to involving the UN was strongly expressed by Vice President Dick Cheney.[22] There was also a widespread view that having too large a role for either the

UN or NATO/ISAF would impede America's primary goal of hunting terrorists. As Brigadier General David Kratzer related, in 2001 CENTCOM Commander General Franks "told me directly, with his finger in my face, that I would not get involved in nation building."[23] This affected development funding as well. For 2002–2003, USAID provided $1.4 billion for economic assistance to Afghanistan, but over 75 percent was for short-term humanitarian assistance—not long-term reconstruction or development.[24]

As a result of these starting assumptions, the military commands in Afghanistan quickly became a many-headed hydra. The United States supported the creation of the International Security Assistance Force (ISAF), but initially refused to put its own troops into it, because of doubts about working with international forces and a broader concern that America would be sucked into nation-building instead of fighting wars. The American forces thus operated as an entirely separate command—US Forces Afghanistan, whose mission of pursuing al Qaeda and the Taliban in the south and the east was related to, but distinct from, the broader efforts of the ISAF coalition. All of this led to parallel bureaucracies and persistent confusion.

Other early assumptions concerned how Afghans would receive the Americans and how long the American public would tolerate the war. The fear of Afghan xenophobia—long thought to be the reason Afghanistan had always been "the graveyard of empires"—was palpable among scholars, pundits, and politicians alike in 2001. Even knowledgeable Afghan-Americans warned of it.[25] Influenced by the massive Afghan resistance to the Soviets during their 10-year occupation, nearly everyone with credibility on Afghanistan warned that if the Americans stayed, they would eventually encounter animosity and armed resistance. This was one of the reasons Washington wanted to avoid a long occupation and state-building mission.

In fact, Afghans turned out to be far more welcoming than the analysts assumed—at least at the start. Many of those who served in the immediate aftermath of the invasion found reactions were very different. So hated were the Taliban that the Americans were greeted with flowers, kisses, hugs, and the question "why didn't you come ear-

Figure 1.1 *Left to right:* First Lady Laura Bush, President Bush, Secretary of State Rice, Ambassador Neumann, and President Karzai inaugurate the new US embassy in Afghanistan in 2006. (US State Department)

lier?"[26] Journalists reported on the feeling of victory, the hope bordering on euphoria, and the freedom of the foreigners to move anywhere in the country.[27] As former special envoy to Afghanistan James Dobbins later put it: "The perception was that Afghans hated foreigners and that the Iraqis would welcome us. . . . The reverse turned out to be the case."[28] For these reasons, there was considerable optimism in the early years of the war—a feeling that was palpable when the new American embassy in Kabul opened in 2006.

What went wrong in the years that followed? Rather than a timeless culture of Afghan xenophobia, a set of specific American mistakes convinced some Afghans to turn away from the coalition and the Karzai government. As Sarah Chayes related in her memoir of the early years of the war, the American military's short-term thinking and focus on hunting al Qaeda badly hindered the establishment of decent governance in the heartland of the Taliban. Enterprising power brokers like Kandahar governor Gul Agha Sherzai took advantage of the Americans' complete ignorance of the tribal affiliations to marginalize his enemies and consolidate power. As Carl Forsberg also noted, once those power networks became predatory, the population turned back to the Taliban for defense. And, as America prepared for the 2003 invasion of Iraq, it pulled out the majority of its USAID experts and other key State Department personnel from Afghanistan—the very experts who could have led to wiser decisions and better relations with local Afghans.[29]

The embassy's own reporting on Afghan dynamics was also inadequate, which contributed to overly simplistic narratives about whether the Afghans wanted Americans to stay. Normally, gathering these fundamental attitudes and reporting them back to Washington would be a staple of diplomatic reporting. But the newly reestablished embassy in Kabul was tiny, with personnel changing rapidly. Only a few Dari-language speakers were present.[30] Worse, communications were largely limited to reporting by telephone, so broader analytical perspectives were difficult to convey and were not broadly disseminated within the government.[31] The result was a broad inability of Washington policymakers to tailor policy to information and on-the-ground realities.

That the American public would reject sustaining a long Afghan occupation was also part of the common sense of the early years of the war, and this too turned out to be false. (After all, for 13 years, Congress sustained—and even increased—the troops and dollars devoted to Afghanistan.) Nonetheless, the presumption of a rapid departure was explicit and strong right from the start, especially from Secretary of Defense Rumsfeld who made it clear that Afghans were "going to have to figure [the future] out for themselves."[32] One consequence of this short-term thinking was that the United States never developed a long-term strategy for ejecting the Taliban and delegitimizing them permanently. Rather, it just kept reevaluating the war year to year, switching commanders and, eventually, changing strategies. It is a strange irony that American short-term thinking has helped Afghanistan become America's longest war.

2005–2008: Famine and Then Feast

Some people were thinking about the long term in those early years of the war, but no one had the ability to force Washington to adopt a workable strategy and to fund it appropriately. Lieutenant General David Barno, who served as the commander of military operations in Afghanistan from 2003 to 2005, authored a 2003 campaign plan that specifically recognized the importance of nonmilitary factors to enable reconstruction and good governance. Barno's plan even named the Afghan people as the "center of gravity" (i.e., the top priority in military jargon) in the Afghan campaign—a point that Washington only embraced in 2009, when the military shifted to counterinsurgency operations.[33] General Barno's counterpart in the embassy, Ambassador Zalmay Khalilzad, agreed but the strategy was never funded. Barno's successor, Lieutenant General Karl Eikenberry, and I continued the effort to integrate civil and military planning into a long-range plan for the country. Our weekly one-on-one dinners regularly ranged across the full gamut of issues without respect to turf or lines of authority. Our proposals to expand police training and economic aid were just two reflections of a joint focus that had long moved beyond the military and assistance assumptions of the early years, but I often felt our proposals fell on deaf ears.

One thing both General Eikenberry and I agreed on was that the effort in Afghanistan was under-resourced. Iraq was the principal reason why—as early as 2003, it had absorbed the bulk of the money, troops, and attention of senior policymakers, and the deteriorating situation there precluded any long-term planning for how to manage two wars at the same time.[34] But another problem—one more endemic to Washington's culture of warfare—had to do with how funding decisions were made and how slowly the American government is able to change course.

The budgeting process in the federal government has something of a feast-or-famine quality to it: when funds are available, departments are urged to spend quickly to clear the books; when requesting funds, the justifications and paperwork to get what one needs seem without end. I experienced this firsthand in the fall of 2005, when I began to report my analysis that the insurgency in Afghanistan would become significantly worse in the spring of 2006. I subsequently requested almost $600 million in supplemental funding for fiscal year 2006 to expand road construction and electric power generation and to promote economic growth both in areas threatened by the insurgency and in other areas where I believed preemptive action was needed.

Over the ensuing months, Washington asked my embassy for reams of supporting economic data. We were asked whether we really needed the money given other funds that were not yet obligated. We were asked for detailed projections of how the money would be spent and how fast projects would be completed. After all of that, all but $43 million was rejected by OMB on the grounds that roads, power, and expanded funding for Provincial Reconstruction Teams did not constitute "emergencies" suitable for supplemental funding. (The definition of "emergency" had never been raised with us as an obstacle during our discussions, and this same issue was subsequently ignored when a very large supplement was approved the next fiscal year.)[35] Thus, at the very moment when conditions were worsening, total US funding on Afghanistan declined from $4.7 billion in 2005 to $3.5 billion in 2006.[36] And while I am convinced that a significant opportunity to manage the downward spiral in Afghanistan was lost, the larger point is that the process of budget allocation and management in Washington was disconnected from operations in the field. OMB bureaucrats badly constrained the implementation of policy in Afghanistan, and the reasons they gave for doing so—meeting a definitional standard for emergency allocations—had no connection to the war's goals or needs.

Things only got worse in the following years. By 2007, the coalition was losing the war in Afghanistan, and Washington finally started to listen to the requests it had ignored over the previous two years. Security was worsening by the day: the British position in Helmand had deteriorated; Taliban forces were in the districts just outside Kandahar city, and bombings and attacks inside the city escalated alarmingly. Taking note of the decline, President Bush in mid-February

2007 tried to make good on his 2002 promise of a "Marshall Plan" for Afghanistan by promising funding that would enlarge the Afghan security forces, strengthen NATO, and help President Karzai improve provincial governance, combat narcotics, and fight corruption.[37] The problem was that budgeting procedures were simply too slow to have the necessary effect. The Bush budget for fiscal year 2007, proposed in February when he gave his speech, contained major increases in economic aid and a giant jump in security funding, especially for the police. But funding only began to reach the field toward the end of the year.

The money did finally begin to appear in late 2007, and continued to arrive thereafter. As just one example, funding for the Economic Support Fund—an essential resource for reconstruction—jumped from $473 million in 2006 to $1.4 billion in 2008 and to $3.3 billion in 2010.[38] However, once the funds arrived, they came with demands to spend quickly, which led to the flawed decisions and inadequate oversight. Tripling the funds in an account can happen with the stroke of a pen; expanding programs responsibly is far more complex. DOD spending—which accounted for over 90 percent of all spending in the war and was 20 times greater than the programs run by the State Department—encountered similar problems on an even greater scale. As other chapters in the volume show, the massive inflows of resources unbalanced the Afghan economy and made the corruption problem worse.[39]

This feast-or-famine quality to funding operations overseas is yet another attribute of how Washington goes to war, and it stretches far beyond Afghanistan. As George F. Kennan once famously explained in a lecture on American diplomacy, Washington has a long history of ignoring problems and then overreacting to them. The United States, he offered, is like a "prehistoric monster with a body as long as this room and a brain the size of a pin: he lies there in his comfortable primeval mud and pays little attention to his environment; he is slow to wrath—in fact, you practically have to whack his tail off to make him aware that his interests are being disturbed; but once he grasps this he lays about him with such blind determination that he not only

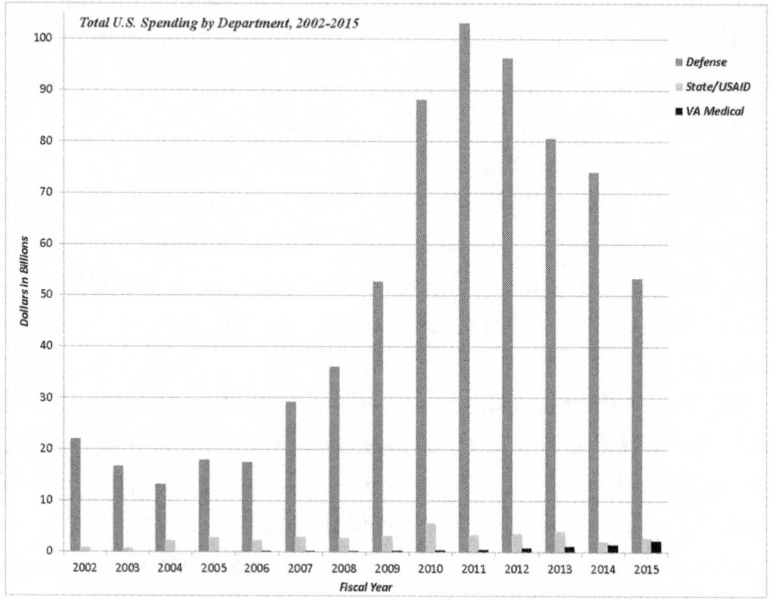

Figure 1.2 Total US spending in Afghanistan, 2002–2015. DOD spending accounted for over 90 percent of the $743 billion spent in the 13-year-long war. (Congressional Research Service)

destroys his adversary, but largely wrecks his native habitat."[40] This is what happened in Afghanistan in 2007, but the tool the dinosaur of American government used was not its teeth or its tail—it was its credit card.

2009–2014: Counterinsurgency and Confusion

Because of the resources required for Iraq, and the slowness of the American government to adapt, the Obama administration took office with a losing war in Afghanistan and pending requests for substantial troop reinforcements. This led to a rapid review of policy led by former CIA and NSC official Bruce Riedel and a longer policy review in the fall, all of which occurred during the fractious Afghan presidential election of 2009. And yet even with a year's worth of debate and analysis, the United States still came to conclusions that yielded an impossible-to-implement plan for how to save Afghanistan.

The most dramatic conclusion of the 2009 review was that the various policy goals that had accumulated over the years—defeating the Taliban, rebuilding the country, ensuring gender equity in the parliament, and so on—needed to be scaled back. Rather than a complete rebuild of the country, President Obama decided that the focus would be to "disrupt, dismantle and defeat al-Qaeda in Pakistan and Afghanistan and to prevent their return to either country in the future."[41] To do this, the military shifted to population-centric counterinsurgency operations, and the president agreed to send some 30,000 additional troops to Afghanistan. This would not be an open-ended commitment to nation-building, however; the surge troops would work on stabilizing communities and building support for the government in Kabul, but after a year on the ground, they would begin to come home. In a sense, the major conclusion of the strategy review was that the United States did not need to win the war outright—it only needed to stabilize the country sufficiently to transition responsibility to the Afghans. To enable all of this, President Obama named three key efforts: "a military effort to create the conditions for a transition; a civilian surge that reinforces positive action; and an effective partnership with Pakistan."[42]

The administration's strategy review was filled with military, intelligence, and political expertise, but it still repeated many of the perennial misunderstandings and assumptions seen in the early years of the war. Leaders still made grand pronouncements of policy with little attention to implementation; funding was now ample instead of lean, but the oversight was terrible; short personnel tours persisted, as did metrics that rarely reflected reality on the ground.

But a few things were new as well. With the shift to a counterinsurgency strategy came a renewed focus on problems of Afghan governance—problems that would take far more time to solve than the president allowed. The decision to bring in a "civilian surge" of nonmilitary experts to strengthen government institutions and curb excesses was also new, but its size was less than expected. More importantly, the notion that governance could be rapidly changed by such intervention was massively ignorant. Finally, the failure to listen to the Afghans—and to President Karzai in particular—became a nearly insurmountable problem for the political relations between the two countries.

The renewed focus on governance and the adoption of counterinsurgency had the potential to reverse the decline in Afghanistan in theory; unfortunately, in practice, the new approach had enormous contradictions. First, at the heart of the policy was a strange irony: even though the president explicitly renounced nation-building, his new strategy funded many of its elements. The training of the Afghan army and police grew exponentially, and advisors were detailed to virtually every Afghan ministry. Efforts to boost agricultural outputs, build roads, electrify cities, and build rule of law and justice infrastructure all increased. Gender programs were expanded as were small grants to civil society organizations. Total US spending in Afghanistan skyrocketed from $43 billion in President Bush's last year in office to $118 billion in 2011.[43] The assumption that the administration could deny nation-building while adopting it in practice produced strategic confusion at all levels—in Washington, in the field, and among the Afghans themselves.

Moreover, the president's new strategy had a critical flaw—an assumption that reflected political realities in Washington, but disregarded events in Afghanistan. In vowing to bring the surge troops home one year after their arrival, President Obama may have assumed that he would ease Americans' exhaustion with the war and perhaps even force the Afghan government to take more active steps to avoid a Taliban victory. But the timeline announcement also effectively removed the surge's credibility before it began. For the strategy to work, Afghans needed to believe America would remain sufficiently engaged until Afghan forces could be built to secure what ISAF gained. Without that assurance, progress seemed ephemeral, and most Afghans stayed on the fence. The one-year announcement only convinced them that the Americans would not be present to protect them over the long haul. Later, at the NATO Lisbon summit in 2010, the United States vowed to remove all of its troops by the end of 2014—another decision that undermined the coalition's ability to convince Afghans to reject the Taliban.

The timeline also had debilitating effects on the governance effort in particular. Everyone agreed that Afghan corruption and poor governance was part of the problem—General Stanley McChrystal had identified this in his initial assessment, as had numerous policy studies and reports—but in the year that the Obama team debated its new approach in Afghanistan, no one seemed to seriously consider the time it would take to actually fix the problem. All the discussion focused on the military timeline.[44] Near the end of the review, former general and then-ambassador Karl Eikenberry warned, "We underestimate how long it will take to restore or establish civilian government. . . . The process is likely to be slow and uneven no matter how many US and other foreign civilian experts are involved. . . . The cadre of Afghan civilians [needed to run the ministries effectively] does not now exist and would take years to build."[45] And yet his message arrived too late and offered no alternative. President Obama announced the surge and one-year timeline in December 2009 at West Point. The result was yet another irreconcilable contradiction: improving Afghan governance was essential to stabilizing Afghanistan, but the new approach demanded improvements on a schedule that no governance expert deemed feasible and that had never previously been achieved anywhere.

The civilian surge was another key element in the president's new approach, and this too had a fundamental flaw—it assumed that the State Department, USAID, and other civilian agencies of government could actually increase their presence in Afghanistan in a fairly timely manner. It didn't happen. In 2009, about 300 civilian federal employees were in Afghanistan, and by March 2010, that number had only risen to 1,000, with another 200–300 on the way. The numbers flatlined thereafter, and by February 2011, still less than 1,200 US government civilians were in the country.[46] As one US division commander caustically remarked to me in 2010, "I feel the civilian surge lapping at my ankles."

Because those in the field had neither the time nor the people to implement the president's policy, the entire effort to improve governance was rushed and ineffective. None of the Afghan ministries had the trained personnel or procedures to meet the goals the United States had set. Several participants of the early civilian surge arrived at their post with neither plan nor direction. Civil-military frictions were intense. The civilian governance experts felt that the rate of progress demanded by the military was infeasible, and emphasized repeatedly that none of the work done would have a lasting impact on Afghan governance if Afghans didn't do it themselves—and on their own timeline. The military demanded that the mission be accomplished nonetheless. Military planners worked to identify some 80 "key terrain districts" and selected 40 of these for intensive work in 2010, but those priorities rarely coincided with the governance and development priorities of the State Department or USAID, which focused on building Afghan administrative capacity. Each side tended to caricature the other, with the civilians complaining that the military was rushing to failure, and the military retorting that the civilians were too slow to move and too small in numbers.

In a sense, both sides were correct, but the vehemence of the disagreement inhibited discussion. I was startled by the freedom with which senior military and civilian officers would criticize the other side in large meetings or settings where their words were bound to be repeated elsewhere. At times I wondered if we were not losing focus on who the real enemy was in the war we were fighting together. Yet the origin of the problem was not the fundamental cultural differences between military and civilian experts; it was the Washington habit of choosing a policy without serious consideration of how to implement it.[47]

The final—and most important—assumption in the Obama administration's new approach concerned President Karzai. After eight years of war, and a steadily worsening security situation, President Karzai

Figure 1.3 Ambassador Neumann on one of his listening tours in Khost Province, ca. 2006. Being responsive to rural Afghans' concerns was a critical element of gaining their support for the ISAF coalition and the Kabul government. (Courtesy of the author)

had an uneasy relationship with the United States, particularly after the 2009 Afghan elections.[48] In an effort to increase US assistance to the country, various Washington pundits opined that President Karzai was either "off his meds" or simply "crazy like a fox."[49] As a result, in the new policy announced in December 2009, Obama's national security team put in writing that they would work "with Karzai where we can and around him where we must."[50] This decision led to serious friction at the highest levels of US-Afghan relations.

President Karzai and I had had our own share of misunderstandings of course, and I too found it hard at times to bridge the two cultures, even though my father had been ambassador to Afghanistan, and I had traveled the country extensively as a young man. But in the years after my ambassadorship, I traveled often to Afghanistan and usually met with President Karzai and some of his closest advisors. In the last five years of the war, I saw an increasing blindness among American policymakers to how US policies appeared to Afghans and a concomitant deafness toward Afghan concerns. During my 2010 trip to Afghanistan, I heard regular refrains from American officials and soldiers in the field that "Kabul doesn't matter." In other words, the United States would do as it pleased in pursuit of its policy, and the Afghans could either cooperate or get out of the way.

This was both ignorant and mistaken: Karzai did matter, far more than most Americans appreciated. For one, even though he was dependent on international aid and support, President Karzai controlled all provincial government appointments and could remove officials at will. He did so for many reasons, sometimes good, but he would not tolerate the United States deciding who would govern or let provincial officials substitute foreign goals for his own. This should have been clear to the United States, as something rather similar had happened before with its closest allies. In 2006, the British task force in Helmand had operated with similar disdain for Kabul. The British relied on then-governor Mohammed Daúd, extolling his virtues and building him up in the British press. When Karzai eventually fired Daúd for various reasons, the British were furious. They failed to understand that Karzai couldn't be bullied in his own country—something the United States tried to do more and more after 2009.[51] I drew on this example repeatedly in efforts to explain in Afghanistan and in Washington why Kabul actually mattered, but I made no impact on US behaviors that steadily worsened our two countries' relations.

Even the way the United States communicated with the Afghan government strained the relationship. The Afghan government was terribly corrupt, and this had been a subject of discussion, pressure, and comment for years. But with the Obama administration, it exploded into sustained, high-level public criticism on television and in the press. This would be embarrassing to any politician in the United States, but in Afghanistan it had more damaging consequences. In a culture where honor translates directly into power, the style of communication can be just as important as the substance, particularly in public. No Afghan would ever engage in the type of public criticism the United States leveled at Karzai unless he was deliberately trying to weaken or undercut a rival. The idea that the Americans would criticize the president so forcibly—and over corruption, for that matter—made sense to no one on the streets of Kabul or in the halls of Karzai's palace. All of this contributed to a narrative that the Americans were working to secretly undermine President Karzai.

One well-reported example of how the style of US communications spoke louder than the substance was then-senator Biden's meeting with Karzai in late 2008. Much of Biden's lecturing and criticism took place not in private but over dinner with the president and his cabinet. The evening ended with Biden's abrupt departure from the dinner when he took Karzai's responses to be untruthful.[52] There may be a nation in which one can repeatedly insult its president in front of others without leaving suspicions about one's intentions, but it is certainly not Afghanistan. Karzai is not alone among Afghans in being conspiratorial in his thinking; after years of warfare and betrayals, second-guessing motives is effectively an Afghan secret to survival. The United States paid no attention to this, and the voices of news pundits, pop psychologists, and uninformed Washington "experts" controlled the narrative. As a result, the mutual mistrust and poor communication increased.

By 2009, US-Karzai relations were at a new low, and one of the reasons for the decline in trust was Richard Holbrooke. During the 2009 presidential election, Holbrooke met with and encouraged various potential Afghan presidential candidates to run. He made no secret of his desire to see Karzai defeated and, according to Secretary of Defense Gates, believed that "Karzai had to go even if it meant disregarding the Afghan constitution."[53] Whether this was an administration decision or just Holbrooke's is unclear but the result was disastrous. Karzai saw Holbrooke's effort to undermine him as proof that the US commitment to democracy was flexible at best, and pursued a predictable counterstrategy. When credible evidence of widespread fraud emerged in the aftermath of the vote, the United States pressed for a runoff election, which Americans saw as obedience to rules, but Karzai construed this as a further deliberate effort to delegitimize him, a view that I found many Afghans agreed with. By 2010,

President Karzai confided to me that he simply did not understand what America wanted. He was certain the United States was trying to weaken him, but he did not understand why.[54]

Eventually, Karzai put together a theory of US interests in Afghanistan, one that gave him an explanation of both the United States' public criticism and its failure to press Pakistan harder on the Taliban sanctuaries that kept the insurgency strong. The United States, he reasoned, deliberately wanted to prolong the war and keep him weak. Doing so would allow the United States to extract basing agreements from Kabul, which it would use to station troops in the country to pressure Afghanistan's neighbors whenever needed for American goals.[55] While incorrect, President Karzai's conclusions were not irrational—they were incorrect inferences born out of the confusions that US policies caused. That the United States actually had no idea how its actions were received was too incredible for nearly any Afghan to accept.

US calls for action on corruption also fueled Karzai's belief that the United States was deliberately trying to keep him weak, and here the cross-cultural confusion was intense. Part of the problem is that patronage—corruption, in American parlance—is a political tool in many societies, and in Afghanistan, it was almost Karzai's only tool: he had little money and no solid political base, and the United States controlled all the military forces. As a result, establishing patron-client relationships was one of the few ways Karzai could maintain influence over the various political and ethnic factions that had a long history of resisting and even overthrowing the government in Kabul. The United States ignored this political imperative and took a zero tolerance approach to corruption that bore no connection to the realities on the ground in Afghanistan. Adding to the problem was the fact that the ISAF coalition's anticorruption efforts appeared hypocritical to Karzai because ISAF had its own lucrative contracts for transportation and logistical services—some of which were with Karzai's rivals or with power brokers who paid the Taliban for protection. Moreover, the Americans rarely distinguished between different types of corruption and had little ability to influence the rapacious predators that used their government positions to settle scores and to steal without building. And the United States only moved to fire Afghan power brokers who held US contracts when it could gather sufficient evidence of legal or financial malfeasance. This meant it could rarely target the worst offenders and its choices for prosecution often appeared arbitrary. As a result, when American officials would ask Karzai to fire one of his corrupt officials or contractors, he would shake his head in confusion and then speculate about what the "real reasons" were for demanding the firing. Viewing each case through his own lenses—where knowledge of each person's status was more important than the legal details of how money moved from patron to client—the Americans' arguments almost never made sense.[56]

The misunderstandings went on in the final years of the war with relations steadily deteriorating and mistrust rising. In a March 2014 visit to Kabul, I found US perceptions and Karzai's to be mirror images of each other. With presidential elections just months away, US policymakers were deeply suspicious that Karzai would pick a presidential candidate to be his successor and intervene with massive fraud to elect him. Karzai had the opposite theory: he was convinced the United States would never remain neutral, but would work to choose its own successor, regardless of the desires of the Afghan people. The trust and communication between the Americans and Afghans had broken down almost completely.

The long-running controversy over the signing of the Bilateral Security Agreement (BSA), which would govern how many troops and bases remained in Afghanistan after 2014, was one more area where mutual suspicion and miscommunication undermined progress. Theories circulated on either side: Karzai was convinced that the United States wanted the agreement because it wanted the military bases, and many Washington insiders assumed Karzai was holding out for more development aid and security assistance.[57] When the two sides could not reach agreement, Karzai refused to sign the BSA, claiming the incoming president would have to make the decision. Based on my many discussions with Afghans and with Karzai, I believe that he thought not signing gave him leverage to prevent the

United States from intervening in the election as, in his view, it had done in 2009. American pressures simply reinforced his perception that the United States was desperate not to leave and wanted the BSA at any cost. US statements of deadlines, first October 2013, then December, then early 2014—none of which were real or acted on—simply reinforced Karzai's belief. That the United States was bluffing was clear. That the administration remained unaware of how its actions were understood in Kabul was equally clear and continues as of this writing.

Other gaffes contributed to the mistrust and poor relations. In May 2014, President Obama visited Afghanistan but stopped only to see troops outside Kabul. The president's last-minute invitation to President Karzai to meet him at the US base at Bagram was rejected. It was unclear whether the White House failed to understand how insulting it was to invite Karzai to visit a foreign base in his own country or whether the administration simply didn't understand how insulting the offer appeared to Afghans.[58] If the insult was deliberate it was senseless; if not, it was ignorant.

Perhaps the administration had simply given up on the Afghan mission. The May 2014 announcement by President Obama that he would delay the complete withdrawal of all advise-and-assist forces until the end of 2016 continued the confusion, even for US military forces in the country.[59] To them, it suggested that they were being risked for a mission that no longer mattered since it was scheduled to end whether it made progress or not. For Afghans, the United States' goals remained utterly confusing and disturbing.[60]

Contradictions in the United States' Afghan policy persisted after combat operations ended in December 2014. Although Operation Enduring Freedom is now officially over, the war has continued, and some US forces are still participating in it, albeit only sporadically. Karzai's departure removed one source of contention, but the political bargain of the 2014 election created new frictions. The US presence and purpose in the country remains uncertain, and after the Taliban briefly seized Kunduz city in September 2015, the Obama administration slowed the troop withdrawals and then reversed the decision to withdraw all forces.

As of the time of this writing, at the end of 2015, the Afghans' war against the Taliban is going badly although it is not yet lost. But as the civilians draw down and hunker down, and the military trains and assists the Afghan army and police, it is not clear that there is a real US exit strategy that will lead to the president's stated goals of a safe and secure Afghanistan that is free from al Qaeda and can govern itself. The Obama administration still clings to its public pronouncement that the combat mission has ended, despite continuing air and Special Forces engagements and steadily increasing Taliban control around the country. And this mixed message continues to confuse Afghans about America's strategic purpose and long-term dependability. There may yet be a way to repair the mistrust and friction in the US-Afghan relationship and to move together toward the common goals of ridding the country of al Qaeda and other militant groups. But as the United States works to do so, one thing should remain clear: cultures are stubborn social phenomena. The civilian and military cultures America takes to war are very different from Afghanistan's cultures, and neither will change easily.

CHAPTER TWO

US Strategy in Afghanistan

A TRAGEDY IN FIVE ACTS

Lieutenant Colonel Colin Jackson, USA

Over 13 years in Afghanistan, the United States explored the full menu of civil war strategies. Operation Enduring Freedom opened in 2001 with a novel combination of Special Forces, local proxies, and airpower. After the fall of the Taliban regime, the United States waged an open-ended counterterrorism campaign against al Qaeda and its allies. When its efforts to delegate development and state-building to its European allies foundered, the United States was reluctantly drawn into training Afghan security forces and sponsoring economic development. When these new measures failed to stem the return of the Taliban, the United States backed into a counterinsurgency campaign.

The counterinsurgency campaign and US ambitions reached their apogee between 2009 and 2011. With the surge, the United States assumed the lead in security, governance, and development, and the ensuing increase in resources and ambitions soon outstripped the perceived value of the object in Afghanistan. With the killing of Osama bin Ladin in 2011, the United States began to disengage from its sprawling Afghan enterprise. During this withdrawal, the United

States sought to buttress its client army as it removed the military, bureaucratic, and financial scaffolding it had built around the Afghan state.

On a deeper level, Operation Enduring Freedom can be seen as two, intertwined tragedies. The first involved the crippling American ambivalence toward intervention in civil war. That ambivalence pitted the evangelical impulse to save Afghanistan through intervention and good works against an equally powerful desire to limit entanglements and transform by example rather than deed. The second tragedy was one that long preceded American intervention: the Afghan war between town and countryside. For much of the preceding century, urban elites eager to modernize and centralize had collided with conservative rural populations equally committed to resisting social change and holding the government at arm's length. That struggle continued throughout the US engagement and did much to undermine the West's efforts to build a functioning Afghan state.

The failure of the US campaign stands at the intersection of these tragedies. The inability of the United States to reconcile its desire to transform Afghanistan with its aversion to entanglement drew it from a modest opening role in 2002, to a dominating one by 2009, and finally to disillusionment and disengagement by 2014. By backing Afghanistan's urban elites, the United States became the underwriter of a renewed war between the center and the periphery. Unable to convert and modernize the countryside with its own resources, the Afghan government substituted American muscle and money; rapid US disengagement left the Afghan government dangerously overextended. The Taliban alliance seemed no more likely to win in a lasting sense. Having failed to govern the center in the 1990s, the Taliban were nevertheless unwilling to forgo a new bid for control of the center.

Following a coherent strategy in Afghanistan required policymakers to answer four fundamental questions. First, what was the purpose of US involvement in Afghanistan? Second, how could that be translated into concrete objectives? Third, what was the value of Afghanistan? Fourth, how much was enough in terms of men and money to achieve the purposes and goals set out? The failure to arrive at firm and consistent answers to these questions explains much of the confusion, waste, and misallocation of resources that bedeviled the US campaign.

While the purpose of US involvement was reasonably clear in 2001, translating this into tangible objectives proved more challenging over time. Early on, punishing al Qaeda and deterring future attacks on the homeland were the rationale for invading Afghanistan. Once the Taliban had been overthrown, the sequel was to pursue the remaining terrorists, destroy their networks, and prevent their return. The problem was that accomplishing this aim demanded the construction of some political order in Afghanistan. From 2002 through 2014, the United States seesawed between minimalist visions of state construction and more expansive ones based on the late stages of the Iraq War.

As resource demands increased, it was logical to ask what Afghanistan was worth. In part, this calculation hinged on judgments about the magnitude of the terrorist threat; in part, this was a question about which theaters were most important to preventing future attacks on the homeland. Thus the perceived value of Afghanistan was rooted in domestic political judgment. As the specter of 9/11 receded, popular sentiment and attention waned, and the high costs and frustrations of Iraq drove down the American appetite for protracted war.

Finally, successive military commanders and ambassadors struggled to specify how much was enough to accomplish the goals set by the Bush and Obama administrations. As the insurgency returned and the challenges of state-building became apparent, leaders often found themselves in holding actions with the Taliban and with political leaders in Washington. Following the pattern described by Leslie Gelb and Richard Betts in the Vietnam era, US leaders invested the minimum necessary not to lose in Afghanistan in the hope that they would muddle through in the end.[1]

It may be too early to know whether the United States can still succeed in its aims or secure its client state in the long run. The object of this chapter is to trace the evolution of US strategy and provide some sense of the relationship between changing theories of victory and the nature of the problems on the ground. US plans and programs were the imperfect products of the great debates (what is the purpose? how much is it worth? how much is enough?) and the practitioners' struggles to stabilize and solve immediate problems. US strategy was in this sense Moltke's system of expedients—one part doctrine, one part experimentation, one part the experience of Iraq.[2] This strategic bricolage meant that US plans seldom corresponded with the problems on the ground.

Act 1: Triumph and Tutelage, October 2001–December 2002

Scene 1: Triumph

The opening act of the US war in Afghanistan was the ouster of the Taliban and the pursuit of al Qaeda. The Taliban's refusal to hand over Osama bin Ladin and his allies in the wake of the 9/11 attacks triggered US preparations for the invasion of Afghanistan.

The purpose of this military action was to prevent a second round of attacks in the United States. The Bush administration translated this into a plan to kill or capture the al Qaeda leadership and fighters inside Afghanistan and topple the Taliban regime. By doing so, it sought not only to punish al Qaeda but to deter other terrorist groups and sponsors from considering attacks on the American homeland.[3]

The strategy that emerged was highly unorthodox. It was conceived and led by the CIA, and it combined small US Special Forces teams and US airpower to amplify the power of the existing Afghan Northern Alliance. The CIA's Counterterrorism Center director, Cofer Black, and his deputy, Hank Crumpton, planned to use US money to rent the allegiance of Afghan warlords and US airpower to overthrow the al Qaeda / Taliban coalition.[4]

The administration's debates hinged on the relative merits of two campaigns for overthrowing the Taliban—one in the north and one in the south. The primarily Tajik Northern Alliance was concentrated in the Panjshir Valley north of Kabul, and its armies were already arrayed in an L-shaped line running south from Tajikistan to the outskirts of

Kabul and then east to the Pakistani border. While it seemed that any ground offensive would need to start in the north, many feared that direct support to the Tajiks would alienate Afghanistan's Pashtuns. Pakistan, the longtime sponsor of the Taliban, echoed these concerns. While the United States sought to balance Tajik and Pashtun interests, the absence of an organized Pashtun opposition meant that a southern strategy would delay US action as winter approached. Presented with the rival arguments, President Bush endorsed the northern strategy on October 16, 2001.[5]

The leading edge of the northern campaign was a CIA team led by officers whose familiarity with the Northern Alliance dated to the 1970s. Gary Schroen and his "Jawbreaker" team arrived in the Panjshir Valley on September 26 and quickly sought to revive the US partnership with the Northern Alliance. Schroen's personal relationships and his distribution of $5 million in cash over the first 40 days secured the support of the leadership and carried the partner forces through the climax of the campaign in the north.[6]

While the CIA took the lead in designing the campaign and forging alliances, the action arm of the strategy was Task Force Dagger: the US Army's 5th Special Forces Group under Colonel John Mulholland. What TF Dagger brought was the ability to partner with Afghan commanders and direct US airstrikes. Each 14-man, Special Forces team brought specialized skills and equipment to identify targets and control close air support.[7] Getting these teams into Afghanistan proved to be a logistical and bureaucratic challenge. Weather delays, safety concerns, undeveloped staging bases, and military conservatism delayed the insertion for almost a month.[8] Two teams entered Afghanistan on October 19, and as late as November 18, there were fewer than 130 US military personnel on the ground in Afghanistan.[9]

While US airpower would ultimately propel the Northern Alliance's ground offensive, interagency arguments over targeting limited the results in the opening weeks. Most of the missions in the first three weeks were "strategic targets" (e.g., air defenses, trainings camps, leadership targets) well behind Taliban lines; the CIA and Special Forces teams lobbied for increased use of observed precision strikes against the Taliban armies. In the last week of October, a shift to direct attacks on Taliban forces helped US advisors prod the Northern Alliance into launching an offensive across the northern front. These air strikes and spirited assaults by the Northern Alliance led to the capture of Mazar-e-Sharif on November 9.[10]

US leaders in Washington had hoped to delay the capture of Kabul to avoid a power struggle among Afghan factions.[11] Instead, the initial breakthrough triggered a swift collapse of the Taliban lines and the subsequent fall of Kabul and Jalalabad. While US airpower and Afghan assaults were the key to the breakthrough, the early victories triggered a wave of defections by onetime Taliban allies. By November 14, the Northern Alliance and its US advisors had effectively secured the northern half of the country.[12]

As the battle raged in the north, the United States scrambled to find Pashtun allies in the Taliban heartland. Before the US invasion, Taliban control of the south had been uncontested. As a result, resistance groups there had to be created from scratch. With the assistance of US advisors, two major Pashtun resistance groups emerged under the leadership of Hamid Karzai and Gul Agha Sherzai.[13] Although these groups were far smaller than the Northern Alliance, US air support and political guile enabled the two leaders to engineer the final victories in the south. Karzai's violent bargaining split the remaining Taliban coalition and made possible the largely bloodless recapture of Kandahar on December 7, 2001.[14]

The results of the two campaigns were staggering in scale, speed, and cost. By the end of the year, there were only 110 CIA and 350 US Special Forces personnel in Afghanistan. These advisors, armed with US airpower and $70 million in cash, had led a coalition of 20,000 Afghans to defeat the 40,000–60,000 Taliban troops and drive the remnants and their al Qaeda allies to the borders of Afghanistan. They had managed to do this in 50 days at a cost of fewer than 25 US lives. By any reasonable measure, this was an astounding success and one that promised to secure US aims at minimal cost.[15]

The sequels to the overthrow of the Taliban underscored the limits of the strategies of the opening campaign. As US-led Afghan forces

Figure 2.1 US Special Forces ride with the Northern Alliance during the opening days of the war. Special Forces and CIA officers helped direct the airpower that toppled the Taliban at minimal cost in 2001. (Department of Defense)

chased al Qaeda forces toward Pakistan, their quarry paused in the Tora Bora cave complex in the mountains of Nangarhar Province. From December 1 to December 17, CIA and Special Forces sought to destroy the al Qaeda forces, which were believed to include Osama bin Ladin and his deputy, Ayman al-Zawahiri. US leaders hoped that the same combination of advisors, precision air strikes, and Afghan ground assaults would be sufficient to kill or capture the remaining terrorists. Unfortunately, the Afghans proved unequal to the task. Individual warlords sparred with each other and the Americans and preferred to negotiate with al Qaeda leaders rather than attack them. Sensing the loss of momentum, Gary Berntsen, the senior CIA advisor, asked CENTCOM to send a battalion of US Rangers to block the mountain passes between Tora Bora and Pakistan; the military was hesitant to commit US troops to a risky operation and declined Berntsen's request. By the third week of December, it was clear that airpower and a porous Afghan cordon would not be enough to prevent the escape of numerous al Qaeda fighters. Bin Ladin's escape was a dispiriting coda to a campaign focused on the destruction of al Qaeda.[16]

The arrival of US conventional forces in early 2002 opened the door to new approaches to the kill/capture mission. In Operation Anaconda, US troops were airlifted in to cordon and search a suspected Taliban stronghold in eastern Afghanistan. While the 2,000 US infantrymen, 1,600 Afghan militiamen, and Special Forces advisors anticipated a lopsided fight, they stumbled into a much larger battle with 1,000 Taliban fighters in mountainous terrain. Over the course of March 2–18, the US force managed to seize and clear the valley, yet American casualties and the escape of many Taliban fighters underscored the difficulties the United States would face as it sought to stamp out resistance in the east and south.[17]

Scene 2: Tutelage

The swift ouster of the Taliban forced the United States to reassess its purpose and objectives in Afghanistan. The administration's commitment to prevent future attacks on the American homeland made a vigorous pursuit of al Qaeda in Afghanistan and Pakistan the logical sequel to regime change. As a result, counterterrorism became the focus of almost all military operations from 2002 through the return of the Taliban in 2005–2006.

If killing and capturing terrorists was a tangible objective, the related goal of denying them sanctuary was more problematic. While it was reasonable to want to eliminate al Qaeda's sanctuaries, denying the enemy access to a vast territory spanning Afghanistan and the tribal areas of Pakistan would be more demanding and more resource intensive than the defeat of the Taliban regime. Furthermore, the denial of sanctuary implied a derivative project—the construction of an Afghan political order to fill the vacuum and support counterterrorism. These twin challenges would bedevil the Americans and their Western allies from 2002 to 2014.

Development of the new order was urgent and improvisational.

As the Taliban crumbled in late November, James Dobbins, the US special representative to Afghanistan, and Lakhdar Brahimi, the UN representative, convened a conference in Bonn, Germany, to determine the shape of the new order and the process that would bring it into being. By bringing the four major Afghan resistance factions together, the organizers hoped to forge a broadly legitimate process for political reconstruction and avert a civil war among the victors.

Over two weeks, the Afghan factions and the Western organizers were able to agree on an interim leader, a multiyear political process, and the distribution of ministerial posts. The victorious Northern Alliance agreed to cede the interim presidency to Hamid Karzai, a Pashtun with a strong tribal pedigree and superior skills in negotiating with the Western powers. In return, Fahim Khan and his Tajik allies retained several of the key ministries including the Ministry of Interior, which controlled the national police force, and the Ministry of Defense, which controlled the army.[18]

The Bonn process, as it would later be called, envisaged a multiyear series of *loya jirgas* (grand assemblies) to endorse the Interim Authority and ratify a constitution. These traditional assemblies, which already had centuries of precedent in Pashtun culture, would then be followed by presidential elections in 2004 and finally parliamentary elections in 2005. The architects hoped that this series of procedural gates would confer lasting legitimacy on the new regime.[19]

The debates among the international sponsors were defined by analogies and constraints. For the United States and the UN, the Bosnia and Kosovo cases loomed large. For many in the State Department and the international community, these missions were examples of costly but successful stabilization. For the Bush administration, the Balkan episodes were examples of the mission creep and unending engagement that it sought to avoid. While Dobbins personally saw the Balkans as a useful model, his marching orders reflected the Bush administration's overriding desire to avoid entanglement: "I had no written instructions and a good deal of leeway. My job was to get an agreement and almost any agreement would do, so long as it resulted in an Afghan government that would replace the Taliban's, unite the opposition, secure international support, cooperate in hunting down al Qaeda's remnants, and relieve the United States of the need to occupy and run the country."[20] The administration feared that deep US involvement would not only inflame resistance but also limit American options to focus its military and financial might elsewhere. In the wake of 9/11, the opportunity costs of entanglement in Afghanistan and the prospect of war in Iraq dominated the policy process.

What emerged from the sponsors' debates was a division of labor. The US rejected Brahimi's calls to disarm the militias and introduce Western security forces; from the administration's perspective, it would be far better to shift the burden of peacekeeping to the UN and the Europeans. The compromise was the "lead nation" approach in which each country assumed responsibility for a specific piece of the reconstruction project. The Germans took the lead on police development, the Italians on the legal system, the UK on counternarcotics, and the United States on training the Afghan army. The United States eschewed direct involvement in reconstruction or political engineering, preferring to leave these tasks to its international partners. It hoped to focus almost exclusively on the pursuit of al Qaeda and depend on the Afghans and Europeans to cement the gains of the 2001 victory.[21] As a result, by the end of 2002, there were fewer than 15,000 foreign troops in the country, of whom roughly 10,000 were Americans.

Act 2: Backing into Counterinsurgency, January 2003–November 2008

Scene 1: Armed Development in the Shadow of Iraq, January 2003–December 2005

From the American point of view, the Afghan project in early 2003 appeared modest. The pursuit of al Qaeda and its allies remained the first priority. The key to erecting an effective Afghan state was the execution of the Bonn process and the fulfillment of Europe's governance and development commitments. As the United States soon discovered, the Taliban resurgence in the south and east upset these plans to complete an orderly restoration.

Dealing with a renewed Taliban offensive would have been complicated enough—particularly given the disconnects created by assigning reconstruction duties to different lead nations—but the largest factor limiting US options in Afghanistan after 2003 was the progressively worsening situation in Iraq. With the fall of the Taliban, the White House's and CENTCOM's focus, attention, and resources shifted from a task seen as largely complete to the challenge of Iraq. The justification, planning, execution, and unexpected sequels to Operation Iraqi Freedom meant that the US campaign in Afghanistan between 2003 and 2008 would be fought as an economy-of-force mission with the troops and resources on hand.

Even without the Iraqi diversion, the creation of a stable Afghan state would have encountered numerous challenges, not least because of the type of government the West was trying to install. The Bonn process not only formalized the ascent of Hamid Karzai but determined the structure of the government. As enshrined in the December 2003 constitution, that government would be highly centralized with the president holding the power to appoint not only ministers but also provincial governors. Western leaders supported centralization as a check on the return of civil war; they found ready allies among those who hoped to use a powerful state to modernize Afghanistan under Pashtun leadership.[22] This formal structure sat atop a reality still dominated by powerful warlords and self-governing locales. Much of the energy of the next decade would be consumed in trying to rationalize the relationship between a weak but highly centralized government in Kabul and the traditional and warlord fiefdoms that surrounded it.

The connective tissue joining these formal and informal structures was financial patronage rather than nationalism or a shared vision for the country. In the absence of a strong, national army, and in the presence of armed rivals, Karzai used appointments and cash to elevate and reward his allies; at the same time, he sought to weaken his rivals through the internationally sponsored disarmament of warlord militias.[23] At a time when the Taliban seemed to be in retreat, Karzai accepted the risks associated with hobbling his allies in the hope that this would secure a solidary, centrally administered state.

The problem was that the state's ambitions for control exceeded its ability to compel obedience, mediate disputes, and resist insurgent challenges. While the demobilization of militias may have prevented warlordism, the state lacked the resources, apparatus, and competence to manage a complex array of local alliances in the face of a rising Taliban threat. As traditional leaders squabbled over land and offices in the wake of the Taliban collapse, the state lacked the strength or facility to limit this feuding and buttress its own authority.[24] It was this turmoil and the weakness of the patrimonial order in the provinces that made the return of the Taliban possible.

The return of the Taliban would strike the Afghan state and the coalition at the low ebb of their military power. The demobilization of militias, while effective in limiting the threats to Karzai from within his own camp, had the unintended effect of reducing the fighting strength of Karzai's coalition just as the Taliban began to return. Attempts to weld the members of various militia forces into a national army were frustrated by the political maneuvering of the Tajik minister of defense, Fahim Khan, and other warlords who feared the emergence of an army under Karzai's control. Ironically, even successful attempts to impose discipline on onetime militias dissolved the web of personal loyalties that had given these units their effectiveness. The strength and coherence of Karzai's Afghan alliances fell, and this slide was not offset by the development of a professional Afghan army or the introduction of foreign troops.[25]

Those other candidate security forces were, for various reasons, unavailable to fill the security vacuum. By 2003, the 10,000 US troops remained squarely focused on the pursuit of al Qaeda in the east and south and did very little to bolster Karzai's standing or legitimacy. With such a small contingent, the only options for American planners were raids of varying size or multiweek sweep operations. The International Security Assistance Force (ISAF) created at Bonn was by design very small (under 6,000 in late 2003) and strictly limited to operations inside Kabul. Eager to prevent mission creep, US Secretary of Defense Donald Rumsfeld resisted calls to introduce more US troops or expand ISAF's boundaries.[26] Thus, from 2002 through the end of 2005, international guardianship took the form of two separate and loosely coordinated foreign forces: ISAF policed Kabul while the American military hunted al Qaeda. This arrangement would persist until early 2006 when ISAF assumed control countrywide and brought most US forces under its control.[27]

As the Bonn process unfolded, it became clear that the political process alone might be insufficient to restore the stability necessary to achieve American goals. The frailty of the Karzai regime prompted American leaders in Afghanistan to explore new ways to buttress the state.

On his arrival in October 2003, the US commander, Lieutenant General Barno, assessed the situation and proposed a shift from counterterrorism to counterinsurgency. Once again, this strategy was the product of demands and constraints. The UN's special envoy, Lakhdar Brahimi, was concerned that the presidential and parliamentary elections in 2004 and 2005 would require greater levels of security in the south and east. In the shadow of Iraq, Barno could not expect to receive the troops necessary to protect the population directly. Given these parameters, Barno sought to develop a "light footprint" counterinsurgency strategy to fill the vacuum and safeguard the upcoming elections.

The inspiration for Barno's plan was historical and experiential. Drawing on the classic 1960s works on counterinsurgency and the experience of British officers on his staff, Barno developed a strategy that identified the population as the center of gravity. To gain the support of the population, he proposed five lines of effort: counterterrorism operations, the development of the Afghan security forces, clear territorial responsibilities, development and governance, and engagement with neighboring states (notably Pakistan).[28]

While Barno saw no alternative to offensive operations against al Qaeda and the Taliban, he sought to apply the Hippocratic principle of counterinsurgency—first do no harm. Barno placed stricter limits on the use of air strikes and developed a list of 15 points governing the conduct of searches. His intent was to temper the pursuit of enemies with an understanding that the blowback from botched operations might easily outweigh their tactical results.[29]

Given the limits on US troop levels, the most straightforward answer to the problem of security was for the Afghans to do it themselves, and this meant developing a competent Afghan army and police force. With just one US maneuver brigade of troops to protect 31 million people across a mountainous country the size of Texas, Barno clearly understood the primary importance of the training mission.[30] Still, for various reasons, the training project failed to meet early expectations. The initial target set in December 2002 for the Afghan National Army (ANA) was 70,000; US planners hoped to complete the fielding of this army by 2008.[31] Unfortunately, the advisors sent to train these forces encountered problems ranging from the material (infrastructure, equipment, and pay) to the political (ethnic divisions, warlord loyalties, involuntary enlistment), as chapter 3 in this volume explains. The result of these complications, and the concurrent failure of attempts to professionalize the warlord militias, meant that the ANA did not reach the battlefield in significant numbers until 2005.[32] The three-year gap between the overthrow of the Taliban and the ANA debut was a missed opportunity that US and Afghan leaders would rue as the insurgency worsened after 2005.

The results of police training were even more dispiriting. While the Germans had agreed to be the lead nation for the effort, their focus on the long-term training of police officers left the regime without trained rank and file to restore order in the provinces. Once the German failure became clear, the United States stepped in to inject greater urgency, resources, and attention.[33] In the interim, the police in many areas were little more than militias. Not surprisingly, these ill-trained forces were often ineffective and corrupt. Far from bolstering the authority of the state, such forces frequently alienated communities and lowered the barriers to Taliban reentry.

Perhaps the most striking aspect of General Barno's campaign was its renewed emphasis on economic development and governance, tasks which had heretofore belonged to the US State Department, US Agency for International Development (USAID), and the United Nations—not the US military. If Barno lacked the troops to protect the population, then one plausible approach was to win their hearts and minds through the provision of public goods and services. In theory, building schools, digging wells, and constructing government buildings might address public grievances, dampen resistance, and foster goodwill and cooperation.[34]

The primary vehicle for this theory of armed development was the Provincial Reconstruction Team (PRT). The PRT had its origins in the early experience of US Civil Affairs teams in Afghanistan. Encouraged by their success, Barno hoped that larger units (of 60–100 personnel) combining US troops, development specialists, diplomats, and Afghan government officials would fill the political vacuum, extend the government's reach, and increase public support.[35] Building on the experiences of the four PRTs in the stable north and west, Barno ordered a tripling of the number of teams and their deployment to the south and east.[36]

While the PRTs were a novel solution to troop constraints, two problems emerged. First, the implicit theories of economic development and pacification were shaky at best. While locals seldom declined the investments and cash the PRTs distributed, these did not automatically translate into sustainable economic growth or lasting goodwill. In addition, studies of Afghan perceptions revealed that these benevolent acts often engendered resentment and amplified competition within and among targeted communities. Building a well in a village might seem uncontroversial, but it might be destabilizing in a community in which water rights are at the heart of political competition.[37]

Karzai and his ministers were also deeply ambivalent about the PRTs and would eventually turn against them. On the one hand, they acknowledged the importance of development and the government's weakness at the district and village levels. On the other hand, they saw the PRTs as they did militias; both were, in Karzai's words, "parallel structures" that usurped the role of the Afghan state and diminished its authority.[38] To the extent that the PRTs succeeded in stimulating development and governance, they might come to serve as separate and foreign objects of loyalty. Karzai preferred and ultimately demanded that all assistance flow through the central government so that loyalty accrued to the state rather than its foreign sponsors.

General Barno's embrace of counterinsurgency was an important conceptual shift but one bounded by resources. Counterinsurgency without troops meant a mix of armed development, Afghan National Security Forces (ANSF) training, and new limits on offensive operations. By his own accounting, Barno considered the strategy a success; the planned presidential and parliamentary elections of 2004 and 2005 were conducted without major disruptions, and this constituted a setback for the Taliban.[39] Other indicators were more mixed. By late 2005, the Taliban had begun to infiltrate the settled areas of the south and east and this translated into increasing attacks on Afghan forces, officials, and schools.[40]

Scene 2: The Return of the Taliban, January 2006–November 2008

While Barno's light footprint, counterinsurgency and the conclusion of the Bonn process appeared to herald a new beginning, the return of the Taliban soon exposed the weaknesses of US strategy and Karzai's regime. Starting in late 2005, Taliban offensives shattered the new order, recaptured large swathes of the south, and forced the United States to reassess what it would take to defend the Afghan state. Tellingly, the US response was to debate resources and implementation more than the underlying strategy.[41]

The leading cause of the return of the Taliban was the fragility of the neopatrimonial order and the Karzai regime's inability to persuade more-traditional rural areas to accept Kabul's rule. On paper, the Bonn process had created a strong central government and had granted the president sweeping powers at the national and provincial levels. In practice, Karzai lacked the resources and muscle to enforce his writ. As a result, his success hinged on his ability to manage a complex network of alliances with local potentates. Under such indirect rule, Karzai used his powers of appointment to install clients and bless existing traditional leaders and warlords.[42]

Though this quasi-feudal system drew on traditional Afghan notions of authority, it was in many ways weaker than the monarchical system it echoed. Installing or accepting one set of tribal or Mujahideen leaders in an area often marginalized other tribes and segments that had supported the Taliban. Their exclusion, however understandable, provided the new Taliban with ready allies. Rivalries among nominally loyal elites had always been an intrinsic feature of the feudal model; what changed after 2001 was the state's capacity to manage and adjudicate these disputes. In many areas, and most importantly in the rural south, the Karzai regime was unable to maintain a tribal coalition sufficient to prevent the Taliban's return. Unable to resolve the disputes on their own, many elites abstained from the coming contest or shifted their allegiance to the Taliban.[43]

Even this feudal confederation might have survived had it not been for the turmoil surrounding the provision of security. After 2001, "centralizers" in Kabul and many international observers saw the return of warlordism, and not the Taliban, as the "principal obstacle to implementation of the political process that was agreed at the Bonn Conference."[44] From the start, there was pressure to remove warlords and demobilize the militias that had been both integral to the victory in 2001 and closely associated with the civil war of the 1990s.

Viewed in isolation, the impulse to remove warlords and dissolve militias was entirely reasonable. Unfortunately, it came at a singularly perilous juncture. By 2003, the efforts to professionalize the militias had failed, and the construction of the Afghan National Army and the police had barely begun. At the end of 2005, there were fewer than 30,000 US and NATO troops in Afghanistan and very few of these were engaged in population security. For these reasons, the demobilization of the militias proved a catastrophic success. In the short run, it further weakened the state and dissolved the militia bulwarks that were the primary obstacles to Taliban infiltration. Removing 60,000–

100,000 militiamen may have weakened Karzai's rivals but it simultaneously opened the door for the Taliban thrust into the south and east.[45]

Events inside Afghanistan were not the only factors facilitating the return of the Taliban, for their resurgence in 2005–2006 would not have been possible without the sanctuary and support of the Pakistani state; this support would remain an indelible feature of the US campaign in Afghanistan for the remainder of the war. The Pakistanis had underwritten the original Taliban movement of the 1990s and had expressed misgivings about an independent, US-sponsored regime in Kabul. While the Pakistanis had grudgingly cooperated in the pursuit of some al Qaeda leaders immediately after 9/11, they had done nothing to hand over Taliban leaders. Instead, Pakistan had offered the fleeing Taliban forces sanctuary to preserve its options in the future struggle for Afghanistan.[46]

Starting sometime after 2003, Pakistan substantially increased its level of material and advisory support to the Taliban and the Haqqani network—a Pashtun group with links to both al Qaeda and the Pakistani Inter-Services Intelligence (ISI).[47] Some have argued that the Pakistanis did so out of fear that the United States might leave Afghanistan abruptly to reinforce Iraq; less charitably, the early success of the Karzai regime may have encouraged the Pakistanis to hobble the emerging state.[48] Whether this was a defensive reaction or an aggressive bid for influence, the ISI provided easy access to cash and weaponry to those fighting the Americans and the ANSF.[49] Absent sanctuary and active state support, the Taliban would have been unable to mount a major offensive in the south and east in 2005–2006.[50]

The results of the Taliban offensive were impressive. The failure of the Karzai regime to consolidate control over the rural areas of the south and east meant that the Taliban were pushing on an open door. The Taliban were again operating in large groups, and they were able to seize control in a number of the rural areas of the south and east. While the Afghans and their Western allies still held Kandahar City and other urban centers, security in the countryside and along major roads plummeted. On the local level, Taliban leaders launched murder and intimidation campaigns targeting local officials, police, and loyalists. By the fall of 2006, the Taliban once again controlled significant base areas in the south as the government and coalition forces retreated to district and provincial centers.[51]

The Taliban offensive coincided with a major expansion of NATO forces into the south and east. Sensing weakness in the south, the UK and Canada agreed to deploy additional forces; between May and November 2006, the number of NATO troops more than doubled to 21,000 while the number of US troops reached 20,000. Unaware of the extent of Taliban infiltration, these new contingents collided with the insurgent offensive. The result was the heaviest fighting since the end of 2001 and heavy use of US airpower in support of beleaguered British and Canadian troops. The number of insurgent attacks in 2006 grew by 200 percent year on year and attacks along the borders of Pakistan grew by 300 percent.[52] While these operations staved off the loss of major cities, they revealed the magnitude of the insurgent threat.[53]

While US decision makers sought to avoid defeat in Afghanistan, they preferred incremental resource injections to major changes in strategy—a choice the United States made in the Vietnam War as well. Starting in the fall of 2006, President Bush ordered a "silent surge" of 10,000 US troops over two years as commanders clamored for additional development spending to improve conditions and foster goodwill.[54] US military and civilian leaders in Afghanistan saw the urgency of immediate action; leaders in Washington were caught between a desire to reinforce Afghanistan and to cope with the growing demands of Iraq. These competing demands would effectively cap the resources devoted to Afghanistan through 2008.[55]

This acute resource scarcity precluded any meaningful discussion of the war's overall strategy. So long as US leaders could blame the return of the Taliban on the lack of money and personnel, few saw a need to reexamine either the foundations of the Afghan political order or the counterinsurgency strategy. Thus, from 2006 through the end of the Bush administration, the United States pursued armed development, counterterrorism, and gradual reinforcement, but this formula did little to slow the Taliban's momentum in the south and east.

Act 3: The Surge, January 2009–June 2011

Upon taking office in 2009, President Obama spent a full year reassessing the Afghanistan strategy, eventually settling on what came to be known as the surge. That surge marked the climax of US involvement in Afghanistan and involved not only a dramatic increase in troops but also major changes in leadership and strategy. US troop levels climbed from 31,000 in December 2008 to over 100,000 by August 2010. The surge was the hallmark of the incoming Obama administration's shift from Iraq to Afghanistan, and the two military leaders charged with its implementation were the leading lights of the Iraq surge—Generals Stanley McChrystal and David Petraeus. With these changes in resources and leadership came an embrace of classical counterinsurgency—an instantiation of the principles General Barno had first proposed in 2003, and a reprise of the late war strategy in Iraq. Six years later, with security declining and corruption growing, a campaign that had been dominated by counterterrorism and armed development now shifted to the protection of civilian populations and the accelerated development of the Afghan state and security forces.

With the three-year surge came profound increases in US aims, costs, and attention. The change in strategy and increased resources had unintended but costly effects on the administration's relationships with military commanders and the Afghan government. President Obama's endorsement of counterinsurgency was quickly followed by buyer's remorse and mounting frustration with Karzai. Within a year, major gaps had opened between the administration and its military leaders, and the Afghan government was subjected to the bullwhip effects of the steep increases in US spending and personnel.

Scene 1: Debating the Surge, January–December 2009

By the end of 2008, the strategy of expedients assembled after 2002 appeared unequal to the task of stabilizing Afghanistan. Despite substantial US and NATO reinforcement of the south and east,

Taliban momentum had continued to build. After a February 2009 trip to Afghanistan, Michèle Flournoy, the incoming undersecretary of defense for policy, privately reported the absence of a unifying strategy: "I saw little to convince me that we have a comprehensive interagency plan or concept of operations. I still believe that many competing—and often conflicting—campaigns are ongoing in Afghanistan: counterinsurgency, counterterrorism, counternarcotics, and efforts at nation building. Interagency planning, coordination, and resourcing are, by far, the weakest link."[56]

This growing unease was punctuated by then ISAF commander General David McKiernan's standing request for 20,000–30,000 additional troops to blunt the anticipated spring offensive and to shield the presidential elections planned for 2009.[57] McKiernan's request set in motion a Bush administration internal assessment whose conclusion was bleak: "We're not losing but we're not winning, and that's not good enough." The report argued that Afghanistan's government was weak, riddled with corruption, and enmeshed in the narcotics industry, and that the existence of Taliban sanctuaries in Pakistan made it difficult to terminate the insurgency inside Afghanistan.[58] While President Bush found the report compelling, he was reluctant to impose its recommendations on the incoming administration. Consequently, he tabled McKiernan's request and left the decision to the Obama team.

After reluctantly endorsing the deployment of 17,000 additional troops, the new administration embarked on a 60-day assessment led by a former CIA analyst, Bruce Riedel.[59] The Riedel report echoed the Bush administration's pessimism but proposed a more sweeping solution. The ultimate aim was "to disrupt, dismantle and defeat al Qaeda, and to ensure that their safe havens in Afghanistan and Pakistan cannot threaten the United States anymore." To accomplish this, Riedel proposed a regional strategy that combined "fully resourced counterinsurgency" inside Afghanistan with cooperation from Pakistan to dismantle the Taliban sanctuaries inside its borders. All of this would be accompanied by renewed initiatives in ANSF development and insurgent reconciliation and a civilian surge to buttress the Afghan state.[60]

President Obama announced his decision to implement the Riedel strategy on March 27, 2009. In unequivocal terms, he highlighted the primacy of pursuing al Qaeda and the importance of Pakistani cooperation. Obama envisioned a comprehensive strategy to strengthen the Afghan state, pursue al Qaeda, and "take the fight to the Taliban in the south and the east, and give us a greater capacity to partner with Afghan security forces and to go after insurgents along the border." Over the longer term, the United States would transfer responsibility to an expanded and improved ANSF.[61]

On the heels of the president's decision, chairman of the Joint Chiefs, Admiral Michael Mullen, and Defense Secretary Robert Gates decided to replace General McKiernan. Neither was confident that the commander was capable of implementing such a sweeping change in strategy; both believed it was essential to have the most adroit commander in place immediately.[62] They recommended the appointment of General Stanley McChrystal, the architect of the highly successful counterterrorism campaign in Iraq. Obama approved of the change and McKiernan stepped down on May 11, 2009.[63]

Unwittingly, this change of command reopened the strategy debate. At Gates's suggestion, McChrystal began his own 60-day assessment. Skeptics of the Riedel strategy, including Vice President Biden and many of the president's political advisors, saw this study as a ploy to force additional troop increases. Secretary Gates, Secretary of State Hillary Clinton, Admiral Mullen, and CENTCOM commander General David Petraeus saw the assessment as a prudent step toward implementing the president's intent. The result was another lengthy bottom-up review that stretched from June through December of 2009.[64]

Based on his planners' work, McChrystal concluded that the only feasible answer to the crisis was population-centric counterinsurgency. Protecting the population and training the Afghan security forces would take precedence over pursuing the Taliban. McChrystal was confident that with such a strategy, and an additional 40,000 troops, he could break the momentum of the insurgency within a year and restore Afghan confidence. Under the prevailing conditions,

McChrystal saw no reasonable alternative to counterinsurgency; if additional forces could not be committed, the only responsible option was to reduce US aims in Afghanistan.[65]

The rival camps in Washington soon coalesced around two strategies. Where Generals McChrystal and Petraeus saw the need for counterinsurgency, Vice President Biden saw an opportunity to step back from escalation. Biden lobbied for 20,000 Special Forces, human intelligence assets, and trainers to pursue al Qaeda and expand the ANSF. In theory, his "counterterrorism plus" strategy would disrupt, dismantle, and defeat al Qaeda while shifting the burden of security to the Afghans.[66]

While the White House was receptive, "counterterrorism plus" met with determined resistance from the Department of Defense, which Secretary Gates communicated to the president in a memo on October 13. As Gates later recounted in his memoir, "Counterterrorism focused solely on al Qaeda could not work without a significant U.S. ground presence in Afghanistan and the opportunity to collect intelligence that this would afford us. 'We tried remote-control counterterrorism in the 1990s, and it brought us 9/11.' 'Counterterrorism plus' or 'counterinsurgency minus,' was what we had been doing since 2004, and 'everyone seems to agree that too is not working.'" In Gates's estimation, the goal should be to deny the Taliban control of the key population centers and develop only those ministries necessary to restore order. Such a focused campaign might blunt the Taliban offensive and reduce violence to 2004 levels.[67]

The debates of the fall oscillated between theoretical discussions of aims and strategy and hard-nosed bargaining over numbers. After two months of haggling, Obama endorsed a surge of 33,000 US troops and 5,000 NATO trainers to pave the way for an ANSF of 400,000.[68] Obama made it clear that he would assess the results in December 2010 and begin troop withdrawals in July 2011. Speaking at West Point on December 1, 2009, Obama expressed the strategy in bellicose terms: "Our overarching goal remains the same: to disrupt, dismantle, and defeat al Qaeda in Afghanistan and Pakistan, and to prevent its capacity to threaten America and our allies in the future. To meet that goal, we will pursue the following objectives within Afghanistan. We must deny al Qaeda a safe haven. We must reverse the Taliban's momentum and deny it the ability to overthrow the government. And we must strengthen the capacity of Afghanistan's security forces and government so that they can take lead responsibility for Afghanistan's future."[69]

While the West Point speech marked a victory for the counterinsurgency advocates, the debate strained Obama's relations with the military and did not settle the underlying arguments about the scale, duration, purpose, and prospects of US intervention in Afghanistan. The president resented his having been "boxed in" by military leaders intent on waging counterinsurgency. On the eve of his speech, Obama privately underscored his fixation on the exit: "This needs to be a plan about how we're going to hand it off and get out of Afghanistan. . . . Everything we're doing needs to be focused on how we're going to get to the point where we can reduce our footprint. . . . There cannot be any wiggle room. It has to be clear that this is what we're doing."[70]

The dissidents seized on the president's ambivalence as an opening to assail the McChrystal strategy.[71] While much of this criticism emanated from the National Security Council, two explosive cables sent by US ambassador and former US military commander in Afghanistan Karl Eikenberry attacked the feasibility of counterinsurgency and Karzai's competence. The subsequent release of those cables fatally compromised Eikenberry's relationships with McChrystal and Karzai; rather than remove Eikenberry, the administration chose to leave a divided country team and a poisoned ambassadorial relationship in place for over a year.[72] The unsettled debate would rage for two years, pitting a skeptical White House against a command eager to win at counterinsurgency.

Scene 2: Implementing the Surge, December 2009–June 2011

In execution, the McChrystal strategy combined conceptual changes and geographical continuities. McChrystal envisioned three main efforts: (1) securing the population, (2) separating the population from the insurgents and restoring government and public services, (3) and connecting secured communities to foster effective governance and economic development.[73] Determined to reduce civilian casualties, he formalized the shift from kill-and-capture operations to population security in a new tactical directive that placed important restrictions on the use of American firepower.[74]

On the operational level, bureaucratic politics and the enemy's recent advances drove the early employment of US forces. The Taliban successes in the south and east made some riposte imperative; McChrystal envisioned an early counteroffensive in Helmand and Kandahar followed by a final push in the east. Operation Moshtarak, launched in February 2010 in the city of Marjah, would serve as the test case of the new strategy.[75]

The fight for Marjah prefigured the possibilities and difficulties of counterinsurgency in Afghanistan, and highlighted once more how difficult it would be to convince the rural periphery to accept Kabul's writ. While the Marines were able to seize the center of the town at limited cost, the fighting along the outskirts became bogged down in a months-long struggle. More troubling was the failure of the first attempts to restore Afghan government control. In an early visit to the city, McChrystal announced the hold and build phases of the operation in technocratic terms: "We have 'government in a box,' ready to roll in."[76] In practice, the attempt to install Afghan administrators and restore public services collided with existing tribal politics.[77] Even well-intentioned efforts to restore the city's irrigation systems provoked violent conflicts over water access and political power. While US forces were eventually able to push the insurgents out, and draw ANSF units into the area, the fighting continued through December 2010. This slow and painful debut of the "clear, hold, build" strategy suggested that securing the south and east would be arduous.[78]

As in all wars, ill fortune can upset the best-laid plans. In the summer of 2010, this came in the form of an acute civil-military crisis. On June 21, 2010, in the opening stages of Operation Hamkari, the long-awaited offensive to secure Kandahar, the publication of a *Rolling Stone* article on McChrystal and his staff set in motion his removal as

US and ISAF commander.[79] While in Paris for meetings with NATO allies, the general and his staff let their guard down with reporter Michael Hastings; the resulting article (entitled "The Runaway General") was a public relations disaster for McChrystal and for the US military more broadly.[80] The article recounted the staff's unvarnished criticisms of the Obama administration; in short order, Obama relieved McChrystal and appointed General Petraeus as his successor. While the proximate cause of McChrystal's relief was his apparent disrespect for the commander in chief, Obama conveyed his underlying doubts to Gates: "Let's talk substance. . . . I don't have the sense it's going well in Afghanistan. He [McChrystal] doesn't seem to be making progress. Maybe his strategy is not really working." Gates sensed that the president, who had six months earlier announced a two-year campaign to turn the tide in Afghanistan, had already begun to back away from counterinsurgency.[81]

General Petraeus took command of the war just as White House support for the campaign began to ebb. As the architect of the counterinsurgency renaissance in Iraq, Petraeus was on one level the ideal successor. Ironically, his greatest contribution came in lifting many of the restrictions on the use of air strikes and artillery McChrystal had imposed in his quest to secure Afghan goodwill. Even more than McChrystal, Petraeus saw the Special Operations task forces as his mobile reserve in Afghanistan, and worked to increase their size, capabilities, and operational tempo throughout his time as ISAF commander. But his overriding conviction was that successful counterinsurgency hinged on getting the right mix of capabilities—both military and civilian—onto the battlefield, a task he referred to in his many briefings to Washington as "getting the inputs right."[82] Petraeus was intensely aware that he was in a race to obtain decisive results in the south and east before US troop withdrawals began in July 2011. Provided he could do this, and keep the pace of withdrawals modest between 2011 and 2014, the country might be stable enough for a successful transition to the Afghans.

By the summer of 2011, the question was whether McChrystal and Petraeus's strategy had worked. If the immediate aim had been to reverse the Taliban's momentum and prevent Karzai's fall, then the surge had succeeded. Special Operations Forces used night raids to capture large numbers of Taliban cadres. As Petraeus noted in congressional testimony, "In a typical 90 day period . . . precision operations by US Special Mission Units and their Afghan partners alone kill or capture some 360 targeted insurgent leaders." The fivefold increase in the prison population of Afghanistan between 2004 and 2012 gives another indication of the scale of the counterterrorism campaign.[83] The most promising results came in the short-term suppression of violence. In those areas where the United States injected very large numbers of troops for 18–24 months (in Helmand and to a lesser extent Kandahar), violence first spiked and then declined precipitously. Equally important, successful clearing operations often made it possible to replace US and coalition forces with Afghan security forces.

Where the surge fell short was in the depth and durability of its results. While there were dramatic local successes, in 2013 insurgent attacks nationwide remained nearly 10 times the 2004 level Secretary Gates had proposed as his own benchmark in the surge debates. Perversely, the number of foreign troops proved the best predictor of violence on the national level; as troop numbers rose, so too did the number of attacks.[84]

Moreover, even if the coalition had been able to break Taliban resistance, the gains would all be impermanent if the Afghan state could not generate and maintain its own competent security forces. Despite dramatic increases in the size of the army and police and determined efforts to resolve problems of quality and desertion, the ANSF remained heavily dependent on external funding and advisory support. The elemental question remained whether the Afghan state could reasonably afford and competently manage a security force large enough to secure the regime.

The American impact on governance and development, the core of the "hold" and "build" campaign, was less encouraging. The much-touted "civilian surge" of diplomats and technical experts was far less extensive, energetic, and effective than planners had hoped. While the

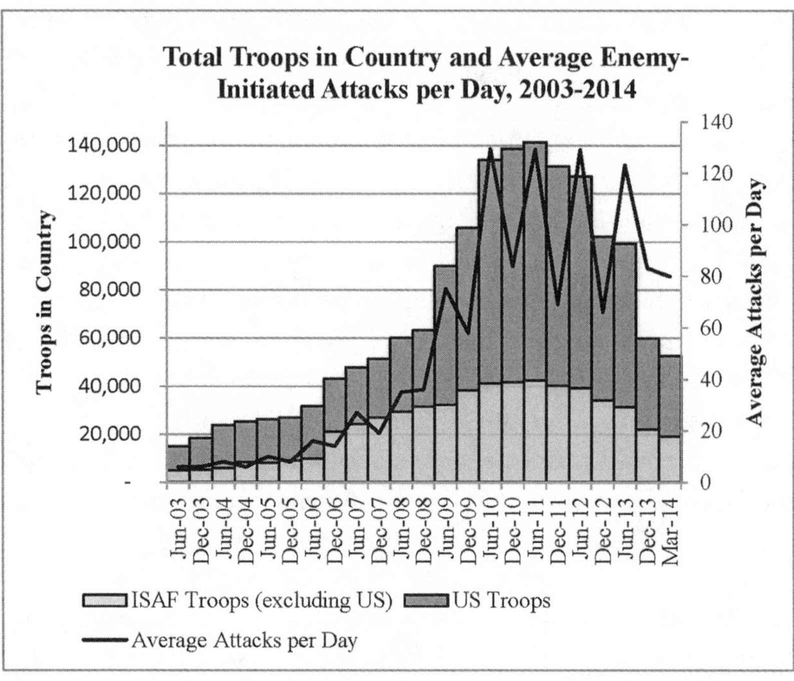

Figure 2.2 Counterinsurgency strategists surmised that with sufficient troops on the ground, the ISAF coalition would be able to protect the Afghan people from the Taliban. However, as troop numbers rose after 2005, so too did enemy-initiated attacks, which always peaked during the summer fighting seasons and declined during the winters. (Government Accountability Office)

Kabul embassy staff swelled, only 400 of the 1,500 civilians deployed at the peak were ever pushed to the district and provincial levels.[85] While the United States continued to promote the elections process, the relationship between these rituals and real political competition was tenuous. Karzai and others had increasingly captured the process, transforming it from an institution of representative democracy into a vehicle for reinforcing elite power.[86] Even where the United States sought to foster local governance and connect those structures to the central government, these initiatives often ran afoul of Afghan leaders. Karzai decried the creation of "parallel structures," while community leaders resisted the intrusion of a central government when resources could be more easily obtained from foreign troops or NGOs. The overall impression was that Afghan politicians entertained US advice as the price of extracting resources; the lasting impact of American institutional tutelage in education and judicial reform remains uncertain.

The impact of the development surge was equally problematic. Implicitly, the United States saw economic development as both a goal and a means to cultivate goodwill in support of counterinsurgency. The crescendo of US aid and US surge spending inflated the Afghan economy in the short run. At the peak of the surge, the United States spent between $15.8 and $16.65 billion per year on Afghanistan assistance; the Afghan economy in 2011 was estimated to be between $18 and $19 billion.[87] Even if a substantial portion of those funds was spent outside Afghanistan, the aid injection was the largest single driver in the economy, and this was enough to push annual growth rates from near zero in 2001 to 9.4 percent between 2003 and 2014.[88] Building infrastructure such as roads, power plants, and markets may have increased the long-term productivity of the Afghan economy. Other aspects of the "war economy" drove both output and inflation in goods and services. The overarching question was how much of this economy could survive the impending withdrawal of US troops.

Development as an instrument of pacification had a decidedly mixed record. In theory, the provision of public goods and services and jobs should have decreased incentives for resistance and increased incentives for collaboration. In practice, small projects and cash outlays bought information and rented short-term cooperation. Over the longer run, the reciprocity norm seldom held.[89] Public works projects often triggered envy and competition between the beneficiaries and those who were excluded. Even when US development assistance fostered lasting goodwill, a basic question was whether this helped or undermined the Afghan state. If US units proved better at delivering goods and services, then this might tarnish the authority of the state and reinforce such "parallel structures."

The final challenge was corruption. Injecting massive sums of money into an economy with limited absorptive capacity induced profound distortions. Afghanistan was transformed into a "rentier state" in which the most promising occupation for enterprising Afghans was to capture the rents associated with lucrative US contracts and development projects. While Americans were quick to decry corruption within the Afghan government, they were less willing to accept that they had unintentionally fueled this behavior with their spending.[90]

Those charged with transforming Afghanistan, whether Western or Afghan, collided with the chasm separating rural and urban opinion on issues of modernization. For many Afghans, the urban boom inaugurated in 2002 and fueled by Western spending appeared to herald a prosperous new age. The urban population swelled as Afghans voted with their feet to seek employment in the cities and particularly the capital. And yet the same things that appealed to these urban immigrants were anathema to the elites of many rural communities. When the Afghan government or its Western partners sought to export modernization to the countryside, these offers were often met with suspicion, resistance, and rivalry. Trading autonomy and established social structures for the possibility of services, education, social upheaval, and government control never appealed to more than a fraction of rural elites; even when certain leaders benefited from state or Western patronage, these gains stimulated resistance and struggle by those left out. For this reason alone, efforts to consolidate Afghan central government control proved maddeningly difficult to achieve and sustain.[91]

The most discouraging aspect of the surge was its negligible influence on the problem of Pakistani sanctuaries. From the Riedel report through Obama's speeches and the campaign plans, US policymakers and strategists insisted that success in the region would hinge on active Pakistani cooperation in the border areas. So long as the Taliban and their allies enjoyed sanctuary and varying levels of support from Pakistan, it would be impossible to defeat the movement inside Afghanistan. By 2011, most US leaders were skeptical that real cooperation would be forthcoming. The existence of these safe havens allowed the Taliban to organize and reconstitute in the wake of successful US and Afghan offensives.[92] The Pakistanis were willing to cooperate against targets that threatened the Pakistani state, provided these operations were not too costly in casualties or domestic opinion. The Pakistanis were unwilling to crack down on militants they considered potentially useful—Lashkar-e-Taiba, the Haqqani network, and the Quetta Shura.[93] The Pakistanis never complied with Afghan or US requests to detain and transfer the leaders of the Afghan insurgency; instead, many of these leaders were provided with safe houses and guarantees of protection. In some instances, Pakistan appeared to exercise veto power over the Afghan Taliban in its negotiations with the Americans. Pakistan successfully resisted US pressure to cut its ties with Afghan militant groups and thus retained the trump cards in any political struggle that might follow US withdrawal.[94]

Act 4: Transition, July 2011–December 2014

As the president's July 2011 deadline approached, the debates of 2009 remained unresolved. The Defense Department and the commanders on the ground saw the reductions in violence in the south and southwest as the tangible, if slow and costly, achievements of the surge. If the surge was indeed working, the key was to maintain high US troop levels to secure those gains and replicate them in the east. The White House saw the situation in entirely different terms. It considered the achievements of the surge underwhelming and was squarely focused on meeting domestic commitments in advance of the US presidential election. All of this played out against the backdrop of the civil-military distrust born during the 2009 surge debates. Commenting later on a March 2011 meeting in which Obama had announced that he refused to be "gamed" by the military, Gates was blunt: "The president doesn't trust his commander [General Petraeus], can't stand Karzai, doesn't believe in his own strategy, and doesn't consider the war to be his. For him it's all about getting out."[95]

The successful May 2011 raid against Osama bin Ladin resolved the administration's strategic dilemma. With Bin Ladin dead, civilian leaders could plausibly claim to have achieved the mission of degrading and disrupting al Qaeda. This made a rapid withdrawal of the US surge forces politically defensible and made the acceleration of the handoff to the Afghans the central focus.

The final decision on troop withdrawals broke along familiar lines. When General Petraeus returned to Washington for his confirmation hearings as the director of Central Intelligence, there were over 100,000 troops in Afghanistan. In a White House meeting in late June, General Petraeus recommended a minimal withdrawal in 2011 and the maintenance and the withdrawal of the bulk of the surge forces in December 2012 after the end of the fighting season. After considerable debate, the president rejected the ISAF/DOD proposal in favor of the accelerated withdrawal of 10,000 troops between July and December 2011 and another 23,000 by September 2012. While Petraeus and Gates publically supported the president's decision, the scale and pace of the drawdown was a pointed rejection of the military's warning of mission failure and marked the end of "fully resourced" counterinsurgency.[96]

As the focus shifted from counterinsurgency to "transition," interpretations of this process reflected the vast differences in outlook between civilian and military leaders in Kabul and the White House. ISAF and the US embassy sought a "conditions-based" transition in which the pace of US troop withdrawals would depend on the readiness of Afghan security forces and the strength of the insurgency.[97] The White House, by contrast, was primarily intent on meeting its previously announced timeline for withdrawals. Both groups described the process as "irreversible"; the military used the word to emphasize the durability of security gains while the civilian leadership used the same word to underscore the impossibility of slowing or reversing the withdrawals. These discussions were eerily similar to the Vietnamization debates between General Creighton Abrams and Secretary of Defense Melvin Laird under the Nixon administration; the political leadership in both cases was intent on capturing the domestic benefits of withdrawal, and the military on minimizing the risk of mission failure.[98]

The US military's original plan was to start the transfer of security responsibility in the areas where stability was greatest. This process was already underway before the US announced its first withdrawals on June 22, 2011. Transition was then to proceed in five "tranches," or packages of districts and provinces, from the most stable to the most unstable areas. This plan was consistent with the ISAF command's emphasis on "conditions-based" transition. The president's decision to pursue rapid withdrawals in 2011–2012 forced US commanders to accept the primacy of the Washington timeline. Consequently, later ISAF commanders, Generals John Allen and Joseph Dunford, chose to begin the handover in the unstable provinces of the south and east much earlier. The rationale was that beginning the transition in restive provinces would give the coalition more time to oversee the process and manage the risks of ANSF failure.[99]

Assessing the success or failure of transition remains difficult in 2015. As in Vietnam, assessing the transfer of security from the intervening power to a client regime has been subjective, and the United States has had positive incentives to overstate the solidity of its Afghan allies. Optimists have pointed out that the removal of US troops has not led to an immediate collapse in security or the outbreak of civil war. Other observers have looked for valid, coincident or leading indicators of stability, the simplest being the level of violence. Between 2002 and 2011, troop increases were associated with increases in the level of violence. After 2011, the converse was not true. Optimists had hoped that the removal of the Western antigen would lead to a reduction in violence. Instead, as US troop levels fell, violence against Western troops fell, but violence against Afghan security forces and civilians increased. According to the ISAF command, the number of enemy-initiated attacks between October 2013 and March 2014 fell 2 percent compared to the same period one year prior. At the same time, the number of high-profile attacks rose 43 percent and included 10 high-profile attacks in Kabul.[100] Outside sources have offered more pessimistic appraisals. In May 2014, the International Crisis Group highlighted increasing violence, the declining hold of the government in rural areas, and the increasing size of insurgent bands.[101] Nine months later, the UN reported that civilian casualties had increased by 22 percent and that civilian deaths had increased by 25 percent in 2014, and attributed 72 percent of those civilian casualties to insurgent attacks. The total number of civilian deaths in

2014—3,699—represented the highest death toll since the UN began tracking these statistics in 2007.[102]

Act 5: A Long Good-bye

In the end, what can be said about Operation Enduring Freedom and the likelihood of a stable Afghan state emerging in its aftermath? From the vantage point of 2015, it is clear that the durability of the Afghan order will depend on three variables: the resilience of the Afghan state, US support, and the strategies of the insurgents and their sponsors.

In late 2014, the United States managed to engineer an orderly political succession despite rising ethnic divisions and allegations of electoral fraud. After both Abdullah Abdullah (a Tajik) and Ashraf Ghani (a Pashtun) claimed victory in the presidential election, the United States brokered a tentative compromise. Ashraf Ghani assumed the presidency and his opponent became the chief executive officer—a specially created position in the Afghan government that has no historical or constitutional precedent. While this averted renewed civil war, divisions within and between the Tajik and Pashtun factions draw into question the durability of the political order established by the Americans from 2002 on.

The Afghan economy will slow dramatically as the foreign spending associated with the Western troop presence declines. While the US and the international community have long supported economic development, donors may become less willing to underwrite these projects if the political order frays. According to the 2014 World Bank analysis, the withdrawal of troops and associated spending will halve Afghanistan's growth prospects, reducing projected GDP growth rates to 4.8 percent per annum through 2025.[103] With the Afghan budget running at four times the level of domestic revenues, Afghanistan will remain heavily dependent on foreign donors for the foreseeable future.[104]

US support will determine the staying power of the Afghan state and its armed forces. Here the early news is mixed. Starting in 2011, the administration and the ISAF command began discussing a range of options for an American "enduring presence" in Afghanistan. On May 27, 2014, President Obama announced a steep, post-2014 drawdown from 32,000 in the summer of 2014 to 9,800 at the beginning of 2015, 5,000 at the end of 2015, and "a normal embassy presence . . . with a security assistance component, just as we've done in Iraq" by the end of 2016. In March 2015, with violence mounting in Afghanistan and pressure increasing from US military advisors and Afghan president Ashraf Ghani, the administration grudgingly agreed to slow its own troop drawdown and maintain 9,800 US troops through the end of 2015. In October 2015, President Obama postponed the final drawdown yet again, promising to keep 9,800 troops in the country for most of 2016 and a minimum of 5,500 at year's end.[105] At the same time, the United States agreed to forgo planned cuts in security assistance so as to maintain an ANSF of 352,000 through the end of 2017.[106]

The debate about the scale and duration of the train-advise-assist mission will likely continue under a succeeding administration. If and when US advisors are withdrawn, US influence over the ANSF will fall dramatically.[107] While President Ghani dodged a crisis by signing the Bilateral Security Agreement, which established a legal framework for US operations after 2014, the Obama administration has continued to signal its desire to withdraw US forces and scale back counterterrorism operations. While the military and the Afghans have lobbied for a larger residual force, the administration has stuck to its timeline even as the ISIS advance in Iraq and Syria has highlighted the risks of complete withdrawal.[108] Only time will tell whether the administration's commitment to a time-based transition and a zero option proves a shrewd reallocation of US resources or an invitation to renewed civil war.

The most encouraging element of US policy has been the stated willingness to honor its commitments on ANSF funding. So long as these funds continue to flow, the ANSF will be able to pay salaries and maintain its cohesion. Absent such funds, most fear that the ANSF would dissolve much as the Najibullah regime's forces did in 1992 after

Soviet funding stopped.[109] Even so, the current US policy suggests that the ANSF will have to face its coming challenges funded but alone. As the collapse of the Iraqi security forces in the summer of 2014 has demonstrated, modern equipment, past US training, and financial support may be insufficient to ensure the survival of client forces once advisors have been withdrawn.[110] If this occurs in Afghanistan, it should surprise no one, for the ISAF commander, Marine General Joseph Dunford, warned Congress of this specific outcome in March 2014: "If we leave at the end of 2014, the Afghan security forces will begin to deteriorate. The security environment will begin to deteriorate, and I think the only debate is the pace of that deterioration."[111]

The survival of the Afghan state will also depend on the actions of its enemies. The Taliban, their coalition partners, and their external sponsors will have choices to make in the wake of US withdrawal. The Taliban offensives in the last six months of 2014 suggest that they will test the strength of the regime by attacking ANSF outposts and recapturing rural areas where the state is weakest. A series of high-profile attacks in Kabul have underscored the vulnerabilities of even the most secure urban areas late in transition. The Haqqani network—perhaps the most capable and deadly terrorist organization operating in Afghanistan today—has shown no sign of seeking reconciliation; like the Taliban, it seems inclined to push harder before considering compromise.

The Pakistanis too will have decisions to make. If their intent is to destabilize Afghanistan by encouraging its proxies in the Haqqani network and the Quetta Shura Taliban, then the Afghan government and the ANSF will have to hope that the institutional and political weaknesses of the regime can be overcome without US ground intervention. If, on the other hand, Pakistan decides that the removal of US troops makes a more harmonious relationship with Afghanistan desirable, then the Ghani regime may win some breathing space. What is clear is that the influence of Pakistan and Iran will only increase as the United States withdraws its forces and turns its attention elsewhere.[112]

It seems reasonable to ask whether the twin tragedies, one Afghan and the other American, could have been avoided. Could the Afghans have forged a more stable and secure political order in 2002 and thus averted a new civil war? Could the United States have accomplished its political aims in Afghanistan without massive and seemingly unproductive investments of money and lives?

The verdict in both appears the same: possible but unlikely. The Afghan tragedy was not foreordained but the seeds of civil war were present from the outset. As Thomas Barfield has observed, the expansion of political participation in modern Afghanistan has increased the scope and intensity of political violence.[113] Once Afghan elites enlisted the aid of the population, violence was democratized and deepened.[114] Whereas Western powers and Afghan modernizers assumed that political participation would release pressure and stabilize the system, such mobilization proved to be a catalyst for a broader and more violent competition for power.

Similarly, the divisions between the autocratic, urban elites and the conservative, egalitarian populations of the periphery made civil war more likely. The choice of a centralized, autocratic political order set the stage for a battle; the limited resources and ability of the government made it unlikely to win such a clash. That the toothless centralizers and modernizers found ready allies in the Western powers provided the key link between the Afghan tragedy and its American counterpart. While a looser structure with significant regional devolution might have reduced the urban-rural tensions, the preferences of urban elites and well-intentioned Western leaders made a centralized but weak and controversial political order the most likely choice in 2001.

In principle, the American tragedy of excessive ambition, frustration, and despair was avoidable. But such a strategy would have required a compromise on one of two rival motives: the evangelical American desire to improve Afghanistan and the countervailing impulse to limit US entanglements. While the Taliban were in retreat, this trade-off receded, and it was possible to imagine an inexpensive victory against al Qaeda and the construction of a modern, Afghan political order. Once the Taliban returned, the tension between expansive goals and the finite American appetite for civil war produced an escalating stalemate. As that war intensified, American leaders had to pour more troops and money into the project. At the same time, those leaders were reluctant to abandon the ennobling aspects of state-building for fear of confronting the sordid reality of a mafia war. In the words of one American officer, "We paid a high price for a clean conscience."[115]

Even as the instability of the new political order became apparent, its foreign architects were reluctant to reengineer it. The watchmakers of Bonn, united in their frustration with the Karzai regime, were unwilling to reopen the mechanism for fear of offending the owners of the broken watch. Instead, as Gelb and Betts had found in Vietnam, the United States consistently did the minimum necessary not to lose even as its leaders understood that such a path was unlikely to end in success.

Were there alternatives? Conceivably, the United States could have curtailed its ambitions for the new Afghan order and relied instead on co-opting national and regional leaders. Such a strategy would have been cheaper but sordid and open-ended. Accommodating warlords and building a sizable but relatively primitive Afghan army might have filled the security vacuum of the 2002–2005 period and forestalled the Taliban return. But such a structure would still have remained vulnerable to Pakistani escalation and the almost irresistible temptation to improve Afghan society. Better by far to embark on an ennobling if improbable quest; after all, it is the Afghans who will pay the bill at closing time.

CHAPTER THREE

In Our Own Image

TRAINING THE AFGHAN NATIONAL SECURITY FORCES

Dr. Martin Loicano and Captain Craig C. Felker, USN

> We are not going to allow them to progressively learn, we are going to leap them forward to the 21st century. We've given every one of them a laptop. Most of these kids have never driven a car, they may not know how to flush a toilet.
>
> —LIEUTENANT GENERAL WILLIAM B. CALDWELL IV, commanding general, NATO Training Mission-Afghanistan

When Lieutenant General Caldwell made the above remarks in 2011, the international community had been at least nominally training and developing Afghan forces for almost a decade.[1] Anthropological explanations of Afghan culture, military histories of the failed Soviet intervention, and an extensive literature on the problems of bolstering weak states with military power were all widely available.[2] And yet, over the 13 years of the war, the United States poured more than $60 billion into an effort to build competent, professional, accountable army and police forces. To date, nearly all indicators point toward Afghan security forces that cannot succeed—or even function—without sustained international assistance.

There are a number of reasons for this failure, but General Caldwell's comment points to one of the most important ones: the American-led coalition wanted to do the work for the Afghans and was almost entirely indifferent to the Afghans' history and concerns. Despite constant rhetoric about the dangers of imposing Western culture on the Afghans, the great majority of those who went to Afghanistan to train the army and police did exactly that, with predictable results. Furthermore, a rushed effort from the outset, differing notions of policing between American and European allies, and an inability to work outside Western concepts of modernity, progress, and bureaucracy led to constant friction with the Afghans and undermined the training effort. As General Caldwell's statement implies, NATO clung to 1950s-era beliefs first codified in modernization theory, which assumed an overly linear notion of societal progress—and could not be mapped onto the maddeningly complex terrain of Afghan culture. Even when the Afghan past presented obvious lessons and warnings, the international coalition pushed ahead with plans that were neither inclusive of Afghan input nor likely to provide security to the Afghan people. The result was an army with terrible attrition problems, a corrupt police force, instability throughout the country, and very little else.

The Afghan National Army, 2002–2009

Just weeks after Kabul fell to the Northern Alliance in December 2001, the United States and its European partners began setting up the infrastructure for training Afghan security forces. Right from the start, the Westerners set the bar impossibly high. At the UN-sponsored Bonn Conference of December 2001, the participants agreed that upon the official transfer of power set for later that month, "all mujahidin, Afghan armed forces and armed groups in the country shall come under the command and control of the Interim Authority, and be reorganized according to the requirements of the new Afghan security and armed forces."[3] The very location of the conference suggested the tenor of the relationship to come—rather than in Afghanistan, the new Afghan administration was formed in Europe, in a small way echoing the 1884 Berlin conference that began the imperial competition known as the Scramble for Africa. Additionally, as former Afghan minister of interior Ali Jalali noted, this reconstruction of the national army was to be the fourth in 150 years of Afghan history.[4]

A year later, the United States and its partners vowed to help build "multiethnic, professionally trained Afghan national army and police forces" as well as to "help establish a working judicial sector, combat the narcotics trade, and demobilize Afghanistan's militias."[5] All four of the major Afghan groups participating in the Bonn Conference asked that the new peacekeeping force be composed entirely of Muslims and that it focus less on policing and more on "control[ling] the borders of Afghanistan in order to make sure it is not violated by neighboring countries."[6] The Afghans' requests had no appreciable impact on US and European planning. This new partnership was far from equal; President Karzai and his cabinet had little role in decision making. As Peter Tomsen observed, "On settling into the presidential palace in January 2002, Karzai found that he exercised no real control over military affairs. Nor did his defense ministers, first the Northern Alliance's Mohammad Fahim and later, his successor, Rahim Wardak. . . . U.S. military commanders decided operational matters."[7] They also determined the composition and purpose of Afghan forces. A decade later, this basic division of labor remained essentially unchanged.

As designed by the United States and its partners in 2002, the new Afghan National Army (ANA) would be 70,000 strong. Roughly 60 percent of the force—43,000 soldiers—would be combat troops stationed in Kabul and the major cities; the remainder would handle training, recruiting, logistics, and other sustainment tasks. An air staff of 3,000 would handle air transportation for the Afghan president. After coalition retesting, Afghanistan's small fleet of Soviet-made AN-26 and AN-32 fixed-wing aircraft and Mi17 and Mi35 rotary wing aircraft resumed operation in early 2002. However, fewer than a dozen aircraft were operational at any time nationwide. The Afghan National Police (ANP) would be slightly smaller—62,000 strong—and its training would be overseen by Germany, with financial and administrative help from the US State Department. In 2002, the United States appropriated $79 million to fund the army and another $26 million for the police.[8] In 2005, it estimated that the entire Afghan National Security Forces (ANSF) program would cost $7 billion to complete and another $600 million to sustain. These estimates were wildly off the mark. In 2012, US spending on the ANSF topped $9 billion and the fuel costs for the ANA alone were $300 million.[9] The general consensus then—and now—among security experts is that unless the United States continues to fund the ANSF for the foreseeable future, it will likely collapse.

One of the principal reasons why American efforts to build and train the ANSF became so inefficient was that there were persistent cultural obstacles plaguing both sides. Afghans and Americans found each other difficult to understand and trust in many instances, as did Afghans of different ethnicities or who spoke different mountain dialects. In many ways, the problem echoed Adrian Lewis's view that "Americans are probably the least capable people for conducting nation-building operations. American culture, political and military power, and status in the world create a psychological blindness that makes it almost impossible for Americans to empathize with people in undeveloped regions of the world."[10] For example, US leaders in Afghanistan "worked closely with northern warlords and regional strongmen, many of whom are reviled by ordinary Afghans, and unwittingly contributed to the emergence of a government that is corrupt, abusive and even predatory."[11] As for the Afghans joining the new security forces, illiteracy was widespread, which required trainers to abandon or radically revamp Western classroom methods that depended on PowerPoint slides and written materials.

Even before the United States assumed responsibility for ANA training in late July 2002, UK and French trainers were spotting the problems that would plague the Afghan army for years to come: severe attrition, underage recruits, and an Afghan propensity to go absent without leave (AWOL) for weeks or months at a time.[12] Mismanagement and corruption at the senior level added to the difficulties; by late 2003, Western observers were describing the foundling ANA as generally "plagued by delays, desertions and political interference from Afghan defense officials."[13] In the summer of 2002, the 1st Battalion, 3rd Special Forces began 10-week training courses for ANA infantry battalions and border guard battalions with some success. Attrition was a problem from the outset. Misrepresentations during the recruiting process led some trainees to leave as soon as they learned more about the actual ANA program. A US Army spokesperson, Sergeant Don Dees, noted, "Some of the recruits were outright swindled to get here. They were under the impression they would be making several times more a month than they actually are. . . . They thought they would be taken to the United States for training, that they'd be taught to speak English, that they'd be taught to read and write. And these are not part of the program, yet."[14] The goodwill flowing from the ejection of the Taliban faded quickly.

As designed in 2002, the American-run training program for the Afghan army was 14 weeks in length. Recruits first endured six weeks of basic training followed by six weeks of advanced individual training. Two weeks of unit training capped off the program, which included specialized classes on logistics, first aid, human rights, and the laws of war. To ensure a smooth transition from the training site to the field, the Americans planned to proceed incrementally—building one Afghan army battalion at a time and then dispatching it to one of the regional commands around the country. The early results were troubling: ethnic tensions and desertions caught the attention of *Foreign Affairs* reporters Anja Manuel and P. W. Singer, who found that the Afghan military's leadership "is unrepresentative of the country's ethnic makeup and the pay is low, so roughly a third of the recruits end up quitting."[15]

The ANA regional commands would also be built sequentially, with the last command coming into existence by 2006. However, as security deteriorated in the run-up to the 2004 Afghan presidential election, the need for combat troops outpaced training. In an effort to speed up the process, the Americans started training multiple battalions simultaneously: three at a time by January 2004, four at a time by May, and five at a time by January 2005. The four regional commands were also stood up simultaneously in 2004, some with as few as 150 soldiers. Fielding infantry forces became the priority at the expense of training the necessary sustainment and support personnel. Complicating the problem was the fact that the training command had less than three-quarters of its assigned personnel on hand, and the US service members' tours of duty sometimes lasted less than four months.[16]

By 2005, it was clear that a rushed and disjointed effort was producing bad results. Attrition remained unacceptably high, and poor logistical support was undermining the army's basic efficacy.[17] Originally, the training command intended to supply the army with the Soviet-era equipment that so many of Afghanistan's neighbors were willing to sell, but much of it was in poor condition or unusable. Equipment donations from wealthier countries brought some benefit but additional complications: Germany, Greece, and the United Arab Emirates all donated vehicles to Afghanistan, but keeping them running required multiple supply part pipelines and knowledge of three different engines. The US entity used to obtain equipment for the Afghans—the Defense Security Cooperation Agency—was not designed to provide ongoing logistical support to an army in the field, and bureaucratic tangles slowed the process of obtaining basic equipment. As a result, the US Government Accountability Office reported in 2005 that the Afghan army suffered from "shortages of useable uniforms, boots, communications gear, infantry weapons, ammunition, and vehicles."[18] In an effort to adapt, the training command bought equipment from non-US providers but failed to ensure quality control. Boots came apart at the soles, and Afghans resorted to sandals, even when hauling equipment in the country's rocky, mountainous terrain. Such problems led the US Department of Defense to begin bringing in large, expensive contingents of contractors to provide maintenance and logistics support to Afghan institutions that were unable or unwilling to provide these services for themselves.

From 2006 to 2009, these problems worsened as violence increased across the country.[19] In response, the United States and its partners increased the ANA's end strength to 80,000 in February 2008, and

Figure 3.1 An example of defective boots acquired for the Afghan army and an Afghan soldier wearing sandals. Hasty procurements and a bureaucracy ill-equipped to adapt led to numerous problems in supplying the Afghan army and national police. (Government Accountability Office)

then to 134,000 in September.[20] Even with renewed focus on the problem of attrition, more than one-third of the army still deserted each year, usually taking their weapons with them.[21] Throughout the first seven years of international partnership with the new ANA and ANP, the United States continued to finance and employ local militias led by local power brokers whose interests had little to do with the national project in Kabul. Seth Jones and Arturo Muñoz observed, "U.S. assistance to warlords—especially when it did not go through legitimate local or national institutions—weakened the effort to rebuild a central government and became deeply unpopular for many Afghans."[22] This pursuit of both the national project based in Kabul and the empowerment of local power brokers and militias made the challenge of building security in Afghanistan even harder as it put different groups of Afghans in competition over both power and international sponsorship.

A few statistics highlight just how unprepared the Afghan National Army was halfway through the 13-year war. By 2008, the army still lacked 40 percent of its basic equipment, including machine guns and vehicles. Just one of 49 combat units and none of the 33 combat support units were capable of performing their missions independently. Reenlistment rates averaged just 53 percent as soldiers were drawn away by higher-paying jobs, sometimes offered by insurgent groups seeking trained, armed soldiers. Trainer shortfalls exacerbated the problems. The ANA had less than half of its embedded trainers on hand, a fact defense officials attributed specifically to the personnel requirements of the war in Iraq.[23]

Poor planning, bureaucratic turf wars, and a tendency to cut the Afghans out of the planning process exacerbated the problems. Even though the US government had already spent six years and $10 billion training the army, State and Defense continued to duplicate efforts and work at cross-purposes. By June 2008, the GAO reported to Congress that "Defense and State have not developed a coordinated, detailed plan for completing and sustaining the Afghan army and police forces, despite our recommendation in 2005 and a mandate from Congress in 2008 that such a plan be developed."[24] Had any such plan been developed, it almost surely would have been done without meaningful input from the Afghan leadership, which was regularly ignored or unintentionally insulted by the senior levels of the American military command. Nothing shows this better than a high-level meeting between Lieutenant General Karl Eikenberry (who later served as US ambassador to Afghanistan) and Afghan minister of defense Abdul Rahim Wardak in 2005. After a lengthy debate on military cooperation with the Afghans, Eikenberry "capped a testy conversation by saying 'Minister Wardak, I know your army better than you do.'"[25] This may have been true—after all, given how much the Afghans had been excluded from the planning process, the ANSF was more Eikenberry's army than Wardak's at that point anyway. But the larger point is the cultural disconnect that General Eikenberry demonstrated with his comments. No Westerner with any awareness of Afghan culture would criticize a Pashtun leader in front of others, let alone claim to "know" his army. All of this stemmed from the Americans' own cultural inclination to do the work for the Afghans instead of truly partnering with them.

The Afghan National Police, 2002–2009

Efforts to train the Afghan National Police (ANP) also encountered serious obstacles in these early years. As with the army, equipment and facilities problems were severe. In 2002, when police training began, German trainers estimated that the police had roughly 10 percent of the required equipment. By January 2005, trainers estimated that the police had just over one-third of the necessary weapons for police work and less than one-third of the required vehicles. Trainees received no firearms training because weapons and ammunition had not arrived. A lack of fuel prohibited the police from conducting vehicle patrols. Communications networks between police stations were mostly nonexistent, and the previous decade of war had rendered most police facilities unusable or in need of repair. Without adequate holding facilities, police occasionally detained criminal suspects in private homes.[26] The Afghan Ministry of Interior, which was charged with managing the nation's police force and should have been addressing these problems, was understaffed and undersupported by the international community. As just one example, in 2003, Germany sent only *one* advisor to work with the ministry. Other countries also fell short on support and ISAF soon shifted its approach. As scholar Anthony Cordesman pointed out, "ISAF initially tried to create a police force based on German models that were hopelessly under-resourced and did not meet Afghan needs and values. This failure was followed by an equally under-resourced effort by the US State Department that largely ignored the fact that insurgent influence now required a police force that could deal with guerrilla warfare."[27]

Entrenched ethnic grievances, local politics, and corruption caused other problems. In a country where the rule of law bends to the strongest man, new police officers had to return to local communities run by militias, some of which had more weapons than the central government. In other cases, militias competed with the government using money and weapons the United States had provided for the purposes of resisting the Taliban. As a result, one US report explained, "newly trained policemen often find it difficult to apply the principles they learned during training. . . . Some recently trained police were forced to give their new equipment to more senior police and were pressured by their commanders to participate in extorting money from truck drivers and travelers." Moreover, the $30–$50 monthly salary police officers received was roughly half that paid to new army recruits, and many police told US contractors it was not sufficient to support their families.[28] Their solution was more extortion, which journalist Kim Barker saw firsthand: while traveling in Afghanistan in 2008, she was forced to pay a $50 bribe to receive assistance from Afghan police when her vehicle was unable to traverse a mountain pass: "I could hardly blame the police—they made only about $60 to $100 a month, not enough to survive without corruption. The month before, one counter-narcotics cop had complained to me: 'Our salary is too little. If you give a hundred bucks a month to a donkey, it will not fart.' So we gave the cops $50."[29]

Dysfunction within the US government also hindered progress with the police, much as it had with the army. Believing police development should not be conflated with military training, the US Defense Department gladly handed over responsibility for police training to the State Department's Bureau of International Narcotics and Law Enforcement (INL), which assigned just one full-time staff member in the embassy to oversee the initiative.[30] This small-scale effort was appropriate at the outset, because the Germans nominally had the lion's share of the police training; however, by 2003, American officials had decided the Germans were focusing too heavily on training police sergeants instead of basic police officers. Germany also offered far too few trainers and trained Afghans too slowly; according to policing expert Robert Perito, the small German effort would have taken decades to produce the internationally mandated force of 70,000 Afghan police.[31] Seeking a quick fix, the Americans brought in a private military contractor, DynCorp International, which set up seven different training centers around the country, each hosting an eight-week training course for new police recruits.

By this point, the full-time State Department supervisor had departed the embassy in Kabul, so State relied on a single temporary staff member to oversee all of DynCorp's efforts. (The same supervisor also simultaneously oversaw all State Department counternarcotics efforts in the country.) A range of US agencies, from INL to US military commands such as the Office of Security Cooperation-Afghanistan (OSC-A) were also too small to provide sufficient assistance, and police advising programs were staffed with retired small-town police officers and sheriffs from the United States who were unprepared to provide the kind of guidance Afghans needed. These problems between State and Defense continued into the war's later years. In June 2006, Major General Robert Durbin told Secretary of State Condoleeza Rice that "there was no office in the United States government that could effectively build a foreign government's police force; INL did not have the experience in rebuilding a large country's police force, nor did the Departments of Defense and Justice."[32] What took far too long to admit was that the United States lacked the knowledge of Afghanistan, Afghans, and how policing should be done to help secure a country ravaged by decades of war. As a result, Afghan police ended up causing more problems than they solved.

By 2008, the United States had already provided $6 billion for police training, but not one ANP unit was judged fully capable of performing its mission without coalition assistance.[33] The training command still lacked one-quarter of its civilian mentors and one-third of its military mentors, which Defense officials attributed to higher priority being given to the Iraq War.[34] The ANP lacked roughly one-third of its essential equipment, including radios and body armor. Corruption increased: A US government audit in June found that 87 percent of weekly reports on police training contained evidence of corruption, including "multiple examples of police personnel providing weapons or defecting to the Taliban and several cases of high-ranking officials engaging in bribery or misconduct."[35] British journalist Ben Anderson found widespread problems on the ground in Helmand Province in 2007: "There were far more police on the payroll than actually existed. Some of those that did exist had been found setting up unofficial checkpoints where they taxed locals until they had enough money to get high. The British police officers (all six of them) who were training the ANP told me they had pulled up at one checkpoint to find a fifteen-year-old with an AK-47 in charge, while the actual policeman lay nearby in an opium-induced coma. Stories of young boys being abducted and raped were common. 'Ninety percent of crime in Helmand is committed by the police,' I was told by one of the British police mentors."[36]

In the latter years of the war, the Taliban realized that the people either feared or distrusted the police, and they began targeting them directly. From 2007 onward, police died in numbers two to three times higher than those of the ANA.[37] Police expert Perito attributed this trend to using "improperly trained, equipped, and supported ANP patrol men as 'little soldiers.'"[38] Planners responded by increasing the size of the force from 62,000 to 82,000, but this only pressured a staff-starved command to do more with less personnel. Administration and accountability, which were never sufficient to begin with, suffered even further. In 2009, the US training command could not provide auditors records verifying the location or disposition of 41,000 US weapons and 135,000 foreign-purchased weapons that had been given to the army and police.[39] Similar problems occurred in later years with police vehicles.[40]

These problems were unsurprising given that few ISAF personnel interacted with Afghans often enough to have the least idea as to what was going on outside the green zone in Kabul. For example, as late as early 2009, 75 percent of ANP units had no embedded mentors.[41] In June 2009, only 2,097 of 5,688 required personnel for Embedded Training Teams, Police Mentoring Teams, and Operational Mentor Liaison Teams were present for duty. That same year, the State Department agreed to turn over police training to the Department of Defense.[42]

After seven years of US-led international efforts in Afghanistan, security had worsened considerably, and international forces continued to take on a greater share of the fighting on behalf of Afghan forces. They had little choice: Afghan forces were simply incapable of—and often uninterested in—providing security to the Afghan people. The entire effort had begun to backfire: as scholar and for-

Figure 3.2 Afghan National Police vehicles in Herat, Afghanistan, that were listed as "in service" on maintenance records. Between 2011 and 2012, the US Army paid $6.3 million to service vehicles that had been destroyed or missing for over a year. Afghans rarely reported destroyed vehicles, because removing them from the rolls decreased fuel allowances. (SIGAR)

mer British officer Robert Johnson argued, Afghan "police abuses and army heavy-handedness were blamed for antagonizing the population, thereby fuelling the insurgency."[43] The reasons were many and complex, yet a few recurred throughout the effort—international neglect, profoundly unsuitable programming, and the simple reality that Afghans and their purported international partners frustrated each other and rarely shared common views on what should be done and how. US military culture and Afghanistan's history with foreigners lay at the heart of many of these problems. Impatience and short tours of duty led international military personnel to attempt to push through complex problems with hard work and artificially simple solutions.

By 2009, it was clear that something needed to change. Afghan security forces simply were not getting enough help and support from the very same international community that had urged Afghanistan to restructure its government and re-create its security forces. And as eager Westerners (mainly US personnel) raced to solve Afghanistan's problems for the Afghans, "the ANA . . . became psychologically crippled by years of watching from the back seat as the Americans took charge of the war, and [did not] learn . . . to operate on its own or ever develop . . . the ability to supply itself or hold the gains U.S. troops achieved."[44] In these circumstances, NATO decided to substantially increase its role in training Afghan forces and to encourage its partners to do the same. The result was a new organization, more money, but little fundamental change in the approach to building army and police forces in Afghanistan.

The NTM-A Era, 2009–2014

On April 4, 2009, the NATO Heads of State and Government announced the creation of the NATO Training Mission-Afghanistan at the Strasbourg-Kehl summit. Instead of supporting the disparate efforts of the American military, the European Union Police Mission, and the International Police Coordination Board, the new arrangement would combine all army and police training into a single, American-led NATO command that would "provide higher-level training for the ANA, including defense colleges and academies, and will be responsible for doctrine development, as well as training and mentoring for the ANP."[45] Spending ramped up almost immediately, and the president appointed a well-respected army general, Lieutenant General William B. Caldwell IV, to lead the effort.

The fanfare associated with this event did not translate into more trainers for NTM-A, however, for most of the trainers came from other NATO countries, and they did not begin surging forces into Afghanistan the way the United States did in late 2009. In fact, six months after NTM-A's creation, only 26 percent of the command's assigned military personnel were present.[46] NTM-A's leaders pushed for a rapid expansion of the ANSF nonetheless. With an operating budget averaging $9 billion a year, NTM-A sought to triple the size of the ANSF, taking it from 110,000 soldiers and police to a total force of over 300,000. To do this, it had to overcome "rampant corruption, widespread illiteracy, vanishing supplies, lack of discipline and the added burden of unifying a force made up of a patchwork of often hostile ethnic groups."[47] But rather than rethinking their approach, the US Army generals who led NTM-A and ISAF simply expanded the size and scope of the training models that had served so poorly from 2002 to 2009.

The new expanded effort quickly became an exercise in waste and haste. Completely illiterate Afghans were given sophisticated weapons and other expensive equipment they could not care for or use properly, while others were taught Western policing models they did not understand or value. Efforts to "professionalize" the police were undertaken through lecture-style courses, taught by English-speaking contractors, most of whom had no experience with Afghans or Afghan culture. In even the best training centers, contractors would belt out instructions to a class of 30–50 students, while an interpreter translated over the noise of the fans or generators just outside. Usually, there was just one translator per classroom, which made one-on-one contact with the students impossible. Even beyond these logistical problems, the subject matter of the classes was at times rushed or just inappropriate for the students. The Basic Patrolman Course, for example, taught an introductory lesson on the role of the police officer. The purported goals of the course were to teach recruits the characteristics of their profession and, in the words of the course's lesson plan, to make them "professional," "impartial," and "objective"—all terms that had little meaning to Afghans who would always be wedded first to tribal loyalties and defense of family before anything else. The teaching objectives also included educating police officers on their obligation to act within the constraints of Afghanistan's constitution and laws and international human rights norms. To do all of this, the curriculum assigned eight one-hour periods of instruction.[48] (How these recruits, many of whom were simultaneously undergoing basic literacy training, were to understand these Western concepts, let alone practice them, remained a mystery.)

Even with these problems, NTM-A and the ANSF senior leadership were nonetheless successful in finding a much larger number of Afghans to put through the training programs that were springing up all over the country. In November 2009, the army and police generated 5,006 new army and police recruits; one month later, 8,766 recruits entered the ANSF. By April 2010, the recruiting commands had reached a new high: 12,398 new recruits in a single month. However, the quality of these recruits remained the same—mostly illiterate and largely disinterested in national service. Many joined to avoid being unemployed, as Rajiv Chandrasekaran found when he probed the reasons why several Afghans joined the ANA: 'Of course we hate the Taliban, but we joined the ANA only because we couldn't find other work,' said Amir Shah, a twenty one year old Uzbek from Balkh province. He was the sole source of income for his family, and he couldn't afford to get killed."[49] These basic facts—that Afghans always put family and tribe before nation, and that the needs of those families meant recruits would stay with the ANSF only until a better opportunity came along—suggests that no amount of lecturing in a contractor-run classroom could have enjoined the Afghans to behave like their Western counterparts.[50]

Between 2009 and 2011, ANSF training programs suffered from several critical and interrelated problems—many caused by coalition decisions and actions. First was the composition of coalition forces and the allotment of effort among them. In March 2010, ISAF still lacked 40 army mentoring teams and 168 police mentoring teams—a shortage of more than 8,300 personnel.[51] Even as US forces as a whole doubled from 2009 to 2010, trainers and mentors could not be found, a clear indication of the importance of ANSF development in the effort as a whole. Even at the height of the surge—the winter of 2011—the coalition was still short 217 police mentoring teams and 10 army mentoring teams.[52] Second, and also critical, was the fact that these personnel shortages in mentoring made it impossible for ISAF and NTM-A to know how the Afghan troops were performing after they left training camps. For example, one NTM-A staff member decried the absence of new ANSF field assessments for almost six months.[53]

As a result, coalition leaders generally made their own plans without accurate information on the performance and requirements of the ANA and ANP in the field.

Adding to these personnel problems were cultural ones. Once various coalition commanders and staffs had decided what Afghan forces should look like and do, leaders undertook the process of securing what they called "Afghan buy-in." But rather than conducting joint planning with Afghans—which would have actually taught their partners the complex skills they already possessed—all Afghan force development and training planning was still led by US officers who by and large had "very shallow knowledge" of Afghanistan.[54] Many Afghan leaders expressed considerable frustration at the coalition habit of doing their planning for them; in one of many instances of such problems, a prominent Afghan minister wondered aloud whether his position was necessary given the constant American micromanagement.[55]

Even when Afghans were actually able to play a role in planning, they found themselves less than equal members of the team. For example, NTM-A included two one-star billets for Afghan assistant commanding generals (ACGs) for transition, who had the job—on paper anyway—of overseeing the handover of army and police functions from the coalition to the Afghans. When the ANA provided a prominent colonel to serve as an ACG, he found himself crammed into a small office with two contracted interpreters, while coalition general officers enjoyed spacious offices and dedicated staffs. Making things worse, the colonel was forbidden from having a computer, because even the unclassified US computer networks were off-limits to the Afghans. All of this had political reverberations that were lost on the American military officers because almost none of them knew that the colonel was both a trusted member of the minister of interior's inner circle and the younger brother of Mohammad Younis Qanooni, the speaker of the Wolesi Jirga (Afghanistan's lower house of parliament). In a society where personal relationships are the key to trust and partnerships, the United States saw only a colonel's rank. As a result, they insulted both the head of the police force and a prominent Afghan politician.

Other small gaffes had similar effects, mostly because Americans were occasionally unaware of who their principal Afghan partners were. In one famous example, the ANA chief of operations, Lieutenant General Sher Mohammed Karimi, was turned away at the ISAF gates after being invited by the ISAF commander, General Stanley McChrystal. As McChrystal observed, "After years of hearing that we were partners with Afghans, and my recent renewal of that promise, the senior Afghan planner couldn't enter a base in his own country—one that had been an Afghan military club at the beginning of his career."[56] More broadly, these occurrences reflected a lack of concern for Afghan viewpoints and a profound detachment from Afghanistan among coalition personnel tasked with winning a war there. ISAF existed to partner with Afghan forces, yet few Westerners knew many Afghans or much about them. As one diplomat remarked, "The only Afghans I meet are either cleaning my office or running the country."[57]

In the absence of accurate knowledge of Afghans and their intentions, needs, and requirements, the US-led coalition fell back on the default options—spending money and providing massive quantities of equipment to fight lightly armed and poorly financed Taliban insurgents. By mid-2011, the Afghan police and army were well supplied with over 58,000 trucks and armored Humvees, nearly 500,000 weapons from M-16s to howitzers, and 230,000 pieces of communications gear. Training sites dotted nearly every province and could accommodate tens of thousands of Afghan soldiers and police daily, with the National Police Training Center in Wardak Province able to train 3,000 police recruits on any given day. Supporting both the training and operational forces was an infrastructure program that amounted to $11.4 billion, with over 51 percent of the construction projects either completed or underway.[58] Spending reached a peak at $10.6 billion in 2011 and declined thereafter, hovering at around $4 billion per year for the final two years of combat operations.[59] By 2016, the United States had obligated over $66 billion to ANSF development and had pledged another $3 billion to sustain the Afghan army

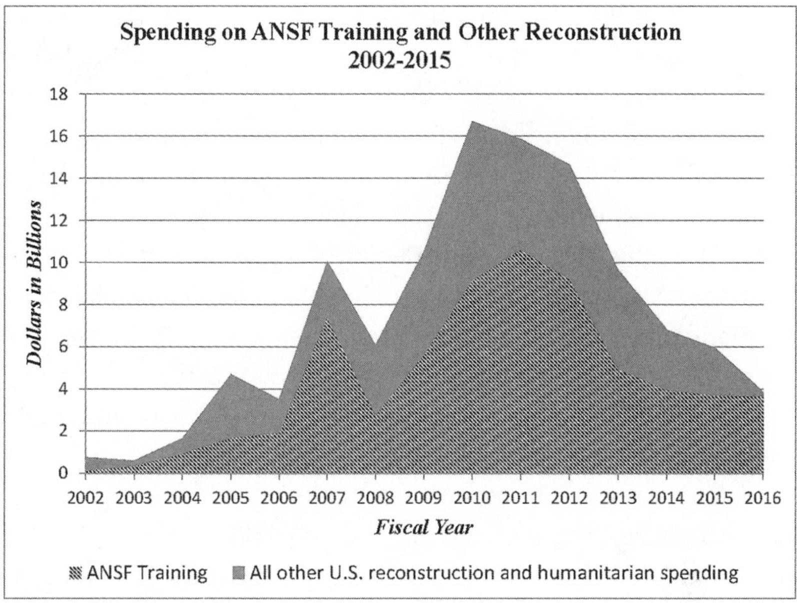

Figure 3.3 Of the $113 billion spent on Afghanistan's reconstruction, almost 60 percent went to training the Afghan National Security Forces. (SIGAR)

and police in 2017.[60] At the time of this writing, most security experts still agree with earlier statements that reducing US funding levels could be "the most calamitous step we could possibly take to destabilize the situation in Afghanistan."[61] After more than a decade and $100 billion in reconstruction spending, the United States continued to believe more money was the answer to stabilizing Afghanistan.

///

In retrospect, it is clear now that the efforts to create a capable army and police force in Afghanistan encountered a number of serious problems. At its heart, the campaign suffered from an almost unsolvable dilemma—ISAF was entirely composed of foreign forces but foreign forces were largely ill-suited for the job of securing Afghanistan. Author Ben Anderson has aptly summarized this problem in his book *No Worse Enemy*: "To begin to understand how hard it was for the British to attempt to carry out this policy, imagine an Indian dropped into Chicago, or a Brazilian dropped into Islamabad. Imagine asking them, without speaking the language or having any idea of who to trust, to create, staff and monitor an entirely new system of government. What's more, imagine asking them to do this within six months, while fighting a war."[62] And yet even this analogy understates the problem, because the training of the ANSF was undertaken by numerous countries, following different strategies, and balancing competing military and political priorities at home. In the end, the various Westerners working on army and police training did not only have problems communicating with the Afghans—they could barely communicate with each other.

Making things worse was the fact that even with these communication problems, the international personnel did a lot more talking than listening, and this created persistent cultural friction and misunderstanding. As American military expert Seth Jones noted, "Many foreigners, including government officials, project[ed] their Western views on Afghanistan. This bias has caused many foreigners, and even some Western-educated Afghan government officials, to look *only* to the central government for solutions."[63] Foreign personnel arrived with little expertise and left shortly afterward, with only slightly greater knowledge of the complexities of power dynamics in Afghanistan. Afghans noticed this ignorance and tried to call attention to it, often without success. As one NATO senior diplomat explained in 2011, "The Afghans kept repeating that there were three different Afghanistans: 'The first is the one you Westerners imagine; another coincides with the city of Kabul; the third is the country of remote provinces, far away from the cities, and of the three, this [the third] is the only real Afghanistan.'"[64] Blinded to the realities of Afghanistan's complexities, the Westerners resorted to a very American fallback plan: substituting money and technical know-how for locally tailored, culturally appropriate, sustainable solutions.

Not only did the Westerners fail to listen to the Afghans; at some points they literally cut the Afghans out of the process of building ostensibly Afghan institutions. And here, they should have known better. Though he was speaking of a different war and of a different people, T. E. Lawrence's "Twenty-Seven Articles" warned of exactly this problem almost a century earlier: "Do not try to do too much with your own hands. Better the Arabs do it tolerably than that you do it perfectly. It is their war, and you are to help them, not to win it for them. Actually, also, under the very odd conditions of Arabia, your practical work will not be as good as, perhaps, you think it is."[65] Numerous academics since Lawrence have issued similar warnings and yet the problem repeated itself in Afghanistan nonetheless.

An overall tendency to rush things probably had the most unintended effects. Because of the competing demands for personnel and resources in Iraq, and political pressures from Washington to demonstrate progress, ISAF rarely took the time to look more than six months to a year down the road. This led to hasty recruiting and training and insufficient accountability that made the army and police part of the problem rather than part of the solution. US efforts to outsource its security problems led to an overwhelming reliance on contractors, most of whom were retired soldiers and retired police officers who had none of the basic knowledge of Afghan society needed to be effective teachers and trainers. In other cases poor oversight led to actions that directly fueled the insurgency; as late as 2010, Congress noted with disdain that "the United States has been contracting with the very warlords who intimidate the people of Afghanistan and undermine our efforts."[66] As Mark Sedra has noted, this short-term thinking "has sacrificed the long-term sustainability of the Afghan security sector to address the immediate security threats of the post-Taliban era."[67]

Adding to these problems was a penchant for Western bureaucracies, institutions, and metrics—all things that are normal parts of America's military, but which have far less utility in Afghan society. And on this point, the sad thing is that the very same problem had occurred in an earlier American war. As James William Gibson's *The Perfect War* explains, one of the critical failures in Vietnam was the Americans' tendency to view the world through the lenses of technical and managerial systems: "In a world where only technology and production count, the enemy begins to be seen *only* in these terms. . . .

Military strategy becomes a one-factor question about technical forces; success or failure is measured quantitatively. Machine-system meets machine-system and the largest, fastest, most technologically advanced system will win. Any other outcome becomes *unthinkable*."[68] The same mentality drove ISAF operations in Afghanistan more than 30 years later—US and international leaders focused on equipment, force numbers, bureaucratic processes, and doctrine as the only viable means to securing Afghanistan. In 2011, nearly 10 years after the coalition began to lead ANA and ANP development and training, NTM-A programs director Major General Peter Fuller admitted the central argument of this chapter. "We realized," he commented to *LA Times* reporter David Cloud in September, "we were starting to build an army based on Western army standards, and we realized they don't need that capability."[69] Fuller was relieved from his post soon after the *Times* article was published.

CHAPTER FOUR

The Impact of Culture on Policing in Afghanistan

Captain Pashtoon Atif, ANP

When I first joined the Afghan National Police in early 2002, the Taliban had just collapsed and a relative of mine, General Akram Khakraizwal, became the police chief of Kandahar Province. Because of this, my cousin and I both got jobs working as police liaisons to the United Nations, NGOs, and other international actors in Kandahar Province—something I could do because I spoke English and knew something of Western customs. In those years, there was no real training program for the Afghan police in Kandahar. We received only basic instruction from a few professional Afghan officers who had been trained a generation earlier by the Soviets. But these individuals were the exceptions. Almost all the rank-and-file police were illiterate villagers who had taken up arms against the Taliban and now were expecting to have a hand in the new Afghanistan. They knew nothing about policing and the rule of law. All they knew was how to fight.

I served in the police force for just 10 months, until the end of 2002, when I joined an Italian NGO and, later, the United Nations Development Program. After four years of NGO work, I went to Boston, Massachusetts, attended Tufts University, and then returned to my home. While I was still in Afghanistan, Akram Khakraizwal was murdered in Kandahar—a story told by my friend and mentor, Ms. Sarah Chayes, in her book *The Punishment of Virtue: Inside Afghanistan after the Taliban*. A major point of that book is something that everyone knows in Kandahar: the Afghan police do not deliver justice or truly protect the people.[1] Since that day, I have thought often about how policing works in Afghanistan and have concluded that the problem is not just one of training programs, or money, or a lack of professional standards. Two things explain the poor condition of Afghan policing: the long history of how police have been used in Afghanistan—by both Afghan rulers and foreigners—and the cultural mindsets Afghans have about what police do and how they should do it.

In 1979, just months before the Soviets invaded Afghanistan, the American criminologist David H. Bayley wrote, "National traditions may affect what the people bring to the police as well as what the police do."[2] Even though Bayley was writing about Europe and America, the point applies to Afghanistan too. This chapter argues that Afghan police forces have always reflected the cultural practices of the societies they emerged from as well as the police trainers they encountered. Using the words of ordinary Afghans who lived under the Soviets, the Taliban, and 13 years of NATO involvement, I argue that each regime's police followed the cultural practices of the government then in power—a practice that has throughout Afghanistan's history consistently inhibited the development of a capable, professional, fundamentally benevolent national police force.

Since it became a state in the 18th century, Afghanistan has never had an effective national police force, and "rule of law," if it existed at all, varied widely according to tribal customs and local balances of power. At the start of the 20th century, Kabul-based elites began creating police forces, but these institutions were used primarily to weaken the tribal structure that ruled in the rural areas. Preventing crime and protecting the people were never the primary goals. A number of attempts to modernize the Afghan state and society occurred in the 20th century with varying results, but no single legitimate national police force ever emerged. When the Soviet Union began advising the Afghan government, and later invaded and occupied Afghanistan from 1979 to 1989, it poured money into building a secret police force, which was modeled on its own KGB. After the Soviets withdrew, rule of law collapsed completely and, eventually, new institutions arose under the Taliban that reflected their misguided interpretation of Islam. While some Afghans appreciated the quick justice the Taliban brought with them, by the end of the 20th century, police in Afghanistan still had many of the same problems they have always had: corruption, brutality, and a basic disregard for the people they were supposed to protect.

When the United States and NATO created the International Security Assistance Force (ISAF) in 2001, a variety of police training efforts began, but the new policing institutions were all shaped by the assumptions and values of the countries providing the trainers: European police trainers had good goals but few resources to implement them; the American effort relied primarily on contractors who advocated a culture of militarization rather than civilian policing. Deep-seated Afghan cultural habits of political patronage continue to undermine the policing institutions brought in from outside the country. As a result of these competing cultures, the Afghan National Police is a hodgepodge of various entities and organizations, none of which are very effective.

Policing in Afghanistan before the Taliban

Afghanistan has never had a strong and professional police force that provides law and order for the population. Since the state's founding in 1747, rulers' authority was confined to the major cities. In rural Afghanistan, the tribal chiefs have always had the greatest influence over the population—not the regime in Kabul. Therefore, Kabul's elites have historically used the police to extend their influence over the rural areas, to extract resources from the outlying areas, and to weaken the tribal chiefs who could rally rural Afghans to oppose Kabul's rule.

When national police institutions began emerging at the end of the 19th century, the main purpose was not preventing crimes and enforcing the rule of law but protecting the regime in Kabul. This practice was followed by subsequent regimes and continues to this day. As a result, Afghanistan suffered—and continues to suffer—from police institutions that are not only ineffective but also highly politicized, and whose service and loyalties are, to a large extent, devoted to a few individuals rather than to ordinary Afghans.

Afghans always tell the international military forces in their country that they need to understand the country's history in order to defeat the Taliban. This chapter attempts to provide that Afghan perspective to the topic of policing. A history of Afghan policing told by Afghans would start with Emir Abdur Rahman Khan, the so-called "Iron Emir," who ruled Afghanistan from 1880 to 1901. Being the first leader to centralize power across Afghanistan, Rahman used his favorite tactic for extending his authority: brute force cloaked in religious benevolence. When tribal leaders resisted him, he destroyed their villages, kidnapped their children, and even instituted forced migration. He also created the nation's first national police force, whose primary purpose was to collect taxes—a task that caused rural Afghans to view police primarily as predators rather than protectors.[3] Even with this repressive approach, the emir never subdued the rural people of Afghanistan.[4] The power and influence of the tribal leaders were so deeply imbedded there that the emir, despite all his efforts, could not win them over.

Two decades later, King Amanullah tried to reform the police, as well as the country's other public institutions, and he put his utmost effort into achieving this goal.[5] Among other things, he increased freedom of the press, expanded rights for women, and signed a friendship agreement with the Soviet Union, which garnered Afghanistan a new source of military support.[6] This was particularly important since the British government had recently stopped directly subsidizing the Afghan state, but the agreement had a domestic purpose as well: strengthening the army would allow the regime to finally control rural areas and collect much-needed taxes. It did not work. The deeply religious chiefs of the rural areas resisted the imposition of central authority and revolted. Amanullah left Afghanistan and died years later in Zurich, Switzerland.

Later regimes encountered similar difficulties. Whenever federal forces—whether army or police—arrived in rural areas, their reason was either to bring violence or to take taxes, and as a result, the rural chiefs almost always resisted. King Nadir Shah (1929–1933) responded by ceding responsibility for security to the chiefs rather than challenging their authority. Muhammad Daúd, who served from 1953 to 1963 as prime minister and again from 1973 to 1978 as the first president of Afghanistan, brought in foreign military trainers in the 1950s; Turkey and the Soviet Union provided training and equipment to various Afghan security forces. During the Cold War, both the Federal Republic of Germany and the German Democratic Republic assisted and trained the Afghan police. Working separately, they built up the police institution using different flavors of a fundamentally European policing model.[7] However, as the International Crisis Group noted in 2008, these efforts were "largely about protecting the state from society. From Kabul's point of view, maintaining order meant first and foremost ensuring that government laws and decrees were enforced in the villages, that taxes were levied and conscription in the armed forces carried out."[8] While Germany and Turkey hoped their aid would lead to a professional police force who could maintain law and order, for the Afghan government, good police were those who could protect the regime, and curb the power of influential people and tribal leaders so that the government could better exercise its power and collect taxes. State weakness was a constant problem, one that led to the assassination of Muhammad Daúd and, eventually, the Soviet invasion and 10-year occupation of Afghanistan.

Policing changed again in the late 1970s, when the Soviets invaded and occupied the country. In April 1978, members of Afghanistan's communist party overthrew and killed Daúd and his family. The Soviet-backed Nur Muhammad Taraki became president and prime minister of Afghanistan, but he too was later overthrown by Hafizullah Amin and assassinated. On December 27, 1979, the Soviet Union invaded the country and installed Babrak Karmal as appointed president, prime minister, chairman of the Revolutionary Council, and secretary-general of the Central Committee of the communist party.[9]

Like Afghan leaders before him, Karmal focused on creating military and police forces that could stifle growing opposition against the regime. He created the military police, the Sarandoy, and the Department of State Information Service, or KhAD (riasat-i Khadamat-i Ittela a't-i Doulat). Although the KhAD was officially working within the prime minister's office, it was actually the most powerful institution in the regime, and it eventually became the Ministry of State Security, or WAD (vizarat-i amaniyat-i doulati).[10]

Modeled after the KGB, this new department would soon become the most effective tool for the regime. At its beginning, about 200–250 of its personnel were sent to Tashkent for professional training. After that, about 80–90 recruits were sent to KGB schools in the USSR. In addition, KGB advisors worked closely with the KhAD, the Sarandoy, and the army in order to provide on-duty training and mentoring. In addition to the KhAD, the Soviets supported the Sarandoy, which included the branch of traffic police, provincial police, and prison facility officers. Trained by the Soviets, the Sarandoy were charged with fighting counterrevolutionary fighters, or the Mujahideen. They also helped the KhAD make arrests and conduct other operations. At one point the number of Soviet advisors reached 5,000, and the total number of Sarandoy were about 100,000, many of whom had been trained in the Soviet Union.[11] Overall, the model was based on a two-track system of career officers and short-term conscripts who served for two years as police officers.[12] Some parts of the system worked: "One thing that was good about the communist regime was that people who were assigned to positions of power were actually skilled in what they were doing," one prominent Kabuli remembered years later. "And there was no nepotism in the system. Everyone had to obey the rules and regulations, unlike the current government."[13] Trained and educated policemen and policewomen were working in every position, and both the officers and foot soldiers were provided with training and mentoring by their Soviet supporters.

But even with relatively skilled police officers, the institution still served the rulers rather than the people. This affected the security services as well, which primarily fought the counterrevolutionaries, Mujahideen, and their sympathizers rather than providing protection and rule of law.[14] The KhAD arrested people who opposed the regime, put them in jails, tortured them, and in some cases killed them. According to Abdul Samad, 65, a victim himself, the KhAD used every method of torture in its prisons, including electric shocks and sleep and food deprivation. "I was locked in a room where I could not stand tall or lay on the ground for 57 days," he recalled in 2014. "A piece of bread and a bottle of water was all I received as daily meal. They beat me and gave me electric shocks at least twice a week."[15]

Another victim reported that the KhAD arrested him for hosting a few of his friends the night before. "Just before I left my home for work in the morning, there was a knock on my door," recalled Ahmad Wali of Kandahar. "When I opened the door, three men in civilian clothes grabbed me by my hand and ordered me to go with them. I followed them to where their vehicle was parked. I was taken to the prison, not knowing what I had done wrong. Nobody told me why I was brought there that first night. The second night, I was taken to a separate place where people were flogged or given electric shocks. They beat me for almost an hour without telling me anything. Then, two officers came to me and asked about the people who were my guests the night before I was arrested. I told them they were my guests from my village, located in Shah Walikot district, to the north of Kandahar. And I assured them that my guests were not linked to the Mujahideen. They did not trust me and thought I was hiding something. After three months in jail and multiple times of being tortured, they released me because they did not find anything on me."[16]

While Wali's story represents only one example of the way the KhAD treated the Afghans, people in every corner of the country suffered, and the majority of Afghans came to despise the communist regime and began siding with the Mujahideen. Abdul Khaliq, a civil servant under the communist regime, said that the "brutality and notoriety" of the KhAD was actually the lesson "our Soviet friends at

KGB have taught" their Afghan counterparts.[17] In the end, while the Soviet-installed regime made some attempts to establish a civilian police force, it did not succeed. The police force, the army, the KhAD, and other security services were all dissolved after the Soviets left in 1989.[18] With no central government in power, a civil war raged for years until the Taliban captured Kabul and established the Islamic Emirate of Afghanistan in 1996.

Policing under the Taliban

As the Taliban came to power in the 1990s, a new form of policing emerged, one that reflected the values and ideology of the new rulers. Although the Taliban government was mainly preoccupied with taking control of all of Afghanistan and fighting its opponents in the north, the regime also did everything possible to impose its interpretation of Sharia law on the areas it already controlled. The authority of the Taliban was total: every Taliban member was given the authority to enforce the regime's law regardless of his position in the government, and the punishments for violations were quick and severe. Torture in the Taliban's prisons was a common way of extorting information, which often led to either murder or permanent disability of the alleged criminal. "The level of cruelty and inhumanity that the Taliban practiced in their jails is not describable," remembered one former Mujahideen commander who was imprisoned and tortured under suspicion of having arms at his home without the regime's permission. "They put me in a dark room and kept me there for more than a month. They gave me one meal per day. After a month they started interrogating me and accused me of weapons that I hadn't informed them about. In fact, I did not even have a single bullet and I told them that, but they wouldn't believe. So they would beat me everyday after my first month in jail. I became so ill and weak eventually that I could not even talk when they were questioning me and only then they realized that torturing me was useless but I did not have anything to talk about. So they released me."[19]

One of the most infamous institutions under the Taliban regime was that of the religious police, which was later turned into an independent body called the Ministry of the Promotion of Virtue and Prevention of Vice. It was this institution that jailed men who had shaved their beard or had grown their hair too long. It forced people to go to mosque for prayers. Listening to music carried a sentence of three to six months' imprisonment.

Women had the most to fear from the Taliban's religious police. The regime banned girls from attending school and isolated women from workplace and public venues.[20] In addition, the Taliban prosecuted women in soccer stadiums where thousands of ordinary people were gathered to watch as women were shot at or stoned to death. "They [the Taliban] forced women to wear burqas, stoned women to death, didn't allow girls to go to school or work," an Afghan woman later recalled. When asked what she would do if the Taliban came back, she said, "I won't live in Afghanistan. I will leave no matter what it costs me; even if I have to sell my body as a prostitute, I'll do it to avoid the brutality of the Taliban."[21]

As another scholar has noted, the short reign of the Taliban was essentially a role reversal in Afghan politics.[22] For all of the 20th century, urban elites in the capital had tried to impose their will on the conservative religious tribes in the south and east and had used the police and military to collect taxes and punish transgressions. Under Taliban rule, the rural power brokers got their revenge, and the police were often the most visible instrument of the Taliban's ire. And while the world knows well how hated the Taliban had become by the time of the US invasion in 2001, most forget that all police forces before the Taliban had been similarly hated. This was the legacy of policing in Afghanistan when international military forces began rebuilding the country in 2002.

From the Taliban to ISAF: Police Training after 2001

People always take their culture with them when they go abroad. The Americans and Europeans who came to rebuild Afghanistan in 2002 were no different. Thankfully, on the issue of creating a professional police force, the Afghans found themselves in broad agreement with their liberators. Rebuilding the Afghan National Police (ANP) was a priority for the new Afghan government, and the interior minister estimated that it should be 70,000 strong.[23] More important than the size would be the training the new force would receive, so that it did not descend into the predatory behaviors that had always plagued police forces in previous years. Everyone also agreed that the ANP should not be another army—it needed training in law and order, public protection, and investigations. But even with these major points of agreement, differences of opinion between American and European trainers and basic problems of overlapping and redundant bureaucracies appeared early on and never went away. Germany took an early lead in police training but proceeded too slowly for the Americans. In 2003, the Americans began a much larger—and less effective—program that relied on DynCorp contractors and retired soldiers, which had a militarizing effect on the training. By 2007, the European Union began supplementing the Germans' efforts with the European Union Police Mission (EUPOL) in Afghanistan, and Canadians and Italians ran their own training programs in western and southern Afghanistan. By 2009, the NATO alliance took over all police recruiting and training when it created the NATO Training Mission-Afghanistan (NTM-A). Because of these changing and uncoordinated efforts, in the end, the Westerners created a host of policing institutions in Afghanistan that were not professional and were not accountable to the people.

When police training began in 2002, the first step was to ensure that the army and police had separate and defined roles. Right from the start, both Afghans and Westerners agreed that the Afghan National Army (ANA) would concentrate on threats coming from outside the nation's borders, and the police force would be responsible for internal security, prevention of crimes, and the preservation of law and order. At this point, however, Afghanistan did not have any kind of professional police. Available recruits were illiterate fighters who had taken control of major cities and operated under the control of their local potentates after the Taliban fled. After several conferences and consultations, the Afghans and their international allies decided to create a new professional Afghan national police force that would include educated commissioned officers, trained career noncommissioned officers, and police officers. The Germans agreed to be the lead nation for training the police, based partly on the fact that they had done similar work with the Afghan police in the 1960s and 1970s.[24] The US agreed to provide financial support to the effort, but to ensure that the police did not become militarized, that support would be supervised by the Department of State, not the Department of Defense.

German police advisors arrived in Kabul in March 2002. After rehabilitating the police academy in Kabul, they instituted a training plan that looked very similar to the ones that produced national police forces in European countries. The commissioned officers would receive a college education, and police sergeants would undergo a shorter, but still academically rigorous, training program. After initial training, the ANP police officers would be dispatched to the provinces for duty, and the best students would be retained as instructors for the next class. This approach to police training was exactly what the Afghans wanted. "We already knew how to fire a gun, but what we did not know was how to behave with people," said Hamid Ahmad, an illiterate police officer who graduated from the police training center in Kandahar in 2006.[25] But because the Germans kept their program so small, they could only enroll 1,500 commissioned officers in each five-year term and 500 noncommissioned officers in each three-month training program. At this rate, meeting the goal of 70,000 police would have taken decades. In addition, the program was mainly focused on Kabul, where law and order was already far better than in most other parts of the country. Even though Germany's method of training the ANP could have provided Afghanistan with the best police force in the country's recent history, the number of police it could produce in a year was only "a drop in the ocean."[26]

Aware of the shortcomings within the German training program, the US Department of State created a separate program in 2003 to provide what it called "in-service" training to the ANP so that the demand for personnel could be fulfilled. Reflecting the decentralized police training system in America—where each state trains its own police—the US program was designed to train the ANP recruits in their respective provinces where they could be close to their duty stations while they learned their basic policing skills. The American-designed training offered illiterate recruits an eight-week course, literate recruits a five-week course, and those with previous policing experience a 15-day transition and integration program. A private firm called DynCorp International was contracted to construct training facilities, hire instructors, and manage the project.[27]

While the new project gave momentum to the police training program throughout Afghanistan, the quality of the training suffered greatly. The DynCorp contractors were mainly former military service members or retired American police officers who had little understanding of Afghans and used military and police jargon which the Afghan interpreters had trouble translating. There was no follow-up from the DynCorp side on its training program, nor was there any positive coordination between the United States and Germany regarding their respective training programs. Moreover, the Ministry of Interior was not properly supervising the program either. When the Pentagon and US Department of State launched a joint study of the police training program in December 2006, they found that the American-trained police were incapable of performing their most basic duties: enforcing the rule of law and protecting Afghan citizens from insurgents. The report concluded that despite the $1.1 billion the United States had spent to that date on the police training program, Afghan officials could not even track how many police were on duty.[28]

Both the Americans and the Europeans next tried to adjust. In the United States, responsibility for training the police shifted from the State Department to the Department of Defense, and in 2007, the DOD's Combined Security Transition Command-Afghanistan (CSTC-A) formed yet another program with the intention of providing supplementary training to the ANP. Unlike the large training centers in the provinces, the Focused District Development (FDD) program offered classes at the district level (equivalent to the county level in the United States), which included an introduction to basic police skills for new recruits, advanced training for former police officers, and management and leadership training for police officials.[29] The same year, the European Union launched its own police mission in Afghanistan, with the aim of contributing to and tracking the establishment of a "sustainable and effective" civilian law enforcement institution in Afghanistan by monitoring, mentoring, and training Afghans.[30] Unfortunately, because road infrastructure and security were so poor in the country, most EUPOL members were unable to extend their role beyond Kabul, and there were persistent problems getting enough trainers to do the job properly. In 2011, more than two-thirds of the 306 EUPOL trainers were located in Kabul, with only 85 operating in 13 of Afghanistan's almost three dozen provinces.[31] Although their mission was to monitor, mentor, and advise the police training programs, those in Kabul mostly worked with high-ranking officers at the Ministry of Interior.[32] Security conditions made it impossible to travel regularly to other provinces, and there were no EUPOL trainers in some of the provinces with the most need.

Even as these new organizations emerged, the old ones did not go away. The nations who had the largest military presences in the country, such as the United States, the United Kingdom, Canada, Italy, and Germany, continued to conduct their own police assistance programs in their respective provinces.[33] Canada, for example, was given the security responsibility for Kandahar Province, and in 2006, its police mentors were sent to Kandahar to train the Afghan police. The UK had a similar role in Helmand Province, while Italy was doing the same thing in the western province of Herat. Coordination between these countries was almost nonexistent. As a result, by 2008, at least six separate countries, as well as the European Union and the United Nations, were all doing police training and advising using different manuals, different curricula, and different priorities.[34] Communication with the Afghans was poor. "The main problem with the police training was that both Europeans and Americans did what they thought was good for us," Afghan National Army General Juma Khan later remarked. "They did not consult with Afghan counterparts on curriculum development of these short-term trainings, for example."[35]

Recruiting and training programs were finally consolidated under one command in 2009 with the creation of the NATO Training Mission-Afghanistan (NTM-A). Led by US Army Lieutenant General William Caldwell, NTM-A worked to standardize training across the country and also promised NATO military protection for European police so that they could move around the country and work in the areas of the greatest need. But NTM-A was a military command, and thus all the police trainers and recruits found themselves in an American-led military command structure instead of a police academy. And because the United States provided the bulk of the funding for NTM-A, its focus on rapidly increasing the number of police in the field took precedence over training quality.

The US approach did achieve its primary goal: it put many more police in the field, which was important given the Taliban's advances across the south and east. When NTM-A commenced operations in November 2009, there were 95,000 police in Afghanistan. A year later, there were 116,000, and by the end of 2011, there were 143,000.[36] But the American effort also had major flaws. To train so many new recruits, the Americans needed more trainers, and most of the ones coming from DynCorp International were former police officers and soldiers who were drawn by the large salaries contractors received. Not all these so-called trainers were professional instructors, and few knew anything of the culture and history of the people they were being paid to instruct. The lectures were delivered in English and required translation through local interpreters, who did not understand the police and military jargon the instructors used.[37] In addition, most of the US-run police training programs allowed only six to eight weeks to introduce the trainees to proper policing. The curriculum looked good on paper; it included courses on police law, police ethics, human rights, and how to engage the enemy. In practical terms, however, it was quite impossible to prepare illiterate former fighters to serve the people in a six- to eight-week training period. Apart from being in the classroom and listening to the instructor, they hardly had any contact with Western troops. Unlike the army, where American soldiers partnered with the Afghans after initial training, in the police train-

Figure 4.1 A US contractor demonstrates restraining holds on Afghan National Auxiliary Police recruits during a two-week training course in Miri, Ghazni Province. US contractors were mostly former US military or US police officers and were rarely sensitive to Afghan culture. (PO1 Scott Cohen / Department of Defense)

ing programs, there were always major shortages of mentoring and advising teams. As a result, the police had little on-the-job training after they completed their initial training.

The Afghans noticed these deficiencies, and a trust gap that had already existed for years grew wider. According to Niaz Muhammad, a former police officer who went through the six-week training program, the training helped Afghans understand the general roles of engagement and tracking the enemy, "but what it lacked was learning about human rights and guidance of civil policing. We were happy [at first] because we thought our foreign advisors will teach us a whole lot of new things, including crimes detecting, human rights, and investigation. However, though we learned a lot of about fighting, we didn't really learn anything about actual police activities."[38]

Niaz Muhammad's observations point out the largest impact of the Americans' consolidation of police training after 2009: a general militarization of the police role in Afghanistan. With the Taliban still resilient throughout much of the country, and the Afghan army struggling with high attrition rates, the police took on a larger and larger role in combating insurgents, and as a result, the police trainers began focusing more and more on military tasks rather than policing ones. The Europeans disagreed with the approach but had little ability to change it. Nigel Thomas, the former EUPOL head, complained in 2010 that 95 percent of training in the six-week course concerned "how to stay alive."[39] A German report released in 2011 warned, "It is easier to militarize the police now than it will be to drive out the spirit of militarization at a later date."[40] But the Americans were providing most of the resources, and the Europeans' concerns were brushed aside. Police deaths rose steadily from 961 in 2010 to 1,400 in 2011 and 2,200 in 2012—all of which were roughly double the deaths suffered by the Afghan army in the same years.[41] Afghans noticed. As a district police chief in Kandahar Province explained, "Neither foreigners [ISAF] nor the ANA cares about the Taliban. . . . We [the police] are the ones who fight them."[42]

The focus on how to kill, rather than how to protect, gave the officers a military mindset—they came to believe that killing the enemy was more important than being responsive and respectful to the citizens whom they were supposed to serve. This war zone mentality and ambiguity with regard to their duties has contributed to a sense of entitlement and impunity among Afghan police; many feel that they can do whatever they want. Professionalism in the ranks is nonexistent. "From the top to the bottom of the organization, corruption is a problem," remarked Nigel Thomas. At the top, the corruption has connections to organized crime, and at the bottom, police officers extort money from civilians at police checkpoints.[43] While visiting just such a checkpoint in 2010, I noticed that only three out of about a dozen of the police officers were wearing uniforms. A fighting dog was tied up with rope in one corner, several police officers were busying cooking in another corner, and others were smoking hashish.[44]

This militarization of the ANP has confused everyone in Afghanistan, from the highest military generals in the Afghan army, to the police officers themselves, to the ordinary citizens on the street. "It is the military who should fight the insurgents," an Afghan army general explained in 2014. "The police should only secure the big cities, and their responsibilities are maintaining law and order, detecting and preventing crimes."[45] Gulam Farooq, an Afghan police officer who attended police training in 2010, had the same idea: "I knew how to shoot. What I expected from the training was to learn more about actual policing, on how to conduct searches, how to investigate, how to behave with people, and what our actual authorities were. But they didn't teach us that stuff."[46] Sabir Ahmad, a businessman in Kabul put it best: "Every time I hear about police dead in an operation I wonder what the hell is the military doing. Fighting the insurgents is not what the police should do. It is the military's job. . . . And no wonder their [police] behavior doesn't match that of a policeman you see in other countries—India, for example. Our police don't know how to deal with their citizens and how to treat a criminal. They only know how to fight and they love abusing people, as if they were confronting a notorious enemy."[47]

The ANP Today: Afghan Culture and Government Misrule

Perhaps because there were so many different philosophies of policing at work in Afghanistan during the years of NATO involvement, a hodgepodge of different units and policing types now exist in the country with different missions and degrees of effectiveness. What began as a plan to create a force of 70,000 in 2002 expanded over time into a variety of plans, run by a number of different countries. By March 2014, the NATO Training Mission-Afghanistan had created an Afghan national police force of 152,000 members and had plans for a future expansion to 157,000. The force is deeply militarized and fragmented. The main force, the Afghan Uniformed Police (AUP), is responsible for maintaining and enforcing rule of law and protecting civilians from crimes, but it seems to spend most of its time battling the Taliban. The 14,000 members of the Afghan Civil Order Police (ANCOP) has an explicitly paramilitary role, as does the General

Directorate of Police Special Units (GDPSU), colloquially referred to as the "Police Special Forces." The 21,000 members of the Afghan Border Police (ABP) controls all border crossings and handles customs. The Afghan Public Protection Force (APPF) is a conglomeration of 22,000 former militia members and private security contractors that were integrated into the government starting in 2011. The Afghan Local Police (ALP)—another paramilitary force fully separate from the ANP—remains another rival force, and the National Security Service (NSS) has some other forces that it alone controls. Despite occasional success stories by some ANCOP units, the ANP has yet to gain the trust of the Afghan people, most of whom—along with international observers—are suspicious of police abilities, integrity, and professionalism.

The new ANP was supposed to be ethnically balanced, politically neutral, professionally skilled, and equipped with all the necessary tools a police force requires. And yet, as of 2014, structural problems are widespread and present major problems for the future of the force. Attrition remains high at 19 percent. The Ministry of Interior, which runs all police in the country, still needs regular coalition assistance to manage its budget, facilities, and logistics. Drug use and basic equipment shortfalls are regular problems. Most troubling, the force remains ethnically imbalanced, which will almost certainly create problems in the future. Police of Pashtun ethnicity are underrepresented, and Tajiks—who are the Taliban's best-organized foes and account for one-quarter of Afghanistan's population—make up 43 percent of the ANP. Just 1 percent of the ANP are women, which hinders investigations and arrests of those who commit crimes against women.[48]

These are serious problems, but they were not created by the Westerners alone. Of course, different decisions might have yielded different results, but even if the Americans and Europeans had agreed on one model of policing and had taken more time to implement effective training programs, creating a professional Afghan national police force would have still encountered serious obstacles. This is because cultural factors inside Afghanistan naturally affect how its police operate. Because of three decades of war, psychological trauma, and destruction of the country's infrastructure, Afghanistan lacks the human capital and organizational skills to create workable institutions. The biggest problems have been a tendency to abuse power for personal profit and a quick resort to brutality when other methods fail.

Corruption and undemocratic promotions are also major problems in the ANP. Assignments to positions of power are based on personal relations and favoritism—not on merit—and this is one of the biggest factors preventing Afghanistan from creating an effective, capable, and professional police force. High-ranking police officers are controlled by people who have close ties with some influential individuals in the government. As Amrullah Saleh, the former intelligence chief for the country, wrote in 2012: "The upper and middle echelons of Afghan forces are filled by people who have not risen to their promotions in a democratic system. . . . Most of them have been placed in their posts through political consultations and personal connections. This directly affects the loyalty and inspiration of the officers at different levels."[49]

The lack of meritocracy affects the lower ranks as well. When police see that their promotions are based off of whom they know, rather than their skills, they lose interest in learning and applying the knowledge acquired in training. South Korean police inspector Won-Hyuk Im, who trained ANP recruits in Parwan Province in 2011, saw this firsthand. The students, he said, have no interest in learning because they know that "no matter how much they learn, there will not be any incentives for them." This means that they will very likely work under someone who may have far less understanding of police work, far less knowledge of the area, but a better social network in the government.[50]

Even those police officers who try to resist corruption sometimes find their efforts thwarted by corruption in the higher levels of the justice system. One former police official in Kandahar City remembered what happened after arresting a suspect who had placed a bomb under his police vehicle. After two days, relatives of the alleged bomber came to him and offered a bribe to secure the prisoner's release. "I told them that I cannot sell my own blood," the police officer said. "But still they were able to obtain his release by paying a smaller bribe after his case went to the prosecution office."[51]

Police corruption also affects national politics. In the 2010 parliamentary elections, the ANP was blamed for helping rig the election. "Twelve district chiefs led a coordinated process [to rig the election], including involvement from high authority, the border police and officials," said one Afghan in Kandahar. "We were told by our agent he saw stuffing boxes one night before the election and the night after and also during day . . . in some areas the polling station was stolen."[52] Similar allegations were made after the presidential election on April 5, 2014, but no investigation followed, which further degraded the image of the police in ordinary Afghans' eyes.

Besides a long tradition of securing favors through bribes, Afghans have also had decades of experience with war and brutality, and this affects how the police conduct themselves as well. Even with all the Westerners' classes on human rights and professional conduct, torture remains a problem. "There is all kind of *zilam* [torture]," one citizen stated in 2010. "There is *wohal, barq,* and *reshwat* [flogging, electric shocks, and bribes],"[53] Electric shocks are used mostly on people who are suspected of larger crimes such as murder, kidnapping, and affiliation with insurgents. "Torture is especially common for suspected antigovernment elements," another police officer explained.[54] According to a local newspaper report online, the police in Kandahar have allegedly killed prisoners under torture without facing any consequence. One Afghan news website reported on May 12, 2014, that tens of people gathered to protest against the torture in the police headquarters of Kandahar.[55] There is very little oversight from other institutions on the police detention centers to ensure that torture is prevented.

///

In the entire history of Afghanistan, never has so much attention been paid to rebuilding its security forces as occurred after the fall of the

Taliban in 2001. But even after a decade of efforts by the international community, the ANP still cannot either provide security for or win the trust of the Afghan citizens. The best explanation for this failure is that each country brought its own culture of policing to Afghanistan and those varying cultures led to incompatible approaches, priorities, and results. The Europeans had ambitious plans to build well-educated, well-trained national police forces like their own, but they did not devote sufficient resources to the effort and moved too slowly. The Americans, on the other hand, poured resources into hastily conceived training programs and rushed to failure. Relying on poorly trained contractors and allowing the military to take over the effort, they ended up producing soldiers wearing police uniforms rather than proper police. This focus on combat, combined with an emphasis on the quantity of recruits rather than their quality, blurred the line between the role of the police and the role of the military and undermined the idea of building a civilian police service.

Afghans have their own culture of policing too, and this also created serious obstacles to building a professional, accountable force. Much like the 19th-century police forces of the Iron Emir and other past leaders, police in the "new" Afghanistan still oppress, extract bribes from, torture, and in some cases kill the very people they are supposed to protect. As was the case in earlier eras, government officials still get appointed to prestigious jobs based on whom they know, not what they know. Even when politicians talk about accountability and rule of law and meritocracy, they don't work in the police stations or have to answer to powerful bosses as ordinary police officers do. Having the right vision for the country's police force means very little if it is not broadly accepted and advanced by the majority of police.

Some skeptics of the Afghan training mission might say that the real problem is Afghanistan's long and brutal history. After generations of Afghans watched those with the power oppress the weak, the theory goes, they eventually lost hope and heart and became culturally conditioned to submit. I am an Afghan and I disagree. Even though corruption, brutality, and predatory behavior all have a long history in my country, the problem should not be explained with simple comparisons between barbarism and civilization, or unhelpful comments about modern societies and supposedly "backward" third-world countries. Culture is a strong force in people's lives but it is not the only force. If all Afghans were truly prisoners of their history, why are millions of girls attending school today—something that was unimaginable only a decade ago? (People like to focus on the Taliban as the reason girls did not attend school, but the truth is there was strong resistance to education for girls across most of the country well before the Taliban took power.) If culture truly determined people's actions, how could seven million Afghans choose to vote in the 2014 presidential elections—sometimes at great personal risk—when there was no previous history of voting for national leaders in Afghanistan's entire history?

It is possible for a nation to escape its history and move beyond the habits of the past. I see good police officers in Afghanistan who do their best to serve the people and protect the weak. The problem is that they are badly outnumbered by the unprofessional and corrupt ones. These corrupt ones cannot be given an easy pass by saying that Afghan culture is the problem. In fact, assessments of the problem need to be more specific and generalizations avoided. Afghans must look honestly at their institutions and work to correct them. A key aspect of democracy is holding leaders to high standards, and in this respect, I think the Afghan government has been allowed to fail its people. From the beginning of the police training program, members of the Ministry of Interior should have been examining the training curriculum and pointing out the flaws. When schools stood up without sufficient translators, the ministry should have protested. When Americans brought in their military contractors who lacked knowledge of Afghanistan and basic social skills for dealing with non-Americans, the government should have proposed another solution. When the Americans prioritized large-group instruction to teach basic literacy instead of holding small-classroom discussions to explain the concepts of policing, the government should have said "thank you, but no thank you." And when the training got more and more militarized, and the roles of the army and police became almost indistinguishable, the Afghan government should have known better than to allow the country to follow the American example.

I want to be optimistic about Afghanistan's future because I believe that both the Afghan government and the international community now realize that there is no future for Afghanistan without a professional, accountable police force. But the truth is that I do not believe Afghanistan will have such a force in the near future. Security continues to deteriorate day by day, and this makes it impossible for the Ministry of Interior to do real long-term work on building a proper civil police force. The government needs more and more fighters to fight the insurgents, and when that is the priority, the rule of law and long-term planning for the police become less important. But once the war ends, there are a number of specific steps that will ensure Afghan's police forces do their job well.

At the national level, the Ministry of Interior (MOI) should make a national training strategy for the ANP that sets goals for training and follow-up training for commissioned and noncommissioned officers as well as for police officers. It should also set criteria for sending officers abroad to international police training programs. The MOI must demilitarize the ANP and also depoliticize it so that its purpose is protecting all Afghans, not those of a certain clan or tribe. Most important, the MOI must demand that the ANP function as a meritocracy. It should have a clear reward system, where those who serve well are promoted and their efforts appreciated. It should have clear, enforceable standards of conduct, that all must obey, no matter how powerful their friends or relatives.

When making a nationwide strategy for the ANP, the MOI should also involve local communities so that the people gain confidence in the police and become invested in their success. Invite representatives from all provinces and seek their consultations so that the police are sensitive to the specific history and problems of the region. Train and equip a criminal investigation division (CID), not only at the ministry level, but in all provinces as well. Without professional investigators, armed with the necessary tools and skills to investigate a crime scene, police abuse and torture will probably continue. Similarly, specific professional trainings are required for counternarcotics police and counterterrorism police. Once these branches are properly equipped and their officers trained, it is possible that the police will detect criminal activities in advance and no longer fight criminals in the same manner the army fights the Taliban.

Within the training command, a number of more specific changes are necessary. First, the curriculum must be revised, both in content and method. Literacy training should continue, but it should be in smaller groups so that the talented students are identified and tracked. This will help identify who can be in a leadership position and who should be given less intellectually demanding duties. More emphasis should be given to community policing and to problem solving through dialogue and regular procedures rather than through guns and violence. Once police enter the field, they will still need refresher training to ensure that they practice what they have learned. Ongoing assessment of the training is needed too, so that the training officials see what has worked and what has not. Finally, it is good that the international community has always included human rights training for police, but like the literacy training, lectures and PowerPoint slides done in translation before large groups are ineffective. Small-group sessions are better, with a discussion leader presenting a scenario that leads to fruitful discussion. This is how Afghans discuss problems every day. Why shouldn't the police be trained in a similar manner?

We Afghans are profoundly grateful for the investments the international community has made in our country, but there is room for improvement here too. If the international community insists on using contractors instead of proper police officers, then there must be more attention to selecting ones that can work across cultural divides and communicate effectively. The training materials must be translated into local languages by professional translators and verified by officers before they are used in the training. Trainers cannot be too dependent on using military and police jargon, and the interpreters must be familiar with the basic police terms that are not often found in a dictionary. This has created many problems in the past, including mistrust between the police cadets and their international instructors and even violence.

Finally, despite these problems, it is important to understand that quitting and walking away is not a real option. The only thing I know for certain about the future of policing in Afghanistan is that without funding from the United States and the international community, the ANP will fall apart in a matter of months. Most of Afghanistan's police are in uniform because they have no other source of income. They are police officers because they need to feed their family. Even with international support, the government still struggles to pay for salaries, fuel, equipment, and the normal costs of operating a police station. If the world turns its back on Afghan police, many will leave or turn to crime to support their family. If they do this, they'll take their weapons with them—weapons the United States and other nations gave them in the first place. When people talk about why they support the insurgents, they always talk about justice and the Taliban's harsh stance against corruption. If the crime and corruption increase, and the police are participating in it, the attraction of the Taliban will grow stronger—something that will be bad for both Afghanistan and the world. But with patience, sound training, and financial help, Afghanistan's police forces can mature into what everyone wants them to be: true civil servants that serve and protect all of Afghanistan's citizens. We need not be prisoners of the past or hostages to the old ways. We must not give up. The costs for the people and for the world are just too high.

CHAPTER FIVE

Building and Undermining Legitimacy

RECONSTRUCTION AND DEVELOPMENT IN AFGHANISTAN

Lieutenant Commander Jamie Lynn De Coster, USN

Shortly after the United States toppled the Taliban regime, the entire international community agreed on the importance of stabilizing Afghanistan and helping it transition from war to peace. The United Nations—after a decade of hard lessons in the peace operations business—quickly took the lead in championing reconstruction. At the UN-sponsored Bonn Conference, participants established guidelines for creating an inclusive Afghan government and committed to assisting in the "rehabilitation, recovery, and reconstruction" of the country.[1] Despite a general wariness of "state-building" in US government circles, the UN had good reason to push for such an aggressive approach, because at the dawn of the 21st century, countries emerging from civil conflict had a nearly 50 percent chance of returning to violence within the first five years of peace.[2] With enough time, money, and people, Afghanistan would hopefully avoid a similar fate.

The United States had similarly ambitious goals. In a speech to Virginia Military Institute cadets in April 2002, President Bush outlined his vision for Afghanistan's reconstruction, which required the United States to help build a stable government, develop an army, educate boys and girls, clear minefields, build roads, and stimulate the economy. He compared his plan to George C. Marshall's in Europe after World War II, which he called a "moral victory that resulted in better lives for individual humans," something he promised for the Afghans.[3] While veiled in moral imperative, this speech also presented a realpolitik argument for state-building: reconstruction was a way to mitigate risks posed by an ungoverned state in the age of global terrorism. Simply put, rebuilding Afghanistan would prevent terrorists from launching another attack on the United States.

But creating the conditions for stability and lasting peace would not be an easy task. After nearly two decades of war and five years of oppressive Taliban rule, the humanitarian situation in Afghanistan was desperate—wars left the physical, social, and political infrastructure in disrepair. As one of the world's most underdeveloped countries, Afghanistan's living conditions were deplorable. One-quarter of all children died of preventable diseases, and other significant health threats such as typhoid, cholera, pneumonia, and malaria were rampant.[4] Gaining access to health care and education often required long journeys by mule over high mountain passes or scorching deserts. Land mines claimed lives and limbs, and millions of refugees roamed back and forth across the border to avoid itinerant violence. To overcome these challenges, 61 countries and 21 international organizations pledged an initial $4.5 billion at the January 2002 Tokyo International Conference on Reconstruction Assistance to Afghanistan.[5] With the resources committed, all hoped that reconstruction would help lift Afghanistan from the ashes.

Over the next 13 years, the United States would spend $113 billion on Afghanistan's reconstruction and development. Almost 60 percent of this—$64 billion—went to recruiting, training, and equipping the Afghan National Security Forces.[6] Another $6 billion went to other DOD-led reconstruction efforts, mostly the Commander's Emergency Response Program (CERP) and efforts to encourage private sector growth through the DOD's Task Force for Business and Stability Operations program. USAID-led reconstruction spending accounted for just $19 billion, with the majority of funds going to roads, energy,

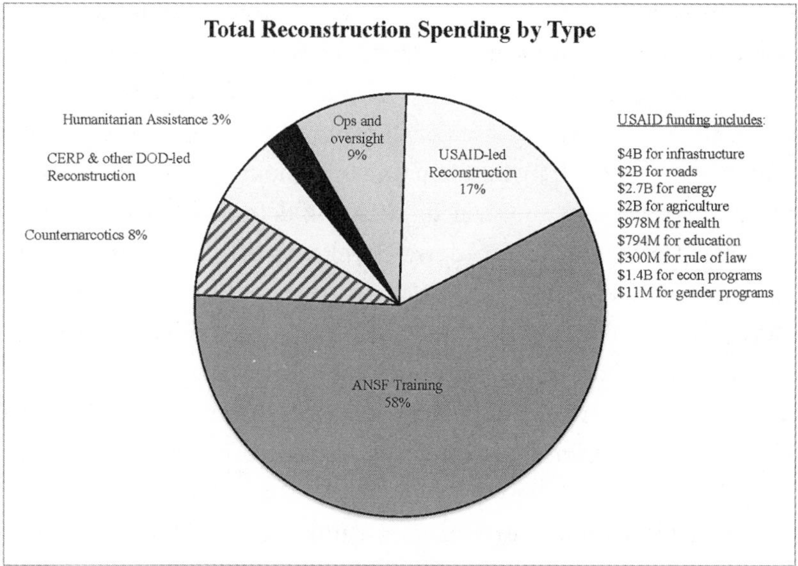

Figure 5.1 Counterinsurgency strategists argued that improvements to infrastructure, education, health, roads, and the private sector would help turn the population away from the Taliban. However, just 17 percent of the $113 billion in reconstruction spending went to these types of USAID-led activities—less than one-third of what was spent on training the Afghan Army and National Police. (SIGAR)

infrastructure, and agricultural programs. Less than $2 billion went to health, education, and gender programs combined. Counternarcotics programs (which were shared across the DOD, the State Department, and the Drug Enforcement Agency) cost the United States another $8 billion. Just $3 billion went to humanitarian relief operations.[7]

Some of these investments produced tangible benefits. When the United States invaded, only 30 miles of road were paved in the entire country; in 2014, nearly 2,000 paved miles made up the Ring Road, which connected Afghanistan's major population areas.[8] Access to midwives grew fivefold and infant mortality dropped precipitously. Life expectancy increased by almost a decade. Thousands of schools and health clinics opened around the country, and international aid helped Afghanistan hire over 140,000 teachers.[9]

This progress notwithstanding, by the end of 2014, Afghanistan was still teetering on the brink between war and peace. Even with this massive investment of time, money, and people, most of the efforts to rebuild Afghanistan were only partially successful. The reasons for this are threefold. First, from 2002 to 2008, the civilian organizations operating under the auspices of the United Nations lacked coordination, were stymied by bureaucratic inefficiencies, and struggled to complete projects as the security situation deteriorated. The United Nations' preference for top-down development—which pushed aid through the nascent national ministries down to the provincial ones—had a goal of strengthening Afghan institutions and creating the infrastructure to facilitate good governance. Unfortunately, for a variety of factors, aid rarely reached the Afghan people through all the layers of bureaucratic interference. Instead of strengthening the connections between the government and the people, the millions of dollars of top-down aid actually encouraged corruption and created perceptions of injustice.

Second, from 2009 to 2014, the United States implemented a counterinsurgency strategy, and its military forces became increasingly hands-on in the country's reconstruction efforts. This brought forth new opportunities, but also new challenges. The military, in particular, executed a bottom-up approach as it "stabilized" areas that were recently cleared of insurgents. Military commanders, not civilian experts, became the primary managers of reconstruction efforts at the district level. Under military leadership, the number of completed projects seemed to take precedence over quality or sustainability, and the desire to demonstrate progress quickly led to poor—or absent—contextual planning.

Third, in the end, the UN's top-down approach and the military's bottom-up efforts never successfully connected, and as a result, military stabilization did not always reinforce the broader framework for reconstruction. While there were many instances of successful cooperation, military officers often clashed with civilians on method and execution, resulting in distrust on both sides. The military also allocated resources to advance military objectives, which rarely aligned with the civilians' development goals. And for the duration of the war, aid money and poor oversight fueled pervasive corruption, undermining the very legitimacy the efforts were intended to build. Combined, these setbacks raise serious doubts about the international community's ability to use development assistance to move countries from war to a sustainable, lasting peace.

Early Reconstruction and Modernization Efforts, 2002–2008

Afghanistan was not the first time the United States or the international community used development and reconstruction to help move a country from war to peace. Herbert Hoover's American Relief Administration saved millions from starving in war-torn Europe after World War I, and two decades later, the Marshall Plan simultaneously rebuilt much of Europe and kept Greece and Turkey from falling to communist insurgencies. Efforts in Vietnam (which occurred while the conflict was ongoing) were far less successful, however; and in the post–Cold War era, reconstruction and development experts began to agree on a number of lessons and best practices. Most now agree that a successful reconstruction program requires at least three things: strategic direction, adequate funding, and proper oversight.[10] Nor can efforts be overly militarized—while security is an essential precondition for development, it must be accompanied by nonmilitary efforts that sustain the peace. History has shown that those things are all easier said than done, particularly when working across agencies, countries, and international organizations.

The early efforts in Afghanistan took note of some of these lessons, ignored others, and consistently encountered four obstacles that hindered success. First, the UN's reconstruction strategy was not a workable one, mostly because the UN could not efficiently manage its resources and personnel. Second, while funding was adequate, big infrastructure projects received the most resources the fastest. These large efforts rarely produced completed projects that could be sustained without long-term international assistance. As a result, what should have been modest reconstruction in carefully selected areas expanded into large modernization ventures that had unintended effects. Third, the metrics used to track progress were misleading;

the number of dollars spent and projects completed did not reflect effectiveness or sustainability. Finally, deteriorating security affected reconstruction in two significant ways: it provided the Taliban ways to interfere with development projects, and it pushed the military to assume an expanded role in what was supposed to be a civilian-led effort.

The United Nations' Strategic Framework for Reconstruction

With the fall of the Taliban regime in December 2001, the international community faced enormous reconstruction challenges in Afghanistan. Decades of war had stunted the country, and it lacked the basic infrastructure, financial resources, and human capital to succeed on its own. At the January 2002 Tokyo conference, members of the interim Afghan government announced six reconstruction priorities: administrative capacity; education, particularly for girls; health and sanitation; infrastructure, with a focus on roads, electricity, and telecommunications; economic and currency restructuring; and finally, agriculture and rural development, including food security, water management, and revitalizing the irrigation system.[11]

Later in 2002, United Nations Resolution 1401 established the United Nations Assistance Mission in Afghanistan (UNAMA), which would oversee all UN activities in the country. Besides mandating recovery and reconstruction as UNAMA's primary efforts, Resolution 1401 also stressed that aid funds—humanitarian or otherwise—should be directed through Afghan government institutions, which set UNAMA on the top-down approach it would use for the duration of the war.[12] With these initial documents, the reconstruction framework was in place. The many donors, including nongovernmental organizations, international organizations, and donor states, enthusiastically set up shop in liberated Kabul. But even though donor states had just signed off on an aggressive reconstruction and modernization plan, no one seemed to notice that the details of how to execute it were not yet fully articulated.

Over the course of the next six years, there would be numerous other conferences and joint declarations to announce reconstruction strategies, renew international commitment, and raise funds. Between 2002 and 2008, three major documents drove Afghanistan's reconstruction. First was the 2006 Afghanistan Compact, which laid out a five-year strategic framework for rebuilding the country and contained 52 benchmarks for success.[13] Second, in 2008, the Afghans came up with their own document—the Afghanistan National Development Strategy—which eventually became the overarching coordination mechanism for international efforts.[14] And lastly in 2008, the United Nations finally recognized a need for better coordination and declared that UNAMA would "lead the international civilian efforts."[15] Its authority was significantly increased in Resolution 1808, but as international investment continued to pour into Afghanistan, it quickly became clear that the disparate efforts of so many civilian and military organizations were coming into conflict with each other.

Unfortunately, UNAMA's expanded mandate was not accompanied by an equal expansion in capacity. Reliant on donor countries to pay the bills and provide the personnel, UNAMA was constantly falling short. The mission was always understaffed, and by 2009, UNAMA only had 8 regional offices and 12 provincial offices.[16] This limited the UN's reach—and its ability to oversee efforts—in the 33 provinces beyond Kabul, which left a leadership void in rural areas. Bureaucratic inefficiencies caused problems too. To function properly, UNAMA had to coordinate the efforts of over 25 of its own internal agencies, each with its own governance, development, and humanitarian assistance programs, as well as work with over 50 separate countries and the hundreds of nongovernmental organizations that were also operating in the country.[17]

Further complicating matters, international donor funding was supposed to flow from the Afghan central government to the provinces—a process that was referred to as "on-budget" aid. Although this was done on purpose to give Afghans ownership of the process, it rarely worked in practice because the Afghans had few capable bureaucrats and technical experts, and those that were capable were rarely immune from corruption. Consequently, only a trickle of international aid arrived in the rural areas where the need was the greatest and support for the Taliban was the strongest.[18]

Thus, while considerable energy went into writing down the UN's reconstruction framework, much less energy was directed at linking ways and means to the strategy. Even though there was a coordination and monitoring body, there was no effective internationally run management structure in place to carefully execute reconstruction activities while the Afghans learned how to do it themselves.[19]

USAID: Prioritizing Critical Infrastructure

The US was the largest donor to the United Nations during the war in Afghanistan, but it also ran its own reconstruction and development programs through the US Agency for International Development (USAID). Besides having far more resources than most other donors, USAID did not have to channel funds through the Afghan government, and thus, its "off-budget" programs were more flexible and accountable than those routed through the Afghans. Thus, with so many resources available, the trouble was not determining how many projects to do, but where to start and what areas to focus on. Some of USAID's initial efforts—particularly in health and education—began early and showed impressive gains.

In early 2002, USAID began building schools and health clinics, training health workers, and working to increase crop yields and access to safe water. Joining with the UN and other agencies, these efforts had demonstrable success. Between 2002 and 2014, access to education dramatically increased—over 8,000 schools opened their doors to millions of children, including over 4 million girls.[20] USAID built more than 500 health facilities throughout the country, trained over 20,000 health care providers, improved women's access to health care, and directly contributed to the lower infant mortality rates observed in 2014.[21] In addition, Afghanistan's GDP grew an average of 9–10 percent each year; wheat production increased 76 percent;[22] and by 2014, nearly two-thirds of Afghans were using cell phones (88 percent of women had them too).[23] That same year, 69 of Afghanistan's 249 parliamentarians were women—a higher percentage than in most Western governments.[24]

These successes were not USAID's largest priority, however, because early in the war, its development experts decided that rehabilitating critical infrastructure was the key to stabilizing Afghanistan. Successes here—in the transportation and energy infrastructure, in particular—would not only stimulate economic development but have compounding benefits elsewhere: that is, in health and sanitation programs, schools, hospitals, markets, large cities, and rural towns. (USAID also had a history in Afghanistan—it had funded large road and electricity-generating projects during the Cold War.)

The infrastructure challenges in Afghanistan were enormous because in 2001 its roads were some of the worst in the world. In December of that year, USAID estimated that 30 miles of paved roads existed in all of Afghanistan. The Ring Road that connects the capital city of Kabul to major cities around the country was essentially a dirt track whose conditions were measured in terms of travel time, not distance covered. Without efficient roads to move goods to markets, the Afghan economy would remain at a standstill. Improved roads would also help the Afghan government reach its people in the outlying areas, facilitating central governance over a country that was traditionally difficult to keep together.

Fixing the Ring Road emerged as the first internationally coordinated reconstruction project with eight nations and international organizations involved.[25] Between 2002 and 2014, the United States provided over $2 billion for the construction or refurbishment of nearly 2,000 miles of national and regional highways, and other international donors provided another $2 billion.[26] USAID's first effort was arguably its most important: connecting Kabul to restive Kandahar where the Taliban's strength had always been strong. The project's funds were obligated in late 2002, and a year later, the Kabul-to-Kandahar section was complete—an achievement that reduced travel time from several days to six hours.[27] Nonetheless, this project

Figure 5.2 Afghans observe the paving of the Kabul–Kandahar road in July 2003. The United States provided over $2 billion to help rehabilitate the "Ring Road" during the 13-year war. A decade later, the World Bank would report that 85 percent of Afghanistan's roads were unsuitable for motor vehicle traffic. (USAID)

cost over double the initial estimate due to security issues and supply shortages. It was deemed such a high priority—and had such high visibility—that additional resources were committed to see it finished.

By 2012, the entire 2,200-kilometer Ring Road was complete, save for a 233-kilometer section in Faryab and Badgis Provinces, which still suffered from persistent Taliban attacks. And although many have touted the Ring Road as one of the prime examples of reconstruction success, the project's results were actually more mixed. Total numbers of kilometers paved and dollars spent paint an incomplete picture because they do not account for the systemic failures of the Afghans to either maintain the roads or manage the Ministry of Public Works. Beginning in 2007, USAID devoted $53 million to improving the ministry's managerial capacity and even created the Road Maintenance Unit. A fuel tax law ensured that necessary funds would be available for maintenance, and once the Road Maintenance Unit was operational, it would oversee upkeep. But when the Ministry of Public Works assumed responsibility for maintenance in 2012, the

Ministry of Finance refused to transfer the fuel tax revenues to the maintenance unit. Disagreements between the Afghan government and the contractors charged with completing the final missing pieces of the Ring Road stalled and then stopped construction. A 2014 law established maximum tonnage for vehicles on the road, but a former minister of public works admitted that his staff regularly allowed overweight trucks on the road in exchange for bribes that equaled roughly $3,000 per day. In 2014, the World Bank assessed that nearly 85 percent of Afghan national roads were in poor shape and that most could not be used by motor vehicles.[28] In 2015, the budget for road maintenance had a $100 million annual shortfall, and the US government estimated that over the course of the war, over $360 million of US taxpayer funds paid to private contractors for road security actually ended up in the hands of the Taliban.[29] Even the Kandahar-to-Kabul Road—USAID's first major success in 2003—is now crumbling. "The road is a disaster," remarked one Afghan commander in 2014. "It causes obstacles and delays and countless casualties."[30]

Efforts to repair portions of Afghanistan's electrical grid had similar problems. The thinking was sound: electricity would have cascading positive effects in business, health, and education, and would show the Afghans that their new government was serious about improving their lives. But rehabilitating a grid would be a multiyear project even in an advanced country, and the security situation in Afghanistan added considerable challenges. As a short-term solution, USAID and the World Bank set up emergency diesel generators in 11 cities while the longer-term solutions were being developed.[31] In the ensuing years, work began on two large endeavors—the North East Power System and the South East Power System—but deteriorating security constantly plagued the effort. Many of these "short-term" generators were still in use in 2014, and the rising fuel costs made them an expensive substitute for a proper, functioning power grid.

Afghanistan's greatest potential for power generation was in hydropower, and the United States' most infamous effort in this area was a $500 million project to refurbish the Kajaki Dam in Helmand Province. (Ironically, the United States had built the Kajaki Dam in the

1950s, and then bombed the plant's transmission line in 2001 during the invasion, only to have to spend more money and build it again.) Kajaki's rehabilitation, it was hoped, would bring electricity to over 300,000 Afghans, increase crop yields by directing water from the dam for better irrigation, and produce jobs.[32] Unfortunately, those dreams never materialized.

The Kajaki Dam project was ill-fated from the start. USAID, pressured to complete the project it had abandoned after the Soviet invasion in 1979, aimed to refurbish the dam's run-down infrastructure—and finally after 25 years—install a third power-generating turbine. For 10 years, violent conditions in one of Afghanistan's most restive provinces thwarted repeated attempts to finish the project. Work commenced in 2004, but by 2006 security concerns halted the project. In 2007, a military operation known as Operation Kryptonite temporarily drove out the Taliban from Kajaki but was unable to secure the logistics pathways needed to transport materials and parts. The new, third turbine was finally transported to Kajaki in 2008 by a robust (and costly) military convoy of 100 vehicles. But on the return trip, one of the vehicles struck an improvised explosive device, killing one soldier and wounding seven more;[33] progress in Kajaki thus came at a tremendous cost in blood and treasure.

The Kajaki Dam project is illustrative of what could and did go wrong with reconstruction in Afghanistan. Three years later in 2011, the third turbine was still crated where the military convoy had dropped it off in 2008 because the Taliban were actively blocking the project's completion. Attacks along logistics routes prevented much-needed turbine installation supplies from reaching the dam. Later that year, attempts to negotiate a cease-fire in the area with local elders and the Taliban fell apart; and rumors of bribing Taliban fighters to allow materials through their turf added further scandal to the project.[34] Any effort to back away from the project proved fruitless; President Karzai insisted that it was essential to stabilization in the south, and it remained one of his priorities throughout his time in office. In 2013, after three other subcontractors failed to get the job done, the United States turned the project over to the Afghans. After an additional $75 million pledge toward the project in 2014, the US special inspector general for Afghanistan reconstruction questioned USAID whether the dam's benefits were worth the costs associated with it; USAID responded that they were.[35] The project is now scheduled for completion at the end of 2016, though even that is an ambitious timeline.[36]

Overall, between 2002 and 2014, the United States spent roughly $2 billion on Afghanistan's power sector,[37] but the actual delivery of reliable, low-cost power needed to stimulate businesses never occurred. Despite the enormous costs and efforts, Afghanistan still had one of the world's lowest electrification rates in 2014, with only 18 percent of Afghans connected to the power grid. Over 75 percent of Afghanistan's power is imported and the Kajaki Dam is still not fully operational.[38]

The reconstruction efforts in the transportation and energy sectors are only two examples of how the already robust reconstruction mandate quickly expanded into an ambitious modernizing program. The two sectors that the United States spent the most time and money on—about $5 billion in roads and electricity over 13 years[39]—were long-term development projects that have not yet produced sustainable results.

Militarizing Reconstruction and Humanitarian Aid

These large modernization projects were not the only efforts to develop Afghanistan; the military also began combining security operations with development work almost as soon as the conflict began. In late 2001, the US Army deployed civil affairs teams throughout the country to assess humanitarian needs, implement small-scale reconstruction projects, and establish relationships with UNAMA and NGOs already in the field. Recognizing a need to help the local governments deliver services to the population, these early Coalition Humanitarian Liaison Cells, dubbed "Chiclets," expanded to include traditionally civilian development roles in late 2002 under the name Provincial Reconstruction Teams (PRTs). The first of their kind, these small civil-military organizations had three broad objectives: extend the authority of the Afghan central government, improve security, and promote reconstruction.[40]

The PRT program had some of the best prospects for success in Afghanistan, and as a result, it expanded rapidly throughout the country. Because they operated at the provincial level (equivalent to the state level in the United States), the PRTs quickly gained the support of provincial governors, who wanted to direct the aid to their communities and claim the successes as their own. Importantly, all PRT resources came from the funding agency directly to the PRT site; they were not channeled through Kabul and thus avoided the large federal corruption machines operating in the capital. The first PRT was established in Gardez, the capital of Paktia Province, in November 2002, and by early 2003, there were PRTs in the major population centers of five other provinces including Mazar-e-Sharif, Kandahar, and Herat City. By 2005, the number increased to 22, and by 2008, the United States was leading 12 of the 26 nationwide PRTs, and 13 other coalition countries were leading the rest.[41] Only 8 of the country's 34 provinces would never have a PRT.

The PRTs were not exclusively military—they were always intended to be civil-military partnerships—but the military provided over 90 percent of the personnel.[42] The DOD also provided most of the funding, although the handful of non-DOD government employees also managed the reconstruction, development, and governance projects funded by their own agencies. A major source of the military funding came from the Commander's Emergency Response Program (CERP), which allowed military commanders to spend up to $25,000 at a time for quick-impact stabilization projects that would improve local conditions and gain them the support of the local population.[43]

The PRTs had more resources than most NGOs and fewer constraints and requirements than the UN. And because they had their own soldiers for security, they could tackle local governance and development issues in places where the unarmed NGO workers could not. Working as a civil-military team, PRT members planned and built small-scale infrastructure projects such as wells, health clinics,

Figure 5.3 The militarization of reconstruction: military members of a Provincial Reconstruction Team (PRT) supervise Afghan engineers as they oversee construction of a new district center in Bakwa, Farah Province, in 2012. While PRTs were designed to be civil-military partnerships, over 90 percent of their personnel were military. (SSGT Jonathan Lovelady / Department of Defense)

roads, or schools. They advised the provincial and district governors in an effort to improve their responsiveness to the needs of their people. They helped deliver public services, such as clean water, sanitation facilities, and electricity generators. With both military resources and development dollars, they were able to overcome security and logistics challenges normally faced while rebuilding in a postconflict area.

The PRTs also aimed to provide a forum for discussion and coordination among the local Afghan leaders, ongoing military operations, and the UN and NGO field offices. In practice, however, their success as coordinators was uneven at best. Personalities, not policies, drove local coordination attempts, and cultural differences between the military and civilians created strife. From the onset, the PRTs were criticized for crossing the boundary into what had been traditionally a humanitarian space. Humanitarian aid was given a military face as uniformed soldiers helped plan and execute development activities.

NGOs felt that the militarization of aid would put civilian aid workers at risk. Unfortunately, this would prove true.

While the PRTs had some successes over the years, they also faced numerous challenges in design and would eventually be a major source of tension between the coalition and President Karzai. Even though the Afghan minister of interior signed off on the creation of the PRTs and their objectives, there was no central coordinating authority and no strategic plan to manage all the different flavors. Individual PRTs were free to interpret the guidelines and conduct operations based on national priorities and local conditions. For example, the British PRTs emphasized security sector reform, while the German PRTs had their civilian aid workers live outside their military camp.[44] No PRTs were directly answerable to Kabul, which eventually convinced Karzai that the coalition was using PRT aid and services to undermine his rule. In 2010, he began to lobby heavily for their removal, and by the end of 2014, all the PRTs had been abolished.

Problems with Metrics and Declining Security

In addition to the UN's labyrinthine bureaucracy and the focus on large infrastructure projects, the ways the coalition measured success also hindered progress. One of the hardest things to do in a postconflict zone is to measure whether reconstruction efforts are making a difference, and in Afghanistan's case, whether the work was reinforcing stability. As it turned out, progress was measured by the number of projects completed and dollars spent, but not by quality, sustainability, or overall effectiveness of the effort.

Between 2002 and 2008, UNAMA touted the following key indicators of reconstruction progress: in the health sector, 85 percent of the population had been given access to basic health services; over 6 million children were enrolled in school; roughly 32,000 villages had benefited from agriculture and rural development projects; more than 3 million people had benefited from rural water and sanitation projects; 8,000 miles of roads had been rehabilitated, improved, or built; 75 percent of voters participated in democratic elections; the gross domestic product per capita had increased by over 70 percent; over 75 percent of Afghans had access to telecommunications and 5 million Afghans were using cell phones.[45] By 2007, Afghanistan moved up a place in the UN Human Development Index, going from the fourth least developed country to the fifth least.[46]

Metrics generated inside the US government looked equally impressive. During the same years, USAID touted the fact that it had rehabilitated over 1,025 miles of national and regional highways (including over 620 miles of farm-to-market and cobblestone roads), increased overall agricultural production by $1.75 billion from 2003 to 2006, supported 50 women-run business associations to provide training and increase opportunities for women entrepreneurs, printed and distributed over 60 million textbooks; constructed or refurbished over 680 schools, built or rehabilitated over 670 health facilities and trained over 10,500 health workers, inoculated 95 percent of all Afghan children against polio, built or rehabilitated 40 courthouses and justice facilities in 18 provinces, trained over 950 judges, established or upgraded 36 independent community radio stations, and helped establish the Independent Electoral Commission and the Afghanistan Independent Human Rights Commission.[47]

The PRTs also put their achievements into numbers. Between 2002 and 2008, over 7,500 civil-military projects had been started in hard-to-reach or conflict-ridden areas, 75 percent of which were already completed by 2008.[48] In 2007 alone, the PRTs were responsible for completing 1,080 projects. Between 2004 and 2008, the US Department of Defense spent $1 billion in CERP projects—yearly expenditures grew over time from $40 million in 2004 to $486 million in 2008.[49]

As impressive as these gains seem, the statistics paint an incomplete picture of progress. First, some of the projects paid dividends to both the government and the insurgents, so it is difficult to claim they actually increased stability in the country. Roads may have helped goods move from farm to market, but they also helped Taliban intimidators and opium smugglers extend their reach throughout southern Afghanistan. While coalition forces provided generators for electricity and guarded some of the infrastructure, insurgents in Helmand Province controlled access to power substations and could extort money from residents or turn the power on or off at will. PRT commanders could rarely distinguish Taliban from non-Taliban, and this led to insurgents benefiting from CERP projects and then picking up weapons to fight the people who funded them.

Moreover, some projects were simply inappropriate, or unsustainable, or lacked basic oversight. In 2011, USAID awarded $70 million to a contractor called International Relief and Development (IRD) to provide tractors, solar panels, and agricultural supplies to Afghan farmers. While the original work plan called for inexpensive ($5,400) two-wheeled tractors that could operate in the Afghans' narrow orchard rows, IRD purchased larger four-wheeled tractors instead—each of which cost $17,600. Not only were the larger tractors less suitable to the local conditions; more importantly, a year later, one-third of the 95 tractors originally purchased could not be located. When questioned, IRD responded that it had no obligation to track tractors after delivering them to the Afghans.[50]

The effort to provide solar panels to shopkeepers in bazaars also proved problematic. When IRD officials correctly reasoned that an alternate power source would allow shopkeepers to use fewer generators and to save money on diesel fuel, their solution was to distribute $700,000 worth of solar panels. Each cost $2,300 but also required a 10 percent buy-in by the shopkeeper, which was far more than most Afghans spent on diesel fuel. The system also required batteries and additional electrical parts that few Afghans could purchase easily, and the panels were also highly vulnerable to theft and resale, as an Army officer involved in a similar program later explained. "As soon as the project was complete, the solar panels would be stolen and put on top of individual homes," Captain Steve Baunuch explained to NBC News. "The thinking was that you bring light at night, the market could stay open, it would boost the economy and win the hearts and minds of the Afghan people. . . . But that just did not happen. If anything, it was a glowing example of American incompetence."[51]

Elsewhere, dining areas were built without a kitchen, and show-

Figure 5.4 Village elders receive USAID-purchased solar panels in Jaji District, Paktiya Province, in 2011. Solar panels sometimes reduced the need for diesel fuel and generators, but they were also often stolen or sold on the black market. (Department of Defense)

ers and bathrooms were erected without plumbing.[52] The Afghan Ministry of Public Works struggled to maintain the newly rehabilitated roads; it lacked the resources to do it, and the ministry's budget was mismanaged. In 2014, US officials estimated that the Ring Road had already deteriorated by 40 percent.[53] Glowing photos, like those of Afghan children attending class, overshadowed the gruff reality on the ground—policymakers loved to talk about girls going to school, but nobody asked what they were actually learning. And when auditors started investigating how the local schools compiled their rosters and statistics—mandated data that determined school budgets—they found that the rosters were frequently forged and that no one was tracking either the number of students or teachers in any systematic way.[54]

What's worse, as security deteriorated rapidly in the latter half of the war, reconstruction became increasingly dangerous. Once the

Taliban realized that the reconstruction efforts were pushing people away from the insurgency, they began targeting development projects and humanitarian workers. In the first six months of 2009 alone, there were over 75 incidents where humanitarians were intimidated, robbed, abducted, and assassinated.[55] Along the Ring Road, the Taliban attacked construction sites, destroyed vehicles, kidnapped workers for ransom, and killed over 200 US-funded construction contractors.[56] Horrible images, like those of new schools bombed, weakened the progress narrative. Aid workers soon began to concentrate in Kabul, and major NGOs forbade their members from traveling to the conflict areas. All the progress in improving education, health, agriculture, and roads was being undermined by a few well-timed Taliban attacks. The Afghan people began to notice. A 2008 Asia Foundation poll of Afghans found that "the most important challenge is seen to be insecurity followed by weak government and corruption."[57] (It was also not helpful that, despite active measures by the international community to prevent it, fraud and corruption marred the 2009 presidential election, worsening perceptions of the Afghan government.)

Thus, six years into the war, the rhetoric of the Bonn Conference had begun to ring hollow. Instead of a peaceful and functioning Afghanistan, the international community faced a persistent and growing insurgency and a crisis of confidence in the government. While the causes of these two threats did not originate with the coalition's development efforts, some development mistakes made the problems worse. Although there were strategic planning documents and numerous conferences to coordinate activities, the projects undertaken by UNAMA were not necessarily linked to the larger plan. Large infrastructure projects were too big and required long-term maintenance that the Afghan government could not adequately provide. Inside the PRTs, even though there was plenty of funding, money was tossed at projects without ensuring they were appropriate, and the lack of oversight in all agencies caused unnecessary reconstruction blunders. Efforts to track progress were haphazard, and deteriorating security made everything more difficult. By mid-2009, it became clear that unless the coalition shifted its approach, NGOs would leave the country and development work would crawl to a halt.

Counterinsurgency and the Shift to Military-Led Stabilization Operations, 2009–2014

Although most of the planning that led to the military's counterinsurgency (COIN) manual was aimed at halting a downward spiral in Iraq, the basic first principle of COIN was something the Afghans had been shouting at the coalition for years: security comes first. Without basic safety, neither development nor governance nor the basics of running a local economy can take hold. In Afghanistan, however, the dangers were not merely physical. Rampant corruption and weak rule of law had not only imposed economic hardship on the Afghan people; at times it threatened their very ability to put food on the table or escape arbitrary arrest or death. With no assistance from the government—indeed oftentimes Kabul supported the worst actors—Afghans began turning to anyone who would protect them from the predations of local power brokers.

To their credit, the American military leaders who took charge of the war in 2009 recognized the seriousness of the problem. Upon his arrival in Kabul, the new ISAF commander, General Stanley McChrystal, conducted an initial assessment that painted a bleak picture of the challenges ahead. To reverse the Taliban's momentum, he concluded, the coalition needed to do much more than use violence against insurgents; it needed to provide for the Afghan people, reduce government corruption, and build effective Afghan institutions all at the same time.[58]

To do all of this, President Obama authorized the deployment of an additional 33,000 troops in 2009, and called for a "civilian surge" to improve the governing and management capabilities of the regime in Kabul. Soldiers have always been good at breaking things down; for the counterinsurgency strategy to work, someone had to come in afterward to build things back up. As a prominent scholar who wrote the preface to the military's COIN manual explained, in counterinsurgency, "some of the best weapons do not shoot."[59]

The US logic of counterinsurgency theory flows from the Western tradition of parliamentary democracies and the American experience in the Cold War. For much of human history, governments facing internal insurgencies have used brute force to either coerce or eliminate threats to their power, but this requires a large expensive army to be forever on guard against attacks from within. Rather than only countering violence with violence, counterinsurgency enthusiasts argue that the more sustainable approach is to earn the support of the population and to bolster the existing government's *legitimacy*. Creating a functioning social contract will lead the people to reject the insurgency, and eventually, defeat it permanently.

The military envisioned the path to legitimacy through a three-stage sequence, known colloquially as "clear, hold, and build." The "clear" phase looks similar to earlier approaches to insurgencies: military forces enter a contested area and use violence to drive out the insurgents. But instead of counting on the threat of further punitive measures to subdue the population, the counterinsurgents next transition to the "hold" phase: remaining in the area, and bringing in interim programs to establish governance and deliver social services that will connect the people to the government. Finally, in the "build" phase, the host government should stimulate the economy, establish mechanisms for justice and governance, reconstruct what has been destroyed, and set the conditions for long-term stability. If successful, the strategy does not subdue the population; it convinces it to choose the government over the insurgency and thereby deny the latter the basic resources it needs to contest the existing regime.

Because so much of this effort involves the will and opinions of the people, civilian instruments of power are central to it. Once the immediate threat of attack has subsided, soldiers with guns can rarely earn the public's trust; that falls to a host-nation government, preferably supported by civilian technocrats and development experts. Furthermore, unlike conventional military operations, counterinsurgency operations have far more direct contact with civilians because the battlefield stretches into the very fabric of a contested society. In the cities and villages, the military and police must protect the people from insurgent attacks and deliver justice and rule of law. Governing officials must be viewed as legitimate and responsive to their people's needs. The economy must function sufficiently to give people enough hope to gamble on the future. All of this depends on the basic security that the military initially provides, but it cannot be done by the military alone. Eventually, the host nation must run its own affairs, and it is the civilian-run efforts—the development projects, rule of law programs, police professionalization courses, and basic government infrastructure—that create the conditions of possibility for long-term peace. Military force is necessary in this process, but it is never sufficient.

Prior to the 2009 surge, a number of stabilization activities were already codified in US policy and doctrine, but few of them were networked into the larger military operations in Afghanistan.[60] And as the above pages have shown, most of them were top-down programs and focused on building capacity in Kabul—very little successful work was being done in the rural areas where support for the Taliban was the strongest. The approach adopted after 2009 sought to increase the number of civilians working on governance and development all over Afghanistan and to stitch together the top-down efforts with the new ones built from the bottom up.

These objectives led to a massive expansion of two programs in Afghanistan: USAID's District Delivery Program (DDP) and the Pentagon's Commander's Emergency Response Program (CERP). The DDP was intended to be a joint international-Afghan venture to improve or initiate government service delivery in 80 priority districts. With support from international civilian advisors, Afghan officials would meet with the local community to identify gaps in the health, education, agriculture, and justice sectors and apply resources to address them. While it depended on population size, a basic DDP package included a staffed district center; a health center; primary, secondary, and adult education facilities; livestock and horticulture for farmers; and a judicial capacity to resolve disputes.[61] In 2010—at the height of the surge—USAID funded 13 districts for the program, at a total cost of roughly $40 million.[62]

To supplement USAID's efforts to hold and build the areas wrested from Taliban control, the US military also increased dramatically its own CERP program, which had already existed for years. Unlike the DDP's effort, CERP was not meant to design long-term development; it sought to knock out quick-impact projects to jump-start reconstruction. Most of the projects were "cash for work"—for example, cleaning out canals, building walls, and clearing rubble—and were done without impact studies, development expertise, or even much of a plan besides keeping guns out of the hands of the thousands of unemployed, mostly illiterate young men who could potentially become a resource for the insurgency. These new efforts came with a hefty price tag. Between 2009 and 2010, US reconstruction funds increased from $2.7 billion to $4.7 billion.[63] Of note, CERP funding reached $1 billion for the fiscal year 2010, which was the total amount spent between 2004 and 2008.[64]

These programs saw their first tests in Helmand Province in 2009 and 2010. And while many writers focus on the better-known Operation Moshtarak in Marjah, the actual first test of what would later be called "government in a box," occurred in Nawa District in July 2009. Following a successful clearing operation, the Taliban melted away and the district government, DDP, and CERP poured in the resources. The Marines and USAID spent $20 million in Nawa in 2010 alone—more per capita than in any other part of the country.[65] Sixteen thousand men were hired for quick-impact projects, farmers received seeds and fertilizer, new tractors arrived to fix the roads, and solar-powered lights appeared on the streets. In the months that followed, violence levels dropped dramatically and stayed down as governance and reconstruction activities reinforced the improved security. Shortly thereafter, Nawa became the counterinsurgency "proof of concept" in Afghanistan.[66]

On the heels of success in Nawa, ISAF sought to repeat that model elsewhere, with considerable difficulty. In February 2010, it moved next to the Taliban stronghold of Marjah. Following the clearing operation, the coalition flowed in all the necessary components of district-level governance in hopes that the residents would reject the Taliban and support the government as had occurred in Nawa. By June 2010, civil affairs officers were dispensing $125,000 a week on public service projects. Military officers paid "tens of thousands of dollars directly to store owners, canal cleaners, litter patrols, and families that lost relatives."[67] At the same time, the DDP was attempting to establish government and commencing work on reconstruction.

But the insurgents fought back in Marjah and progress was elusive. By June, the levels of violence were higher than in the first month of the operation, and the Taliban had murdered more than a dozen civilians for cooperating with the coalition. USAID had money and plans to hire 10,000 civilians for local work, but just over 1,000 braved the Taliban's intimidation campaign and enrolled. Development projects floundered because of the worsening security.[68] The civilian-military team on the ground was increasingly pressured to produce results for policymakers back in Washington. Expectations concerning the time it would take to create effective and legitimate governance were unrealistic; establishing a new local government in Marjah "proved even more complex than [ISAF] thought."[69]

Marjah's key lesson for counterinsurgency was that the "hold" and "build" phases were going to take time. Expending the resources to build the physical infrastructure like district centers, schools, or clinics was the easy part. But staffing them with enough capable Afghan administrators who were willing to live austerely and brave Taliban intimidation was excruciatingly difficult.

Finding enough American civilians to do governance and development work in the field was also a challenge. In December 2009, when President Obama announced the shift to a counterinsurgency strategy, 626 US government civilians were stationed in Afghanistan. A year later, there were just over 1,100—far too few to run the programs needed to "hold" and "build" Afghanistan.[70] Moreover, most of the State Department employees were in the large embassy complex in Kabul—far from the rural, violent areas that were so in need of reconstruction and development. In July 2009, when the Nawa operation began, there were just 8 US civilians operating alongside the military in southern Afghanistan. By May 2010, several months into the Marjah operation, there were still only about 100. This meant that in most districts and villages, junior officers and senior enlisted soldiers were negotiating, building infrastructure, and advising on governance, economic development, and rule of law—mission-sets they were not traditionally trained to do, particularly without expert civilian supervision.[71]

The ISAF counterinsurgency campaign next turned to Kandahar Province, the birthplace of the Taliban. In the summer and fall of 2010, Operation Hamkari cleared insurgents out of the populated districts, and subsequently focused on reconstruction projects to increase the influence of the provincial governor, whom most residents viewed as an outsider. Each district of focus had a corresponding DDP package, and the support of the Kandahar PRT. The Kandahar PRT even deployed civilian advisors to live at the district centers and work with and directly mentor the Afghan leadership.[72] The US budget for stabilizing Kandahar was estimated at roughly $1 billion and was funded by various US civilian and military agencies.

Kandahar was a good example of civil-military cooperation; the civilian infrastructure proved to be a valuable platform for coordination of governance and development efforts. Even so, corruption and predation significantly affected international efforts there, something the civil-military team was not fully prepared to address. From the onset, the Kandahar PRT visibly struggled with convincing the residents that they could *trust* the representatives of the Afghan government. Whereas Nawa and Marjah suffered from a total absence of state government, Kandahar had some functioning institutions. But the people of Kandahar saw these institutions as predatory and illegitimate.[73] Counterinsurgency was ill-equipped to counter the Kandahar elite's culture of impunity and criminal activity that eroded the legitimacy of the efforts there.

While the military and civilians generally depended on each other and sometimes cooperated well together, these three examples of US counterinsurgency also illuminate some of the major shortfalls faced by the civil-military team in attempting to "hold" and "build" after the military's initial clearing operations. Ultimately, tensions between the military's preference for short-term quick-impact projects and the civilians' desire to strengthen government capacity in the long run created incompatible timelines and an unfocused effort. The military exerted significant pressure on both the State Department and USAID to get the local governments up and running in as many districts as quickly as possible. This pressure was reinforced by White House and congressional leaders who demanded to see whether the counterinsurgency investments were producing results. USAID staffers felt bullied and ignored when they pushed back about needing more time to establish governance and develop primitive institutions. Although the DDP was supposed to be Afghan-led, the demand for fast results forced the US military and civilians to keep tight reigns on the programs. As a result, the governance and development initiatives were hastily implemented, and the Afghans never got to run things themselves under the watchful eye of a patient mentor. Civilian experts in the field began calling the hold and build efforts a well-intentioned "bridge too far" that consequently fell short of meeting objectives.[74]

Coordination with other development entities was also a problem. Besides the DDP, USAID also funded 15 other subnational governance programs in Afghanistan; the United Nations and the World Bank's National Solidarity Program funded others as well.[75] The Afghans had two separate ministries responsible for reaching out to strengthen subnational governance.[76] These programs all worked in parallel, and rarely congruently. While the provincial and district centers provided a forum for coordination, there was never the capacity to keep track of it all.

Eighteen months after the initial shift to counterinsurgency, it was clear that even Nawa District—the early success that had been touted as the proof that COIN could work—was having problems. Between August 2009 and August 2011, the coalition poured roughly $30 million into the district.[77] At the height of the resource surge there, over half of the working-age men were receiving salaries from US government sources.[78] While direct attacks by the Taliban remained low, crime and intimidation never went away. In late 2010, one reporter noted that half of the USAID-installed solar lights had had their batteries stolen, and President Karzai still remained deeply unpopular. The abundance of aid dollars inadvertently created a dependency in Nawa and, arguably, atrophied Afghan creativity and innovation in addressing its problems. Inevitably, as resources thinned, so did the prognosis for sustainable peace there. "If the Americans end their cash-for-work programs," the district governor warned in late 2010, "people will go back to fighting for the Taliban."[79] If the surge yielded increases in both resources and possibilities, the final four years of the war were marked by unmet expectations, dwindling resources, and pervasive corruption. Just one year after President Obama's surge announcement, the coalition began planning its exit. At the November 2010 NATO Lisbon summit, the international community agreed that combat forces would remain until 2014, but that thereafter the bulk of the support would be financial. Securing enough funding for the future would not be easy. Even after several donor conferences, by 2014, there were still only modest pledges to fill the reconstruction trust funds managed by the World Bank and the Asia Development Bank beyond the end of ISAF's mission.[80] In 2011, the US State Department unveiled a regional development initiative, dubbed "the New Silk Road," which was intended to integrate Afghanistan further into the region by "reconstructing significant infrastructure links broken by decades of conflict."[81] By early 2014, however, the artificial economy already showed signs of looming trouble as aid wound down and troops withdrew,[82] and the New Silk Road development plan was criticized as a road to nowhere.[83]

The military continued to pour money into development during the final two years of the war, but these projects were usually connected to its own narrow military objectives and not to the civilian reconstruction framework that was supposed to be guiding the process. By 2012, the special inspector for Afghanistan reconstruction found that the military's infrastructure projects were 6 to 15 months behind schedule and warned that "these projects may result in adverse [counterinsurgency] effects because they create an expectations gap among the affected population or lack citizen support."[84]

USAID also encountered few demonstrable successes in the final years of the war. The agency spent over $400 million on two new programs—the Stability in Key Areas Program and the Community Cohesion Initiative—but a 2015 USAID-funded study found that in the aggregate, stability had actually *declined* in the villages where USAID had been operating since 2012. Subindices such as local governance, government capacity, and quality of life—all of which were meant to gauge Afghans' faith in the government—also declined. Most troubling, in 13 villages with USAID projects, "stabilization programming actually had the perverse effect of increasing support of the Taliban," because villagers assumed the Taliban had acquiesced to the projects.[85] Almost everywhere that USAID operated, corruption remained rampant. USAID responded by managing the projects through US-contracted partners, which led Afghan government officials to throw up obstacles and create delays to express their displeasure. "The Afghan government did not want this program," one USAID official admitted. "They would often not cooperate with us in getting basic services for villagers." Even when USAID avoided direct government interference, Afghans at every level found ways to appropriate US taxpayer dollars for themselves. "The money is going out, but it's hard to track," another USAID official explained. "A lot of projects got captured by Afghans who steered aid to where they wanted it to go, to their villages."[86]

///

Overall, it is clear that Afghanistan reconstruction was an expensive enterprise for the US government. Of the $113 billion spent between 2002 and 2015, the vast majority was controlled by the Department of Defense: $72 billion went to training the Afghan National Security Forces (ANSF) and other DOD-led reconstruction efforts. USAID spent roughly $19 billion and the State Department spent less than $5 billion. A smattering of other agencies (the Department of Justice, Drug Enforcement Agency, Department of Agriculture, and so on) spent another $17 billion.[87] (None of this includes the costs of combat operations, which add another half a trillion dollars to the war's final bill.)[88] But what exactly did the reconstruction money pay for?

In hindsight, it seems that most of those dollars did not produce enduring and sustainable gains, and the reasons for the shortfalls are numerous. First, the grand development and reconstruction strategy was not executed in practice. Because of the sheer number of organizations involved—the UN, the World Bank, the major donor countries, and the ISAF military coalition—efforts were not coordinated or managed effectively. Second, the projects chosen were not necessarily the best or most sustainable for the Afghan context. The reconstruction strategy was an incredibly ambitious plan to modernize Afghanistan at an accelerated pace without considering whether it was prepared to handle such a jump in development. Third, an unfortunate consequence of militarizing the development agenda was that humanitarian workers and projects were targeted. And, overall, there was very little appreciation or patience for the amount of time it takes for the reconstruction and development process to have effect. This led to a misguided and haphazard approach that lasted for six years.

Once the United States shifted to a counterinsurgency strategy in 2009, there was some initial progress but also new difficulties. By shifting to a bottom-up approach, the military was able to deliver aid to the most insecure areas of the country and to defend the people doing development work. With its enormous budget, ability to operate in insecure areas, and contingency planning skills, the military could adapt quickly and persevere under extraordinarily difficult circumstances. But the counterinsurgency shift also caused a number of other problems. Attempts to stabilize and reconstruct from the bottom up did deliver some services to rural areas, but only by flooding those areas with overwhelming resources—an unsustainable approach that also distorted the local economy and never yielded sufficient security to completely eject the Taliban. Earning the Afghan people's trust and bolstering the central government's legitimacy was difficult and hard to sustain, particularly with corruption rampant throughout the country. Over time, the large amounts of international funding also created a dependency culture—peace in an area started to hinge on where the next dollar would come from and whose hands it would fall into. All of this made it difficult to put lasting, sustainable systems in place.

For both the military and civilian organizations doing development in Afghanistan, there were also problems with metrics. As a general rule, the major successes were explained through numbers and not narratives or context. It is generally agreed that the greatest achievements were in the health and education sectors—both worthwhile endeavors that improved Afghan livelihoods. But while the work to pave roads was both expensive and impressive, the lack of maintenance for the roads has already undermined the earlier progress.

These problems have led some pessimists to conclude that reconstruction and development cannot work in an active conflict area. That charge is overly simplistic. Some things did work: health improved dramatically during the years of coalition involvement, as did access to education. Afghans have noticed the difference too: long-term survey data managed by the Asia Foundation showed in 2015 that nearly three out of four Afghans were satisfied with their access to drinking water, and two-thirds of those surveyed were satisfied with the quality of education for their children. Some small-scale endeavors that did not disrupt the local economy had positive effects, and should the large-scale infrastructure projects ever be completed, they too will likely lift some Afghans out of poverty and give them ways to improve their everyday lives. But even if this occurs, it will have come at a tremendous cost. And part of the reason for that cost is the military doctrine of counterinsurgency, which posits that armed forces can increase a government's legitimacy and thereby disempower an insurgency by providing basic services to the population. If Afghanistan proves one thing, it is that this premise needs to be refined, or perhaps discarded altogether. As one US Institute of Peace analyst summarized the militarized development experiment in Afghanistan: "We got confused. . . . We fooled ourselves into thinking that money could stabilize the situation, rather than create instability. . . . Trying to redirect a lot of development assistance to achieve security objectives instead of development objectives was a major cause of waste."[89]

CHAPTER SIX

Rule of Law and Governance in Afghanistan, 2001–2014

Colonel Abigail T. Linnington, USA, and Lieutenant Colonel Rebecca D. Patterson, USA

On April 30, 2014, three weeks after the Afghan presidential election, former ISAF commander General John R. Allen appeared before the Senate Foreign Relations Subcommittee to testify on the future of Afghanistan. Though the winner of the presidential election had not yet been decided, the general gave his testimony in the form of a letter to the new president-elect, offering advice for the future US-Afghanistan relationship. In his letter, Allen conceded that "for too long we focused our attention solely on the Taliban as the existential threat to Afghanistan. . . . The battle for Afghanistan, the real fight, will be won by righteous law enforcement, a functioning judiciary and an unambiguous commitment to the rule of law."[1]

The controversy and instability surrounding the 2014 Afghan presidential election demonstrated how fragile and interdependent the rule of law, governance, and security are in Afghanistan. The process of choosing a successor to Hamid Karzai dragged on for more than five months. After numerous runoffs and recounts, and despite repeated interventions by US and European heads of state, the two frontrunners—Dr. Ashraf Ghani and Dr. Abdullah Abdullah—refused to budge. President Karzai continued to insist he would step down on September 2, until that date came and went. On September 19, Ghani and Abdullah finally struck a deal to divide executive power—a compromise that appeased their constituents but confused Afghan legal experts, since the power-sharing arrangement had no historical precedent or justification in the Afghan Constitution. After announcing the agreement, the two men hugged stiffly but later refused to appear together at a joint press conference. The Afghan government never released the tallies of the nationwide vote as doing so would have added to the widespread accusations of voter fraud on both sides.[2]

After 13 years of international assistance and billions of dollars invested, the fundamental question of who rules Afghanistan and with what legal framework is still largely unresolved in practice. In this chapter we explore the attempts to reestablish or create rule of law mechanisms in Afghanistan since 2001 and conclude that the international community's efforts in the justice sector have not yet demonstrated sustainable progress. Moreover, in some cases, and despite the best of intentions, international efforts have hindered Afghanistan's ability to build a responsive justice system, increase government transparency and accountability, and reduce corruption. In the crafting of this critique, we acknowledge that tens if not hundreds of thousands of civilian and military personnel from more than 50 countries joined millions of Afghans to devote their time, labor, resources, and in some cases their lives to rebuilding a more secure Afghan state governed by the rule of law. We offer this critique to document and assess the rule of law efforts made to date in the hope that we may apply these lessons to future international assistance in Afghanistan as well as justice sector development in other countries.

We argue that the efforts to improve rule of law in Afghanistan passed through three stages during the 13-year war in Afghanistan. From 2001 to 2005, the countries, nongovernmental organizations (NGOs), and international organizations working on rule of law adopted a "light footprint" approach that sought to provide technical expertise and advice while encouraging Afghan leaders to take ownership of the process. From 2006 to 2008, the international community became increasingly aware of the linkage between rising insecurity and the absence of accountable dispute resolution practices. Funding for justice programs rose dramatically, but the international community failed to create a unified strategy with Afghan partners to prioritize and focus limited resources on limited objectives. From 2009 to 2014, ISAF adopted a counterinsurgency approach that brought more resources for rule of law development but also resulted in a greater role for military forces. Each of these three approaches had advantages and disadvantages that resulted in a patchwork of often unrelated programs that were largely unsustainable given the limited consultation with and support from Afghan leaders.

Running through each of these stages were three persistent problems or debates that have made progress in the justice sector extremely difficult. First, Afghanistan's experience in the 20th century was marked by violent disagreements between urban leaders, who pushed for a Western-influenced, constitution-based justice system, and traditional or religious authorities in rural areas, who resisted efforts to centralize state power or change social norms. This debate reignited when Westerners showed up in force in 2001. Laid upon this fragmented foundation was a second disagreement between Afghan leaders and the international community concerning the priorities and methods for improving rule of law. From the beginning, international rule of law experts imported their own cultural ideas about law and justice and disregarded the region's history; as a result, the experts failed to incorporate Afghan ideas into international strategies and actions, resulting in numerous unsustainable initiatives. Lastly, the expansion of the US-NATO military mission after 2009 substantially increased the military resources for rule of law efforts, and this led to a disagreement inside the ISAF coalition over the civilian and military divisions of labor on rule of law matters. As a result of these three disagreements, no coordinated, sustainable approach to rule of law development ever emerged. Instead, a range of disparate programs run by different entities competed for scarce resources, sent mixed signals to Afghan partners, and frequently worked at cross-purposes.

Rule of Law in Theory and Practice in Afghanistan

Much has been written on how to promote rule of law in conflict-ridden societies in general and in Afghanistan in particular.[3] In theory, "rule of law" refers to a "principle of governance in which all persons, institutions, and entities, public and private, including the State itself, are accountable to laws that are publicly promulgated, equally enforced and independently adjudicated, and which are consistent with international human rights norms and standards."[4] In practice, however, a successful rule of law regime requires more than principles. It needs institutions: an independent judiciary, the infrastructure for public and fair trials, dependable bureaucratic administration, a professional and accountable police force, and a safe and humane detention system.[5] And while societies must account for differences across countries and cultures, in the end, a successful rule of law regime should be able to do five things: make the state abide by the law, ensure equality before the law, supply law and order equally and consistently, provide efficient and impartial justice, and uphold human rights.[6]

These were always ambitious goals for Afghanistan, not least because of internal disagreements extending back to the early 20th century, when Afghan reformers like Emir Amanullah Khan tried to impose "modern" values on the deeply religious Pashtuns of the east and south.[7] The history of frequent political turnover has also thwarted efforts on the part of the central government to extend rule of law beyond the capital. But it is Afghanistan's recent experience that is perhaps the most relevant cultural context; since 1978, Afghans have had at least three types of legal regimes imposed on them: a Marxist regime backed by Soviet occupation forces (1979–1988), a hard-line Islamist rule enforced by the Taliban (1996–2001), and multiple Western models introduced by the ISAF coalition after 2001. What each of these regimes had in common was the goal to centralize rule of law in the capital and to delegitimize the traditional, customary practices that 80 percent of Afghans have historically used to resolve disputes. And in all three cases, Afghans resisted.

Because of this history, the country's rule of law mechanisms are best described as a patchwork of formal and informal frameworks, all of which are subject to constant renegotiation between urban elites in Kabul, tribal elites in the provinces, and religious elites in both areas.[8] Quite simply, there have never been any hard-and-fast written rules concerning the rule of law in Afghanistan, and this has made it very difficult to help Afghans build a system that will be acceptable to them all.

Even with these problems, it is incorrect to say that there has been no justice or rule of law in Afghanistan either now or in previous eras. Despite the absence of formal institutions, anarchy has not reigned. Individuals seeking justice rely on tribal, religious, or other community leaders to adjudicate disagreements, and the tenets of *Pashtunwali* and the strictures of Islamic law provide guidelines and centuries-old practices for resolving grievances.[9] As late as 2013, with corruption affecting more than half the country, 67 percent of Afghans considered local *shuras* and *jirgas* more fair, effective, timely, and consistent with local values than the country's formal justice institutions.[10] Outside the few major cities, village councils or tribal elders play the predominant role in both resolving disputes and meting out justice.[11] The problem has always been to balance the formal and the informal systems and to create working nationwide mechanisms that do not alienate the rural population. For, as history shows, Kabul-driven initiatives seeking to dictate new social norms beyond the city centers provoke widespread, often violent resistance in the conservative countryside. This fundamental dispute, of who rules and with what rules, has been a constant in Afghanistan's history. More importantly, it has been one of the principal obstacles to the coalition's efforts to build a nationwide modern rule of law regime in Afghanistan.

2001–2005: A "Light Footprint"

Because of these internal arguments over justice and authority, when international rule of law experts arrived in Afghanistan after 2001, they sought to use a "light footprint" approach: providing advice and resources but little else in the hope that the Afghans would take ownership of the process. Because the advisors focused their efforts in and around Kabul, the initiatives that saw modest gains in 2001–2005 were at the federal level and concerned the basic processes for ratifying a constitution, electing a president, and establishing a national assembly. Although there were several attempts to begin justice sector reform in those early years, few took hold because the international community applied too few resources and powerful Afghans resisted. The "lead nation" concept which allowed specific countries to take ownership of all activities in a given rule of law sector also created overlapping efforts and poor results. Despite the calls for Afghan ownership, poor coordination—both with the Afghans and between the countries offering support—yielded numerous rule of law initiatives that were designed by Westerners and then imposed on the Afghans.

The first major effort to improve rule of law in Afghanistan began with the 2002 Bonn Agreement. In addition to creating the Afghan Interim Authority, Bonn also authorized the formation of the Afghanistan Judicial Reform Commission with the task to "rebuild the domestic justice system in accordance with Islamic principles, international standards, the rule of law, and Afghan legal traditions."[12] Thus, just a few months after the fall of the Taliban, Afghanistan had a road map to create a liberal, accountable parliamentary democracy, and the international community showered it with robust attention, technical support, and resources.

There were some early successes. President Karzai was inaugurated later that year; the Afghans ratified their constitution in 2004 and held parliamentary elections in 2005, which led to the convening of the National Assembly. But even these early federal efforts gave insufficient attention to the most important element of rule of law: the justice system. The first Judicial Reform Commission (JRC) was established in May 2002, but it quickly became deadlocked and was disbanded. In November 2002, a presidential decree reestablished the JRC with a new mandate to "organize a comprehensive law reform programme, survey the human, technical and logistical needs of the justice sector and develop selection and training programmes for judges, prosecutors and other lawyers."[13] But even with President Karzai's backing, the JRC had little support from the president's cabinet and soon became an isolated faction competing for scarce resources. With every ministry clamoring for more international assistance, the 12-person JRC was a lonely and ineffectual voice, one that some in government worked deliberately to marginalize. In 2005, the JRC was disbanded.[14]

The international community's light-footprint strategy had good intentions but the result was a disjointed effort that quickly became unmanageable. As this volume's chapters on Afghan National Security Forces (ANSF) development show, the lead-nation concept caused a number of inefficiencies, and this affected rule of law as well: Italy took the lead on the justice sector, including Afghan prisons; Germany headed up police training and reform, and the United Kingdom led counternarcotics-related efforts. The United States and Canada initiated their own justice sector projects, as did the United Nations Development Program and the United Nations Office on Drugs and Crime.[15] Coordination between the countries was poor, and the Afghans found themselves in bilateral consultations with every country supporting a rule of law program.

Overlapping efforts were not the only problem. Despite early admonitions that Afghan law should reflect Afghan culture, several countries suggested new government legal systems cut from the whole cloth of their own societies. After Italy promulgated an interim Afghan criminal code, the US Institute of Peace reported that the "code has been subject to some controversy, as it was prepared by Italian officials with help from U.S. military lawyers but [with] relatively little input or support from the Afghan justice institutions, and was reportedly adopted under strong foreign political pressure."[16] Similarly, after conducting interviews with Afghan legal experts in Kabul, the International Crisis Group argued that Italy's lack of consultation with Afghans has led to "one of the international community's most egregious failures."[17]

US rule of law interventions were even more hands-off than their European counterparts in these early years. Although American leaders expressed broad support for justice sector reform, most of their focus was on hunting al Qaeda and senior Taliban members; thus they were reluctant to take the lead on any international nation-building or development efforts in Afghanistan. Instead, America's contributions were almost entirely financial. In 2002 and 2003, the United States spent an estimated $15 million on rule of law assistance programs, most of which was for rebuilding federal institutions in Kabul. After the successful ratification of the Afghan Constitution in January 2004, US assistance doubled to $29 million in 2004 and was $21 million in 2005 but remained largely separate from the United Nations Assistance Mission-Afghanistan (UNAMA) and Italian efforts. By 2004, the United States was the single largest donor of rule of law development aid, as well as aid to related security sector reform efforts such as policing. Yet as a matter of policy, the United States remained reluctant to take on a leadership role or to ensure that its dollars were spent in a focused manner. As the various, disjointed rule of law programs began to take shape across the country, the lack of any functioning coordination mechanism made it difficult for fledgling Afghan ministries to communicate with donors and respond to their interests in any coherent manner. A variety of programs emerged, each with a limited connection to one another and in many cases with minimal Afghan engagement or support.[18] Little aid trickled down to the rural provinces where, by 2005, justice concerns had already begun delegitimizing the Karzai regime.

None of this was kept secret; it just didn't capture the attention of policymakers the way the war in Iraq or the ongoing hunt for al Qaeda did. As the US Department of State inspector general reported several years later:

> Since 2002 the different civilian and military agencies engaged in aspects of ROL [rule of law] development have approached their tasks with different goals, methodologies, and timelines, and have often been unaware of each other's efforts. . . . By 2004 serious questions were raised regarding how well the U.S. government and its allies were communicating with one another, coordinating their efforts, and monitor-

ing their expenditures. . . . At the [U.S.] embassy in Kabul, according to individuals both in and out of the U.S. government, by late 2005, internal U.S. coordination meetings on ROL were best characterized as shouting matches between representatives of different agencies.[19]

2006–2008: Rising Insecurity and Overlapping Efforts

Five years into the Afghan War, the link between rising insecurity and the absence of rule of law became increasingly apparent. Despite the noteworthy political and social gains since 2001, insecurity escalated in 2006, and this was felt most profoundly outside Kabul. The Asia Foundation's Survey of the Afghan People saw markedly different concerns on the part of the population between 2006 and 2007. For example, in 2007 the survey identified insecurity as the largest problem facing Afghanistan, with 32 percent of respondents citing security issues as the major problem.[20] Just one year earlier, the poor economy was the respondents' biggest concern. At the same time the security situation was deteriorating, respondents had little confidence in the formal judicial system: only 11.2 percent reported having a great deal of trust in the judicial system and 26.8 percent reported a fair degree of trust. Only one-fifth reported bringing their disputes to a formal government court for settlement; the majority instead favored local leaders and tribal elders for dispute resolution.[21] Even when Afghans did turn to formal institutions, "the lack of an effective police force, poor infrastructure and communications, instability, and insecurity hampered investigations of unlawful killings, bombings, or civilian deaths."[22] Despite judiciary reform efforts, the Afghan people did not have faith in their justice system.

As security deteriorated, the Afghans and the international community sponsored donor conferences and created strategy documents, but did little else. With all efforts focused in Kabul, the source of the problem—rural Afghans' lack of access to workable justice systems—went unaddressed. The "facile optimism" the international community brought with it increased funding for rule of law development but no long-term, nuanced assessments or engagement with Afghan partners.[23] Overlapping bureaucracies continued to create inefficiencies both inside Afghanistan and in the international community—and an increasing reliance on contractors created basic management and accountability problems. The only efforts that made some connections with rural Afghans—the Provincial Reconstruction Teams (PRTs)—were resisted by President Karzai and were chronically underfunded.

In May 2005, the Afghan Ministry of Justice, working in concert with the reinvigorated Justice Sector Consultative Group, published the first substantive Afghan assessment of the justice sector, titled *Justice for All*. The report noted what was readily apparent by that point: despite fairly robust funding for rule of law, Afghanistan still lacked "a comprehensive plan for the reconstruction of the justice sector," and the efforts undertaken using the lead-nation concept had not yielded any permanent, well-functioning justice institutions. Noting the importance of empowering traditional justice systems, the report also reminded the international community that justice reform "must reflect Afghan political circumstances, social and legal traditions and aspirations for the future." The report concluded by requesting $600 million over 12 years to implement a nationwide legal aid program; provide wages to justice officials; build justice centers, court rooms, and prisons around the country; and provide ongoing legal education to create a professional justice work force.[24]

Justice for All was not the only report on rule of law to come out of the Afghan government; nor was it the only request for more support. In 2005 and 2006, key leaders from across the Afghan government, and in consultation with numerous government, private sector, civil society, and nongovernmental actors and experts, drafted the interim Afghan National Development Strategy (ANDS) organized around three pillars: security; governance, rule of law, and human rights; and economic and social development. At the London conference in February 2006, the interim ANDS was unveiled alongside the Afghanistan Compact, which set benchmarks for achieving ANDS objectives within five years and included metrics for assessing rule of law efforts. The Afghans also drafted the National Justice Sector Strategy (NJSS) and the National Justice Program (NJP), which guided ministry and donor participation and funding.[25] On paper anyway, the Afghans and their partners were taking rule of law seriously.

The international community responded by convening more conferences and spending more money. In 2006, UNAMA sought to reestablish the International Coordination Group on Justice Reform, and the following year, donors met in Rome and pledged $360 million over five years for rule of law efforts in Afghanistan—more than half of what the Afghans had requested for the next 12 years. The United States continued to be the single largest donor of justice sector aid with $30 million invested in 2006, a sum which nearly doubled in each subsequent year to $65 million in 2007, $126 million in 2008, and $207 million in 2009.[26]

The London and Rome conferences made other advances as well. The best change was the decision to terminate the lead-nation strategy that had led to such disjointed efforts in years past, but all of the international community's ambitious objectives for rule of law development still lacked a realistic implementation plan. Afghan ministries continued to compete with one another and continued to be overwhelmed by the proliferation of international actors. No donor country or international organization stepped forward to lead rule of law assistance efforts, and no mechanisms existed to hold donors and Afghan ministries and leaders accountable.

Problems of bureaucracy and competition over resources grew fiercer after the Rome conference—probably because with the new pledges, there was now a larger financial pie to carve up. Because the Afghan Constitution had created a highly centralized Afghan state, all budget decisions for nationwide services were controlled in Kabul, and the ability to secure resources was largely tied to ministers' relationships with President Karzai. As a result, even after the dollars for rule of law increased dramatically, they rarely made it to the right place. As just one example, the Ministry of Justice in Kabul had all responsibility for case management, the prisons, legal assistance, and mediation services, including the local Huqooq officials who mediated conflicts at the district level.[27] And yet even with these responsibilities, the ministry remained chronically underfunded, as resources flowed to the Ministry of Defense and the Tajik-controlled Ministry of Interior (which oversaw the police). The Afghan Supreme Court had a similarly unwieldy portfolio—as the court of last resort and the chief administrative body for all court personnel including judges and clerks, it was charged with overseeing the appointment, transfer, promotion, and punishment of judges, and held budgetary authority over all subordinate courts and court staff.[28] Despite this wide-reaching mandate, it too found itself chronically short of the most basic supplies. In the deeply centralized Afghan government, very few services ever made it outside Kabul to the areas where the lack of justice was turning rural Afghans toward the Taliban.

Separate entities within the American government—and a heavy reliance on contractors—also created overlapping layers and miscommunication. Most US rule of law efforts were nominally led by the State Department's Bureau of International Narcotics and Law Enforcement (INL), but the Department of Defense, Department of Justice, and US Agency for International Development also had their own programs that either directly or indirectly involved rule of law. State's INL ran the Justice Sector Support Program and the Corrections Sector Support Program and relied mostly on contractors from PAE Incorporated, whose performance it could not properly manage or oversee.[29] Some PRTs also provided technical assistance to train and equip local police, and after 2006, State Department INL advisors in the PRTs began sponsoring multiday provincial justice conferences, which brought together police chiefs, judges, prosecutors, and prison officials to assess local capacity, discuss priorities for assistance and infrastructure projects, and work high-profile cases.[30] Many US PRTs also added an advisory ROL position to their ranks after 2007. The Department of Defense did most of the mentoring and coordinating with the Ministry of Interior, which controlled all the police, but civilian contractors did almost all the police training. The US Department of Justice led the Senior Federal Prosecutors Program, which sought to bolster the Afghans' ability to investigate and prosecute major crimes. A separate USAID program focused on the development of the formal court system, training and salaries for

Figure 6.1 A US contractor from BAE Systems describes fingerprint types to Afghan legal professionals during a forensics course in Parwan Province. A heavy reliance on contractors, high-technology solutions, and overlapping efforts between different US agencies hindered rule of law development for the entirety of the Afghan War. (Staff Sergeant Jerry Saslav / Department of Defense)

judges, and programs to educate citizens on their rights. By the end of the war, everyone claimed to be doing something about corruption and governance in Afghanistan—the State Department, DOD, FBI, ATF agents, Immigrations and Customs Enforcement, and even forensic analysts from the Treasury Department—but no one agency was ever placed in charge of the multiple and overlapping efforts.[31]

2009–2014: The Militarization of Rule of Law Efforts

In 2009, President Obama took over the war in Afghanistan and dramatically increased the resources for reversing the Taliban's momentum. A series of strategic assessments followed, all of which noted corruption, weak rule of law, and poor governance as major obstacles to a functioning, legitimate Afghan state.[32] When General Stanley McChrystal arrived in May 2009, he specifically acknowledged the cultural rift between the international community and the Afghan people: "We have operated in a manner that distances us—physically and psychologically—from the people we seek to protect. . . . We must . . . change the operational culture of ISAF to focus on protecting the Afghan people, understanding their environment, and building relationships with them. . . . The weakness of state institutions, malign actions of power-brokers, widespread corruption and abuse of power by various officials, and ISAF's own errors, have given Afghans little reason to support their government." Rule of law failures had become as large of a threat to success in Afghanistan as the Taliban.[33]

That August, nearly eight years after the initial US invasion, Ambassador Karl Eikenberry and General Stanley McChrystal published the first comprehensive US strategy for the Afghan War, titled the "Integrated Civilian-Military Campaign Plan for Support to Afghanistan." In it they articulated, among 11 priorities, three closely related to rule of law: access to justice, expansion of accountable and transparent governance, and countering the nexus of insurgency, narcotics, corruption, and criminality.[34] The new campaign plan ushered in a period of renewed US interest and resources for the Afghan intervention. At the United States' and NATO's urging in the fall of 2009, the international community's involvement in Afghanistan shifted from a minimalist patchwork of peacebuilding and reconstruction activities to a concerted counterinsurgency campaign.[35] This paved the way for increased personnel and resources for civilian rule of law development, and simultaneously called for an expanded military role in supporting justice sector efforts. But shifting the military's operational culture from counterterrorism to counterinsurgency would prove difficult, and major divides between military and civilian justice sector efforts hindered cooperation. What began as an earnest effort to bolster Afghan rule of law and counter corruption soon devolved into bureaucratic turf wars and a civil-military debate over issues of implementation.

Other decisions made in Kabul hindered progress as well, particularly during the contested Afghan presidential election in 2009. Certain that the United States was intent on replacing him, President

Karzai tightened his grip on power, consolidated his executive branch networks, and co-opted the Independent Electoral Commission. The United Nations observer mission failed to combat widespread voter fraud, and the United States' demand for a runoff election resulted in a progressively hostile relationship between Karzai and the United States—as well as almost all international actors funding rule of law development in Afghanistan. With Karzai's reelection and rising indicators of government corruption, the United States and other partner nations began looking for ways to bypass Kabul and to expand access to justice at provincial and district levels.[36]

Because of the mistakes of earlier years, 2009 was the first year that all three cultural clashes noted at the outset of this chapter were undermining rule of law in Afghanistan. The internal argument grew louder as Afghans continued to distrust their own government's ability to rule and counter corruption, and to resent Kabul's intrusions into the rural areas. The international argument also became more heated as the contested elections and poor coordination between countries increased tensions between the Afghans and their international supporters. And with more military resources being devoted to rule of law after the shift to a counterinsurgency approach, tensions within the ISAF coalition—between civilians and military officers in particular—began adding a new layer of friction to the effort.

Part of the problem was that the State Department rightly felt it should be running the US government's rule of law efforts in the country, but it lacked the people to radically expand its efforts. Despite the president's call for a "civilian surge" to augment the military's troop increases, the best State could provide was more money and better leadership. Thus, as the civilian and military surge peaked in mid-2010, the Department of State appointed Ambassador Hans Klemm as the first coordinating director of rule of law and law enforcement at the US embassy in Kabul, and assigned him the task of overseeing all US civilian and military activities in the justice sector.[37] Most US civilian program expansion remained focused on the formal justice sector: providing technical assistance to ministries, rebuilding infrastructure, and addressing shortfalls in human capital through education, salaries, and protection for Afghans serving in the provincial and district courts.[38] Funding for the State Department's justice and corrections sector support and counternarcotics programs and the Justice Department's prosecutor program reached a high-water mark of $589 million in 2010.[39] The State Department expanded rule of law support to ISAF Provincial Reconstruction Teams and newly created District Support Teams; worked alongside Afghan ministries to train and protect investigators, prosecutors, and the courts; and helped the Afghan Ministry of Justice create a case management system.[40]

As welcome as these changes were, they were dwarfed by the US military's expansions across the country. US force levels rose to over 100,000 troops in 2011 and Department of Defense funding expanded precipitously.[41] Given General McChrystal's assessment that rule of law issues were central to the counterinsurgency campaign (an opinion shared by his successors), the military began its own programs to tackle corruption, improve detentions, and establish local justice centers. Across the international community, a growing number of donor nations, government and nongovernment organizations, and military commands began feeling that the military was treading on their turf and doing so without any of the training, experience, or sensitivity that improving justice systems required.

One of the first areas where the military dramatically increased its activities was in the Afghan prison system. In January 2010, NATO/ISAF created a new command, Joint Task Force-435, with the mission to craft "a country wide, coalition supported, corrections and detentions plan to help establish unity of effort, [and] ensure meaningful corrections reform in both U.S. and Afghanistan detention/prison systems." The US detentions regime was arguably the most prominent symbol of the US commitment (or perceived lack thereof) to the rule of law. As one of the three most sensitive political issues raised by President Karzai (alongside civilian casualties and night raids), ISAF sought to transition all coalition detentions to Afghan control once the Afghan government "had developed the requisite sustainable capacity to run those detention systems in accordance with international and national law."[42] The new command and its ambitious agenda

Figure 6.2 Commander Kevin Messer (*right*), the officer in charge of the Justice Center in Parwan, describes the center's planned expansion to the US deputy ambassador to Afghanistan, Tina Kaidanow (*left*), as two senior officers listen in the background. Although US support to foreign prison systems is normally overseen by the State Department, in Afghanistan a military command ran the justice and detention centers until 2013. (Staff Sergeant Faiza Evans / Department of Defense)

had its skeptics in the US government and NATO capitals, in large part due to the history of US detention policy and practice during the Bush administration.[43] The command launched several initiatives to increase the transparency of the US detentions with Afghan leaders and the population, the International Committee of the Red Cross, and human rights groups. Arguably the embassy and JTF-435's two greatest contributions were the development of evidence-based requirements for US or coalition forces to hold Afghan detainees and the creation of a national security court, known as the Justice Center in Parwan (JCIP), to transfer detainees from coalition forces to the Afghan government through a process of investigation and prosecution.[44] Together these two initiatives led the way for the full transfer of all Afghan detainees to the government of Afghanistan in March 2013 and substantive reforms of the Afghan criminal procedure code and penal code to criminalize insurgent activities.[45]

As important as detentions were, the biggest threat to peace and legitimacy in the country was corruption. By 2009, 68 percent of Afghans judged that the government was doing a poor job of fighting corruption. Half the population had experienced corruption in the judiciary, and less than half had any confidence in the justice system as a whole. Roughly one-third (29 percent) thought the inability to counter corruption was the government's biggest failing.[46] Many of the corruption problems seemed small—padding the roles of the army and police to siphon off salaries; selling US-provided equipment, vehicles, and fuel; and overcharging the US government to guard facilities. But even these issues became serious problems over time as the scale of the corruption grew. In 2010, a massive Ponzi scheme in the country's largest bank resulted in over $900 million in losses and almost collapsed the country's financial system.[47] And because the brothers of both President Karzai and First Vice President Fahim Khan were major shareholders in the bank, Kabul regularly obstructed the investigations. (As of 2014, roughly one-third of the funds had been recovered, and no close allies of the Karzai or Fahim family had been prosecuted or convicted.)[48]

Even though a bevy of Afghan and international programs already sought to reduce corruption, starting in 2009, both the Afghan government and the ISAF military coalition added more. The Afghans created the Afghan Anti-corruption Tribunal, the Major Crimes Task Force (to investigate high-level corruption and organized crime), and the Sensitive Investigations Unit (to investigate complex drug-related cases). Some enjoyed a few successes and maintained good collaboration with their Western partners, but nearly all the Afghans in these units had to contend with frequent interference from the presidential palace and intense political risks for targeting powerful actors.[49] Adding to these new units were three new DOD-led interagency task forces created in 2009 and 2010: Task Force Spotlight, Task Force 2010, and Task Force Nexus, all of which were under the umbrella of Task Force Shafafiyat (which means "transparency" in Pasto and Dari). Leading these efforts in 2010–2011 was Brigadier General H. R. McMaster, a celebrated regimental commander in the

Iraq War who held a PhD in history from the University of North Carolina-Chapel Hill and had authored a book about the US military's failures in the Vietnam War. Under McMaster's leadership, DOD-led anticorruption efforts got renewed vigor, but his blunt style and the military-heavy team also faced criticism from embassy personnel and other civilians for not doing enough to bring Afghans into the anticorruption effort.[50] The task forces' results were mostly monetary and legal—by 2012, ISAF's investigations had led to "$25.4 million in fines, $3.4 million in seizures from allegedly fraudulent contractors, and . . . [the] disbarment or suspension of more than 125 American, Afghan, and international workers for alleged fraud."[51] But none of these task forces were empowered or equipped to counter the daily corruption in rural areas that continued to turn Afghans away from the government and toward the Taliban.[52]

As relations with the Karzai administration soured in 2010 and 2011, ISAF and embassy leaders sought alternate avenues for expanding justice sector reform and countering corruption beyond the central government. The new strategy called for expanding access to justice by creating linkages between formal and informal dispute resolution mechanisms, a move seen by its advocates as a creative, Afghan-owned program for transformative change but judged by its critics to be highly controversial because of the risk of a backlash against foreign and central government interference in local political and social disputes.[53] Though it was endorsed by the Ministry of Justice, Minister Sarwar Danish admitted that "implementing it will be very difficult. The goal is to take advantage of the positive elements of the informal system in order to increase all citizens' access to justice, and to proscribe the negative parts, which too often result in human rights violations."[54] In 2010, USAID received the authorization and resources to lead the US program in support of this expansion through a combination of civilian, military, and contracted efforts.

Perhaps the most detailed and thoughtful military effort to support rule of law development was the ROLFF-A, or Rule of Law Field Force-Afghanistan. One of the few programs to tackle rule of law reform at the local level, the ROLFF-A was the brainchild of General

David Petraeus's former legal advisor in Iraq, Brigadier General Mark Martins. A Rhodes Scholar and lawyer from the Army's Staff Judge Advocate ranks, Martins wanted to expand rule of law to the rural areas by linking local dispute resolution mechanisms (usually led by tribal, religious, or community leaders) to formal justice institutions in district and provincial capitals. Working closely with the ISAF leadership and NATO embassy partners, Martins built consensus around the organization's aspirational mission: to increase the capacity of the formal criminal justice system, increase the number of Afghans with access to local dispute resolution, and reduce public sector corruption with the ultimate aim of promoting the functionality and legitimacy of the Afghan government.[55] General Martins described the objectives and mandate of the organization during the ceremony marking his departure from the command after two years in Afghanistan:

> This organization was formed in recognition that assisting Afghans in building the rule of law requires more than high sounding ideals. While all units must work toward the rule of law—and the ISAF Joint Command strongly directs this in its orders—there is need for a component of field support, liaison, and security to be dedicated to the justice sector during this period of transition. Make no mistake: justice sector capacity-building must be Afghan-government-owned and civilian-led and predominantly civilian-manned in order to succeed. But during armed conflict, the security, logistics, administrative, procurement, communications, and other field projection capabilities of the military—Afghan as well as coalition—must be leveraged. This is particularly so where the government is competing for the peoples' minds and hearts with armed groups that use corruption as their battle cry and justice as their calling card.[56]

In practical terms, the field force provided Afghan, US, and international civil-military experts with security, transportation, and coordination for rule of law activities as well as engineering and contracting oversight for justice sector infrastructure projects with particular emphasis on those geographic areas in the south and east where security forces held terrain and sought to build stability long term. With limited personnel and resources that grew modestly over the course of its first year, the command focused its efforts on deploying small teams (less than 10 personnel) to consult with leaders in 52 districts, identify justice-related gaps in personnel and infrastructure, accompany Afghan justice sector officials to conflict areas, and oversee infrastructure development. The ROLFF-A also contributed heavily to civil-military efforts to craft a civil law enforcement process as an alternative to military detentions—arguably the most important joint Afghan and international initiative in the justice sector.[57]

Even though the ROLFF-A was following the ISAF commander's intent to "work with its civilian and international counterparts to enable justice sector reform . . . at the local level,"[58] it encountered resistance from all sides. Coordinating support with US and coalition forces proved difficult; commanders were often reluctant to devote personnel in support of governance or rule of law activities as doing so took troops away from what they perceived as their primary mission of hunting down Taliban units.[59] At the same time, partners at the Department of State and USAID preferred to devote their few civilian personnel and resources to more stable areas of the country, while those personnel serving in the conflict areas of the southern and eastern provinces wanted to flood those areas with development assistance as soon as the security situation stabilized.[60] No one had enough troops to do everything, and those fighting the Taliban always prioritized those efforts over the rule of law work that most military personnel thought belonged to the civilians anyway. A separate effort to get NATO buy-in for the ROLFF-A failed in 2013, and the unit became another consequence of the steady drawdown of forces that marked the final years of the war.[61]

While the militarization of rule of law efforts provided vastly more resources than had been seen in the earlier years of the war, problems of coordination and pacing undermined international support. As the military strategy and force levels increased, funding for military operations far outpaced the resources and attention devoted to other rule of law functions managed by the Ministry of Justice, the Supreme

Court, the Attorney General's Office, and the High Office of Oversight and Anti-corruption.[62] Critical segments of the justice sector essential to building local security and thus government legitimacy in the eyes of the Afghan people were unable to deliver even the most basic law enforcement functions, including administrative services, case management, criminal prosecution, and safe, secure detentions. The result has been a continuation of the system that has operated in Afghanistan for centuries: an unreliable and often corrupt formal rule of law system in the cities with limited reach, and informal traditional systems in the rural areas where people pay little mind to Kabul as long as it leaves them alone.

///

In the ninth century, Ibn Qutayba, a notable Islamic scholar, wrote that "there can be no government without an army, no army without money, no money without prosperity, and no prosperity without justice and good administration."[63] Afghanistan in 2014 is a tragic tribute to the truth of those words. At the close of 2013, Transparency International ranked Afghanistan 175th out of 177 countries on its corruption index, alongside North Korea and Somalia. The 2013 Asia Foundation Survey of the Afghan People found that concerns about corruption were at their highest levels and nearly on par with concerns about insecurity.[64] And as the resolution to the 2014 presidential election showed, even the Afghan Constitution—held up as one of the great collective successes in rule of law development—was pushed aside to reconcile the interests of the country's two most powerful politicians. In light of these facts, it seems easy to argue that the effort to build a capable, responsive rule of law regime in Afghanistan has been more of a failure than a success, but it is likely too soon to judge what is undoubtedly a multigenerational challenge.

Nonetheless, at the end of combat operations in 2014, it is fair to say that the progress of bolstering rule of law in Afghanistan has been—at best—uneven. What went wrong? First, the bulk of the blame rests with the Afghan government itself, for despite the many problems of bureaucracy and mismanagement, the simple fact is that members of the government—or people close to them—engaged in the theft of billions of dollars that were meant for their own people. In fact, it is estimated that at least one in every eight dollars provided by the international community has been pocketed by individual benefactors; millions of dollars have simply never reached their intended destination and have since disappeared.[65] While donor countries have made efforts to ensure better accountability in the future, and international pressure has risen for the Afghan government to punish those responsible, little progress has been made in terms of permanent systemic or institutional change for the better.[66]

But the government should not bear all the blame, for the various organizations doing rule of law work in Afghanistan also made serious mistakes. The international community's initial response and strategy for rule of law development did not appreciate the full scope and scale of the reconstruction task and gave insufficient attention to Afghan culture. The lead-nation concept divided efforts instead of uniting them and overwhelmed the nascent Afghan government. International rule of law experts systematically failed to include the viewpoints of Afghan leaders and citizens and tried to install Western systems of law in a country deeply resistant to such impositions. Over time, the size and scope of international involvement raised Afghan expectations for a legitimate and just central government, expectations that were rarely satisfied.

Moreover, the international community did not fully appreciate the relationship between security and rule of law, and this badly undermined Afghanistan's progress. Even after ISAF understood that extensive government corruption and criminal behavior were alienating the Afghan people, it did not have a clear vision for what to do about it, particularly given contributing countries' limited political support for military involvement in rule of law efforts.[67] If the first half of the Afghan War was driven by the failure to understand the links between security and rule of law in Afghanistan, the last five years were marked by disagreements over how to address the problem. As a result, the few successes that did occur happened at the national level, and subsequent efforts to create local rule of law mechanisms in the rural areas are likely to be unsustainable in the wake of the military's withdrawal. By the time several important civil-military organizations emerged to focus ISAF/NATO support to the justice sector—a decade into the conflict—the international community had lost its will. Given these problems and the general complexity of Afghan society, it is no surprise that success has been so elusive.

Finally, it is fair to say that the ISAF coalition, NATO, and international partners struggled because of a basic catch-22 in Afghan culture. Rural Afghans resented the predatory behavior of corrupt Kabul officials, and thus turned away from government centralization, and in some cases turned toward the Taliban out of frustration and a sense of injustice. This, in turn, drew more of the coalition's resources toward security and away from rule of law, which allowed the predatory behavior to continue. As the argument between the urban center and the rural and religious areas continued, the coalition was caught in the middle. None of this was a truly new development. As one scholar explained in 2008, "A quick review of Afghan history would have shown [the international community] that implementing a system of nationally applicable laws and courts was a state-building project that had never been successfully completed in Afghanistan."[68] Another scholar hinted at this five years earlier when she wrote, "Rural Afghanistan is the root of tribal powers that have frequently doomed Kabul-based modernization efforts."[69] The efforts of the Taliban since 2006 show that history has been repeating itself in Afghanistan, and one wonders why the international community did not pause and plan a bit more before trying to do exactly what had failed before—even when it had been led by Afghans.

CHAPTER SEVEN

Liberalism Does Its Thing

Captain Aaron MacLean, USMC

In August 1972, RAND published a lengthy analysis of the conduct of the Vietnam War titled *Bureaucracy Does Its Thing*. The author was Robert W. "Blowtorch" Komer, a former CIA officer, deputy national security advisor, and the first director of the Civil Operations and Revolutionary Development Support (CORDS) program in Vietnam. In a publication that would shape thinking on Vietnam for years to come, Komer argued that certain structural shortcomings of American institutions—"institutional constraints" in his language—bore a critical share of the blame for failure in Vietnam, as did the inattention of policymakers, who failed to be aware of those constraints or to adjust for them appropriately.[1]

Here I make a related argument: certain characteristics of liberalism bear a critical share of the blame for the more recent disaster in Afghanistan. By "liberalism," I do not intend the colloquial sense of the politics of the American center-left, but instead something more akin to what people mean when they say "liberal-democracy": the broad political consensus that applies to most Westerners, whether they consider themselves on the political "right," "center," or "left," and which certainly applies to those who have made or executed Afghan policy since September 11, 2001.

Liberals tend to assume that there is a common human desire to live in a system governed by laws that promote both equality and liberty, and that even if all people are not actively conscious of this desire, they would nevertheless lead happier and more fulfilling lives in such a condition. Like Christianity, from which it sprang, liberalism is a universalist doctrine—just like Islam, but unlike *Pashtunwali* tribalism or Judaism. Indeed, liberalism has been so successful that those who are raised as liberals rarely question the fundamental assumptions that underlie it, or recall the violent conflicts that were required to bring about the present flourishing of the modern West and the world system that it sponsors.

From political efforts to rebuild the Kabul-based government after the ouster of the Taliban to military efforts aimed at bringing order to outlying districts, Western policymakers and practitioners generally failed to have a healthy wariness of their own assumptions about how political order is established or allowed to flourish. This lack of self-awareness was combined with regular and dramatic ignorance among Western actors regarding Afghan assumptions about the nature of politics. Though other factors played important roles in bringing about a situation in 2016 in which the Taliban, al Qaeda, and even the Islamic State are on the march (factors such as the existence of a Pakistani sanctuary, the incompetence of the Kabul government, and plain inattention), much of the trouble can be traced back to this failure of political theory, or, put another way, of cultural understanding. Liberalism contains its own ideological and institutional constraints, and those constraints go a long way in explaining how the war in Afghanistan unfolded as it did.

The West did not originally go to Afghanistan to nation-build, but—despite some dissenting voices—found itself involved in such an effort, culminating in the peak counterinsurgency (COIN) years of 2009–2012. Was any effort at nation-building doomed from the start? Could more resources and better coordination among the United States, NATO, and their Afghan allies have generated a better result? Perhaps, if combined with a more sustained, aggressive posture toward the elements of the Pakistani state that backed (and continue to back) elements of the insurgency, but, critically, not without a serious examination of just what kind of "nation" could possibly be built in Afghanistan at the start of the 21st century. The poor quality of thought that evidently went into this critical question proved counterproductive for the Afghan nation-building effort from the first days of the Bonn Agreement onward, and led to some spectacularly dissonant moments a decade later, the best example of which may be Marjah's infamous "government in a box," which I witnessed firsthand.

The argument proceeds in three stages. I begin with a brief overview of some of liberalism's main tenets and claim that the West's modern assumptions about individuals, states, sovereignty, and human nature led to a fundamental misunderstanding of what was both desirable and possible in Afghanistan. Second, I very briefly examine Afghanistan's own political assumptions and ask how fertile the ground was for the liberal seeds the Westerners found themselves sowing. Finally, I discuss what happened when these two ideological complexes clashed on the ground during the years of Western involvement.

Liberalism, Violence, and Inevitable Progress: Western Political Assumptions

Ernest Gellner once observed, "Men and societies frequently treat the institutions and assumptions by which they live as absolute, self-evident, and given."[2] Those raised in the West are as susceptible to this description as any other group, even despite the relatively recent arrival of their form of government on the historical scene. The result is that Westerners tend to consider liberal political institutions to be natural, when they are in fact the products of conscious, careful labor. Put another way, these institutions are artificial—works of art or, in another sense, products of technology. And, like all political institutions, they have a dark side, a foundation of coercion and violence that is easy to forget in lands characterized by sustained economic growth and the widespread satisfaction of individual aspirations. The result, as far as Afghan policy has been concerned, has been a forgetfulness of the role of force in building sustainable political systems, and a related, deep-rooted assumption of more or less inevitable human progress toward a liberal political system.

In failing to observe the highly artificial nature of our own civilization, we Westerners are like people who were born and grew to maturity on a passenger jet flying high above the ocean. Having spent our entire lives within an aluminum tube hurtling through the air, propelled by engines attached to each wing, we think that this experience of being suspended in the atmosphere is perfectly natural, normal, and inevitable—certainly not the human-made consequence of centuries of scientific progress and immense wealth, certainly not dangerous, or fragile, or dependent on fire and fuel and controlled explosions.

The many strains of politics and social thought within the broad category of liberal or "Western" states may seem to preclude the possibility that we could speak of a single airplane that carries both a libertarian from Montana and a socialist from the Parisian *banlieues*. But Westerners do tend to share a set of broad political assumptions, including four beliefs about what constitutes a legitimate state. First, all liberals believe that such a state is sovereign: that it exists within clearly established borders and divides the labors of its citizens such that some of them, with the consent of everyone else, become agents of state institutions that maintain a monopoly on legitimate violence. Second, the state is republican: its agents and institutions are expected to represent the public interest—the state is not the private property of, for example, a family, a military clique, or a particular social class. Implicit in this condition is that the rule of law, not the rule of men, prevails, and that the rulers are thus accountable to the same laws as all other citizens. Third, the state is liberal in a specific sense of the word: it secures the rights of its citizens, who are equal in these rights, and is tolerant of minority practices, including religious practices. Finally, the state is democratic: within the boundaries established by its liberalism, it is procedurally majoritarian, and regularly secures the explicit consent of the governed through the mechanism of elections.

This is all to say that Westerners tend to vest political legitimacy in states that are sovereign, liberal-democratic republics and to condemn or at least disapprove of those that are not. This broad consensus was not handed down from heaven—quite the opposite in fact. It developed slowly on earth, and more specifically in Europe during periods of regular and turbulent wars. Fear and violence were critical to its formulation and had roles to play in its long creation, as in the creation of any system of political order—something the first canonical political philosophers writing in the liberal tradition well understood. Yet over time the role of illiberal factors like force has been obscured and minimized as a necessary foundation of liberal states—an occurrence that goes far in explaining how and why the West mismanaged the state-building project in Afghanistan.

Any college course on the history of Western political thought begins with the city-states of Greece and the Roman Republic. This is appropriate, as the origins of several important elements of the modern Western consensus can be found in those communities: majority rule, for example, and the notion that state mechanisms should be directed for the public good of all citizens. But in important ways, the political assumptions of those societies were entirely different from those that came to hold sway in the modern West. In particular, most Greeks or Romans had a shared understanding that the real rules for human conduct came from transcendent sources—from the heavens. There was such as a thing as "the good," and, in a sense, it was decided by the gods.

This notion that heaven, in whatever specific conception, was the ultimate authority concerning the affairs of men remained in force in Europe for at least a thousand years after the fall of Rome, and led to any number of wars fought either in the name of religion or under the cover thereof. But just as early modernity witnessed decisive breaks with the past in mathematics and what came to be called the natural sciences, so too there was a break in conceptions of politics—a break that has not occurred for Afghan politics. The break concerns the authority of "heaven" or "the good," and its origin is in the writings of Machiavelli (d. 1527). In *The Prince* and *The Discourses on Livy*, Machiavelli proposed a theoretical basis for an entirely new kind of political order. To oversimplify (as I will throughout this section), Machiavelli relieved Western political theory of classical or medieval morality by asserting that, in reality, the universe neither rewards nor punishes moral goodness. For Machiavelli, the real man, the man of *virtù*, recognizes his alienation from the universe and chooses to make his own luck rather than awaiting its arrival from heaven. Indeed, these real men of *virtù* are the proper leaders of the state, men comfortable with imposing their wills violently if need be, and who expect to be obeyed out of fear, if not also out of love. One of Machiavelli's most quoted (and by today's standards, disturbing) remarks makes this point well. Men should not wait for fortune to arrive from above, because "fortune is a woman, and if you wish to keep her under it is necessary to beat and ill-use her. . . . She is, therefore, always, womanlike, a lover of young men, because they are less cautious, more violent, and with more audacity command her."[3]

Machiavelli's contribution was a sea change in political philosophy in the 16th century, for it rejected both Christian doctrine and the first principles of classical politics, which imagined that the universe was a good place for men, and would reward them for living in accordance with its ethical rules. For Machiavelli, men—not gods—made history. Force was an essential tool, but did not require divine justification.

A later philosopher—Thomas Hobbes (d. 1679), whose *Leviathan* became a foundational text of liberalism—also appreciated violence's role in politics and understood human betterment as the contingent product of human effort (and not, as would later be theorized, a function of inevitable progress). Hobbes lived nearly his entire adult life in a time of religious conflict. Born in 1588—the very year the Spanish Armada was destroyed in Phillip II's crusade to reconquer Protestant England—he wrote *Leviathan* during the Thirty Years' War and the English Civil War. As Machiavelli did, Hobbes theorized about the causes of political phenomena he witnessed around him, and set forth principles through which a political order should be understood and maintained.

One of the most important contributions of Hobbes's work was a suggestion that politics be divorced from religious authority, for if each side could perpetually claim authority from a transcendental source, there could be no end to the debate—or the killing. Hobbes described a system that would prevent conflicts started by men who claimed that their understanding of the divine gave them grounds to challenge an unjust political order. In metaphysical terms, this doctrine implied that multiple interpretations of the divine will were acceptable throughout Christendom, and hinted at the idea that divine will possibly had no real grounds at all. (Given these beliefs, it is not surprising that Hobbes was accused of harboring a secret atheism.)

But removing religious authority was only part of Hobbes's solution, for without any constraints on their desires and actions, men would revert to a "state of nature"—an anarchic condition where all pursue their own wills violently and without restraint. To avoid this, societies must have a man-made substitute for divine authority—a commonwealth, a state, a Leviathan—that men would submit to voluntarily for the simplest of purposes: to avoid the total chaos of a world without rules. In this commonwealth, man surrenders his right to do anything he pleases in order to enjoy security from the predations of others. Thus, Hobbes's system theorized about the existence of a minimalist social contract founded on the most selfish of desires: the avoidance of violent death.

In *Leviathan*, Hobbes did much more than try to separate religion from politics. He also promoted a doctrine of the equality of men, and suggested that there is such a thing as a natural law or right. But even with these familiar, modern elements, he was also very far from presenting democracy as something that was natural or desirable. States still needed rulers—Hobbes preferred absolute monarchs—who would have total supremacy over all temporal and spiritual matters. Moreover, and more important to the US intervention in Afghanistan, coercion and fear remained integral to the functioning of the state even if the rules came from people instead of God; it is no accident that his metaphor of the state, and the title of his book, is a sea monster.

Westerners living in a sovereign liberal-democratic republic today might not recognize much of Hobbes's Leviathan or Machiavelli's princely rule in their own nation-states, but that is precisely the point: the coercive elements in the liberal political system have not disappeared, but they have been obscured through softening—hidden in such a way that later practitioners failed to appreciate just how central they are. Hobbes, in a sense, softened Machiavelli's teaching, and in turn found his own teaching softened by Locke; later revisions and critiques came from Rousseau, Kant, and Hegel. Each of these philosophers wrote in a specific time and place, but over time, their ideas have transformed into a hidden assumption—a basic certainty of practical liberalism—that some version of the modern Western state is natural rather than artificial and voluntary rather than coercive. This is an idea that deserves analysis, particularly before an attempt to introduce liberal institutions like democratic elections and minority rights into a new and foreign culture.

In the *Second Treatise on Civil Government*, Locke expanded Hobbes's minimal contract to prevent a war of all against all into a more benevolent vision of states as entities that preserve life, liberty, conscience, and property. With Locke, the political tradition begun by Machiavelli reached a stage frequently referred to as "classical liberalism": an intellectual trend that favors states where citizens voluntarily relinquish a share of their theoretically unlimited freedom while retaining certain natural rights; mixed constitutions with elements of monarchy, aristocracy, and democracy; tolerance for multiple religious traditions; and—made explicit by the later elaborations of Adam Smith—a preference for relatively free markets. Capitalism and classical liberalism were allies from the start.

It would be crude but not, for our purposes, useless to describe these 17th-century teachings, which in the 18th century became the doctrine of the American revolutionaries, as the Spirit of 1776, or as an Anglo-American or Atlanticist theory of politics. The same would apply to descriptions of the reaction and critique that followed, initially at the hand of Rousseau, as the Spirit of 1789 and the foundation of a Continental theory of politics. Both trends are today much in evidence, and much in tension, in Western politics, even if they retain important, shared assumptions.

Confronted with the practical consequences of the teachings of the first wave of liberals, Rousseau recoiled at what he held to be the removal of virtue from politics. Men were no longer encouraged by their political communities to be brave or good, but rather were formed to become bourgeois: shopkeepers and moneymakers, ruined by the luxury brought about by the improvement of arts and sciences. The development of civil society and the concurrent rise of natural science had not relieved man's estate, but had degraded it.

The truly radical difference between Rousseau and his predecessors is his assertion that man has no nature, only a history. That is to say that, unlike the Hobbesian vision of a troubled nature made better but never quite changed by politics, Rousseau proposed a conception of humanity that is fundamentally alterable. He argued that, prior to civil society and the state, man in his original state was a "noble savage." This noble savage was not morally good (for what would "good" mean before civil society?) but preceded goodness and even rationality. It was history that brought about language, morality, rationality, and civil society as groups of men were forced to live in close proximity. With this proximity, one sees the origins of the family, private property, the state, and war and inequality as some men seek to acquire more property than others. With each new political order, each new conception of virtue and the good, the raw matter of man is reformed. This is true, in a more limited sense, of all living things, but what makes men unique is their freedom to alter their own matter, to change their own way of life. Thus the goal of politics is not the amelioration of man's nature but the direction of history toward a politics that grants him something approximate to his original freedom to be his best self—leading to a future that carries the potential for man's perfectibility.

Contained in Rousseau's thought is the secularization of a Christian ideal that still holds sway across Europe and the United States:

progressivism—the idea that humans are traveling along a trajectory to a more perfect condition. Subsequent authors like Kant and Hegel provided further elaboration, while yet a third wave of theorists, most famously Nietzsche, attacked the foundations of both classical liberalism and its early critics. But a generally progressive attitude seems to have survived these later assaults. Hegel had entertained the notion that the French Revolution's universalization of a secularized Christianity had ushered in the final stage of human political development. Marx thought that the late capitalism of the 19th century was only the penultimate stage of History, and that soon, with international socialism, the State would at last wither away. Writing in the immediate aftermath of the collapse of the Soviet Union, and reworking the thought of Alexandre Kojève, American political theorist Francis Fukuyama argued that the triumph of democracy and capitalism was the true "end of history," and that their spread in the late 20th century proved such systems reflected the natural, universal desires of all people. In all these ideas we find the core tenet of progressivism: the idea that societies are moving linearly, ascending an escalator, if you will, from less perfect to more perfect systems of human organization and development.[4]

Thus, by the end of the 20th century, with the Soviet Union in ruin and democratic movements in the ascent worldwide, most political leaders in the United States and Europe were firmly convinced of a few key concepts that helped set their goals and approaches in Afghanistan. Gone was the emphasis on fear and compulsion to restrain people's violent ways. In their place came a benevolent vision of human organization and a complaisant sense that this vision would eventually become a reality. The varieties of liberal regimes were not just forms of a time-tested functional political system but the natural order of things—the *only* just regime. Humankind's progress was inevitable, so much so that to oppose it put one on the "wrong side of History"—a perilous political place to be. Versions of this belief could be detected on both the political "left" and "right." As President George W. Bush explained in 2005: "We believe that liberty is the design of nature; we believe that liberty is the direction of history. . . . And we believe that freedom—the freedom we prize—is not for us alone, it is the right and the capacity of all mankind."[5]

Lineage, God, and Swiss Cheese: Afghan Political Assumptions

As pleasing as the president's notion may have been, very little of it has come to pass in Afghanistan. Among the most important reasons was a fundamental incompatibility between institutions that Westerners worked to introduce and the history and culture of the receiving population. In fact, there was an equally strong set of assumptions about states, rulers, rights, and violence in Afghanistan that stretched at least as far back as the modern liberal project's origins in early modernity. Grounded in regional traditions, Islam, and *Pashtunwali*, these assumptions were as obviously natural and right to the Afghans that held them as liberal ideas were to the Westerners. Therefore, when the two ideologies collided, both sides struggled to understand why the other supported its own approach.

Aaron O'Connell's introduction has already detailed the key components of Pashtun history and *Pashtunwali*—points that do not need repeating here. But it will be useful to consider how Pashtun culture deals specifically with violence and killing, for with these topics the dictates of *Pashtunwali* are highly inflexible.

A brief thought experiment will illustrate just how differently Western and Pashtun societies understand violence. Imagine that you and a companion are walking on the French side of the Franco-Swiss frontier. For some reason, you purposefully shoot your companion, who dies. In order to evade the negative consequences of your actions, you now must worry about the French state and its many agents. Whether in the form of the local, provincial, or national authorities, barring extraordinary efforts on your part to obscure the fact that a killing has occurred, someone will be coming to arrest you. It makes no difference if you flee across the border to Switzerland. The agents of the Swiss state will work to arrest you and send you right back to France. This is true if you flee most anywhere in Europe, or, for that matter, any of the numerous countries around the world that have extradition agreements with France. It is also true that, insofar as there is no statute of limitations for the crime of murder in France, you will never be able to rest assured that you have run long and far enough. In theory, the French state will look for you forever. There is no escaping its search, no refuge in either time or space.

In some sense, the reason why the French state is looking for you so doggedly is not just the single act of killing but the challenge you present to the state with that act. You have not only taken a life but also arrogated to yourself that privilege which makes Leviathan sovereign: the monopoly on violence. It does not matter much if your companion had dishonored you in public or killed a member of your family years earlier. Retributive violence is not within your power as an individual residing within the borders of France: violence is the power of the state alone.

Transpose the entire scenario to the Afghan-Pakistan border, however, and your prospects change. If, for some reason, you believe that because you have killed your companion you might run afoul of the agents of the Afghan state, you may well succeed in obscuring the evidence of your crime, as the Afghan police at all levels lack training and forensic resources. If you fail in this, crossing the border into Pakistan and seeking refuge in the Federally Administered Tribal Areas will very likely keep you out of the hands of Afghan authorities—a tactic Osama bin Ladin himself used. And, of course, you could always remain in Afghanistan and pursue any number of strategies to remain free from negative repercussions from the government, including bribery of state officials.

These strategies are, however, somewhat moot, for the plain fact is that the government is the least of your worries. You are much better advised to be more concerned about possible repercussions from the dead man's family than the impersonal machinations of the state. If your companion was not related to you at all—that is, if he was from an entirely different tribe—you may have just begun a violent conflict of substantial proportions. If he was related—say, a second cousin—those male relatives who are more closely related to him can be counted on to seek revenge or compensation for his death. You are well advised to seek assistance from and refuge with those male relatives who are more closely related to you, and, if possible, seek mediation from an elder member of the tribe who is roughly equally related to both lineages.[6]

Such mediation may make excellent sense in your case, as the list of reasons why you might have been justified in your killing is far longer than it is in the French scenario. Revenge, preemptive defense, the preservation of your family's honor in the face of a slight: all might, depending on the circumstances, justify your act in the eyes of influential power brokers. It may well be the case that your act was still, in some technical sense, a crime under laws promulgated in Kabul, but it is certainly not likely that the government will make an effort to interfere in a tribal dispute. There are already institutions in place—the balanced opposition of segmentary lineages, the institution of mediation by elders, not to mention the religious influence of village mullahs—to mitigate and control the violent souls of men.[7]

As different as these practices may be, they are not unique to Pashtuns or to Afghanistan; in fact, they may be found in some form or another wherever Islamic tribes are found. Yet it is the case that, in the face of the historical weakness of the Kabul-based state, such institutions are particularly easy to see at work in Afghanistan. While Westerners debate whether aspects of sovereignty should be elevated from the nation-state to international institutions, the Afghan government does not monopolize violence on a state level; it is not "sovereign" within its own borders.

Anthropologists describe such societies as *agonistic*—that is, characterized by a constant, low-grade presence of violent competition, which can flare for a time to more significant levels. The state acts not as the sovereign force within all areas colored in on an internationally determined map, but as a sort of magnet, exerting great influence close to the center and much less as it encounters resistance farther afield.[8] An important point to note is that, contrary to Hobbes's state of nature where, in the absence of a sovereign power, the life of man is nasty, brutish, and short, the situation in Afghanistan has not historically been quite so dire. Indeed, life there is measurably more brutal and shorter than life in a modern, sovereign state. But the institutions of balanced opposition, mediation by elders, *Pashtunwali*, and indeed Sharia provide limited and widely accepted solutions to the problem of insecurity. These solutions are imperfect: it is, for example, easy to see how wealthier, larger lineages would regularly be able to get away with violent aggressions that poorer, smaller lineages would not. But they are nonetheless solutions that command legitimacy, even with the substantial stress placed on the tribal system by decades of foreign-funded Islamic radicalism and the warlordism that has arisen during long decades of conflict.

This is the true political system of Afghanistan's Pashtun regions, and it is a system based on long years of tradition and practice. Other regions have their own cultural patterns, some more amenable to centralized state control than others—but even those areas have little in the way of an appreciation for liberal politics broadly conceived. Sovereignty in Afghanistan, Thomas Barfield has explained, is more like swiss cheese than American cheese, which is to say that it has holes in it that are neither defects nor mistakes (in fact, the holes are an integral part of what makes swiss cheese what it is). It is a whimsical but useful metaphor: for centuries, the Afghan state has maintained control in some areas (usually the urban areas and strategic points) but has left other areas alone—the "holes" in the state's control, the unproductive areas that have few resources.[9]

But the Westerners who came to Afghanistan after 2001 typically failed to appreciate the power and rootedness of local patterns. They had some awareness of it, of course; most were in some way familiar with the notion that Afghan politics were complicated by the existence of different ethnic groups, many of whom did not share a common primary language. Additionally, most military officers and senior noncommissioned officers were familiar with the notion that tribalism was politically significant, and that the most important system of Afghan tribalism, that of the dominant Pashtun ethnic group, was critical to the ways in which Afghan politics function. However, Westerners habitually failed to take seriously how Afghans lived their beliefs in practice, and how alien such notions as minority rights or democratic elections premised on individual choice in fact were. As a result, year after year, the Westerners approached their project with a set of assumptions about people, communities, and governments that did not really describe the actual human beings they were trying to persuade, or control, or cooperate with.

Theory in Practice: Liberalism in an Illiberal Land

Critics will exclaim that many policymakers recognized perfectly well that Afghanistan was not a Western country and that it likely would not become one in short order. This is true: the policymakers made exactly those points repeatedly. However, rhetoric did not determine practice, and the nation-building policies pursued by the UN, the International Security Assistance Force (ISAF), and, eventually, the US military tended to be liberal in their structure anyway.

Nation-building was not the reason why the US military and its NATO allies originally came to Afghanistan. They came to destroy al Qaeda and to punish the Taliban for harboring the terrorist organization, but nonetheless they quickly found themselves (often halfheartedly) participating in a nation-building project that was flawed in its theoretical foundations. Westerners often found Afghan allies of liberalism, particularly among exiles and well-educated urban Afghans. But in practice, older illiberal practices remained firmly in place.

In 2016, the Western-backed Afghan government functions much like Afghan governments have always functioned. It has control of Kabul and a few other productive centers but lacks authority throughout the country. There is no broadly accepted social contract between citizens and government: those that cooperate with the government do so mostly out of fear or greed, and almost every government institution has serious problems with corruption. There is little separation between religious or ethnic identities and politics, and indeed, if we are to believe the opinion polls, Afghans increasingly want more religious participation in politics—not less. Finally, as the Marines learned in Helmand beginning in 2009, the only widely accepted method of preserving peace is through exerting outright domination, or leasing peace through subsidies, just as rulers have done since the earliest days of the Afghan state.

This was not what the Westerners had in mind at the outset. Despite some dissenting voices and the occasional gesture in the direction of recognizing the illiberal quality of Afghan politics, from the start Western policymakers tended to pursue a course of making the Afghan state sovereign within its borders, creating public-spirited government agents, introducing liberal conceptions of minority rights, and using democratic elections as the principal method of securing legitimacy. Below, I provide a snapshot of each of these four tendencies and then conclude with a discussion of how the US military went all in on a certain kind of liberal state-building outlined in US counterinsurgency doctrine.

To be a functional and sovereign state, the Westerners believed, the Afghan government needed to extend its writ into the rural tribal areas, gain something approaching a monopoly on violence there, and provide enough basic security to allow the people to stand with the government and against the Taliban. Such was the justification for the establishment, funding, and tasking of any number of state security and legal organizations, and by any reasonable standard, these goals were at no point achieved. The various national police agencies and the army have generally been staffed by members of northern ethnic groups as foreign to the Pashtun tribal belt as American troops, but for their (usually) shared religion. Even in those cases—as within some police organizations—where locals occupy the ranks, the public good is often far from their minds, supplanted by the demands of the dominant tribal or criminal networks that supplied the personnel in the first place.

Partly because of this misplaced emphasis on filling the sovereignty "holes" in the swiss cheese, violence increased almost uniformly throughout most of the war, and the levels in 2014 were still higher than before President Obama's 2009 surges.[10] That same year, 65 percent of Afghans reported that they were "always, often, or sometimes fearing for their safety or security or that of their family." And, unsurprisingly, the ongoing violence has led many Afghans to be skeptical of the Kabul government. In the most insecure areas of the country, more than 50 percent of men surveyed in 2014 reported still having sympathy for the armed opposition groups, whether Taliban or other antigovernment forces.[11]

Extending the government's authority beyond Kabul requires more than just a monopoly on violence, however; a functioning liberal state should also have a way to enforce its rules through a functional police force and court system. The West put considerable resources toward this end during the 13 years of combat operations, including billions of dollars to improve the justice sector and to train and deploy the more than 100,000 police across the country. But those police have always been as much a part of the problem as they were the solution. Primarily because there has been little tradition of benevolent or professional policing in Afghanistan, when the thousands of new police officers descended on Afghan villages (even their own villages), no one trusted them. The United Nations Development Program took note of this in its 2011 Police Perception Survey, which found that just 38 percent of Afghans would turn to the police as their first resort to report a kidnapping and fewer than 2 in 10 "would turn to the ANP first to report violence against women, an unpaid loan or a problem with an employer."[12] The people rarely take their grievances to the state courts that are financed by the West; the most popular dispute resolution mechanisms are the informal ones—the consultative councils (*shuras*) and mediations by elders (*jirgas*) that preceded Western involvement.[13]

The key point here is not just that the Kabul government lacks both control of the country and legitimacy in the eyes of its people. The point is that sovereignty in Afghanistan has never been one-size-fits-all, and by assuming it could or should be, the West wasted resources and failed to pursue more creative strategies that were sensitive to local realities. The mistake Westerners made, especially in the era of peak COIN, was to overlay an American cheese model of sovereignty onto Afghanistan—a model that assumed the government's writ must be uniform and ubiquitous. This misunderstood the problem, for Afghanistan's resource-poor areas—the holes in the swiss cheese—

were never truly empty, and were certainly not devoid of order. The attempts to cram the American cheese model into what the Westerners all perceived to be empty holes of lawlessness was generally an exercise in futility.

Next, what of efforts to ensure that agents of the Afghan state behaved as agents of Western states are expected to behave, that is, by elevating the public good over their own private interests? Here, too, older systems remained deeply rooted and new ones failed to take hold regardless of the resources thrown at the problem. Since Afghanistan's creation in 1747, the government, whether based in Kabul or Kandahar, has acted like most premodern Turko-Persian states—as an extractive monarchy.[14] The state did not exist for the benefit of the ruled, and peasants who lived within the state's area of influence were treated primarily as economic assets by the monarch and his agents. The individual's relationship with the government never involved a Kennedyesque question about what your country would do for you. The question was, what would you do for your monarch, and more specifically, what would he do to you if you refused?

That remained the case throughout the entire Afghanistan war. In 2014, 76 percent of Afghans thought corruption was a "major problem," and "all long-term measures for both perception and exposure to corruption have risen since the survey began" in 2006.[15] And in fact, even this notion of corruption—which we should think of as the use of public resources for private ends—makes little sense in Afghanistan's cultural context, as the state has never been seriously concerned with the public good and has always viewed the "public" as a source of private revenue. Thus, the best way to describe the relationship between the state and the people is as "that of the shepherd to his flock: the state fleeces the peasants, making a living off of them, and protects them from other predators, so that they may be fleeced again."[16]

Put simply, the government agents the West began supporting in 2002 were much like those who had preceded them: intrusive, violent, and predatory. They did not believe that they had a role in securing any natural rights of the Afghan people; rather, they took much of the property they were supposed to be protecting. For their part, Afghans responded to this new government much as they had responded to the old one. They gave the government what it asked for out of fear, not a sense of civic duty. And of course one of the few responsibilities Afghans *did* expect from their government—security from foreign invaders—was something that Kabul had already abdicated by allowing an international force of thousands of its non-Muslim backers to move unimpeded throughout the country, while still failing to stop the steady flow of foreign fighters coming to the insurgency from Pakistan and Central Asia.

Third, what of liberal protections for the rights of ethnic and religious minorities? This was a major focus of the human rights groups that descended on Kabul, and a subject that received substantial lip service from Western diplomats, but that never took root in Afghanistan in any meaningful way. What prevailed instead was a conceptual muddle that is captured well by the text of the first three articles of the 2004 Afghan Constitution:

1. Afghanistan shall be an Islamic Republic, independent, unitary and indivisible state.
2. The sacred religion of Islam is the religion of the Islamic Republic of Afghanistan. Followers of other faiths shall be free within the bounds of law in the exercise and performance of their religious rituals.
3. No law shall contravene the tenets and provisions of the holy religion of Islam in Afghanistan.[17]

The contradictions here are obvious. Article 2 gives "followers of other faiths" freedom in the exercise of their religions only within the "bounds of law," and Article 3 hastens to add that the law must not contravene "the holy religion of Islam." To call this a loophole is somewhat to understate the case: Islam, and its Sunni-Hanafi school, in particular, is a vast body of doctrine and law that touches on almost every aspect of human life. One need not exhaustively demonstrate that it is doctrinally and historically intolerant of other religious traditions in order to suggest that, if there are enough Afghans who believe that it is, then the language of Articles 2 and 3 allows substantial leeway for the suppression of non-Sunni-Hanafi religious practice. We see here a somewhat wan gesture in the direction of liberalism—just enough to incite critics of Western influence—smothered in its crib by an overt appeal to heaven.

Without a bright line separating religion and politics, Afghanistan remains more or less where it was before the Taliban: intolerant of non-Muslims, and even non-Hanafi Sunnis. As the State Department's US Commission on International Religious Freedom reported almost a decade after the 2004 constitution became law: "Religious freedom conditions continued to be exceedingly poor for dissenting Sunni Muslims, as well as Shi'i Muslims, Hindus, Sikhs, Christians and Bahai's . . . and the Afghan constitution fails explicitly to protect the individual right to freedom of religion or belief." Christians must conceal their faith and are sometimes arrested for apostasy; "members of Afghanistan's small Baha'i community lead an essentially covert existence, particularly since May 2007 when the General Directorate of Fatwa and Accounts ruled the Baha'i faith blasphemous and all Muslim converts to the Baha'i faith apostates." During a 2010 visit to Kabul by the commission members, "government ministers and government-backed religious leaders repeatedly explained that, in their view, Islamic law trumped the constitution's human rights provisions, as those references come later in the document and do not take precedence. In addition, Afghanistan's highest religious body, the government-backed Ulema Council, stated in November 2012 that it wants the power to issue legally binding decrees."[18] And in fact, most Afghans seem to support this level of religious authority in politics: in 2014, the Asia Foundation found that 65 percent of Afghans reported believing that religious scholars should have a hand in politics and that "over time, Afghans appear to consistently favor religion and politics mixing over the alternative."[19] How were members of minority communities ever meant to peacefully assent to majority rule in such circumstances?

From these first three snapshots, it should be clear that Afghanistan was never fertile ground for the fourth element of liberal states, democratic elections, and that the international community's involvement since 2001 has not moved the society far from its earlier illiberal moorings. In fact, the compromises of the Bonn Agreement and the 2004 constitution not only failed to establish a workable foundation for government but also gave the Taliban proof positive that the invading infidels were intent on destroying Islam and replacing it with foreign rule—something that helped its recruitment and reentry into Afghanistan. National elections, rather than being expressions of the aggregate of equal, individual wills, were generally manipulated by tribal, ethnic, and criminal networks.

With the Americans increasingly preoccupied with another insurgency in Iraq, President Karzai had insufficient military resources to remove the rising challenges to his rule and thus relied on older methods: making bargains with local strong men to keep them from actively opposing the government. There were no Western troops to spare, and absent a credible threat of force from a functioning Afghan army, the Kabul government gained a reputation for weakness. The predations of its local representatives continued to alienate the Afghan people and to push them back into the arms of the Taliban. Beginning around 2004, levels of violence and measures of insecurity in Afghanistan began to increase, and by 2007, Helmand and Kandahar Provinces were again effectively coming under Taliban control.[20]

The Taliban's return after 2006 brings us to a final example of how incompatible Western and Afghan political theories were, and to a theme that has often appeared throughout this chapter: the role of illiberal tools like violence and coercion in creating functioning states. Here, we see that progressive ideals were not only in the minds of policymakers but also part of the military doctrine of counterinsurgency that shaped how Western military personnel interacted with Afghans during the second half of the war.

If any entity in the US government is capable of grasping the role of coercion in creating working states, one would expect it to be the US military. *The U.S. Army/Marine Corps Counterinsurgency Field Manual* is the closest approximation to a military "theory" of nation-building, even though the manual only covers military actions and acknowledges at the outset that the military cannot defeat an insurgency alone or grant a government legitimacy. Written by a combination of military officers and academics, it reflects many of the same liberal assumptions that this chapter takes as its subject. And while it acknowledges the role of force, fear, and coercion, it misses something too. "Legitimacy is the main objective," the COIN manual explains in its introduction.

> All governments rule through a combination of consent and coercion. Governments described as "legitimate" rule primarily with the consent of the governed; those described as "illegitimate" tend to rely mainly or entirely on coercion. Citizens of the latter obey the state for fear of the consequences of doing otherwise, rather than because they voluntarily accept its rule. . . . In Western liberal tradition, a government that derives its just powers from the people and responds to their desires while looking for their welfare is accepted as legitimate. In contrast, theocratic societies fuse political and religious authority; political figures are accepted as legitimate because the populace views them as implementing the will of God. . . . Illegitimate states (sometimes called "police states") typically cannot regulate society or can do so only by applying overwhelming coercion.[21]

In this passage, we see that the writers of the counterinsurgency manual have used ideas that have broad appeal in the United States to make a universal claim about what makes states legitimate. There is a basic formula at work here—ruling through consent equals legitimate government, and ruling through force or religious authority does not. But while that may be largely the case in Western societies today, it is not a universal truth. All states rely on force to varying degrees, and the degree of violence used typically reflects the norms and history of the society. In Afghanistan, and Pashtun culture in particular, there has always been a high tolerance for violence in problem solving—consent may come entirely voluntarily in some cases, but more often it comes when a credibly strong opponent demonstrates that he can and will use violence to compel obedience. And while the ISAF forces in Afghanistan understood well that violence was necessary to secure the people from the Taliban, they saw little role for coercion anywhere else. Legitimacy would come, they assumed, by giving the Afghans the same things Westerners had: working roads and wells, assembly halls, jobs, and education.

Nowhere was this soft approach to building legitimacy more evident than in the first major operation of the counterinsurgency campaign: Operation Moshtarak, known popularly to Americans as the Battle of Marjah. The operation was conducted primarily by the Marine Corps, and because strengthening the authority of the Kabul government was paramount, the Americans strove to include the Afghans from beginning to end. Planners even incorporated the idea into the operation's name—*moshtarak* means "partnership" or "together" in Dari (a language spoken in Afghanistan, but these days rarely in Marjah). The plan was clear: American and Afghan forces would clear the town of insurgents, after which representatives from Kabul, aided by the Western foreigners, would deliver all the basic services the modern liberal social contract requires: representative political institutions, development assistance for roads and agriculture, education, and basic health and sanitation items. Because the Afghan government would be directly involved at every step, the theory went, the population would choose to break with the Taliban and reward Kabul with their full support.

I fought in Marjah as an infantry platoon commander during the first six months of the operation and can testify, as other authors in this volume have also explained, that the effort did not go as planned. The Taliban melted away at the end of the initial assault, and then resorted to sniping, improvised explosive devices, and small harassing attacks. Even though the West had been supporting the development of the Afghan National Security Forces since 2002, the Afghan army was entirely incapable of taking the lead on the attack, and the combat skills of average Afghan soldiers were so poor that Marines often considered them to be liabilities rather than assets. (It should be added here that the army was, by far, the most reliable of national Afghan

Figure 7.1 Marjah district elders and US Marines watch *Why We Are Here*, a US-funded video "that serves to educate the Afghan population on the purpose for the continued presence of coalition forces in Afghanistan." Despite constant outreach to the local population, most Afghans did not believe the promises made by the coalition and trusted the Kabul-appointed politicians in Helmand even less. (Department of Defense / SSgt Andrew Miller)

institutions.) In the months that followed the "clearing" phase of the operation, violence steadily rose, and by April, prominent local leaders were disillusioned and complaining. During a meeting with the Kabul-appointed district governor at the end of April, Haji Muhammad Asif, a Wardak tribal leader and one of the district's leading power brokers, explained that "the situation is bad here, the President and Provincial Governor had lots of promises, but in fact nothing happened."[22] When my Marines met with local power brokers—tribal elders, drug traffickers (not mutually exclusive groups), and religious officials—our script was almost always the same: the Afghan government would, before the departure of the Marines, be able to provide security and basic services. Even carefully crafted videos explaining why the Americans had come to Afghanistan had little effect.

The locals saw no evidence to support the Americans' arguments. No one believed the Afghan government was up to the task—even the agents of the Afghan government I worked with on a daily basis. (My Afghan army counterpart, a remarkably brave officer by any standard, once said to me that he intended to return to the mountains and fight on there when the army ultimately dissolved.) Among the Afghan institutions meant to be involved—the army, the Afghan National Civil Order Police, and civilian elements of the government under the leadership of Kabul-appointed district governor Haji Zahir—very few had any appreciable effect on the conduct of operations. The civilian presence was essentially absent; the mayor was afraid to travel far afield of his heavily fortified offices, and many key officials failed to appear in the district at all. My fellow officers and I found ourselves promising something for which there was little demand and little expectation of delivery. As the gaps between rhetoric and reality grew, substantial amounts of terrain lost by the Taliban in February were recaptured. Shortly before being relieved as the ISAF commander in the summer of 2010, General Stanley McChrystal described Marjah as a "bleeding ulcer," and by October, reporters were calling Marjah a "full blown" insurgency. "It's hearts and minds versus fear and intimidation," Marine Lance Corporal Chuck Martin told an AP reporter. "And right now, [the Taliban's] fear and intimidation are winning."[23]

It was not just that the ANSF were often incompetent or that the Afghan officials refused to govern, though these were problems, to be sure. But permeating all of ISAF's efforts were cultural incompatibilities that caused the very actions taken to win "hearts and minds" to occasionally backfire. In some cases, the attempts to conciliate tribal leaders were taken as signs of weakness rather than genuine concern, and the reflexive use of liberal rhetoric more often confused its targets than advanced any sort of goal.

I saw this firsthand while helping deliver a $10,000 condolence payment to Afghans who had lost four family members to Marine firepower—a scene that was captured on film in the HBO documentary *The Battle for Marjah.* As a young Marine sergeant handed over the money, $2,500 for each death, he delivered to the grieving family the only message he had for explaining the American presence in Marjah—a message that drew heavily from the intellectual wellspring of liberal democratic capitalism: "Gentlemen, this is for you, for your losses. You know, the US Marines, the citizens of Afghanistan, and the government of Afghanistan together can achieve great things to make Afghanistan a safer and more prosperous place for all." The Afghan who had just lost his children remained silent for a long time. When he spoke, it was clear that our words had made little difference. "My heart still bleeds because of what happened," he said.[24]

But in the fall of 2010, things began to shift. Violence dropped off dramatically, and by March 2011, the men of Marjah elected a district council. Economic activity started to flourish. Testifying in front of the House Armed Services Committee just two weeks later, General David Petraeus praised the turnaround, claiming that "as a result of improvements in the security situation there [in Marjah], the markets, which once sold weapons, explosives, and illegal narcotics, now feature over 1500 shops selling food, clothes, and household goods."[25]

What had changed? Had the people finally recognized the Kabul government as legitimate and chosen it over the Taliban who ruled as thugs only through coercion, as the COIN manual posited? No. In fact, the Afghans did not change at all; the Americans did. In the autumn of 2010, working quietly and without fanfare, company- and battalion-level Marine officers began to reduce levels of violence by buying off local power brokers directly. The principal mechanism for this effort was an initiative being used throughout Helmand Province: the Interim Security for Critical Infrastructure (ISCI) program. None of this was illegal or even improper, even though it looked like something inspired less by the *Counterinsurgency Field Manual* and more by television series like *The Sopranos* or *The Wire*. Through the ISCI, Marines hired Afghan locals ostensibly to guard things like wells, mosques, and markets from insurgents. But, in fact, this was a variation on a much older practice: paying tribes not to attack. Local elders—most of whom were heavily involved in the opium trade (prominently, Haji Baz Gul in the center of the city and Haji Muhammad Asif in the southern part)—provided the men from their own tribal networks and collected substantial chunks of the salaries for themselves. Some of it they kept, but the bulk was likely redis-

Figure 7.2 A US Marine and two Afghans clear a canal in Marjah in September 2010 while another Marine provides security. Using programs like the Commander's Emergency Response Program (CERP) and Interim Security for Critical Infrastructure (ISCI), the Marines temporarily quieted Marjah through work programs—a new variation on the older Afghan tradition of using tributes and subsidies to prevent tribes from rebelling. (Department of Defense / PFC Andrew Johnston)

tributed to the various patronage and smuggling networks that had existed long before Operation Moshtarak began, a technique by which Afghans have always secured loyalties and created alliances. The Taliban likely also received payments from these tribal networks, either as cuts of ISCI income, cuts of poppy income, or both, and thus found no reason to mount major attacks on the foreigners as long as the money continued to flow. Thus, in the end, Marjah was temporarily quieted, but only by sidelining the Kabul government and strengthening the patronage networks that included both ordinary Afghans and the insurgents themselves.

This pattern played itself out repeatedly across the various surge operations in Afghanistan in the latter half of the war. Whether through the ISCI or other programs—the Commander's Emergency Response Program (CERP) was also popular—ISAF rented peace through subsidies, which convinced Afghans further of something they already knew: the Kabul government was often irrelevant; the

Americans were the new mark for fleecing. The Taliban reduced their use of violence when the economic benefits of doing so redounded to them, either directly or indirectly. On occasion, Taliban supporters masqueraded as government supporters; at other times, they struck deals with the proxies ISAF was already paying, and other times they just extracted their share from ISAF proxies through intimidation and force. Violence did not come to end; it simply went into hiding while there was money to be made.

After 2010, the ISCI program was largely supplanted by the more robust Afghan Local Police (ALP) initiative, which formalized and regularized the practice of raising tribal militias—often constituted by the same people who had been fighting ISAF and the government only months before. The program met with substantial success in the Pashtun tribal belt, especially when in the hands of officers who had a good understanding of the realities of Afghan political practice.[26] (It also met with more acceptance from Kabul, as the money that funded the ALP, though Western in origin, was routed through the central government.) In the opinion of one Marine officer who served in Marjah twice, and who was intimately involved with the management of the ALP program on his second tour, the financial incentives provided to local power brokers were the key to the eventual—but temporary—pacification of Marjah:

> What actually secured Marjah was not that [the Afghan Government] established its legitimacy, but that it became more lucrative to work with the government and the Marines than it did to continue to participate in the poppy trade and work with Taliban elements. . . . Through extending ISCI and CERP payments, relying on the large amount of authorized ALP members, and then intentionally overpaying for contracts, we were able to hire all the former fighters over to the government's side, further entrench and legitimize the traditional leadership structure under the guise of democracy . . . and kept the loyalty of those leaders by making it financially lucrative. The most dangerous thing for the future of Marjah is . . . [if] the funding streams are disrupted or cut off.[27]

And of course, in the end, that is exactly what happened. As Marjah calmed, ISAF withdrew most of the troops and spent significantly less money. Operational units had succeeded in temporarily quelling violence by working within the strictures of traditional Afghan political practice and ignoring the interests of the Kabul state. And of course, when ISAF turned its focus elsewhere, violence and intimidation in Marjah skyrocketed. As one Marjah resident explained at the end of 2012, under the Taliban "if you had a box of cash on your head, you could go to the farthest part of Marjah and no one would take it from you, even at night. . . . [Now,] they are standing in police and army uniforms with weapons and they can take your money."[28] By 2016, Marjah District was again effectively under Taliban control.

///

"Like the political institutions historically preceding it, the state is a relation of men dominating men," sociologist Max Weber opined in 1918, for "if the state is to exist, the dominated must obey the authority claimed by the powers that be."[29] This is something that all political theorists seem to grant in principle, but in Afghanistan, Western policymakers and counterinsurgency practitioners were not able to apply either coercion or persuasion effectively to change the fundamental nature of Afghan society. As I have tried to illustrate here, an unwritten constitution was already in place in that country, one that long preceded ISAF's presence and which remained in force after its departure. It consisted of traditional ethnic, tribal, state, and religious patterns, all of which had been partially transformed by modernization and traumatically stressed by decades of war and the rise of Islamic radicalism. It was not liberal in ideology or democratic in practice, and it never had been.

Across the 13 years of Western combat operations, policymakers and practitioners generally failed to incorporate this reality into effective, creative plans that could succeed within Afghanistan's cultural landscape. They attempted to establish a sovereign state that sought a monopoly on violence throughout Afghanistan—perhaps an impossible task in itself—and they largely ignored the illiberal actors who already commanded legitimacy at local levels. Most problematic, both the Bush and Obama administrations tended to approach Afghanistan, in practice, with the assumption that Afghans themselves wanted to be liberals. Making Afghanistan better, it turned out, meant making it more like the United States. And while most policymakers saw some role for violence and coercion in all of this, they rarely incorporated an understanding of how Afghans use their own levers of power—patronage, *Pashtunwali*, and Islam—into the heart of their strategy.

Western policy often seemed as though it was being pursued without any awareness of a basic fact about politics, well described by Thucydides, that the "strong will take what they can and the weak will suffer what they must."[30] Afghans, on the other hand, were always aware of this basic fact; they saw it in their daily interactions with both the Taliban and agents of the Kabul state. Faced with the harsh reality of their incompetent and corrupt rulers, Afghans were deeply skeptical of robust foreign support for the "rule of law." In their skepticism, they were more realistic about politics than their American and European patrons, who had forgotten that the structural problem with the rule of law is that, in practice, it is always the case that one group must apply the law to everyone else. They had forgotten that wars—and politics—necessarily have winners and losers.

Much of the Western political tradition, especially the wave of critique initiated by Rousseau that culminated in the notion of the "end of history," implicitly seeks to deny the necessity of this fact, despite the obvious existence of social winners and losers in even the most socially just Western states. The earliest, and darkest, visions of liberalism—those of Machiavelli and Hobbes—understood the necessarily coercive and often violent nature of political affairs, and those segments of the American right most closely aligned with that earlier vision were always skeptical of the task of nation-building in Afghanistan. Those on the left who were skeptical of the task—for example, President Obama—seemed to feel that neither the task nor its goal was in principle undesirable or unachievable, but rather that the United States was an inappropriate standard-bearer for the project.

But nation-building occurred nonetheless. Assuming the justice and inevitability of the initial invasion, and taking for granted that the West would not tolerate a purely punitive expedition that did nothing to help the Afghans in the aftermath of military action, what could have been done differently? The reestablishment of a limited state, perhaps rooted in a Barakzai monarchy, with more accommodation of illiberal actors, acceptance of the control of vast areas of the country by tribal and ethnic networks whose practices are objectionable to the Western conscience, combined with solicitude toward the conservative beliefs of rural Pashtuns and a recognition that Pakistan, facing the threat of India to its east, has no natural interest in a prosperous state capable of conducting its own independent foreign policy to its west: perhaps that could have succeeded.

This alternative should not be taken as an argument for American "realism" over "idealism." Both of those approaches to foreign policy are essentially impossible in total purity, and indeed, there are real practical and moral problems with realism: considering the idealism of the American founding, a truly realist foreign policy is quite literally un-American. To be an American is to be a liberal, and to be a liberal is to be an idealist. What was needed in Afghanistan was not realism but prudence, in the sense intended by the classical philosophers. The modern Western political project, even in its imperfections, is noble, and worth preserving and extending. But noble regimes require noble circumstances. In ignoble circumstances, ignoble regimes are not only necessary but can be legitimate and, in a sense, just.[31] In ISAF's 13-year war in Afghanistan, prudence was blinded by unexamined political and cultural assumptions, and the result was a massive and avoidable waste of time, lives, and resources.

CHAPTER EIGHT

Organizing like the Enemy

SPECIAL OPERATIONS FORCES, AFGHAN CULTURE, AND VILLAGE STABILITY OPERATIONS

Lieutenant Commander Daniel R. Green, USN

When US Special Operations Forces (SOF) first arrived in Afghanistan following the attacks of September 11, 2001, they encountered an Afghan cultural context ostensibly well suited to their doctrinal heritage of working with indigenous security forces and conducting both unconventional and counterinsurgency warfare. Tasked with partnering with local Afghan allies, and facing an enemy that hid among the population, SOF were uniquely poised to exploit their inherent capabilities to counter the insurgency threat.[1] However, the narrowly defined counterterrorism mission, typified by one Special Forces soldier's attitude of "go get them, get them all, make them pay," eventually gave way to a renewed Taliban insurgency, and SOF were forced to rethink their approach not just to counterterrorism specifically but also to counterinsurgency more broadly.[2] While SOF units continued to conduct "man-hunting" operations in one form or another throughout the Afghanistan War, after more than a decade of war, their mission-set and mind-set changed appreciably, reflecting a deeper understanding of Afghan culture and the requirements for stability. Toward the end of Operation Enduring Freedom, most SOF units were no longer helicoptering in to conduct direct action raids or solely performing military clearing operations of insurgent areas; they were embedded in Afghan villages conducting community engagement and raising indigenous forces to fight the Taliban threat. This alternate strategy to fighting the Taliban insurgency reflected SOF's deeper understanding of the requirements for stability in Afghan culture and a greater appreciation for using a holistic strategy to confront the Taliban's military and political strategies.

Having returned to their roots of raising indigenous security forces—actions known in doctrinal circles as foreign internal defense—US Army Special Forces teams, in particular, applied their increased knowledge of Afghan culture to create a tailored local security program. The initiative they began was called Village Stability Operations (VSO): a collaborative approach that raised local security forces while working with village elders to improve governance, foster development, build justice mechanisms, and protect communities from Taliban intimidation. The VSO initiative empowered local decision making, allowing village elders to address community problems in a comprehensive fashion, and facilitated their selection of military-age males to serve as defensively oriented security forces who, in return for training by SOF , became legitimate local police. While different from the Afghan National Police, these forces were paid for and logistically supported by the Ministry of Interior and were answerable both to local villagers and to the Afghan government. This population-centric approach of organizing Afghan villagers supplanted an enemy-centric counterterrorism view that had initially dominated SOF thinking about the security threat in Afghanistan. Instead of viewing security as something that was done *to* the local population, SOF adapted to the Afghan cultural context and saw security as something that was done *with* it.

The evolution of SOF during the war in Afghanistan reflects changing US strategy in the conflict as much as it does the adaptation of the organizational culture of SOF to the challenges of al Qaeda and the Taliban insurgency. At the outset of the conflict, SOF teams were constrained by the cultural baggage, institutional priorities, and mission-sets of an earlier era, and therefore entered Afghanistan with a focus on counterterrorism.[3] As this approach caused friction with local Afghans and was unable to provide enduring security, and as other elements of the coalition civil-military effort failed to adapt, the Taliban returned, seizing the initiative across the country. Exploiting the gap between the aspirations of the Afghan people and the ability of the government of Afghanistan to provide enduring security, governance, justice, and development, the Taliban instituted a robust political program focused on leveraging the population to achieve their goals. The insurgent movement used its deep understanding of Afghan culture to turn many Afghans away from both their own government and coalition forces. As the insurgency worsened, SOF went through a process of changing how they thought about the insurgency and how they organized to confront it. They adapted their approach to a wide variety of tasks (targeting, partnering with indigenous forces, leveraging relationships with the population to exercise influence, and confronting the insurgency's soft-power strategy) and incorporated Afghan cultural priorities and concepts into their tactics and institutions. The cumulative effect of this process eventually led SOF to adapt to both the Taliban threat and Afghan culture with a strategy informed by and organized like the insurgency. As a result of these efforts, Special Operations Forces built a set of institutions and programs that were responsive to Afghan culture and incorporated the tribal and village structures that had been the basis of legitimacy in Afghanistan for centuries. By organizing like the enemy, and incorporating Afghan cultural priorities and concepts, the SOF community put together one of the most successful mechanisms for improving security, governance, development, and legitimacy in the Afghan War.

A Brief History of US Special Operations Forces

Special Operations Forces perform a variety of roles within the US Department of Defense using specific units that, while sharing a number of core functions, have unique capabilities for particular missions. Many SOF units began during World War II as specialized capabilities created by US military and intelligence services to confront the German and Japanese militaries. In the Cold War, many SOF units focused on partnering with indigenous resistance groups in order to conduct unconventional warfare. This type of warfare focused on coercing, disrupting, or overthrowing a government through US sponsorship of a resistance movement or insurgency.[4] The soldiers required for this work were not just physically tough and resilient but also had an advanced ability to understand indigenous cultures and to work with local forces. In particular, the US Army's Special Forces—a separate special operations community within the US Army known colloquially as the Green Berets—developed a command culture that emphasized adaptability, improvisation, and unconventional thinking and encouraged risk taking when achieving their missions.

With the election of Senator John F. Kennedy (D-MA) to the presidency in 1960, US Army Special Forces units expanded their missions beyond unconventional warfare and began to focus on foreign internal defense. This mission required SOF units to collaborate with foreign governments as they fought to "protect [their] society from subversion, lawlessness, insurgency, [and] terrorism," and to work with civilian and military agencies in order to "assess, train, advise, and assist host nation military and paramilitary forces."[5] Under this new mandate, US Army Special Forces teams expanded their capabilities even further as part of President Kennedy's strategy of "flexible response." The president wanted to have a continuum of options beyond conventional warfare to address the irregular warfare challenge—a range of military tools that would employ the "full spectrum of military, paramilitary and civil action" to confront the enemy's use of "economic and political warfare, propaganda and naked military aggression."[6] This strategic shift required units to focus on civil affairs, psychological operations, and intelligence gathering in order to influence local populations, and to develop doctrine for similar conflicts in other regions of the world.

While US Army Special Forces teams became the principal force for partnering with foreign militaries and indigenous resistance groups, the Department of Defense also created additional SOF units to both contend with specific security threats and to institutionalize highly specialized capabilities. Many of these capabilities included counter-terrorist and maritime operations, reconnaissance and surveillance, direct action, hostage rescue and recovery, interdiction and offensive operations against weapons of mass destruction, and security force assistance, among other tasks.[7] Each of the military services developed its own respective units reflecting its unique roles and missions. The US Navy, for example, created a specialized commando unit under the rubric of Naval Special Warfare called SEALs (Sea, Air, and Land) that concentrated on executing maritime as well as air and land missions such as boarding and securing naval vessels, infiltrating enemy shorelines, conducting small unit combat, and surveillance and reconnaissance, among a number of other missions. The Air Force and the Marine Corps also created elite units, and the Army created Ranger units, which are light infantry units distinct from the US Army Special Forces.

US Strategy in Afghanistan and Special Operations Forces

When US Special Operations Forces first entered Afghanistan in late 2001, their primary mission was to function as an unconventional capability in support of the indigenous forces that were already fighting the Taliban regime. Units initially deployed to northern Afghanistan to partner with the United Islamic Front for the Salvation of Afghanistan (the so-called Northern Alliance) and to southern Afghanistan to partner with prominent Pashtun leaders such as Hamid Karzai. In addition to direct combat assistance, SOF also provided leadership and military expertise, targeting support, medical and civil aid, and enhanced communication capabilities. Once the Taliban government fell and its leadership adopted an insurgency strategy, US Special Operations Forces shifted to a foreign internal defense approach while simultaneously pursuing insurgent fighters and their leaders. However, this approach was narrowly focused on killing or capturing the remaining members of the Taliban in direct action raids and clearing operations.[8] After the initial combat operations against Taliban forces largely ended in Afghanistan in 2002, SOF units had established themselves at major bases or in key provincial capitals in Afghanistan and began working with a series of Afghan allies, many of whom were local strongmen or "warlords" who frequently provided intelligence, fighters, and logistical support to US units.[9] The dual tasks of counterterrorism and indigenous partnering dovetailed well with the foreign internal defense doctrine of US Army Special Forces, but this approach had within it the seeds of future instability.

Part of the problem was that Afghanistan's past conflicts had made the state too weak for SOF units to partner with effectively. The country had suffered greatly during the previous two decades of warfare, which had produced large-scale fighting and death, massive population displacement, and major challenges to the traditional, agrarian, and tribally organized social order. Additionally, educated professionals—the "literate class"—had departed, leaving Afghan society bereft of their talents, moderating influence, and leadership. This social upheaval contributed to the "rise of the khans"—militarily adept Afghan militia commanders who had forged extensive military followings through hard work, ruthlessness, luck, and outside patronage. These men frequently took on many of the functions of the state at local levels by providing a modicum of services to their followers, but their rise as power brokers did not always respect, and frequently weakened, tribal hierarchies. Furthermore, tribes and tribal leaders benefited and suffered unevenly during this time, with certain groups seeing a rise in status whereas others became marginalized, contributing further to tribal friction. As the state grew weaker or disappeared altogether, tribal identity and solidarity increased. The "khans" filled the vacuum and warlordism grew stronger throughout the country.[10] This environment had been propitious for the rise of the Taliban in the 1990s, when Afghans sought any way out of the chaos of civil war and the predatory behavior of warlords.

Faced with a military force they were unable to defeat directly, the Taliban adopted a strategy of insurgency that sought to weaken the will of the Afghan government and the Western coalition through targeted operations. By blending in with the population and striking at security forces at times and locations of their choosing, the insurgents hoped to make the costs in blood and treasure intolerable to the Afghan government. However, the armed element of the insurgency was simply, as author Bernard Fall described it, "a tactical appendage of a far vaster political contest and that, no matter how expertly it is fought by competent and dedicated professionals, it cannot possibly make up for the absence of a political rationale."[11] Since Taliban insurgents realized that the population was the true prize in this type of warfare (a point that was not yet apparent to US forces), they worked to maneuver the population away from the government and toward the insurgency.[12]

Special Operations Forces initially focused their efforts on finding and finishing the Taliban enemy as part of what one senior Special Forces officer referred to as a "pressure, pursue, punish" strategy.[13] This required the development of intelligence packages on Taliban leaders and insurgent groups based on human sources (e.g., interrogations, recruited sources, walk-ins), technical intelligence capabilities, and information from indigenous partner forces. These packages led to direct action raids against suspected insurgent leaders, which required SOF units to infiltrate a village either by helicopter, military vehicle, or foot, or to conduct larger clearing operations against Taliban groups, which generally required SOF units in small convoys accompanied by Afghan militia or government forces. This initial strategy focused almost exclusively on confronting the Taliban's military arm, and except for some allied tribal security forces, local villagers were largely bystanders to their own defense. While US forces developed some additional knowledge about Afghan culture in these types of operations, and sometimes conducted minimalist stability operations, much of SOF's initial understanding was still very limited. The intelligence they gathered frequently came from Afghans who had scores to settle and used US ignorance to their advantage.[14] The basic concept in the SOF approach during these earlier years is captured well by their insignia, which emphasized the most kinetic aspects of the mission in Afghanistan (fig. 8.1).

Figure 8.1 The Combined Joint Special Operations Task Force-Afghanistan insignia in the early years of the war, which emphasized the role of violence in Special Operations. (Department of Defense)

As this approach failed to quell the insurgency, the Americans began to completely rethink how they did intelligence. There were too few interrogators, human intelligence collectors, and targeting cells to address the terrorist and insurgent challenges. Intelligence cycles reflected a traditional mode of warfare where intelligence supported operations, but in this new type of conflict, operations increasingly drove intelligence, creating a feedback loop between both sections. Similarly, the top-down model of organization had to be adjusted, reflecting the more horizontal and dispersed nature of the enemy; in the words of General Stanley A. McChrystal, "It [took] a network to defeat a network."[15] The coalition needed a deeper cultural understanding of Afghan tribes to properly locate insurgents, develop sources, and leverage community sentiment against the insurgency. Interrogation methods that had been honed during the Cold War and focused on conventional military personnel had to be adjusted to focus on Afghan insurgents. Human intelligence networks had to be dramatically expanded after atrophying during the end of the Cold War, and a deeper understanding of Afghan culture was required in order to better use human sources to find insurgents hiding among the population. Focusing on the human terrain led to improved knowledge of Afghanistan's tribes, villages, key leaders, culture, and group dynamics.[16] Units also improved their knowledge of Afghan cultural dynamics by working with indigenous partners.

As the war in Afghanistan progressed, SOF units increasingly spread out to larger numbers of smaller forward operating bases in outlying provinces and districts and expanded their missions beyond "man-hunting" tasks.[17] These bases provided SOF with an unprecedented opportunity to engage with the Afghan population and allowed other capabilities within Special Operations, such as civil affairs, information operations, and intelligence, to come into use.[18] This expansion of SOF responsibilities prompted a thoroughgoing review of many aspects of Afghan culture such as community engagement strategies, tribal structures, farming practices, land ownership, and local politics, among other subjects.[19] It also prompted a review of the requirements for enduring local security since formal Afghan security forces were not numerous enough to provide security and frequently lacked crucial community connections and even legitimacy.[20] Additionally, key innovations from not just targeting but also tribal engagement and the organizational adaptations of the SOF units in Iraq began to inform Afghan SOF approaches. The SOF community was beginning to become more knowledgeable about Afghan culture.

Return of the Taliban Insurgency and the Evolution of Special Operations Forces

Security conditions throughout Afghanistan significantly worsened in 2006 as a resurgent Taliban movement seized control of large swathes of the country, calling into question the effectiveness of the "warlord" strategy as well as coalition and SOF counterterrorism approaches.[21] Throughout southern Afghanistan in 2006, the Taliban insurgency returned with a size, intensity, and lethality not seen since the US invasion in 2001.[22] The insurgency was larger, more disciplined, and increasingly operating as a conventional military force. The Taliban were now overrunning district centers, directly attacking coalition forward operating bases, and using more-advanced tactics, such as sniping, suicide attacks, and combined operations, many of which were extremely rare in previous years. The level of skill required to undertake these types of attacks and the experience level of the insurgency's leadership indicated that the Taliban had gained new strength and training. They also had new friends and foot soldiers, composed mostly of local Pashtun villagers who had been marginalized and preyed upon by the Karzai government or who resented constant US direct action and clearing operations. Even some who opposed the Taliban found themselves forced to turn against the coalition because they had no local security forces of their own to counter the Taliban's intimidation. By 2006, the relatively peaceful five years since the American invasion now seemed a false peace, and the United States realized it needed to rethink how to stabilize the country.

One of the first key lessons concerned the role of violence. While SOF units could easily clear the Taliban from an area temporarily, without a viable local partner who could hold it thereafter, the insurgents would inevitably reinfiltrate. Additionally, Afghan villagers were motivated by a variety of reasons to join the Taliban insurgency, many of which had nothing to do with the Islamist movement's religious ideology. Some villagers joined because of tribal and village frictions, others because they were disappointed by the Karzai government, and others because they were intimidated into doing so or because they sought a steady paycheck. What was becoming clear was that the United States and the Afghan government had to confront the Taliban insurgency holistically, addressing its political, tribal, and economic aspects as well as its military wing. In a sense, the United States had to use the Taliban's structure and strategy against them. Some of this process of learning benefited from the US experience in Iraq where US forces actively enlisted with Sunni Arab tribes against al Qaeda in the western Iraqi province of Al-Anbar, leading to significant security gains. A revised US approach would need to blend military and political strategies relatively seamlessly and would be based in the villages and districts where the people lived. It would have to be nested in a "shape, clear, hold, build, and transition" strategy enlisting local Afghans in their own defense in a partnered manner alongside Afghan police and military forces. Instead of constantly clearing villages, US forces would now have a "persistent presence"; instead of engaging in direct combat, the United States would support Afghans doing so; and instead of using a top-down approach to building stability, the United States would adopt a simultaneous bottom-up or grassroots strategy as well. The strength of the Taliban movement at this stage in the war was its ability to mobilize the population by capitalizing on their grievances or through intimidation in order to bolster its organizational strength—a people's war.

Even though the Taliban's strategic goals of uniting the Pashtuns, ejecting the foreign military occupation, and imposing Sharia law were well known, their tactical political program was less well understood and their popularity among many Pashtuns even more so.[23] The key reason the Taliban were able to come back with such force in 2006 was their ability to wage an insurgency campaign using a political strategy targeted to winning the support of the population. The Taliban carefully crafted a political program that tapped into *Pashtunwali* traditions, took advantage of US, coalition, and Afghan government mistakes, and capitalized on the weaknesses of the Afghan state in the villages.[24] Though substantial efforts had been expended by the United States to promote good governance in the provinces, they had been unequal to the task, cumbersome, bureaucratic, and sometimes even counterproductive. The Taliban's positive political program had at least five aspects to it, all of which tapped into Afghan cultural mores: justice, micropolitics, reconciliation, laissez-faire, and village empowerment. While the Taliban imposed their will on villagers and often did so violently, they also had a positive agenda that sought to entice supporters to their banner. In the face of corrupt and sometimes murderous government officials, a nonfunctioning judiciary, and the perversion or suspension of *Pashtunwali* traditions, typical villagers had a limited ability to seek justice for the things that bothered them most: murder, theft, assault, rape, and land and water disputes.[25] For Taliban political agents, this was a rich vein of discontent that could be mined by appealing to the structures of justice created by Sharia law. While villagers may not have been inclined to support Sharia law in its totality, they were likely to do so in the absence of a viable alternative. Because the Taliban agents were sitting in the villagers' homes, soliciting their grievances, and then quickly seeking to remedy them, the villagers were hard-pressed to support a government that was often distant and abused its authority. Along these same lines, the Taliban practiced micropolitics with a remarkably high degree of sophistication.

Taliban political agents would find any problem that a village or individual had and make it their own. If a village was hoarding water from a stream causing a downstream village's crops to fail, the Taliban enlisted with the aggrieved party. If the Afghan government had abused a tribe, the Taliban joined with it to seek justice. This political granularity stood in marked contrast to the frequently inept and ineffective efforts of the Afghan state and the sometimes counterproductive work of the coalition. The Taliban's political program was also furthered by a nuanced approach to the central drivers of local politics and economies. If farmers wanted to cultivate poppy, the Taliban allowed it; if someone once worked for or supported the Afghan government, reconciliation with the Taliban was allowed; if tribal leaders wanted their authority respected, the Taliban did so if it furthered their agenda. Additionally, if villagers felt that "their" government did not represent them or had unfairly attacked their interests, then the Taliban preached inclusion, grievance, and justice. Against this well-crafted, flexible, dynamic, and pervasive program, US, coalition, and Afghan efforts lagged significantly and clearly needed to be revised, although the specific requirements of a new strategy were not yet known. In light of the successes of the newly resurgent Taliban, how then could SOF simultaneously confront the Taliban's military arm and their political strategy in a way that was supported by Afghan communities, protected them from intimidation, was vertically integrated yet horizontally dispersed, and leveraged influence in a way that accounted for the weaknesses of the Afghan state?

Understanding and Mobilizing the Afghan Population

With a renewed Taliban insurgency able to capitalize on local grievances, SOF placed greater emphasis on understanding how villages worked, why some were stable while others weren't, and how SOF might be able to leverage the population in support of the Afghan government.[26] One of the first areas SOF focused on was gaining a better understanding of Afghan tribes, especially in light of the successes from the Anbar Awakening movement in western Iraq that had begun in 2005–2006.[27] The tribes also received new attention because the United States did not then have enough troops in Afghanistan to undertake a proper counterinsurgency campaign largely because of existing Iraq personnel requirements and the need to give units time at home between deployments. But as tribes assumed a more central role in SOF strategy, it was essential that the US strategy going forward be informed by US military experiences in Iraq, not dominated by them, and that a pragmatic approach based on Afghan societal dynamics achieve enduring security effects for the local population. Additionally, it was crucial that the enlistment of the population through tribal protective forces be able to actively confront the insurgency without being overwhelmed by it and to maintain the active support of the population without giving in to tribal infighting. All of this had to be done while simultaneously building the capabilities of the Afghan state without creating a parallel tribal or militia system.

The effort to recruit and train local forces went through several stages, all of which provided important lessons. The initial effort began by working with warlords and their militias who were supportive of the government of Afghanistan. These forces were unaccountable to the people, abusive of the population, and not representative of community groups. As a result, many of their actions prompted Afghan villagers to join with the Taliban in 2006 out of a sense of injustice and because they were unable to defend themselves from Taliban intimidation.[28] Early efforts to build the Afghan National Police (ANP) mirrored this initial warlord strategy as well, especially when recruits came from one particular tribe or faction. These early efforts were never sufficient to secure local communities and the forces were not mentored effectively.

The next step in the evolution of providing local security was the creation of the Afghan National Auxiliary Police (ANAP) in 2006. This was a reaction, in part, to the decision by then ISAF commander Lieutenant General Karl Eikenberry to demobilize the approximately 11,000-member Afghan Militia Force (AMF) that had assisted SOF units since the beginning of the war. This demobilization created a security vacuum, which the ANAP hoped to fill.[29] The ANAP was a Ministry of Interior–led program that included 10 days of training focused on basic policing and military skills as well as instruction on ethics and morality. Upon completion of the training, recruits received an AK-47, a police uniform with an ANAP patch, and the equivalent of $70 per month in salary, which was the same as that of ANP recruits.[30] The ANAP's missions included guarding checkpoints and providing community policing, and its approximately 9,000 members were assigned areas at locations in six southern Afghan provinces: Farah, Helmand, Kandahar, Uruzgan, Zabul, and Ghazni.[31] As the program was implemented, it suffered from a number of problems including poor oversight, a weak and ineffective recruitment and vetting process, and predatory behavior against the local population.[32] It also suffered from the lack of local character in its forces (it was a national program), an absence of community and Ministry of Interior vetting, infiltration by insurgents, the presence of petty criminals and drug addicts, monopolization by local power brokers, and friction with the ANP over areas of responsibility.[33] The program was eventually dismantled in 2007, but a number of valuable lessons had been learned from the experience.

The next version of local police, called the Afghan Public Protection Program (AP3), began in Wardak Province in January 2009 and was overseen by a Special Forces company commander. Recruits came from the communities they would protect, were vetted by local *shu-*

ras and the National Directorate of Security, received three weeks of training from SOF, and earned half the salary of a regular police officer. They received AK-47s from the Ministry of Interior as well as uniforms and other support from the Afghan government. The AP3 forces had a fundamentally defensive orientation; their job was to protect mosques, schools, bazaars, and other local sites. While the initial results of the program were positive, several factors contributed to AP3's demise. The program's recruiting, vetting, training, and oversight role was transferred from SOF to a conventional forces unit in the province, and the unit did not properly mentor the AP3 members. The force was then used improperly and transitioned from a self-defense effort to a highway police force defending the Ring Road. Additionally, recruits from other provinces began to join the program diluting its local character, and its members began to engage in "bribe-taking shakedown" behavior. The program eventually fell under the control of a local Wardak strongman named Ghulam Mohammad Hotak, a former Taliban commander, which further undermined the program. Although the AP3 program began with SOF mentoring and a focus on establishing local security by mobilizing the local population, as time passed its mission changed.[34] Special Operations Forces were no longer involved in the program, and the eventual commander of the force largely disregarded local sentiment and never emphasized governance and development, which doomed the initiative.[35]

The next step in the evolution of local defense efforts was the creation of the Community Defense Initiative, later renamed the Local Defense Initiative. Approved in July 2009, the CDI/LDI program emphasized the defensively oriented nature of the local protective force, sought to reduce the influence of power brokers through community engagement, and nested its forces within the government of Afghanistan by making them answerable to the Ministry of Interior (even though the program was technically administered by another element of the Afghan government called the Independent Directorate of Local Governance). The LDI program attempted to identify communities who had actually sought out Afghan government and coalition support against insurgent intimidation or had resisted insurgents on their own. The villagers would have to provide their own weapons, and in lieu of salaries they would receive development projects and other assistance as a collective benefit. If members of the LDI site required additional assistance against the Taliban, they could rely on a nearby SOF unit for support as well as members of the ANP. While the LDI program was implemented in a number of sites throughout Afghanistan and initially proved effective, it also suffered from a lack of comprehensive oversight, limited Ministry of Interior resourcing, corruption, and a perception that it was not as effective as it needed to be against the Taliban.[36] While success was elusive, many lessons had been learned, which proved vital to the later success of the Village Stability Operations / Afghan Local Police program.

Village Stability Operations and the Afghan Local Police

As civilian and military leaders shifted their attention back to Afghanistan in 2009–2010 following security successes in Iraq, SOF leaders sought to incorporate the lessons that had been learned not just from previous community security initiatives but from Afghan culture as well. It had become clear that no matter how effective direct action and clearing operations by SOF were at destabilizing the Taliban insurgency, absent a viable local partner to maintain security, the effects of SOF efforts would always be short-lived. Additionally, if the sources of instability (e.g., tribal feuds, poor governance, lack of development, etc.) were not simultaneously addressed as well, security effects would remain temporary. As one SOF commander put it: "It seems like every time I come back here [to Afghanistan], the security situation is worse. . . . Maybe we need to do something different."[37]

In March 2010, a new commander took over Special Operations Forces in Afghanistan, but unlike his predecessors who had come from the US Army's Special Forces community, this commander came from an even more elite commmunity, which had long specialized in direct action raids. However, instead of continuing with a narrowly focused counterterrorism strategy, the new commander embraced a holistic approach that sought to address the drivers of instability in Afghanistan's villages as well as the insurgency's political and military strategy.[38] Following a comprehensive review of past security efforts conducted, in part, by his predecessor, he proposed a new local security initiative that represented the accumulated wisdom, learned from both mistakes and successes, from the challenge of raising local security forces that were accountable to the people, answerable to the government, and effective at fighting the insurgency.[39] Initially named the Afghan Local Police (ALP) program, it was approved by Afghan president Hamid Karzai by official decree on August 16, 2010, with an original authorized strength of 10,000. This number was increased to 20,000 in order to properly protect the number of sites the government of Afghanistan's National Security Council had prioritized.[40] The final ALP numbers were eventually increased to 30,000 with the initial three-year program extended to five years.[41]

The program would be administered by the Afghan government's Ministry of Interior in close partnership with US SOF and would concentrate on recruiting, vetting, training, and logistically supporting locally raised security forces. Subsequently renamed the Village Stability Operations / Afghan Local Police (VSO/ALP) initiative, the overall approach was a synchronized delivery of population security, local governance, and microdevelopment to rural populations through active community engagement.[42] Special Operations Forces would embed directly in Afghan villages that met four basic criteria: (1) villagers had to request SOF help, (2) they had to demonstrate a willingness to resist Taliban intimidation, (3) the location had to be logistically sustainable, and (4) the location had to be "consequential to the overall fight."[43] The SOF teams would focus their efforts on "improving informal governance through village shuras, establishing or co-opting village defense forces, and improving development."[44] By adopting a bottom-up approach to establishing stability, the VSO program fought Taliban forces where they were, with an approach based on their structure, and organized the population to resist insurgent intimidation and the appeal of their political program.[45]

The VSO approach achieved several effects simultaneously. It was partly a (1) local protective force, (2) a tribal rehabilitation program, (3) a tactical governance initiative, (4) an economic program (through salaries and greater economic activity), (5) a reintegration program for local part-time Taliban, (6) a means for synchronized delivery of population security, governance, and development, and (7) a link for villages to the government.[46] By fighting the Taliban on their own terms with a village-based, long-term, decentralized strategy that blended civil and military approaches and enlisted the population in their own defense, VSO/ALP prevented the Taliban from accessing the population physically, appealing to their grievances to separate them from the government, and enticing them to fight through economic incentives.[47] It took many years to craft this strategy, but its subsequent success was due to the ability of SOF to adapt to Afghan cultural norms and use a strategy informed by them to defeat the Taliban insurgency.

Before a single villager joined the VSO/ALP program, a process of community engagement took place as well as an assessment of the area by SOF in partnership with the government of Afghanistan and Afghan National Security Forces.[48] The point of this endeavor was to determine the sources of community instability that the insurgency fed off of that, if addressed, would lead to a sustainable model for local security. These engagement efforts were helped by additional SOF enablers: civil affairs members, military information support operations units, and cultural support teams (e.g., women's outreach).[49]

ALP recruits were nominated by village elders, vetted by the district chief of police and SOF team, and then had their names forwarded to the Ministry of Interior for a final check. Village elders vouched for each recruit's character, and each recruit agreed to abstain from drugs and to undergo a SOF-administered training regimen. To protect against fraud, recruits had their photo taken, provided a detailed family history, and were biometrically enrolled by having their iris scanned. Recruits then began a several-week term of training involving weapons familiarization and safety, physical endurance, small unit tactics, ethics, checkpoint construction, and the duties that came from

Figure 8.2 The door sign of the Village Stability Coordination Center in Kandahar Province in 2012. Once the Village Stability Operations / Afghan Local Police program was activated in 2010, the special operators began emphasizing local knowledge, cultural awareness, and respect for Afghan values instead of violence. (Courtesy of the author)

being a member of a local protective force. Once trained, the new ALP members reported to the ALP district commander who answered in turn to the district chief of police.[50] In addition to uniforms, ALP also received trucks and motorcycles for mobility, and those at vulnerable checkpoints sometimes received PKM machine guns. Each ALP member received a regular salary, which was slightly less than a regular ANP paycheck, and logistical and security support from the district chief of police to ensure a basic level of government control of these forces.

In order to better connect these local stability efforts with district, provincial, and national initiatives, SOF needed relationships with Afghans at all levels of the government. They had to be able to reach as many villages as possible, continually liaise and embed with government officials, conduct political action, and exercise persistent presence and performance. To do this, SOF used District Augmentation Teams, Provincial Augmentation Teams, regional Village Stability Coordination Centers, and the Village Stability National Coordination Center to partner with Afghan officials and to undertake essential nonkinetic stabilization tasks to improve governance, connect villages to the central government, and facilitate development programs.[51] Personnel assigned to these positions—typically Afghan Hands who had multiple military tours in Afghainstan—focused on the key political tasks required to defeat the Taliban's political program as well as supplementing other VSO operations. This integrated approach blended civil and military approaches with a detailed understanding of the Afghan human terrain and a political action arm that was able to influence Afghan officials.

Evaluating Village Stability Operations and the Afghan Local Police

As with any new initiative, initial implementation of VSO/ALP across Afghanistan encountered some difficulties. Some SOF units simply rolled existing militias into the ALP program or used them exclusively as security to protect checkpoints rather than to protect villagers. Eventually, many of these problematic ALP units were either disbanded, recertified, or re-formed in some manner consistent with VSO/ALP planning. In areas where the program was implemented properly, significant security, political, and development effects were felt relatively quickly.[52] In one RAND study, violence levels initially increased as teams embedded in the district, but after five months, the rate of attacks decreased to pre-embed levels and continued to decline. Five months later, the rate of attacks was "statistically significantly below pre-embed levels despite the ongoing presence of the SOF team actively contesting the insurgency."[53] Additionally, once the number of ALP members had reached the tipping point to make security an enduring reality and not a temporary condition, economic activity increased and informal and formal local governance improved significantly.[54] Having successfully organized local communities through directly embedding with them, SOF units were able to actively enlist villagers in their own defense and empower elders to conduct local governance. The cumulative effect of doing so enabled local Afghans to resist Taliban intimidation and brought them closer to the Afghan government by creating space for governance and development activities to take place. Unable to effectively mobilize the population, the Taliban increasingly resorted to suicide attacks, assassinations, and insider attacks. With the Afghan people actively enlisting in their own defense, the Taliban began finding it increasingly difficult to win.

The efforts of VSO/ALP in Shahid-e-Hasas District, Uruzgan Province, in 2010 show well what the program could do when implemented properly. By the end of 2006, the insurgency had surrounded Forward Operating Base (FOB) Cobra. Insurgent fighters had mined the main roads between the base and the surrounding district and were emboldened by their greater numbers, stronger discipline, and the foreign fighters that had joined them on the battlefield. As a result, local villagers fled the area, enlisted with Taliban forces, or were coerced into working for them. Beginning in 2010, there was a concerted effort by US and Afghan forces to push out beyond FOB Cobra, engage local leaders, and raise ALP forces. It began by increasing the number of Special Forces teams in the area from one to four and establishing small operating bases throughout the district's valleys and mountain passes. These soldiers operated as the forward edge of FOB Cobra, engaging local communities and establishing an enduring presence in areas that had never known it. Once constant contact with village elders was created, the ALP recruiting process began, and regular *shuras* were convened with area villages to explain the initiative and to identify sources of tribal, economic, and village grievances that alienated the people from their government. As the work progressed, what began in fits and starts cascaded into success as area villagers joined the ALP program, accepted a regular paycheck, embraced the pride of wearing the uniform of a respected force, and used their local knowledge to protect their own community.

As the police established checkpoints at bridge crossings, at valley choke points, at bazaar shop entrances, and in key villages, the Taliban were slowly squeezed out of the area. The district chief of police, who had worked in the provincial capital of Tarin Kowt as a police officer, led the ANP and was in charge of the local ALP program. He visited local *shuras* to promote the program, and area elders respected him because he was one of their own. He also had resources—pay, weapons, and other support—and this gave him the respect of the community and the ability to help his people in a direct and positive manner. As the program grew in the surrounding districts, roads that had been impassable because of the insurgency opened up, commerce reemerged, and the signs of a community wresting off insurgent oppression abounded. As much as the ALP program removed the freedom of movement for insurgent fighters through constructing and operating a network of checkpoints, it also enlisted the population in their own defense, robbing the insurgency of a ready-made recruiting pool of poor and unemployed military-age males.

By 2012, the district of Shahid-e-Hasas had largely been pacified due to the success of the Village Stability Operations / Afghan Local Police program. There were over 380 ALP members in the district working alongside 120 ANP members and 60 Afghan National Army soldiers at over 40 checkpoints at bazaars, key geographical points, and major roads. Efforts were underway to raise the authorized local police levels beyond 400 to about 450. Although some work remained to be done north of the district in Dai Kundi Province, the area was largely free of the Taliban, and while the insurgents still attempted to get traction with the villagers, the fact the local population enthusiastically participated in the VSO program really demonstrated who was winning.[55]

The VSO/ALP program was initially intended to run for five years with the goal of recruiting 30,000 ALP members by 2015. Each selected district was authorized a *tashkil* (paid position) of 300 ALP members with the goal of 100 out of a total of 398 districts countrywide benefiting from the program. Four months after the initial approval of the program, which had been in August 2010, approximately 3,000 ALP members were in 15 different districts. A year later, this number had grown to approximately 10,000 in 57 districts. By mid-2012, nearly 17,000 ALP members were in over 80 districts, and by January 2013, that number had increased to approximately 19,600 ALP members in more than 100 districts. As the program developed, the number of authorized ALP members per district was adjusted and additional districts were added to the program. By early 2013, the number of ALP members was expected to grow to approximately 22,000 in July 2013 and to 30,000 by July 2015.[56] In February 2013, US officials announced that the Afghan government had agreed to extend the VSO/ALP program another five years to 2020 and to support an increase in ALP numbers to 45,000. Subsequent SOF planning envisioned the complete transfer of control and logistical support of VSO/ALP to the Afghans by the fall of 2014.[57] While the substantial increase in ALP numbers indicates that the program enjoyed broad support within Afghanistan, it was not without its problems.

As with most Afghan security forces, there were concerns about potential human rights abuses by ALP members.[58] One mitigating factor in this respect was that since the ALP members answered to local elders and protected their own home villages, abuses were limited since some local accountability existed. Additionally, efforts were continuously made by SOF to prevent abuses from taking place through effective recruiting and training as well as fostering a culture of the rule of law. All ALP members were registered with the Ministry of Interior and also received ethical training in how to work with community residents. When abuses took place, it was relatively easy to identify those responsible.

Additionally, concerns about fostering militias and empowering warlords were central to the VSO program as it was being created. In this respect, SOF adopted several safeguards to prevent this from taking place. ALP forces were drawn from the communities they protected in a way that balanced tribal affiliations and village clusters, preventing one group from dominating others. All logistical support, including pay, weapons, vehicles, and uniforms, was controlled by the ANP, to which ALP reported. This arrangement mitigated the growth of militias by allowing the state to retain control of its resources.

Additionally, ALP was organized as a defensive force, which meant it received weapons consistent with a local protective force such as AK-47s, which most Afghans already possessed. As a program that confronted the insurgency militarily, politically, and economically, VSO harnessed the Afghan people against the Taliban in a manner that was more sustainable than alternative approaches since the people were successfully enlisted in their own defense in a manner they supported.

A key challenge for the VSO/ALP program was providing the logistical support ALP members required: pay, weapons, fuel, uniforms, vehicles, spare parts, and building materials, among other items. Since local ANP officials were charged with distributing these supplies and support, implementation was sometimes inconsistent. Local ANP leaders, including district and provincial chiefs of police, would sometimes sell equipment intended for the ALP program, horde items, keep pay intended for ALP members, or otherwise avoid fully supporting the program.[59] Even if equipment and pay were going to be distributed, the isolated nature of some ALP districts caused timely assistance to be delayed. Additionally, because of low literacy rates and limited training, administrative support to ALP logistics was frequently inadequate unless SOF personnel were directly involved. As districts achieved their assigned ALP quota or security conditions improved and became sustainable, SOF teams would transition either the Village Stability Platform (VSP), the site SOF used to conduct VSO/ALP, or the district to an Afghan unit. Once SOF departed and transitioned to an oversight posture, logistical support became more difficult as Afghans assumed greater responsibility. Additionally, as active SOF oversight diminished, ALP performance became difficult to monitor, leading to some decline in effectiveness.[60]

Even though the VSO/ALP program was innovative, its effectiveness was still evaluated in a manner consistent with the culture of the US military, and this posed some problems. One metric that was frequently used to determine VSO success was the number of ALP recruits in a specific area. If a SOF unit had met its allotted quota for ALP members, the unit's activities were deemed a success; however, the VSO emphasized a holistic approach to defeating the Taliban insurgency. Other efforts such as political outreach, tribal mediation, and other nonkinetic approaches were often not measured adequately. Thus, determining the effectiveness of these types of actions was difficult and especially challenging to generalize across all SOF units throughout Afghanistan. In this respect, the relatively easy metric of the size of the ALP program became a substitute for counterinsurgency success. While traditional measurements of a unit's actions such as inputs and outputs provided a useful metric of the unit's achievements, it was an incomplete method of measuring progress against an insurgency. The central goal of a counterinsurgency strategy must be how the community responds to both the counterinsurgents' actions and the insurgents' actions. In this respect, the behavior of an indigenous community indicates how truly effective operations are, for they accurately reflect the outcome of actions. When villagers take the proactive decision to enlist in their own defense as well as participate in governance and development activities, they make a conscious choice to reject the insurgency both because they want to and because they can. Determining the tipping point of when a villager or community makes this decision to join the government and reject the insurgency, and the right mix of inputs and outputs to achieve this outcome, is the greatest challenge a unit confronts when it comes to measuring success against an insurgency. Unless the community participates in its own security, governance, and development, all actions by the counterinsurgent force, no matter how aggressive, will be ephemeral and the military campaign will be no closer to victory. While SOF had done much to adapt to Afghan cultural priorities as well as the unique characteristics of the insurgency, they still could not fully divorce themselves from their own institutional culture of measuring success in a traditional military manner.

///

When US Special Operations Forces first arrived in Afghanistan, they encountered an Afghan cultural context that matched both their doctrine and their earlier history. However, pursuing a narrowly defined counterterrorism mission eventually gave way to a renewed Taliban insurgency, and SOF were forced to rethink their approach not just to counterterrorism specifically but also to counterinsurgency more broadly. The central insight developed by SOF leaders was that local security in Afghanistan was something that had to be done *with* the population, not *to* it, and that enlisting villagers in their own defense in a manner that empowered community decision makers would be necessary to defeat the Taliban holistically. This required SOF to reorganize to better confront the Taliban's political strategy and military capabilities. By reengineering their approach to focus on a bottom-up stabilization strategy, SOF became more like the Taliban in organization, resources, tactics, and measures of success. In many respects, the process SOF went through is well captured by four key questions that former ISAF commander General Stanley McChrystal put forth about SOF in his March/April 2013 interview in the journal *Foreign Affairs*: "Where is the enemy? Who is the enemy? Why does he fight? How can I defeat him?"[61] As one Special Forces officer summarized this transition: "My theory at the time was pressure, pursue, punish. My three Ps now: presence, patience and persistence."[62] Reflecting the success of this new strategy in Afghanistan, then-commander of US Special Operations Command Admiral William McRaven said that the Village Stability Operations / Afghan Local Police program was the "the most promising effort we have in Afghanistan right now."[63] In adopting a strategy informed by the Taliban's structure and then using it against the insurgents, Special Operations Forces were able to leverage the strength of Afghan culture and society to confront the Islamist movement in a holistic manner, which fundamentally shifted the course of the Afghanistan War in favor of the Afghans.

CHAPTER NINE Leaving Afghanistan

Lieutenant Colonel Benjamin F. Jones, USAF

Khordi burdi . . . na khordi murdi. (If you grabbed it, ate it, or looted it, you won it. If you didn't, you lost it.)
—Afghan proverb

In the movies, wars always end with a battle, or a treaty, or perhaps a homecoming parade. In Afghanistan, it ended with *inteqal*, or "transition"—a confusing, multiyear, partially successful handover of security duties from the International Security Assistance Force (ISAF) coalition to the Afghan government and the Afghan National Security Forces (ANSF). A political process driven principally by the White House, it began when President Barack Obama announced his troop surge in 2009 and insisted that the troops would begin coming home starting in July 2011. True to his word, the US president and his ISAF partners began a drawdown that summer and steadily withdrew forces until December 2014, when combat operations officially ended. In coalition capitals, transition boiled down to troop withdrawals, but in the mind of the coalition commander, transition meant handing over the war to an Afghan military and security forces that were well prepared to wage it.

This chapter explains how ISAF left Afghanistan. In the end, transition occurred because everyone wanted it to, but all the key players—American and Afghan politicians, as well as each nation's military leaders—saw transition differently and tried to shape the process according to their own goals. For President Hamid Karzai, a successful transition meant full sovereign control over his nation, guaranteed future international support, and a military and government that could defend the nation without interference from enemies or friends. For President Obama, transition meant a steady withdrawal of troops and a battle handover of security functions to the Afghans according to a timeline set in Washington. Military commanders in both Afghanistan and the United States wanted the drawdowns to occur as well, but only when conditions on the ground ensured the changes would stick. These different approaches were never fully reconciled.

Adding to these differences in interests and end states were problems of politics, bureaucracy, and culture. For even on matters on which all parties agreed, there were arguments over process that steadily inhibited transition. ISAF needed the Afghans to take over the job of securing the country so that neither al Qaeda nor the Taliban could control it. This was a goal that the Afghans shared (indeed, they had considerably more at stake in the matter than the Americans did), but the two parties' methods for achieving that objective differed radically. Afghan leaders faced crippling poverty, at least one hostile neighbor, and a political system that sought stability through personal fealty and financial patronage. President Karzai's fragile coalition government (which relied on a web of bargains with Tajiks, Uzbeks, and disparate Pashtun groups that would make pre–World War I European politics look easy by comparison) needed one resource above all others to keep key players from jumping ship: money. Thus, in the transition negotiations, the Afghans pursued the strategy hinted at in the above proverb—"Khordi burdi . . . na khordi murdi"—using whatever tools were available to maximize the future flow of dollars into the cancerously corrupt Afghan economy.

The ISAF coalition—a cobbled-together entity authorized by the United Nations but dominated by NATO—had its own key players to satisfy, and they all wanted a say in when and how military forces left Afghanistan. And here, a variety of overlapping bureaucracies had neither the obligation nor the will to cooperate with each other. NATO had one set of timelines, checklists, and reporting requirements; the United Nations had others. The US government made some transition decisions unilaterally, worked others bilaterally with the Afghans, and brought still others to NATO and the non-NATO ISAF partners for resolution or endorsement. Layered on top of these already-ossified decision-making bodies were new, but equally ineffective institutional hybrids like the Joint Afghan-NATO Inteqal Board (JANIB) and the Joint Coordination and Monitoring Board (JCMB)—bureaucratic Frankensteins whose failings will soon be apparent. The West's need for timelines and transparency created rules, checklists, and countless stakeholder meetings of governments in 50 coalition capitals around the world but also sent mixed messages to the Afghans, who were themselves trying to drive the process according to their own priorities. Like so many other things in the overly rationalized processes of Western bureaucracy, the results looked good on a PowerPoint slide but rarely translated into effective policy on the ground. One full year after the end of combat operations in Afghanistan, a residual military force of 10,600 Americans remained in Afghanistan, along with approximately 2,000 troops from Germany, Italy, and other nations.[1] Billions in promised aid backed up and sustained the Afghan army and police.

Envisioning Transition

To understand how ISAF left Afghanistan, one must first grasp how it came, and with what legal authorities and permissions. As soon as the Taliban collapsed, one of the first priorities of the newly created ISAF coalition was to codify in writing the relationships and authorities that would govern the international forces' relationship with the Afghan transitional government. Thus, on January 4, 2002, representatives of both parties signed the Military Technical Agreement (MTA), which remained the governing document for the ISAF presence in Afghanistan for the duration of the war. The MTA gave ISAF "complete and unimpeded freedom of movement throughout the territory and airspace of Afghanistan" as well as unrestricted use of the entire electromagnetic spectrum. It made ISAF free from all taxation and customs fees and rendered all personnel immune from any Afghan legal process. It gave the Afghan Interim Authority responsibility for maintaining law and order in the country, but gave the ISAF commander "the authority, without interference or permission, to do all that the Commander judges necessary and proper, including the use of military force, to protect the ISAF and its Mission."[2]

With this agreement, the Afghan Interim Administration signed away the sovereignty of Afghanistan before it even truly possessed it. This may have seemed a reasonable bargain in 2002, when ISAF was restricted to just 80 bases for its 5,000 troops between Kabul and Bagram Air Base, but over the years, as the ISAF mission and force structure grew, so too did ISAF's reach. In 2003, the UN authorized ISAF to expand across the entire country (despite its inability to do any such thing), and by 2008, there were 63,000 international troops in Afghanistan.[3] In 2009, when ISAF adopted a counterinsurgency mission, managing governance, development, and rule of law all became military tasks too. Thus, by the end of President Karzai's first term, ISAF had legal authority to intervene in almost every element of the Afghan government, as long its actions could be loosely connected to one of the many components of ISAF's wide-reaching mandate. Even more frustrating to Karzai was the fact that the MTA made the ISAF commander the only—and final—authority regarding the interpretation of the agreement, which gave the Afghans no way to amend it.[4] When a new ISAF commander arrived in Afghanistan in 2009 to oversee the implementation of the counterinsurgency strategy, he had more resources and fewer constraints than any other person in the country, including the US ambassador and the Afghan president.

Future historians focusing on an American-centric view of the war will probably name December 1, 2009, as the start of the transition process, for it was on that date that President Obama announced the 18-month troop surge that, he claimed, would "accelerate handing over responsibility to Afghan forces, and allow us to begin the transfer of our forces out of Afghanistan in July of 2011."[5] But, in fact, President Karzai had been talking about an ISAF departure for almost a year at that point. Perhaps because of the steady loss of control over the activities of the foreign forces in his country, President Karzai made sovereignty the centerpiece of his 2009 reelection campaign and asserted repeatedly thereafter that the Afghan government—and not ISAF—should determine the focus and scope of international assistance in Afghanistan. Following his reelection—which was accompanied by massive fraud and an aborted runoff election that soured US-Afghan relations badly—the UN and British ambassadors to Afghanistan worked with Karzai to put together a transition plan. Two international conferences followed in 2010—the first in Kabul and the second in Lisbon—which outlined a "sovereignty agenda" that would gradually give Karzai's government more authority, capability, and resources in both domestic and international affairs.

The UN-sponsored Kabul conference in 2010 was the more important of the two meetings, for it was there that participants agreed to the Kabul Process—a multiyear effort to facilitate "Afghan leadership and ownership" of the major functions of government.[6] Among other things, the Kabul Process committed member states to help train Afghan security forces, strengthen civilian institutions, enable sustainable economic growth, begin a peace and reintegration policy, and bolster Afghanistan's regional relations.[7] Most important for handing power back to the Afghans was the agreement to draw up a "phased transition plan jointly developed between the Afghan government and NATO."[8] NATO Secretary General Anders Fogh Rasmussen expressed what all members sought: "We have to make sure that . . . transition to lead Afghan responsibility should be irreversible," he said. "We'll not be in a position to take responsibility back afterwards. That would be a disaster."[9]

General Petraeus agreed. A few weeks later at Lisbon, the NATO countries set down some rough milestones for transition. As the president had demanded, it would start with an announcement in early 2011, and the Lisbon summit's final declaration also affirmed that "transition will be conditions-based, not calendar-driven, and will not equate to withdrawal of ISAF troops." Even more important than the inclusion of the "conditions-based" caveat was the schizophrenic wording regarding the transition's end date: "Looking to the end of 2014, Afghan forces will be assuming full responsibility for security across the whole of Afghanistan."[10] From the point of view of the US and Afghan militaries, having such loose language put more time on the clock, time that would be necessary to further weaken the Taliban, and allow the Afghan forces in more challenging areas to become proficient at prosecuting the war. But in the end, the Lisbon Declaration would cause extensive friction within the ISAF coalition in the ensuing months, as various parties tried to turn the "conditions-based" caveat and the language on end dates toward their own purposes.

Envisioning transition was relatively easy in theory but effecting it in practice proved difficult because of the differences between Afghanistan's goals and those of the various members of the coalition. From the start, transition was burdened by the numerous, overlapping bureaucratic institutions operating with conflicting mandates and disparate purposes. Overseeing the entire Kabul Process, of which the security transition was just one part, was the Joint Coordination Monitoring Board (JCMB)—a governing body created in 2006 that was co-chaired by the Afghan minister of finance and a UN representative.[11] However, the factor most relevant for transition—security—would not be assessed by the JCMB; that task fell to an entirely separate entity: the Joint Afghan-NATO Inteqal Board (JANIB), which included the ISAF commander, the senior NATO representative for ISAF, an Afghan representative, and the ambassadors of the various coalition nations. There were other competing organizations as well. Inside Afghanistan, President Karzai created his own transition office—the Transition Coordinating Commission. And since NATO's leadership wanted independent information on the security conditions in the country, it required its own quarterly NATO transition report, which was generated entirely by ISAF and without input from the Afghans. The result was four different entities, with four separate leadership structures, following different metrics, all which felt they had the right to direct or at least contribute to decisions on transition.

Adding to the problems were the differing agendas of each participant in the process. Perhaps the most authoritative voice on transition at the outset was that of the ISAF commander, General David H. Petraeus, who had easy access to the senior leadership of NATO and every country involved. With over three decades in uniform, Petraeus's principal concerns were security oriented: Which provinces were safe enough to withstand a withdrawal of ISAF forces? Which cities had a sufficient police presence? Which territories provided the Taliban resources or access to major population centers? Where were the Afghan National Army and Police reasonably effective and where were they not?

The Afghans shared these goals in principle, but they had other, and in their minds, more pressing concerns. Chief among these was how to keep Western dollars flowing into the country after the coalition departed, and to turn transition into a long-term plan for investment in, and support for, Afghanistan. To advance Afghan interests, President Karzai selected Dr. Ashraf Ghani Amadzai—a former Johns Hopkins professor, World Bank executive, and international economic development scholar—to lead the Afghan Transition Coordinating Commission (TCC). A deeply intellectual man, Ghani seemed the perfect choice, for he had strong connections in Washington and had also helped craft the Afghan Constitution.[12] Thus, he could marshal legal and academic arguments for why more money and decisions should be channeled through the Afghans rather than controlled by the various donor nations.

Ghani took a very different approach to transition than General Petraeus. He acknowledged that security was a precondition for a successful transition, but argued that sustainable security would only come when the various provinces had the infrastructure for prosperity: jobs, roads, education, health and sanitation facilities. A development-based transition process, he argued, would not only allow ISAF forces to leave; it would provide sufficient long-term peace and prosperity to ensure they would never have to return. To plan for this more expansive transition mission, Ghani proposed a TCC staff of several dozen economists, engineers, development specialists, local planners, and experts in banking and international aid. The United States agreed to pay for the staff and transferred the necessary funds to the Afghan Ministry of Finance so that Ghani's staff could get to work.

Ashraf Ghani was a learned scholar and a master negotiator, but his selection as the Afghan lead for transition had drawbacks as well. As a prominent Ahmadzai Pashtun, he had been one of Karzai's principal rivals for the presidency and had his eye on the 2014 election. He thus kept his distance from the Karzai government, which he believed to be a wholly corrupt criminal enterprise. Even while serving as the TCC chairman, he refused a salary or formal position in Karzai's administration so that he could present himself as his own man in a future election. This set off a feud within the Afghan government, and Karzai's finance minister responded by withholding the US-donated funds for the transition staff because Afghan law barred dispersing money to a nongovernmental office. (Considering the massive corruption around the Kabul Bank, and the documented outflows of funds out of the country, the stubborn enforcement of the law in this case left coalition members shaking their heads in amazement.)[13] As a result of these tensions within the Afghan government, the Afghan contribution to transition was hobbled from the start. Instead of a staff of 60 experts, Ghani had only 7 young, well-educated Afghan assistants, to whom he rarely delegated decision-making authority.

Ghani's personality also slowed the process. He distrusted the Afghan military and seemed genuinely disinterested in its need for decisions, which slowed transition to the speed of one man. Petraeus's staff often found themselves waiting while Dr. Ghani personally read over transition implementation documents, and planning ground to a halt if the chairman was out of the country. Furthermore, powerful Afghan ministers were unwilling to cross Dr. Ghani and delayed making key decisions unless they received authorization from him. As a result, key transition deadlines were missed or adjusted constantly.

Turf wars within ISAF also hampered the transition process, and here the friction was not between nations but between the military and civilians. The fact that transition planning fell mainly to the military commander confused and frustrated diplomats and political leaders in capitals throughout the world because they found themselves with little means to influence events—events they viewed as largely political and economic in nature. Meanwhile, coalition military leaders often bristled when diplomats asked questions about military strategy, budgets, and troop levels. Civil-military friction also hampered the American leadership, between President Obama and his commander in Afghanistan in particular, where there was regular misunderstanding and a profound lack of trust.[14]

Planning Begins

Once the Lisbon summit had set down the basic parameters of transition, General Petraeus ordered his deputy chief of staff for operations, Major General John Nicholson, to begin planning. General Nicholson's first step was to create an ISAF military transition planning group—the Strategic Transition and Assessment Group (STAG)—and in March 2011, he appointed British Royal Marine Brigadier Timothy Bevis as its director. Bevis's group's job was to evaluate security in each province, liaise with the Afghans, and figure out exactly how to hand over operations to a far less capable military in the middle of a war. Also, because transition was both a security and political matter, General Nicholson and Brigadier Bevis worked closely with NATO's senior civilian representative, Ambassador Mark Sedwill, who provided a link to the coalition embassies in Kabul. But the key decision-making body remained the JANIB. That meant that Nicholson's boss, General Petraeus, and Ambassador Sedwill had an outsized influence on the process. The various nations' embassy staffs would be kept informed, but they would not actively participate in preparing their bosses for key decisions. The US embassy staff in Kabul, located just across the street from the sprawling ISAF headquarters, complained regularly that they were being left out of the transition decisions.[15]

The military's proactive approach to transition planning also caused problems with NATO and President Obama. Even though the NATO coalition had agreed at Lisbon that the pace of transition would be determined by conditions rather than a specific timeline, it had also agreed that Afghan security forces would have full responsibility for security by the end of 2014. These two understandings quickly came to grief as both sides could read the Lisbon Declaration as they wished, with military leaders usually emphasizing the need for flexibility and civilians typically interpreting the timeline more strictly.

That incompatibility first appeared in early March 2011 when General Petraeus presented a tentative transition timeline to NATO leaders in Brussels and discussed his vision for how ISAF would hand over security to the Afghans. In a surprise to the ambassadors, Petraeus's timeline assumed that transition would *start* in every Afghan province by the end of 2014, but would only be complete when the security conditions permitted a full handover. In his mind, this was entirely congruous with the Lisbon Declaration's tortuous language. But it was not what President Obama had in mind, and US permanent representative to NATO Ivo Daalder reacted. He first asked General Petraeus to explain how this transition plan "squared with the agreement of NATO and ISAF Heads of Government that Afghanistan have full responsibility for security throughout the country by the end of 2014," but "received no clarification." Daalder then cabled this "discrepancy" to Washington.[16] Having seen Daalder's cable, President Obama raised the issue during a National Security Council meeting on March 3, and made clear to Secretary of Defense Robert Gates that transition would begin in July 2011 and would be complete by the end of 2014.[17]

Later attempts to explain that a calendar-based transition process risked irreversibility fell on deaf ears.[18] President Obama was intent on recovering the surge forces and ending the war according to the timeline laid out in his 2009 West Point speech. The specific security trends in Afghanistan, the Lisbon agreement's wording about "conditions based" transition, and perhaps even the overall success of the military campaign against the Taliban all became less important than bringing the troops home.

This was exactly what General Petraeus had worried would happen. As commander of the Multi-National Force in Iraq, he had watched a hurried transition of power to the Iraqis and had known that it would not result in sustainable institutions or a workable government. Now in Kabul, he warned in meeting after meeting that rushing transition would lead to failure. As he testified in front of Congress in March 2011, he made the same point again, arguing that the transition must be "irreversible. . . . We'll get one shot at transition, and we need to get it right."[19] His warnings went unheeded.

On March 21, 2011, the Afghan New Year holiday known as Nowruz, President Karzai announced the first transition "tranche," which would begin its handover that July. The first group contained two of the most peaceful provinces—Bamyan and Panjshir (which would transition in their entirety), as well as the cities of Herat, Mazar-e Sharif, Lashkar Gah, and Mehtar Lam. Most important, Kabul Province would also begin transition, except for the restive Surobi District, which would remain under ISAF control. While this first transition tranche had been coordinated with ISAF well in advance, what came next was not. Now that transition was about to begin, "our partnership with the international community will change," President Karzai insisted in his televised address. "Improvements in the lives of our people are the important preconditions for our partnership with NATO and the United States. The functions of parallel structures, the Provincial Reconstruction Teams, militias, Private Security Contractors, and arrest and house searches must be stopped. These are the prerequisites of our partnership and transition."[20] With these preconditions and prerequisites, President Karzai sought to determine the pace of transition and to link it less to security and more to funding sources, as Ashraf Ghani had been recommending for some time.

This was not the first time ISAF had heard Karzai's complaints about "parallel structures"—the term he used for any service provider in Afghanistan that he could not control directly. While the Military Technical Agreement gave ISAF the right to contract directly with Afghans for services and supplies (and to have such contractors rendered immune from prosecution and taxation), President Karzai worried—with good reason—that many of the Afghan private contractors hired for road security could easily morph into militias that would challenge his rule. Furthermore, Karzai badly wanted to dismantle the Provincial Reconstruction Teams, which were hybrid military-civilian development teams located throughout the country. In Karzai's mind, the PRTs were rivals to local government, because with their expansive resources, they attracted more local legitimacy than his own ministries. In the end, Karzai and the coalition reached a muddled compromise: the PRTs would remain in each province until the withdrawal date of the ground troops, and their priorities and projects would be coordinated with the provincial governor. Even with this compromise, the PRTs remained a sticking point throughout transition, with the Afghans, coalition military leaders, and diplomats disagreeing on their purpose, scope, and issues of control.

Following the Afghan president's Nowruz announcement, detailed staff work began. Instead of only meeting with Dr. Ghani, ISAF staffers now began reaching out to the various Afghan ministries to formulate plans for how to hand over authority in the various provinces. Bureaucratic hurdles appeared almost immediately. Planning for transition required direct meetings between STAG and the security ministries, working relationships with government officials, and shared office spaces for meetings and planning. After over a decade of war, those relationships existed, but most did not exist in the ISAF headquarters. Since this was a strategic headquarters, most of its activities were aimed upward—toward NATO, Washington, US Central Command in Florida, and the senior levels of the Afghan government. Almost all the day-to-day cooperation between ISAF and the security ministries happened through two entirely separate and subordinate commands: NATO Training Mission-Afghanistan (NTM-A), which had the job of recruiting, resourcing, and training the Afghan army and police, and ISAF Joint Command (IJC), which ran the day-to-day operations of the war. Although both commands were located in Kabul—indeed, both were within five miles of the ISAF headquarters—they might as well have been in another country because the staff officers in these subordinate headquarters closely guarded their relationships with the Afghans. If the transition staff wanted to reach out to the security ministries, they would have to work through NTM-A and IJC.

In the end, instead of creating whole new networks for STAG, Brigadier Bevis simply incorporated the liaisons from the subordinate headquarters. As a result, by the end of the summer, transition planning meetings could involve up to a half dozen general officers from ISAF, NTM-A, and IJC alone. When combined with the representatives from the Afghan Ministry of Defense (which ran the army), Ministry of Interior (which ran the police), intelligence service, and Transition Coordination Commission, transition meetings were so full of senior brass and interpreters that they became unwieldy. But getting the meetings to happen at all was the first aim, and by July, they were a regular weekly occurrence.[21]

Bureaucracy also slowed the Afghans' activities, but it was a bureaucracy of a different sort. Within the coalition, everyone wanted to be in charge or at least have input; none of the meetings could happen unless all the relevant parties were present and represented. Among the Afghans, no one wanted to be charge—except Dr. Ghani. And in ways completely traditional to Afghan society and culture, Afghanistan's government was highly centralized and hierarchical. Nothing happened without a letter authorizing it, and gaining approval for even a minor decision often required a phone conversation or visit with a high-ranking official. As a result, even after President Karzai ordered transition to begin and Dr. Ghani authorized meetings between the security ministries and ISAF, very little work actually took place.[22] With this latest snag, the coalition planners began to realize that it was going to be impossible to hand Afghanistan off to the Afghans without the Afghans.

Because of these challenges, planning for the first two tranches of transitioning provinces proceeded slowly. As paperwork requested by the Afghans worked its way through drafts, then legal review, then translation and distribution for approval, all STAG could do was hold more meetings and work on developing relationships. And as ISAF assessments of which provinces were ready for transition remained primarily focused on security, they continued to diverge from Afghan assessments, which focused heavily on issues of aid and development. Making things worse was the fact that when General Petraeus returned to Washington in June 2011, President Obama refused his request to extend the surge forces beyond their original one-year authorization.[23] As General John Allen took over command of ISAF, he had fewer forces than his predecessor. But despite indications that enemy activity was declining, Dr. Ghani's dream of a development-focused transition plan now seemed impossible due to the certainty of diminishing ISAF forces.[24] A handover of security responsibility became the only goal, and conditions-based planning had become a fiction. The calendar drove the process. Perhaps to save face, or just to prioritize their efforts, ISAF planners began speaking of two separate processes: transition, which referred exclusively to security, and transformation, which referred to all the aid, development, and governance requests they had neither the time nor the resources to address.

By mid-2011, the transition planning process was functioning at the working levels; though, in typical Afghan fashion, the lines of authority and communication were hard to discern—at least for Westerners. Planning meetings had representatives from all the key coalition organizations and Afghan security ministries. Brigadier Bevis remained ISAF's point person for transition, but on the Afghan side, the leadership was somewhat less clear. Ashraf Ghani remained Karzai's appointed transition coordinator, but his representatives rarely came to the meetings.

There's a common expression in Afghanistan that "the West has the watches but we [Afghans] have the time," and that was certainly true concerning transition.[25] By the start of tranche 2 planning, President Obama had already thrown out conditions-based decisions and forced ISAF to adopt a hastier approach. President Karzai, realizing that Obama wanted to hurry the process while not making the economic concessions he sought, began to delay his public announcements. With the two presidents now wholly divorced from conditions-based transition, Afghan military input to transition planning broke down completely. In the end, the tranche 2 decisions were made even before the Afghan army had the opportunity to offer an assessment. As a result, the NATO leadership made several major decisions regarding transition planning without any substantial input from the Afghan military or the very ISAF office charged with transition planning. This arrangement only further demonstrated to the Afghan generals that their participation in the working group was irrelevant since the tranche was determined without their recommendations. Thereafter, Petraeus's staff in Kabul found themselves in the difficult position of telling nervous Afghan generals that despite the language of Lisbon, the first condition of the transition's "conditions-based planning" was the calendar.[26] Ironically, the push for a faster pace made it more difficult for Afghan security ministries to take over control of their nation.[27]

Even though ISAF had lost the fight with President Obama and President Karzai on how quickly it must hand provinces over to the Afghans, it still managed to refine the four-stage process that was intended to keep the coalition engaged based on Afghanistan's military and police readiness while keeping the Afghans accountable for being ready to conduct operations at predictable times and increasing levels of complexity. In the first stage, the "local support" stage, the Afghan army and police would take formal control of the area and put up the Afghan flag, but would still have regular and extensive ISAF support and mentorship. During the second stage, "tactical support," the Afghan security forces would conduct small-unit operations, but activities with other units would still be coordinated by ISAF. In the third stage, "operational support," Afghan forces would be responsible for more and more of the coordination and route planning, and would handle major operations from the battalion up to the regional army command. The Afghan National Police would also take over security of the tranche's cities and towns from the Afghan National Army. The final stage was the "strategic support" stage. Forces at this point in the transition process would be integrated into the national campaign plan approved by the ministries in Kabul, and coalition forces would conduct only occasional missions outside their bases.

As Brigadier Bevis envisioned it, this incremental approach minimized risk, and allowed the Afghans the necessary time and training to organize, plan, and conduct a national-level campaign to secure Afghanistan from the Taliban. Additionally, each stage would naturally mean greater resources of vehicles, radios, weapons, and other capabilities. Conducted this way, transition would be gradual and attuned to the needs of the security forces on the ground. Had the four stages been adhered to, the transition may well have gone differently. But timelines in Washington and different priorities at the senior levels of the Afghan government drove the entire process, and the result was a quicker and riskier transition than either the US military or Afghan military would have wished.[28]

Handing Over the Flag

The first provinces to enter transition did so in July 2011, a year and a half after President Obama announced the surge, and the very week that General John Allen took command of ISAF from General David Petraeus. Unlike Petraeus, who argued explicitly against making transition the mission, General Allen saw little value in fighting what he could not change. He spoke often of transition as not only an essential element of his mission but the actual end state of the campaign. In fact, he made transition one of the four themes in his first message to his troops saying, "We will set the conditions to support the process of transition."[29] Under his leadership, President Obama got what he had demanded in 2009: a firm timeline and a gradual troop withdrawal. Six months after the first provinces began transitioning, President Karzai announced the second tranche. Succeeding announcements occurred in six-month increments with tranches 3 and 4 beginning in 2012 and the final tranche commencing in mid-2013. American troop levels dropped to 90,000 at the end of 2011 and stayed at that level through the middle of 2012. By the start of 2014, just 38,000 remained, and by the end of the year, only a residual force of 10,000 Americans was still in Afghanistan.[30] The Americans closed over 300 bases, turned the Provincial Reconstruction Teams over to the Afghans, and disposed of over $36 billion in military equipment, often by donating it to the Afghans or selling it at deeply discounted prices.[31] But just as General Petraeus had warned, these metrics were not real indicators of a successful transition. In ways eerily similar to Iraq, the military was good at sticking to timelines, but simply handing over the flag on time was no indication of Afghan readiness or capacity to take the lead for security across the country.

Even though the process of handing over the flag began as soon as Allen took command, it had been President Karzai, General Petraeus, and Ambassador Sedwill who determined the details of the first tranche, and they specifically designed it to be low risk. Most of the provinces to transition first—Kabul, Bamyan, and Panjshir—had no combat troops in them, and major cities like Herat, Mazar-e Sharif, and Kabul were already largely peaceful and under the control of the Afghans. Here, the problem was to make sure the Afghans noticed the change. To that end, ISAF organized transition ceremonies, and the military increased its CERP spending to ensure provincial governors would support the new (and substantially poorer) government in Kabul.[32]

Five provinces began transition as part of tranche 2, as well as specific districts in 11 others—some of which were still struggling with ongoing violence.[33] As with the first tranche, the driving factors in the selection were the lack of enemy activity, the preparedness of the Afghans to secure the areas, and ethnic balancing (to demonstrate that Pashtun areas were progressing as much as the rest of the country). ISAF resisted some of the choices—the city of Jalalabad, at the entrance to the famed Khyber Pass, in particular seemed a risky choice, but once the Afghan army and police had successfully secured the road leading to the pass, General Allen was glad to include it. As the Afghans took over in these areas in late December 2011, approximately 50 percent of the Afghan population's security became the responsibility of the Afghan National Security Forces.[34]

But unlike the early efforts, which had proceeded smoothly, "conditions-based" transition hit some snags in 2012. The pace of American withdrawals quickened, and throughout the year, the total number of American troops in Afghanistan declined from over 100,000 in 2011 to just 68,000. This helped reduce American deaths, which dropped from 418 to 310 for the year, but 2012 was still the third-deadliest year of the war for Americans.[35] Enemy-initiated attacks (ISAF's principal metric for violence) declined by a fraction compared to 2011, but steady attacks by the Taliban in June made it more violent than any previous June since the war began.[36] Fewer American troops also meant less contact with the Afghans and less ability to influence their behavior. Poppy production skyrocketed in 2012, growing from 115,000 hectares of cultivation to 180,000 hectares, according to US estimates.[37] With fewer Americans to shoot at, the Taliban began targeting the Afghan National Security Forces directly, and in 2012, the ANSF surpassed the ISAF coalition in casualties for the first time in the war.[38] In the fighting that year, 2,700 Afghan civilians died and almost 5,000 more were wounded (80 percent of these casualties were caused by the Taliban).[39] Asylum applications increased by 30 percent that year alone, with almost 50,000 Afghans asking for political refuge in the United States and elsewhere.[40]

A series of coalition-caused incidents also strained the transition process that year. In February 2012, American soldiers disposing of library materials from the Parwan prison mistakenly incinerated some religious texts, including copies of the Koran. Riots broke out in several cities across Afghanistan, killing 32 Afghans and wounding many more. The affair soon became politicized as Afghan lawmakers urged citizens to take to the streets, and in the wake of the violence, 13 coalition troops were killed by ANSF troops—the very troops the coalition was trying to transition security to.[41] The number of "insider attacks" (incidents where Afghan troops targeted coalition personnel) rose dramatically, and in 2012, 41 of these attacks took 57 American lives—the most of any year of the war.[42] One month after the riots, Staff Sergeant Robert Bales, an American soldier with several combat deployments and a history of drug use, killed 16 Afghan civilians and set some of their bodies on fire. While he was later sentenced to life in prison by a military court-martial, his atrocities further strained US-Afghan relations.[43]

As disruptive as these events were, they did not slow the now firmly "calendar-based" transition. The third tranche, which had begun in May 2012, was the most ambitious thus far; it included much of the heartland of the Taliban, including Kandahar city and portions of Khost, Kunar, Paktiya, and Paktika Provinces. Tranche 4 followed six months later and included the most troublesome parts of Ghazni and Wardak Provinces in the east, restive sections of Faryab and Badghis Provinces in the west, and the Kunduz-Baghlan corridor in the north. When General Allen handed command over to Marine General Joseph Dunford in February 2013, only the toughest district along the Pakistan border—the home of the pro-Taliban Ghilzai Pashtuns and the Haqqani network—had yet to begin the process.

Unsurprisingly, the coalition's ability to keep to a timeline set in Washington did not translate into calm or confidence on the ground. Uncertainty about the future, and in several districts, palpable fear, caused additional problems through 2013. Fewer international troops meant fewer dollars and less demand for services. As a result, real estate markets in Kabul declined, and a currency sell-off depleted reserves and drove up prices by as much as 25 percent. Over 100,000 more Afghans fled their homes for safer parts of the country in the first half of the year.[44] In 2013, 38 percent of Afghans felt the country was going in the "wrong direction"—up from 31 percent in 2012—and 46 percent reported "always" or "sometimes" fearing for their personal safety and that of their families.[45]

In fact, the Afghans' concerns were understandable, because security in the transitioning provinces varied. In 2014, the International Crisis Group conducted a detailed study of transition in four provinces and found that the "overall trend is one of escalating violence and insurgent attacks. . . . In all transitional areas there is a variety of unfinished business that may result in further violence post-2014." The best news came from turbulent Paktia Province, where pro-Taliban Ghilzai Pashtuns and the Haqqani network had a powerful presence. There, attacks along the road to Khost Province dropped to one-tenth of previous highs, and attacks in Dand and Patan Districts fell to just one-third of earlier levels. Even the provincial capital of Gardez saw a 25 percent reduction in violence. Coalition military operations dropped to just one-quarter of the number conducted in 2011, and while violence did not disappear, it moved away from the roads—where most Afghans lived—and into more-remote districts. When the Taliban attempted to halt traffic on key roads, they failed, and both civilian and government vehicles could pass during daylight hours, provided they had armed guards. But even with these improvements, local Afghans were skeptical the peace would last. "They are just keeping the Afghan government busy now with a few attacks," a tribal leader told analysts from the International Crisis Group in 2013. "They are waiting to make a big attack after 2014."[46]

The news from Kunar Province—home of the Korengal and Pech Valleys and the site of some of the fiercest and most regular fighting in the early years of the war—was mixed. Since the province began transition, security incidents in the capital of Asadabad had declined precipitously, and the presence of more Afghan security forces allowed civilians to travel safely on major roads that were too dangerous only a year prior. The province remained violent with roughly three to four attacks per day, but local bargains between the Afghan security forces and the Taliban led to an informal division of the province, with the government holding the provincial capital and most of the roads and the insurgents controlling the remote areas. Revenge killings occurred in some districts, but overall, having fewer Americans in the province seemed to make a difference. As one provincial official explained in 2013, "When more Americans came, we had more fighting."[47]

In Kandahar, the spiritual homeland of the Taliban, the news was troubling. The key southern province, which houses the ancient capital city of Afghanistan, was part of the third tranche that began transition in May 2012, and the most violent districts joined the process in mid-2013. The coalition kept 40,000 troops in the province but violence continued to escalate nonetheless, with levels of security incidents "rising to levels that exceeded even the peak years of troop surges." Provincial officials in Kandahar echoed Dr. Ghani's security-through-development argument and pleaded for more resources, but as troops began to depart, so too did the jobs that had come with them. One police officer lamented in 2013 that as many as 200,000 young men were now unemployed. "These young men will become thieves and insurgents and my forces must fight them," he said. In response to the coalition's departures, the ANSF flooded the urban areas with army and police, which kept the city relatively calm. Violence dropped to one-third of previous levels in the city and surrounding neighborhoods, but the insurgency grew stronger west of the city. Violence doubled in Maiwand District in 2013 and Panjwai became the most violent district in the country. Tribal disputes continued between the generally pro-Kabul Durrani Pashtuns and pro-Taliban Ghilzais—an expected outcome given the fact that these two tribal confederations have been warring regularly since before the founding of the Afghan state in the mid-18th century. Allegations of torture, kidnappings, summary executions, and sexual abuse of boys continued as well. "The problem is tribal," a Ghilzai elder told the ICG investigators after the police beat a boy to death in Arghandab District. "If they capture you, and you're from the wrong tribe, they can do anything to you."[48] Partly because of these problems, by April 2014, when transition was supposed to be in its final stages, the Department of Defense reported to Congress that every province in Afghanistan had begun transitioning but none had completed the process.[49]

Adding to the security troubles were political ones. With the Afghan Constitution barring President Karzai from a third term, there was no incumbent in the presidential elections held on April 5. The first round of voting showed a clear frontrunner—the urbane Tajik Dr. Abdullah Abdullah who had opposed Hamid Karzai in the previous election and now held a 13-point lead over his Pashtun rival, the former Transition Coordinating Commission chairman Dr. Ashraf Ghani. Even though Abdullah received 45 percent of the popular vote, he failed to capture a majority and a runoff began in June. The runoff election followed nearly the same pattern as the 2009 election; both sides accused the other of wholesale fraud and ample evidence for either claim lay in plain sight. When the runoff's preliminary results were released, they showed a dramatic reversal that gave a substantial lead to Dr. Ghani. The Abdullah campaign responded by arguing that vote tallies in pro-Ghani areas sometimes exceeded the total population estimates for those regions, and released voice recordings that implicated the head of the Afghan Independent Electoral Commission in orchestrating a Ghani victory. Abdullah Abdullah withdrew from the electoral process and threatened to create a parallel government—a move that could have easily pushed the country back into a Tajik-Pashtun civil war. Following a visit by Secretary Kerry and 96 other meetings by US diplomats with the key players, both sides agreed to a power-sharing government that appointed Ghani as president but ceded numerous powers to Abdullah, who would serve in the newly created position of chief executive officer.[50] Ghani was sworn in as president of Afghanistan on September 29, and he signed the Bilateral Security Agreement with the United States the very next day. Both parties agreed to a post-2014 American military presence of 10,000 troops that would stay in Afghanistan through 2016, and if President Ghani made progress on corruption, the funding would continue.

In the final months of 2014, the metrics showed a decline in violence, but the total number of security incidents for the year still exceeded the pre-surge levels of 2001–2009. Perhaps mindful of President Obama's oft-repeated promise to withdraw all forces by the end of 2014, in the final months of that year, the Taliban unleashed a spate of attacks across the country. Two Americans died in a bombing near Baghram Air Base, and insurgents on motorcycles gunned down the head of the Supreme Court Secretariat in Kabul. A teenage suicide bomber blew himself up during a school play about nonviolence and democracy, and other suicide bombers attacked army buses. Taliban insurgents also stormed compounds that housed foreign contractors, attacked those removing landmines from roads, and tried to assassinate the Kabul police chief and a women's rights activist. "What is going on in this country?" an Afghan mechanic asked a *Washington Post* reporter two weeks before President Obama's December 31 dead-

Figure 9.1 Secretary of State John Kerry works to broker a political settlement in the wake of the 2014 presidential election. After eight dozen meetings with US diplomats, Dr. Abdullah Abdullah (*left*) and Dr. Ashraf Ghani (*right*) finally agreed to a power-sharing arrangement. (Associated Press / Rahmat Gul)

line for withdrawing troops. "No one is safe anymore. The Taliban are targeting schools, playgrounds, mosques, roads. I do not know what will happen to this country."[51]

Evaluating Transition

In the end, what can be said about the transition process—the final act of America's latest longest war? First, it is clear that transition happened because all the key constituencies wanted the Americans out of Afghanistan: the American people, the Afghan people and their leaders, both military and civilian. But underneath this umbrella of consensus, there was disagreement about what transition was and how it should occur. To President Obama, transition meant the withdrawal of American troops on a schedule unencumbered by any other consideration. To President Karzai, transition meant the reduction of foreign troops, full sovereignty in practice as well as in official recognition, but no diminution of international financial support. Dr.

Ghani had similar goals, but the former World Bank bureaucrat naturally foregrounded development, international aid, and anticorruption over symbolic defenses of Afghan sovereignty. These differences were never fully reconciled.

A second point is that even with the serious bureaucratic hurdles and cultural obstacles, Afghan and coalition military officers agreed on how to conduct transition. Unfortunately, their counsel was mostly ignored by their civilian leaders. Major General Payenda Nazim—the Afghan general who had been instrumental to getting the ANA to take transition seriously—saw the JANIB process break down entirely as the careful work of the security ministries was cast aside or preempted by political calendars. The infrastructure of deliberate planning was present—working groups, boards, liaison officers, and so on—but at the end of the day, decisions on transition were made in the small circles around Presidents Karzai and Obama, not by the generals and security experts. The result was a job half-done. "One can argue," Payenda wrote in 2014, "that the last stage of the agreement (Strategic Support) isn't fully fulfilled." Moreover, "the elements of good governance and development . . . were ignored during the phases of transition," and the lack of key capabilities such as air, intelligence, and logistics would probably "negatively affect the success of the transition process."[52] Another Afghan—a civilian planner from the agency that linked the government in Kabul to the provincial and district governments—believed that only 30 percent of what was promised by the coalition had ever been delivered. The result was raised expectations, and little else.[53] The fault for this lies not with the Afghans, but with the Americans and their coalition partners.

The same civil-military friction that hampered Afghan planning also affected the Americans. General Petraeus believed—and insisted repeatedly—that the pace of transition must be governed by conditions on the ground to ensure a sustainable peace. Despite these efforts, Petraeus could not convince President Obama to disaggregate his goals from his calendar. In the end, given such fundamental differences and confusion between the two, it is striking that General Petraeus left ISAF to become the president's director of Central Intelligence. For both men, it seems, political ambition was more important than good policy. Later commanders probably shared Petraeus's skepticism of the president's withdrawal plans but saw no benefit to criticizing what they could not change. The result was a transition process that gave the appearance of consultation and deliberation to decisions already made. As one American STAG officer put it, "There was a transparent untruth to the JANIB process—when exactly would [remote provinces like] Nuristan achieve those goals? And was Nuristan, in fact, transitioning from ISAF control to Afghan control? When I figured that out about Nuristan, I assessed that transition was a political fig leaf to allow the war effort to politically transition to Afghan control."[54]

In the end, both nations' presidents won their arguments with their military commanders, as they should in countries that extol the virtues of civilian control over the armed forces. But what may be good for civil-military relations may be more problematic for Afghanistan's long-term security, as events in 2015 demonstrated. That year, the Taliban attacked and temporarily held the city of Kunduz, and made major gains in Helmand Province. Al Qaeda camps continue to be discovered on occasion, and the Islamic State established a small presence in eastern Afghanistan. There were 19,000 ANSF casualties that year alone—a 25 percent increase over 2014—and attrition rates continue to rise. "We have not met the people's expectations," Chief Executive Abdullah explained to the Afghan National Security Council. "Our forces lack discipline. They lack rotation opportunities. We haven't taken care of our own policemen and soldiers. They continue to absorb enormous casualties." By the end of the year, the Taliban held more ground in Afghanistan than it had in any year since its toppling in 2001.[55]

President Obama's Afghanistan policy shows just how much he was willing to risk in order to end a war he claimed to support when he ran for president in 2008. To bring the troops home from Afghanistan, President Obama did more than disagree with his military leaders; he was willing to ignore and alienate the Afghan president, diminish the Afghans' abilities to defeat the Taliban, and perhaps risk the long-term sustainability of the fragile Afghan government. Time will tell whether his decisions are best characterized as a prudently swift walk to the exit of an unwinnable war or, as former secretary of defense Robert Gates has put it, the actions of a president who "doesn't believe in his own strategy, and doesn't consider the war to be his. For him, it's all about getting out."[56]

Even with all the confusion and bureaucratic ineffectiveness, it is fair to say in 2015 that transition worked in a narrow sense. Even if it was merely a "fig leaf" to facilitate Washington's political objective, the Afghans are now in charge of their own war against the Taliban—an undeniable change from the 13 years of substantial US and NATO involvement. Once President Obama made it clear what he wanted, subsequent ISAF commanders—Marine Generals Allen and Dunford and, in the end, Army General John F. Campbell—saluted smartly and complied. ISAF's challenge of working directly with the Afghans (and NATO, and the UN, via numerous subordinate headquarters, while fighting the Taliban) made transition unwieldy, but each side muddled through. Despite a fraud-ridden election and a shaky patchwork government, Afghanistan is not now a safe haven for terrorism or an Islamist theocracy as it was before 2001.

These recent events provoke the larger question of whether Obama and Karzai's calendar-based transition will last. President Ghani has a number of challenges in front of him: he must keep the international aid flowing in, slow corruption, and grow his government's effectiveness and basic legitimacy with its various ethnic and tribal communities, while holding his security forces together as they fight the insurgency more effectively. Afghanistan's military leaders must keep the ANSF at least one step ahead of the Taliban while curbing the military's and police's predations on the Afghan population—a practice as old as the Afghan state itself. Helping in this will be the single greatest strategic advantage a military can have over an enemy—the Afghan people's hatred for the Taliban.[57] If all that holds, even Pakistan's considerable support for the Taliban may not drive Afghanistan back into war.

In the years ahead, the international community—the United States in particular—should continue to help Afghanistan emerge from three decades of near-constant warfare. Two years before assuming the presidency, Dr. Ghani pointed out the fundamental, long-range dilemma for security in Afghanistan: "Our security forces last year cost $6 billion while our national revenue was $1.7 billion."[58] Without sustained support that actually responds to conditions on the ground, Afghanistan will likely not survive. While the Afghan economy has the potential to generate the needed revenues—initial surveys show it is rich is gemstones and minerals—it must have international support. Some positive steps have been taken: At the 2012 NATO summit in Chicago, the alliance agreed to continue funding the ANSF, at a strength of 228,500 personnel to the cost of $4.1 billion per year. That funding will gradually decrease over time, and by 2024, Afghanistan will have "full financial responsibility for its own security forces."[59] If that international will and financial support is sustained for the next decade, Afghanistan may yet escape the fate of Iraq, which descended into chaos just three years after the United States departed in 2011. If not, Americans may yet find themselves back in Afghanistan in the future at a greater cost in both lives and treasure.

CONCLUSION

Our Latest Longest War

Lieutenant Colonel Aaron B. O'Connell, USMC

On December 28, 2014, General John F. Campbell walked to a podium at the International Security Assistance Force headquarters in Kabul and performed his final act as the last ISAF commander in Afghanistan. As he began his remarks, he acknowledged that even though the day's ceremony marked the end of Operation Enduring Freedom, Afghanistan's war against the Taliban was far from over. He listed the reasons why the United States would continue to fund and train the Afghan army for the foreseeable future: "The Afghan people have spoken. They've chosen progress over backwardness, education over ignorance, and transparency over criminality. They've roundly rejected the insurgents' senseless destruction and murdering. This year the Afghan people reasserted their sovereignty and they've asked for, and need, our sustained support. And we will give it to them. We're not walking away." When he finished speaking, soldiers lowered and cased the ISAF colors, and the combat operations of America's longest war formally came to an end.[1]

The Taliban issued their own statement that day. Vowing to fight the residual force of Americans left to train the Afghans and hunt al Qaeda, a Taliban spokesperson claimed that "the infidel powers who thought they would turn Afghanistan into their strategic colony" had been "pushed to the brink of defeat."[2] In the months that followed, insurgents stepped up attacks around the country and security deteriorated precipitously. In September 2015, the usually calm city of Kunduz in northern Afghanistan fell briefly under Taliban control. By the end of the year, the Department of Defense reported to Congress that "fighting has been nearly continuous since February 2015," and the insurgency "remains an enduring threat to U.S., coalition, and Afghan forces, as well as to the Afghan people." There were 28 "high-profile" attacks in the Afghan capital in 2015, and all around the country, "effective enemy-initiated attacks hovered around 1,000 per month." Despite ongoing support from the new operation—a train-and-assist mission known as Operation Freedom's Sentinel—in December 2015, the *Washington Post* reported that the Taliban "now holds more territory than in any year since 2001."[3]

Al Qaeda wasn't defeated either. According to the Defense Department's own assessment, the group begun by Osama bin Ladin still had "a sustained presence in Afghanistan primarily concentrated in the east and northeast" in 2015, and the Islamic State in Iraq and the Levant (ISIL) established a presence in Afghanistan that year as well. Perhaps the only good news about the arrival of ISIL was that in addition to conducting attacks against the Afghan National Security Forces (ANSF) and the United Nations, it also spent the year battling the Taliban, whom it was competing with for recruits.[4]

For the Afghan people, 2015 was the deadliest year of the conflict. Over 11,000 civilians were killed or wounded that year, including 1,246 women and 2,829 children. These numbers bring the total Afghan civilian casualties to 58,736 since the United Nations began tracking deaths and injuries systematically in 2009.[5] Another 335,400 Afghans were displaced by fighting in 2015, bringing the total number of conflict-induced internally displaced persons (IDPs) in Afghanistan to 1.7 million.[6] While the Taliban caused the vast majority of the casualties, many civilians continue to blame the Afghan government

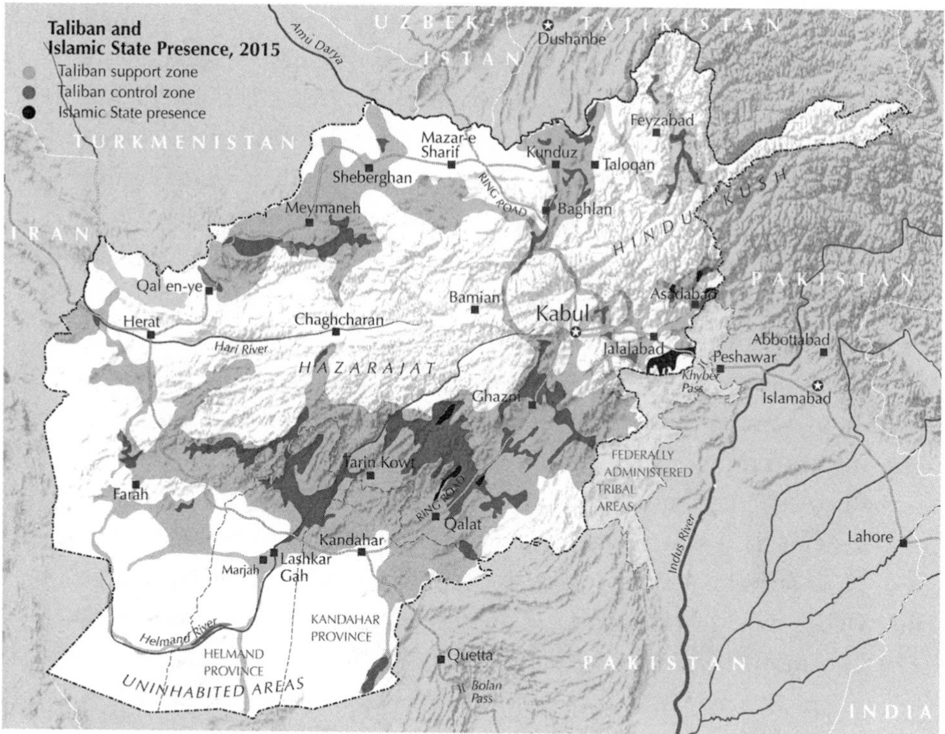

Figure C.1 Areas of insurgent influence and control, December 2015. (Chicago CartoGraphics)

for failing to keep them safe.[7] Public opinion data gathered that year revealed that "only 28 percent of Afghans say that security in their local area is good" and fully 67 percent of Afghans "fear for their personal safety or that of their families"—the highest percentage since polling began in 2007."[8]

By contrast, the 10,000 Americans that remained in Afghanistan to advise and assist the government suffered only three hostile deaths in 2015, but two of them were at the hands of the Afghan security forces they were sent to mentor and train.[9]

The Afghan army and national police continue to fight the Taliban and al Qaeda, but they still have serious deficiencies in almost all areas. ANSF casualties rose in "virtually every province" in 2015, as did desertions and other forms of attrition, which together caused the ANSF to lose over one-quarter of its total strength in a single 12-month period.[10] Maintenance and accounting problems plague all units, and while the Afghan air force now has 161 trained pilots, it struggles to maintain its aircraft, in part because maintenance facilities too often experience water outages and electrical failures.[11] Afghans throughout the security forces continue to resist Western ways: a NATO gender support office has been established to ensure that the ANSF has an "appropriate gender perspective," but "many women" in the ANSF still "receive threats and are subject to harassment," because so many Afghans "actively oppose any initiatives to improve the status of women." American bureaucracy and accounting procedures do not seem to be taking hold either: "A reluctance to embrace technology, reliance on inefficient processes and paper systems, and centralized decision-making authority hinder effective MoD bureaucratic processes." Developing sustainable processes, the DOD's most recent report to Congress concludes, "will require a cultural shift at all levels" of the Ministry of Defense.[12]

The Special Forces–trained members of the Afghan Local Police who were the subject of such intense vetting and screening also appear to be having serious problems. The DOD's 2015 end-of-year report found that ALP members were being "frequently misemployed" as personal bodyguards for warlords and government officials. Over 20 percent of the 28,000 names on ALP rosters still remained untrained in 2015, another 10 percent had deserted or never entered the ranks in the first place, and another 8 percent were "under the control of local powerbrokers."[13] A separate DOD investigation found that "ALP-ordered supplies are often diverted to ANP units, delayed significantly, of inferior quality, or heavily pilfered." ALP salaries are still being siphoned off by superiors or middlemen. Reporters interviewing Afghans during the September 2015 battle for Kunduz found that ALP members in the area "had been supplementing their salary by selling drugs, collecting a 'tax' from residents, and killing citizens in crossfire during skirmishes with other ALP members."[14] As an Afghan academic from Kunduz University explained just after the battle: "The main problem is that some people in our city are Taliban and some are local police. . . . They both do the same thing."[15] According to the Special Operations task force that created and trained the ALP, "Misuse of the ALP is the strongest indicator of larger problems within a district, such as collusion with insurgents, human rights violations, or other illegal actions."[16]

Reconstruction and development have shown some gains over the years, but still remain plagued by mismanagement and corruption. USAID has put $2.2 billion into power sector assistance since 2002, but only 25 percent of the population is now connected to the energy grid, and Afghanistan still imports over 80 percent of its power.[17] Despite $2.4 billion from American taxpayers for road construction, 85 percent of Afghan roads are currently in poor shape and the majority of them are "unsuitable for motor vehicles."[18] The Afghan government reports that 8.3 million students are now in school, but this number includes "both present and absent students," and absent students can remain on the rolls for three years "because they might return to school." Basic accounting is terrible, and audits have found that the required attendance sheets (which help determine school budgets) "are frequently forged." Parliamentarians occasionally trade their votes on the education budget for a certain allotment of teacher positions to hand out as political favors, and the entire education system is "significantly undermined by bribery and nepotism."[19]

Despite a decade of funding rule of law development in Afghanistan, corruption remains debilitating throughout the country. In 2015, 9 out of 10 of Afghans reported that government corruption was still a problem in their daily lives.[20] Two-thirds of Afghans paid a bribe when interacting with municipal officials that year and more than half paid bribes to the police. Half of all Afghans experienced demands for bribes when applying for jobs, interacting with judicial or customs officials, or visiting a health care facility. "The overall trend since 2007," one study found, "is a steady increase in reported corruption."[21] Transparency International now ranks Afghanistan as the fourth most corrupt country in the world.[22]

Even with these problems, there have been some success stories in Afghanistan, particularly in the areas of health and life expectancy. By 2015, roughly 85 percent of Afghans had access to basic medical services, compared to just 9 percent during the Taliban era. The 680 health clinics built around the country have helped cut infant mortality in half. Maternal mortality is now at one-fifth of its Taliban-era levels, and individual life expectancy has increased by two decades. Eighteen million Afghans have cell phone service. Despite the corruption problems with school enrollments, there are now 17 universities in Afghanistan—up from two during the Taliban era—and the literacy rate has improved dramatically since 2001. By almost any standard, these are major improvements in the Afghan people's quality of life and are directly attributable to the United States' and other coalition partners' many years of aid and investment in Afghanistan.[23]

These outcomes must be weighed against the costs of the war to the US people, which were both financial and human. The direct financial costs of all operations in Afghanistan between September 2001 and December 2014 was $743 billion, 95 percent of which was spent by the Department of Defense. This does not account for the indirect costs: long-term VA outlays for treating those disabled in the war, interest on war debt, or postconflict assistance to the Afghan government. Adding those figures to the total brings the cost of the war very close to $1 trillion.[24]

The human costs are far lower in number but significant nonetheless. In the 13 years of combat operations in Afghanistan, 2,216 American military personnel were killed and another 20,049 were wounded. This is just a fraction of the casualties of earlier and shorter wars—Vietnam had almost 10 times as many killed and wounded, and World War II had almost 50 times as many (in one-third as many years). The Army and the Marine Corps account for 95 percent of all casualties in Afghanistan, and three-quarters of those killed were age 30 or younger.[25] Of course, this number does not account for the psychological wounds of war or the damages to families caused by multiple deployments over 13 years.

The Lessons of History

Given these realities, what can be said about the United States' latest longest war? Policymakers often ask historians for lessons from the past—a request that makes some more nervous than others. As the esteemed military historian Sir Michael Howard reminded the faculty at Oxford University some years ago, the most honest answer is that history teaches no lessons. "History" is merely what historians write, and those that do it for a living come to understand over time that any lessons they choose will always be overly reductive and marred by bias because they cannot free themselves from the cultural lenses that shape how they interpret the past or describe it to others. That advice is true for all historians in all times, but it is particularly important for those that write about wars they themselves have participated in (something Sir Michael knew a good deal about as well).[26]

There may never be lessons from history but there are lessons for historians—best practices and professional standards for seeking wisdom from the past or offering it to others. Sir Michael offered four: Don't generalize from false premises or from inadequate evidence. Strive to re-create your subjects' "structure of beliefs" that either determined their actions or made some actions more likely to occur than others. Be mindful of the cultural differences that separate you from the people you seek to explain. (And when dealing with foreign cultures, never substitute timeless "laws" from the social sciences or grand theories for a basic cultural literacy regarding the societies you wish to comprehend.) Finally, and most importantly, do not succumb to the "reigning dogmas" and "socially convenient myth[s]" that those in positions of power use to erase the past or appropriate it for other purposes.[27]

Of course, these lessons can never be adhered to perfectly. Any narration is already a generalization. Historical arguments are never proven definitively; they are always subject to reinterpretation in light of new or better evidence. Foreign culture will always be misinterpreted to some degree, and a firm commitment to escaping the reigning dogmas may lead historians to discard those ideas that reign precisely because they are right. Nonetheless, these four guidelines for the historian's craft provide a way to assess the contributions of this volume—to draw initial conclusions, note shortcomings, posit a few generalizations, and point the way for future research.

The first guideline is really twofold: avoid false premises and don't generalize from inadequate evidence. On the evidence issue, we are surely guilty, for we have only used what is available now: unclassified government reports, news stories, interviews, and other firsthand accounts, supplemented by our own experiences as participant-observers. The US and NATO operational reports will remain classified for decades, and one wonders when—or if—Afghan government sources will be available. If our work has evidentiary gaps, we hope later scholars will investigate and correct them. We view this volume as an early postmortem on the war, not a definitive autopsy.

On the issue of generalizing from false premises, we feel somewhat more confident. Here are the two foundational assumptions that have guided this work: The first is that in the 13 years of Operation Enduring Freedom, the United States and its allies did not achieve the goals of creating a stable and secure Afghan state with a "representative and accountable government."[28] Those objectives were not just flowery rhetoric: President George W. Bush named them as the war's strategic end states and committed to them formally in diplomatic agreements with the Afghan government. The United States Congress provided funds and oversight, and the military designed its campaign plans according to them. President Obama revised his predecessor's goals downward in 2009, but still vowed to defeat al Qaeda and to effect a "responsible transition" so that Afghans—and not Americans—"could secure and govern their country."[29] As of December 2015, that hasn't happened. Therefore, any reasoned analysis of Operation Enduring Freedom must conclude that, thus far, America's longest war has been an extremely costly half success at best, or at worst, a failure.

This volume's second premise is that problems of culture were central to the war's outcomes. To defend this claim, we offered evidence-based accountings of the major lines of effort in the war and interrogated the assumptions that undergirded those efforts. We found numerous mismatches of ideas and institutions both within the ISAF coalition and between the coalition and the Afghans. Together, these incompatibilities produced more enduring friction than enduring freedom at all levels. They help explain why ISAF did not achieve its goals.

As we strove to re-create the belief structures at work in the Afghanistan War, we found some that shaped the war's initial goals and others that hindered their pursuit. At the outset, American leaders suffered not from ignorance but from informed hubris. Senior policymakers knew the challenges of Afghanistan before and during the war. Afghan experts like Barnett Rubin raised them to NSC officials and the State Department's director of policy planning just four days after operations against the Taliban began. Nonetheless, both military and civilian officials argued that the United States had a moral obligation to build a legitimate Afghan state and a functioning economy—"nation-building lite," they called it.[30] The president understood the challenges too but pursued a grand transformative vision all the same. As he explained to cadets at the Virginia Military Institute in the opening months of the war:

> The history of military conflict in Afghanistan . . . [is] one of initial success followed by long years of floundering and ultimate failure. We're not going to repeat that mistake. . . . We will stay until the mission is done. We know that true peace will only be achieved when we give the Afghan people the means to achieve their own aspirations. Peace will be achieved by helping Afghanistan develop its own stable government. Peace will be achieved by helping Afghanistan train and develop its own national army, and peace will be achieved through an education system for boys and girls which works.[31]

As the president's remarks make clear, it was not a lack of information that led America to overreach in Afghanistan; it was an ideology—a deeply held belief that "the way to a peaceful future can be found in the non-negotiable demands of human dignity." That dignity rests on key principles, the president argued, that the United States must defend everywhere and at all times: "the rule of law, limits on the power of the state, respect for women, private property, equal justice, religious tolerance. No nation owns these principles; no nation is exempt from them."[32]

We have argued that this Enlightenment vision drove tactics, operations, and strategy in the Afghanistan War under both Democratic and Republican administrations. In the beginning, it justified end states that would have been ambitious under any circumstances, but that became entirely untenable when the Bush administration refused to commit the necessary resources and then began a costly and unnecessary war in Iraq. President Obama partially abandoned his predecessor's transformative vision, but by then, the same progressive assumptions were already baked into the military's counterinsurgency doctrine. As a result, the military campaign plan still pursued the foundational elements of a modern Western state: a centrally controlled, technology-enabled national military; a secular, written, rule of law regime; and a Western social contract maintained through elections and a majoritarian political system. Even with the Obama administration's more narrowly scoped mission of defeating al Qaeda and degrading the Taliban, the billions spent after 2009 still sought to install the infrastructure of liberalism in a deeply illiberal land.

In retrospect, it seems clear that America's post–September 11 grand strategy (of which Afghanistan was only a part) erred in a critical sense: human dignity may be universal in its existence, but its understanding and interpretation are deeply culturally contingent. Americans may wish it were not so, but the hard truth remains that not everyone wants their daughters educated, or to tolerate different religions, or to accede to even seemingly reasonable laws (particularly when those laws are enforced by urban elites, predatory police, or foreigners with guns). For many Afghan men, the "non-negotiable demands of human dignity" are precisely what caused them to resist America's vision for their country, and that resistance will likely continue for some time to come. The Westerners' deafness to these

Afghan concerns—a point made in almost all the chapters in this volume—only made the problems worse.

While some of us focused on the many ways that American and Afghan belief structures were incompatible, most of us spent more time on the cultural friction within the Western coalition—clashes of ideas and institutions between Washington and the field, State and Defense, NATO and ISAF and the US government. These too shaped action, particularly during the second half of the war. Nearly every chapter in this volume highlighted problems with bureaucracy and disjointed, uncoordinated efforts. Nearly every author explained how the military came to dominate decision making, even in areas that didn't initially belong to the military, such as police training and rule of law development. A number of us also noted the Americans' careless approach to spending, which caused the United States to overpay underskilled contractors, purchase expensive, high-tech equipment the Afghans couldn't use, and demand immediate dispersals that encouraged corruption and unbalanced local economies. Incompatible time scales were another repetitive theme in most chapters, with the military usually demanding speed and results to capitalize on momentum, even when there were indications that the hasty pace was creating new problems or aggravating old ones. And almost all of us argued that in a variety of endeavors—combat operations, ANSF training, and reconstruction, in particular—a reliance on, and politicization of, overly quantitative metrics misrepresented the progress of the war.

These problems were either produced or exacerbated by ingrained cultural frameworks in US foreign policy and military affairs—frameworks that determined the boundaries of the possible and shaped the path from thought to action. The clearest proof of this claim is the fact that these very same institutional problems occurred a half century earlier in the Vietnam War. There, too, bureaucratic turf wars and rigid adherence to procedures created disconnects between policy and implementation. There, too, short rotations and bad metrics impeded understanding of conditions on the ground. Overspending and poor planning led to corruption and enormous waste. Incremental approaches led to worsening security; domino theories about the dangers of withdrawal justified more resources still. In both cases, the United States spent lavishly on a technologically advanced army that the host nation could neither manage nor sustain. There, too, the majority of dollars spent and lives lost occurred after the United States vowed to withdraw.[33]

How could such parallels exist across time and space, unless common underlying factors produced them? Afghanistan is not Vietnam—not least because the Afghanistan War proceeded directly from an al Qaeda attack that killed thousands of Americans on American soil. We do not believe that timeless principles of strategy or universal laws of human behavior explain the similarities between these wars—those are attempts to impose order on things that are fundamentally contingent and subject to emotion, ideology, and chance. But for all the differences between Afghanistan and Vietnam, it is important to remember that at least two common factors were affecting both: the United States government and the Department of Defense. Those institutions and the cultural currents that flow through them shaped policymakers' objectives for both wars as well as the tactics the military developed to pursue them. In both conflicts, the narratives of American exceptionalism led to outsized goals, framing Vietnam and Afghanistan as battles between freedom and tyranny. A benevolent—but impractical—urge to liberate the oppressed produced grand transformative projects that promised more than they could deliver. Undue faith in military technology led policymakers to believe that with enough dollars, gadgets, and troops, they could stabilize foreign societies and remake them using an American blueprint. An obsession with credibility framed withdrawal as falling dominos and an intolerable threat to global stability. All of these are cultural forces, and they are integral to any explanation of why both wars fell short of their goals.

Further proof of the power of culture is the fact that the very military officers who wrote the counterinsurgency (COIN) manual in 2006—and the general who ran the war during the surge—were already steeped in the scholarship of the Vietnam War. These officers did not miss the "lessons" of Vietnam or forget its tragedies; in fact, they were better informed of them than almost anyone else in America. Three of them—General David H. Petraeus, Lieutenant Colonel John A. Nagl, and Colonel Conrad C. Crane—all wrote PhD dissertations, books, or scholarly articles on Vietnam and its failings, lessons, and misconceptions.[34] They were educated at West Point, Princeton, Stanford, and Oxford, and had direct experience in warfare and with military bureaucracy. They spent years teaching undergraduates, as well as researching and writing on precisely the problems the US military would later encounter in Afghanistan. They had read *The Pentagon Papers* and the reflections of Edward Lansdale, Robert Thompson, George Kennan, Arthur Schlesinger, McGeorge Bundy, and Roger Hilsman. They had corresponded with General William Westmoreland, Secretary of Defense Robert S. McNamara, and many of the Vietnam War's major decision makers. They had spent time in the archives pouring over the division reports, the oral histories, and the personal papers of key officers. They knew and used the works of Richard Betts, Samuel Huntington, George Herring, Stanley Karnow, Robert W. Komer, Andrew Krepinevich, Ernest R. May, Richard E. Neustadt. Lewis Sorley, Ronald H. Spector, Harry G. Summers, and Martin Van Creveld.[35]

In brief, these officers understood—as well as anyone in America—what had gone wrong in the earlier war and worked to apply that knowledge toward new best practices for later ones. They knew well and warned explicitly against "mirror-imaging," just as *The Pentagon Papers* had four decades earlier.[36] They grasped the need for unity of effort and close coordination with civilians; indeed, as a young major, David Petraeus published an article on this subject and discussed it again in his doctoral dissertation.[37] The COIN manual devoted an entire chapter to "integrating civilian and military activities," and cited the Vietnam-era Civil Operations and Revolutionary Development Support (CORDS) program as a "successful synthesis of military and civilian efforts."[38] They knew they must not "build and train host nation security forces in the U.S. military's image," and that doing so would result in "poor administration and rampant corruption."[39] They warned against militarizing nation-building, noting that "it is better to entrust civilian tasks to civilians" and cautioning that military personnel should only step in temporarily "to address urgent circumstances."[40] And yet awareness of these problems did not prevent their recurrence. This, too, is evidence that deep structural forces were shaping events in Afghanistan, forces that the best and the brightest of today's military thinkers could not overcome.

Writing the History of the Afghanistan War: Directions for Future Research

What of the final caution to avoid reigning dogmas and to use the writing of history to "demolish myths rather than to create them"?[41] With military history, this is always a tricky business, for wars involve killing and dying in the public's name, and this raises the stakes for how they are remembered and understood. Too often, military history devolves into polemics that cast blame on one party or president, or rest on impossible-to-prove assertions of lost opportunities or triumphs forsaken. Memory activists too often reframe criticism of the war's conduct as an attack on those who fought it or draw overly broad conclusions removed from specific evidence or experience.

We reject such approaches. We sought to explain what happened in the war, not to posit what could have happened or to offer alternatives. We were not interested in arguing whether theories of counterinsurgency can ever work anywhere; rather, we sought to chronicle what happened when they were applied in one specific time and place. We acknowledge this is only a first step toward understanding the Afghanistan War, and we hope that neither our explanations nor other accounts from participant-observers will be immune from criticism simply because we served in the war. The tools for demolishing myths are well-reasoned arguments supported by carefully considered evidence. If there is any place for loyalty in the writing of history, it must be to the facts and the sources—not to any one particular interpretation of them.

As more sources become available in the coming decades, other scholars will continue the work begun here. As they do, diplomatic, political, military, and cultural historians must take up a number of critical questions. First, diplomatic historians should explore the deep structural causes of the war, of al Qaeda, and of the inaptly named Global War on Terrorism. Did the United States really "abandon" Afghanistan after the Soviet intervention, and more importantly, would sustained American support have prevented the creation of al Qaeda or the rise of the Taliban? Did President Bush ever intend to transform Afghanistan into a democracy as he claimed as early as 2002 and often thereafter? Or was that just an intermediary step in a broader agenda of transforming the Middle East, containing Iran, and protecting Israel? If there were no ulterior end states, did the president apply the right mix of pressure and incentives to allies and partners in the region to promote Afghan stability? Did he leverage the full strength of the State Department, USAID, and other entities to build the institutions needed for Afghan self-rule? If so, critics of state-building will have stronger arguments concerning the challenges of installing liberal institutions in illiberal countries. If not, harder questions should then follow about the administration's priorities, and criticisms of the military's failures in Afghanistan should perhaps be tempered.

Questions about the initial goals of the war concern the Bush administration, but the shift to counterinsurgency in 2009 does not. That decision lay with President Obama's administration, and here we have only memoirs and a few journalistic accounts that detail how and why the president arrived at his decisions. The narrative that is now crystallizing in Washington—largely because of the writings of journalist Bob Woodward—is that even though Vice President Joe Biden argued for a much cheaper counterterrorism strategy focused only on al Qaeda, the president chose counterinsurgency, in part because of sustained pressure from senior military officers.[42] If true, the Pentagon will have much to answer for. But here, we must avoid loose accusations and demand concrete evidence. Who—specifically—pressured the commander-in-chief and how did they do it? Are moments of strong disagreement inappropriate political pressure or appropriate military advice? Absent evidence of purposeful misrepresentation of the military situation, or threats (either implicit or explicit) to undermine the president, it seems unreasonable at this point to place responsibility for the shift to counterinsurgency anywhere but at the president's desk.

The formulation of the war's goals and major decision points were settled in Washington and will be taken up by diplomatic and political historians. But what of the conduct of the war? What should military historians focus on in the coming years? A critical first question is to evaluate whether the United States provided President Karzai the necessary military and nonmilitary resources to consolidate control over his country in the early years of the war. A current theory—one that became politicized in the 2008 US presidential campaign—holds that the United States "got distracted by Iraq" and that inattention to Afghanistan was the critical error that allowed the Taliban to return.[43] There is some evidence to support this theory, but much more is needed.[44] Did insufficient US support force President Karzai into Faustian bargains with predatory power brokers that undermined his legitimacy in the south and east? Why weren't Lieutenant General David W. Barno's counterinsurgency proposals implemented fully when he proposed them in 2003? Did White House insiders understand Afghanistan's deterioration from 2006 onward? If so, why were the president, NATO, and the US military so slow to respond? In theory, President Bush could have called up more reserves, blanketed Afghanistan with troops, and denied the Taliban freedom of movement even as he poured resources into Iraq. Had he done so, would the additional troops have halted the deterioration or only produced greater resistance?

After the 2009 surge decision, the military finally shifted to resource-intensive counterinsurgency tactics—a phase of the war that we have given considerable attention in this volume. When more evidence is available, military historians will also have to test and expand on some of the arguments made here. Were there sufficient numbers of State Department and USAID personnel in Afghanistan during the war, and if not, why? What happened with the so-called civilian surge, which President Obama called for in his West Point address and which the State Department never produced? Why were the Americans so profligate with money, especially when there was ample evidence of how overspending had caused so many problems in Vietnam (and in the First Anglo-Afghan War as well)?[45] What factors caused the Americans to agree to fund an Afghan air force complete with helicopters and planes that the Afghans could neither fly nor maintain? Was the Afghan Local Police program truly a novel—and potentially game-changing—approach to foreign internal defense or just a new way to rent militias, as Afghans have done for centuries? Perhaps most important, was President Obama committed to withdrawal regardless of conditions on the ground, as Secretary of Defense Robert Gates—and several of the volume's contributors—have argued?

Cultural historians—both of America and Afghanistan—will have different questions to explore in the coming years. We have spent considerable time discussing the effect of military culture on operations, particularly problems of bureaucracy, metrics, time scales, and civil-military friction. More work on this topic will be possible in the future when declassified documents reveal more fully the assumptions at work in the ISAF headquarters, regional commands, and local outposts. More on the Afghan government's decision making will be illuminating as well, particularly work that uses Afghan sources to recreate the belief structures at work in Kabul and among key officials in Kandahar and Helmand Provinces.

As important as the opinions of government elites will be, the essential questions concerning the war's feasibility or folly will best be answered by probing the narratives of ordinary Afghans who lived through America's attempts to bring them security through liberal state institutions. As pacification theorists have argued (directly and indirectly) for years, counterinsurgency is a cultural endeavor and the culture that matters most is that of the civilian population. They are the center of gravity in counterinsurgency—only when the people are persuaded to reject the insurgency and support the central government will it attain legitimacy and move toward a sustainable peace.

The early evidence collected here indicates that, for a variety of reasons, the Western seeds cast in Afghanistan's mountains never took root. Too many elites fell back on old patterns of using public institutions for private ends, and a pervasive sense of injustice alienated moderates and hard-liners alike. Centuries-long divides between Durranis and Ghilzais, and between urban elites and rural villagers, were patched at times but never repaired, and the cultural imperative to resist foreign occupation remained part of most Afghans' commonsense understanding of the war. Even the Afghans who shared our liberal democratic vision never accepted Kabul's writ or trusted that ISAF forces could keep them safe. In the future, military historians, cultural historians, and anthropologists from the United States and Afghanistan will have to work together to understanding the Afghans' stories of the war. Doing so may provide the clearest answer as to why America's state-building enterprise in Afghanistan fell short of its goals.

No More Afghanistans?

In a 1968 piece ominously titled "No More Vietnams?," Samuel Huntington wrote that America's "bureaucratic machine" ensures that "our operations in Vietnam will always be vigorous, will never grow tired, but also will never grow wiser."[46] We have suggested here that the machine that kept pushing the United States down a path to failure in Afghanistan was not just "bureaucracy" (or, in Robert Komer's phrasing, "institutional constraints")—although those terms do capture some of the problems we have discussed in this book. Rather, it was the shaping force of American culture that caused the United States to repeat the errors of earlier wars, even as it worked assiduously to avoid those specific errors.

The sad truth is that the United States *did* learn from Vietnam; it changed many things from the ways it had fought a half century earlier. Policymakers went to great lengths to identify how Afghanistan and Vietnam were similar in some ways and different in others. President Obama offered a list of the wars' principal differences in his December 2009 West Point speech. The US military learned and innovated too. The US Army may have tried to wish away Vietnam's memory in the 1980s, but by the time it shifted to counterinsurgency in Afghanistan, it was acutely aware of earlier failures and worked hard to take lessons from them. There are 21 vignettes in the *Counterinsurgency Field Manual* that explain best practices or serious errors through historical examples. Four come from Vietnam. The manual has 16 specific references to the Vietnam War, which together warn against the principal problems that had already or would soon reoccur in Afghanistan: imposing values on the host nation, using misleading metrics, allowing overmilitarization, and relying too much on "high-technology equipment and computer-based systems."[47] Platoon and company commanders studied the manual and trained their troops in small-group sessions that combined lectures, discussions, and practical application exercises. Marine infantry lieutenants went through week-long counterinsurgency training packages at The Basic School and then again at the Infantry Officer's Course. Before deploying, every major unit practiced interacting with civilians and talking to rural elders in elaborately staged scenarios involving hundreds of (albeit Arabic-speaking) role players. The Marine Corps established the Center for Operational Cultural Learning and revamped its entire officer education curriculum in an effort to understand Iraq and Afghanistan and to prepare its officers for counterinsurgency operations. In short, no lack of training or information or intelligence explains the repetitive patterns we have identified here.

The United States neither forgot Vietnam nor refought it nor ignored it. The United States just never escaped the prison of its culture or quit the habits of mind that have been operative in American society long before either war began. The United States was committed to American exceptionalism and to a benevolent vision of how Afghans would understand its presence in their lands. It took its culture's stories—narratives that link freedom with elections and dignity to prosperity—to be nonnegotiable and universally accepted. September 11 brought the US military into Afghanistan, but the power of these narratives kept it there, turning the hunt for al Qaeda into a grand strategy of transformation that overpromised and underdelivered.

"We have seen so much of this since the Second World War," Sir Michael Howard concluded in his remarks on the lessons of history. "People often of masterful intelligence, trained usually in law or economics or perhaps in political science, who have led their governments into disastrous decisions and miscalculations because they have no awareness whatever of the historical background, the cultural universe of the foreign societies with which they have to deal." Many of the arguments in this volume suggest that Afghanistan is the latest example of that cultural myopia. But as important as looking outward is, Americans must also look inward in the years ahead and work to understand their own culture better, for they will always take it with them when they go to war. If there is any lesson from America's latest longest war, it is that American policymakers, soldiers, and civilians should rigorously examine their assumptions and values before attempting to export them or promote them abroad.

The military does not—and should not—get a vote on when to use military force; all it can do is try to win when ordered to fight. As we have shown here, the cultural forces at work in the Afghanistan War created problems that were larger than the specific tactics, doctrine, resources, and technologies used on the battlefield. The counterinsurgency manual's authors were experts in the profession of arms and steeped in the experiences of Vietnam, but they—like all Americans—were also inheritors of Hobbes, Locke, Rousseau, and Hegel, as well as their American intellectual descendants: Thomas Jefferson, William McKinley, Theodore Roosevelt, Woodrow Wilson, and Franklin Roosevelt. As a result, they produced a quintessentially Western and American product: a road map for nation-building through political enfranchisement, effective state institutions, and free market capitalism, all of which would be guaranteed by a professional and disinterested military. It was not a new vision, and in some circumstances, it is not a bad vision either. Nor is it the whole world's. If the United States continues to believe that it is, and uses force to advance it, Americans are very likely to find themselves in more Afghanistans in the future.

Acknowledgments

This project began as a conversation with Ambassador Ronald Neumann in Kabul during the height of the surge in the spring of 2011. Later conversations that year with Sarah Chayes, Dr. Stephen Biddle, and a number of military officers and State Department officials convinced me that cultural factors were some of the biggest obstacles to success in Afghanistan.

I found broad support for this hypothesis when I began discussing it with other Afghanistan veterans who were also trained academics. Some of us presented early versions of our chapters at the Society for Military History, the Society for Historians of American Foreign Relations (SHAFR), and the Naval History Symposium in Annapolis, Maryland. A SHAFR panel with Marilyn B. Young, Lloyd C. Gardner, and Michael Cotey Morgan yielded a number of useful suggestions, as did visits with John Lewis Gaddis, Paul Kennedy, and Charles Hill at International Security Studies at Yale. A symposium at Temple University's Center for the Study of Force and Diplomacy allowed us to explore our ideas with Richard H. Immerman, Beth Bailey, David Farber, Petra Goedde, Greg Daddis, Robert K. Brigham, Conrad C.

Crane, and Tammi Davis Biddle. A number of excellent historians also pushed me to refine my thinking on American cultures of warfare and diplomacy, and I am particularly grateful to Michael Allen, Brooke L. Blower, Hal Brands, Charles N. Edel, Jeffrey A. Engel, Katherine M. Epstein, Gretchen Heefner, Daniel Immerwahr, Julia Irwin, David Kieran, Melani McAlister, Lien-Hang Nguyen, Andrew Preston, Daniel Sargent, Ronald H. Spector, Jeremi Suri, and Jenifer Van Vleck.

Several of my colleagues at the US Naval Academy in Annapolis, Maryland, discussed the major themes of this book with me and helped me hone my own contributions. Richard A. Ruth and Brian VanDeMark were valuable resources for testing the parallels to Vietnam, and Ernest Tucker was always helpful in sorting through the complexities of Afghan history. Marcus O. Jones and Jeffrey R. Macris always had time to talk through strategy and foreign policy with me, and faculty with deployments to Afghanistan—Nick Schmitz, Carlo Scott, Mark Thompson, and Tom Robertson—offered ideas and criticism as well.

All the arguments and evidence in this volume were derived from unclassified materials, and the Department of Defense reviewed the manuscript before publication to ensure that there were no inadvertent disclosures of classified information. All the arguments and opinions are our own; none of them should be construed as the official policies of any portion of the Department of Defense or the United States government.

Tim Mennel at the University of Chicago Press had an early faith in the project and was patient and understanding with the numerous delays. Ambassador Ryan Crocker read the entire manuscript and had a number of suggestions and critical comments that made the final product better. Kelly Finefrock-Creed was a master copyeditor whose careful eye made the final version much improved. Finally, I am most grateful to the contributors, who suffered through seemingly endless rounds of edits and questions. Without them, this project would never have become a reality.

Abbreviations

ABP	Afghan Border Police
ACG	assistant commanding general
ALP	Afghan Local Police
AMF	Afghan Militia Force
ANA	Afghan National Army
ANAP	Afghan National Auxiliary Police
ANCOP	Afghan National Civil Order Police
ANDS	Afghan National Development Strategy
ANP	Afghan National Police
ANSF	Afghan National Security Forces
AP3	Afghan Public Protection Program
APPF	Afghan Public Protection Force
ASFF	Afghan Security Forces Fund
ATF	Alcohol, Tobacco, Firearms (US)
AUP	Afghan Uniformed Police
AWOL	absent without leave
BSA	Bilateral Security Agreement
CDI	Community Defense Initiative
CENTCOM	Central Command (US)

CERP	Commander's Emergency Response Program
CIA	Central Intelligence Agency (US)
CID	Criminal Investigative Division (Afghanistan)
COIN	counterinsurgency
CORDS	Civil Operations and Revolutionary (later Rural) Development Support
CSTC-A	Combined Security Transition Command-Afghanistan
DDP	District Delivery Program (USAID)
DOD	Department of Defense (US)
EUPOL	European Union Police Mission
FDD	Focused District Development
FOB	forward operating base
GAO	Government Accountability Office (US)
GDPSU	General Directorate of Police Special Units (Afghanistan)
ICG	International Crisis Group
IDLG	Independent Directorate for Local Governance (Afghanistan)
IJC	ISAF Joint Command
INCLE	International Narcotics and Law Enforcement
INL	Bureau of International Narcotics and Law Enforcement
IRD	International Relief and Development
ISAF	International Security Assistance Force
ISCI	Interim Security for Critical Infrastructure
ISI	Inter-Services Intelligence (Pakistan)
ISIL	Islamic State of Iraq and the Levant
ISIS	Islamic State of Iraq and Syria
JANIB	Joint Afghan-NATO Inteqal Board
JCIP	Justice Center in Parwan
JCMB	Joint Coordination and Monitoring Board
JRC	Judicial Reform Commission (Afghanistan)
KGB	Committee for State Security (USSR)
KHAD	Afghan State Information Service (Taliban-Era)
LDI	Local Defense Initiative
MACV	Military Assistance Command, Vietnam
MOI	Ministry of Interior (Afghanistan)
MOJ	Ministry of Justice (Afghanistan)
MTA	Military Technical Agreement
NATO	North Atlantic Treaty Organization
NGO	nongovernmental organization

NJP	National Justice Program (Afghanistan)
NJSS	National Justice Sector Strategy (Afghanistan)
NSC	National Security Council (US)
NSS	National Security Service (Afghanistan)
NTM-A	NATO Training Mission-Afghanistan
OMB	Office of Management and Budget (US)
OSC-A	Office of Security Cooperation-Afghanistan
OSS	Office of Strategic Services (US)
PDPA	People's Democratic Party of Afghanistan
PRT	Provincial Reconstruction Team
ROL	rule of law
ROLFF-A	Rule of Law Field Force-Afghanistan
SEAL	Sea, Air, and Land (US Navy)
SIGACTS	significant activities
SIGAR	special inspector for Afghanistan reconstruction (US)
SOF	Special Operations Forces
SRAP	special representative for Afghanistan and Pakistan (US)
STAG	Strategic Transition and Assessment Group
TCC	Transition Coordinating Commission (Afghanistan)
TF	task force
UN	United Nations
UNAMA	United Nations Assistance Mission in Afghanistan
USA	US Army
USAF	US Air Force
USAID	US Agency for International Development
USDA	US Department of Agriculture
USMC	US Marine Corps
USN	US Navy
VA	Veterans Affairs (US)
VSO	Village Stability Operations
VSP	Village Stability Platform
WAD	Ministry of State Security (Taliban-Era)

Notes

Introduction

The views in this chapter are the author's own and do not reflect the policies of the Department of Defense or the United States government.

1 Although most assume this aphorism comes from the Islamic tradition, it is originally from a British Enlightenment philosopher. See Sir Francis Bacon, "On Boldness," in *The Essays of Francis Bacon* (New York: Charles Scribner's Sons, 1908), 52.

2 As of late 2016, almost 10,000 American troops were still in Afghanistan, but the combat operations ended in December 2014. In 2015, a new mission began, Operation Freedom's Sentinel, the purpose of which is to train and assist the Afghan National Security Forces (ANSF) and conduct counter-terrorism operations against al Qaeda and its associates. On whether the United States is still legally at war in Afghanistan, see Department of Defense, *Enhancing Security and Stability in Afghanistan* (Washington, DC: The Pentagon, December 2015), 7.

3 Troop numbers are listed in Ian S. Livingston and Michael O'Hanlon, figure 1.1, "American Troops Deployed to Afghanistan," and figure 1.2, "Other Foreign Troops Deployed to Afghanistan," in *Afghanistan Index* (Washington, DC: Brookings Institution, November 2015), 4. For war spending, see Amy

Belasco, *The Cost of Iraq, Afghanistan, and Other Global War on Terror Operations since 9/11*, CRS Report RL 33110 (Washington, DC, December 8, 2014), 14, 19.

4 For a discussion of these issues, see the following essays from *Anthropology and Global Counterinsurgency*, ed. John D. Kelly, Beatrice Jauregui, Sean T. Mitchell, and Jeremy Walton (Chicago: University of Chicago Press, 2010): David H. Price, "Soft Power, Hard Power, and the Anthropological 'Leveraging' of Cultural Assets," 245–60; Hugh Gusterson, "The Cultural Turn in the War on Terror," 280–95; and Dustin M. Wax, "The Uses of Anthropology in the Insurgent Age," 153–67. For a more controversial narration, see Montgomery McFate, "Anthropology and Counterinsurgency: The Strange Story of Their Curious Relationship," *Military Review*, March–April 2005, 27–37. See also Amy Mountcastle and James Armstrong, "Obama's War and Anthropology: Ethical Issues and Militarizing Anthropology," *Social Justice* 37, nos. 2–3 (2010–2011): 160–74.

5 On the involvement of American studies programs with the US government before Vietnam, see Robin W. Winks, *Cloak and Gown: Scholars in the Secret War, 1937–1961*, 2nd ed. (New Haven, CT: Yale University Press, 1996); and Michael Holzman, "The Ideological Origins of American Studies at Yale," *American Studies* 40, no. 2 (Summer 1999): 71–99.

6 A fine summary of the various schools and methods for studying culture is found in Michael Denning, *Culture in the Age of Three Worlds* (New York: Verso, 2004), 75–96.

7 These ideas are adapted from Immanuel Maurice Wallerstein, *The Essential Wallerstein* (New York: New Press, 2000), 265; and Warren Susman, *Culture and Commitment, 1929–1945* (New York: G. Braziller, 1973), 1–24. These scholars owe something to the pioneering work of Clifford Geertz as well. See Clifford Geertz, *The Interpretation of Cultures: Selected Essays* (New York: Basic Books, 1973), 448–53.

8 On this point, see Benedict Anderson, *Imagined Communities: Reflections on the Origin and Spread of Nationalism* (London: Verso, 1983), 5–7.

9 The light and dark sides of Enlightenment thought are explored in Max Horkheimer and Theodor W. Adorno, *Dialectic of Enlightenment* (Palo Alto, CA: Stanford University Press, 2007). On the arrival of parliaments and scientific laboratories, see Bruno Latour, *We Have Never Been Modern* (Cambridge, MA: Harvard University Press, 1993). On modernity and military technology, see Philip K. Lawrence, *Modernity and War: The Creed of Absolute Violence* (London: Palgrave MacMillan, 1997). On modernity's dialectical relationship with freedom, see Paul Gilroy, *The Black Atlantic: Modernity and Double Consciousness* (Cambridge, MA: Harvard University Press, 1993).

10 These ideas are explored in Anders Stephanson, *Manifest Destiny: American Expansion and the Empire of Right* (New York: Hill and Wang, 1995), xii–

27. See also Richard Slotkin, *Regeneration through Violence: The Mythology of the American Frontier, 1600–1860* (Tulsa: University of Oklahoma Press, 2000). On the long history of denying American empire, see Amy Kaplan and Donald E. Pease, *Cultures of United States Imperialism* (Durham, NC: Duke University Press, 1994).

11 The phrase "errand into the wilderness" comes from an election sermon by Reverend Samuel Danforth in 1760 and is explained in Perry Miller, *Errand into the Wilderness* (Cambridge: Harvard University Press, 1952), 1–15. The phrase "city on a hill" comes from John Winthrop's sermon "A Model of Christian Charity," delivered en route to the Massachusetts Bay Colony in 1630. The full text is available at http://winthropsociety.com/doc_charity.php (accessed December 17, 2015). See also Alfred A. Cave, *The Pequot War* (Amherst: University of Massachusetts Press, 1996); and Jill Lepore, *The Name of War: King Philip's War and the Origins of American Identity* (New York: Vintage, 1999).

12 The Jefferson quotations are from, in order, Thomas Jefferson to James Monroe, November 24, 1801, in *The Writings of Thomas Jefferson*, ed. Paul Leicester Ford, 10 vols. (New York: G. P. Putnam's Sons, 1892–1899), 4:574;the Declaration of Independence; and Jefferson, 1807, quoted in Benjamin Madley, "Reexamining the American Genocide Debate: Meaning, Historiography and New Methods," *American Historical Review* 120, no. 1 (February 2015): 109.

13 Charles S. Olcott, *William McKinley* (Boston: Houghton Mifflin, 1916), 2:111. See also Paul A. Kramer, *The Blood of Government: Race, Empire, the United States and the Philippines* (Chapel Hill: University of North Carolina Press, 2006).

14 For Wilson's quotation on Latin America, see Lester D. Langley, *The Banana Wars* (Lexington: University of Kentucky Press, 1983), 81. President Wilson's quotation concerning democracy is found in his war message to Congress, April 2, 1917. *War Messages*, 65th Cong., S. Doc. No. 5 (1917). The Caribbean occupations are discussed in depth in Max Boot, *The Savage Wars of Peace: Small Wars and the Rise of American Power* (New York: Basic Books, 2014). See also Aaron B. O'Connell, "Defending Imperial Interests in Asia and the Caribbean, 1898–1941," in *America, Sea Power, and the World*, ed. James C. Bradford (New York: Wiley Blackwell, 2016), 149–62.

15 The Reagan quotations are from his 1989 farewell address and his 1964 speech "A Time for Choosing." Transcripts of both are available at http://millercenter.org/president/speeches (accessed December 18, 2015).

16 President George H. W. Bush, inaugural address, January 20, 1989, accessed December 22, 2015, http://www.presidency.ucsb.edu/ws/?pid=16610.

17 These ideas are discussed at length in Francis Fukuyama, *The End of History and the Last Man* (New York: Simon & Schuster, 2006); and Francis Fukuyama, *Political Order and Political Decay: From the Industrial Revolu-*

tion to the Globalization of Democracy (New York: Farrar, Straus and Giroux, 2014).

18 President George W. Bush, *The National Security Strategy of the United States of America* (Washington, DC: The White House, September 2002), iv–vi (quotation on p. vi).

19 James R. Blaker, *United States Overseas Basing: An Anatomy of the Dilemma* (Westport, CT: Praeger, 1990), 10–33. See also Aaron B. O'Connell, "An Accidental Empire? President Harry S. Truman and the Origins of America's Global Military Presence," in *Origins of the National Security State and the Legacy of Harry S. Truman*, ed. Mary Ann Heiss and Michael J. Hogan (Kirksville, MO: Truman State University Press, 2014), 189–211.

20 Barry M. Blechman and Stephen S. Kaplan, *Force without War: U.S. Armed Forces as a Political Instrument* (Washington, DC: Brookings Institution, 1978), 23–57.

21 The information on uses of force after 1973 is collected in Richard F. Grimmett, *The War Powers Resolution: After Thirty-Six Years*, CRS Report R41199 (Washington, DC, April 22, 2010); and Richard F. Grimmett, *Instances of Use of United States Armed Forces Abroad, 1798–2009*, CRS Report RL32170 (Washington, DC, January 27, 2010).

22 Grimmett, *Instances of Use*, 27, 30.

23 The quotation appears in ibid., 29. See also O'Connell, "An Accidental Empire?," 202.

24 These ideas are discussed in Steven Pinker, *The Better Angels of Our Nature: Why Violence Has Declined* (New York: Penguin Books, 2012). See also John Lewis Gaddis, *The Long Peace: Inquiries into the History of the Cold War* (New York: Oxford University Press, 1989).

25 On the political power wielded by the military during the surge debate, see Bob Woodward, *Obama's Wars* (New York: Simon & Schuster, 2010), 280, 303, 301–20. The quotation appears on p. 312.

26 Morris Janowitz, *The Professional Soldier: A Social and Political Portrait* (Glencoe, IL: The Free Press, 1960), 21, 27–29, 263.

27 Komer served as the first head of the CORDS program from 1967 to 1968 and was later the ambassador to Turkey and undersecretary of defense for policy. See Robert W. Komer, *Bureaucracy Does Its Thing: Institutional Constraints on U.S.-GVN Performance in Vietnam* (Santa Monica, CA: RAND, 1972), v–xiii, 76. The phrase "institutional constraints" is first mentioned on page iii, "business as usual" on page xii, and "a significant adverse impact" on page 76.

28 These points are discussed in Andrew J. Bacevich, *The Pentomic Era: The U.S. Army between Korea and Vietnam* (Washington, DC: NDU Press, 1986), 120–27; Martin Van Creveld, *Command in War* (Cambridge, MA: Harvard University Press, 1985), 232–60; Paul N. Edwards, *The Closed World: Computers and the Politics of Discourse in Cold War America* (Cambridge, MA:

MIT Press, 1996); and James William Gibson, *The Perfect War: The War We Couldn't Lose and How We Did* (New York: Vintage Books, 1988).

29 Edwards, *Closed World*, 4.

30 The number of general officers in the ISAF headquarters is listed in Department of Defense, *Report on Progress toward Security and Stability in Afghanistan* (Washington, DC: The Pentagon, 2014), 8. I am grateful to State Department foreign service officer Marlin Hardinger for the data on US ambassadors in Afghanistan.

31 Ben Connable, *Embracing the Fog of War: Assessment and Metrics in Counterinsurgency* (Santa Monica, CA: RAND, 2012), 154–70.

32 General John Campbell, US Army, "The State of Afghanistan and Prospects for the Future: A Discussion with General John Campbell" (discussion, Brookings Institution, Washington, DC, August 4, 2015). On Afghan civilian casualties, see UNAMA, *Afghanistan: Protection of Civilians in Armed Conflict, Annual Report 2014* (Kabul: UNAMA, February 2015), 1–2, available at https://unama.unmissions.org/sites/default/files/2014-annual-report-on-protection-of-civilians-final.pdf (accessed December 29, 2015).

33 Connable, *Embracing the Fog of War*, 171 (brackets in original).

34 Martin Ewans, *Afghanistan: A Short History of Its People and Politics* (New York: Harper Collins, 2002), 17.

35 The four tribes are the Durrani, Ghilzai, Ghurghusht, and Karlanri. For more, see Thomas Barfield, *Afghanistan: A Cultural and Political History* (Princeton, NJ: Princeton University Press, 2010), 24–26.

36 At this time, the Durranis were still known by their earlier name, the Abdalis, a point I have omitted in the name of clarity. The tribal name changed when Ahmad Shah was given the sobriquet "Durr-e-Dauran" (Pearl of Pearls) in 1747.

37 This paragraph draws heavily from Louis Dupree, *Afghanistan* (Princeton, NJ: Princeton University Press, 1978), 322–34; Barfield, *Afghanistan*, 96–98; and Ewans, *Afghanistan*, 29–33.

38 Ewans, *Afghanistan*, 44. See also Barfield, *Afghanistan*, 107.

39 Dupree, *Afghanistan*, 343–405; Barfield, *Afghanistan*, 110–34; Ewans, *Afghanistan*, 45–85.

40 Ewans, *Afghanistan*, 89–90.

41 Dupree, *Afghanistan*, 403–13; Barfield, *Afghanistan*, 134–45; Ewans, *Afghanistan*, 87–97.

42 Ewans, *Afghanistan*, 98–109; Barfield, *Afghanistan*, 160–63; Dupree, *Afghanistan*, 417–29.

43 Barfield, *Afghanistan*, 164–210. On the model for stability, see Ewans, *Afghanistan*, 143.

44 Barfield, *Afghanistan*, 205.

45 Ahmed Rashid, *Taliban*, 2nd ed. (New Haven, CT: Yale University Press, 2010), 130.

46 The Soviet occupation is covered in Ewans, *Afghanistan*, 206–37. On Osama Bin Ladin, see Lawrence Wright, *The Looming Tower: Al Qaeda and the Road to 9/11* (New York: Vintage, 2007), 131–38.

47 On the Taliban conquest of Afghanistan, see Rashid, *Taliban*, 17–80; Barfield, *Afghanistan*, 258–70; and Ewans, *Afghanistan*, 249–71.

48 This explanation of Bin Ladin's motives and his partnership with the Taliban is in Wright, *Looming Tower*, 171–72, 213–14, 238–39, 374–75. See also Rashid, *Taliban*, 133–34.

49 Thomas H. Johnson and M. Chris Mason, "No Sign until the Burst of Fire: Understanding the Pakistan-Afghanistan Frontier," *International Security* 32, no. 4 (Spring 2008): 41–77. The authors do not suggest that all Pashtuns are violent extremists, and they account for other influences, such as the deliberate policies of the Pakistani Inter-Services Intelligence during the Soviet invasion of Afghanistan. Their point is that Pashtun culture is particularly amenable to those who use religion to organize military forces for the purpose of defending Islam and honor.

50 On violence and honor in the early United States, see Joanne B. Freeman, *Affairs of Honor: National Politics in the New Republic* (New Haven, CT: Yale University Press, 2002). For the quote on Afghan honor, see Johnson and Mason, "No Sign," 62.

51 My discussion of *Pashtunwali* is adapted from Johnson and Mason, "No Sign," 58–64. The quotation on discord and alarms is found on p. 50.

52 Johnson and Mason, "No Sign," 63.

53 Ibid.

54 On DOD opposition to a large US footprint in Afghanistan, see Donald Rumsfeld, *Known and Unknown: A Memoir* (New York: Sentinel, 2011), 395–409, 681–91. See also Sean M. Maloney, "Afghanistan: From Here to Eternity?," *Parameters* 34 (Spring 2004): 8; and Sean M. Maloney, "The International Security Assistance Force: The Origins of a Stabilization Force," *Canadian Military Journal*, Summer 2003, 6–7. On candidate George W. Bush's opposition to nation-building, see his remarks in the second presidential debate, October 11, 2000, accessed December 29, 2014, http://www.debates.org/?page=october-11-2000-debate-transcript.

55 President George W. Bush, "Joint Statement by President George W. Bush and Chairman Hamid Karzai on a New Partnership between the United States and Afghanistan," January 28, 2002, accessed August 10, 2015, http://avalon.law.yale.edu/sept11/joint_014.asp.

56 The full text of the Afghanistan Compact is available at http://www.nato.int/isaf/docu/epub/pdf/afghanistan_compact.pdf (accessed August 10, 2015).

57 For evidence of President Obama's resistance to nation-building, see Woodward, *Obama's Wars*, 387.

58 *The U.S. Army/Marine Corps Counterinsurgency Field Manual* (Chicago: University of Chicago Press, 2007), 49. For specific discussions of culture, see pp. 27, 35, 37–39, 89–97.

59 On the military's efforts to incorporate culture into the profession of arms, see Barak A. Salmoni and Paula Holmes-Eber, *Operational Culture for the Warfighter: Principles and Applications* (Quantico, VA: Marine Corps University Press, 2008). For a critical perspective, see Roberto J. González, *Militarizing Culture: Essays on the Warfare State* (Walnut Creek, CA: Left Coast Press, 2010).

Chapter One

1 William Colby with James McCargar, *Lost Victory: A Firsthand Account of America's Sixteen-Year Involvement in Vietnam* (New York: Contemporary Books, 1989), 75. For the discussion on institutional constraints, see Robert W. Komer, *Bureaucracy Does Its Thing: Institutional Constraints on U.S.-GVN Performance in Vietnam* (Santa Monica, CA: RAND, 1972).

2 The neglect of governance as an underlying cause of failures in Afghanistan is argued extensively in Vanda Felbab-Brown, *Aspiration and Ambivalence: Strategies and Realities of Counterinsurgency and State Building in Afghanistan* (Washington, DC: Brookings Institution, 2013).

3 Dov Zakheim, *A Vulcan's Tale: How the Bush Administration Mismanaged the Reconstruction of Afghanistan* (Washington, DC: Brookings Institution, 2011), 2.

4 A summary of the workshop is on the website of the American Academy of Diplomacy: http://www.academyofdiplomacy.org/program/arthur-ross-discussions-of-american-diplomacy/2011-diplomacy-education-discovering-and-teaching-reality/ (accessed July 2, 2016).

5 John R. Ballard, David W. Lamm, and John K. Wood, *From Kabul to Baghdad and Back: The US at War in Afghanistan and Iraq* (Annapolis, MD: Naval Institute Press, 2012), 181–82.

6 Bob Woodward, *Obama's Wars* (New York: Simon & Schuster, 2010), 211. Jonathan Allan and Ami Parnes, *HRC: State Secrets and the Rebirth of Hillary Clinton* (New York: Crown Publishing, 2014), 121–27. Vali Nasir also speaks extensively of Holbrooke being excluded from meetings; see Vali Nasir, *The Dispensable Nation: American Foreign Policy in Retreat* (New York: Doubleday, 2013), 5.

7 Zakheim, *Vulcan's Tale*, 9.

8 Robert M. Gates, *Duty: Memoirs of a Secretary at War* (New York: Alfred A. Knopf, 2014), 114 (quotation), 116, 121–26, 127–35.

9 Zakheim, *Vulcan's Tale*, 5, 173 (on Haass), 284, 294.

10 Lise Moraje Howard, *UN Peacekeeping in Civil Wars* (Cambridge: Cambridge University Press, 2008), 14.

11 Author interview with David Sedney, then deputy chief of mission and later deputy assistant secretary of defense, April 21, 2014.

12 Komer, *Bureaucracy Does Its Thing*, 67.

13 Not every SOF unit rotated this way, but many that I visited from 2005 to 2014 did so. One of the most informed briefings I ever received on Afghan local politics came from a SOF team in Kandahar Province.

14 Author interview with General George Casey, US Army (ret'd), May 1, 2014.

15 One senior officer involved in setting up the program told me that the Army personnel office refused to allow helicopter pilots to serve because they could not be promoted if they were to spend five years out of the cockpit. The idea that war might need some bending of the system was rejected. At the time of this writing, training for Afghan Hands is being reduced and positions for civilians are rapidly being shed.

16 Gates, *Duty*, 118

17 Carlotta Gaul, *The Wrong Enemy: America in Afghanistan, 2001–2014* (New York: Houghton Mifflin Harcourt, 2014), 60–61, 94–99.

18 Author interview with Afghanistan veteran and NSC staffer John K. Wood, May 13, 2014.

19 Author interview with David Sedney, then deputy chief of mission and later deputy assistant secretary of defense, April 21, 2014. This is also my experience and that of many others. I heard of the problem repeatedly when I was ambassador, both from President Karzai and from American ground forces commanders who felt that months of work were ruined by raids not coordinated with them.

20 Gates, *Duty*, 206. It is also worth noting that fixing the chain-of-command problems was greatly complicated by NATO nations' reluctance to place all aspects of allied troop operations under US command.

21 Condoleezza Rice, "Promoting the National Interest," *Foreign Affairs*, January–February 2000, 45–62; Zakheim, *Vulcan's Tale*, 7. On George W. Bush, see Commission on Presidential Debates, "Debate Transcript, October 11, 2000," accessed September 14, 2014, http://www.debates.org/index.php?page=october-11-2000-debate-transcript.

22 Zakheim, *Vulcan's Tale*, 9.

23 Ballard, Lamm, and Wood, *From Kabul to Baghdad and Back*, 101.

24 GAO, *Afghanistan Reconstruction: Deteriorating Security and Limited Resources Have Impeded Progress; Improvements in U.S. Strategy Needed*, GAO Report 04-403 (Washington, DC, June 2004), 2–3.

25 Author interview with David Sedney, then deputy chief of mission and later deputy assistant secretary of defense, April 21, 2014.

26 Ibid.

27 Carlotta Gall drove all over Helmand in 2004. See Joel Hafvenstein, *Opium Season: A Year on the Afghan Frontier* (Guilford, CT: Globe Pequot Press, 2007), 101, 112, 133.

28 David Rohde and David E. Sanger, "How a Good War in Afghanistan Went Bad," *New York Times*, August 12, 2007.

29 Sarah Chayes, *The Punishment of Virtue: Inside Afghanistan after the Tali-*

ban (New York: Penguin Books, 2006),155–56; Carl Forsberg, *Politics and Power in Kandahar* (Washington, DC: Institute for the Study of War, April 2010), 21, 27, 51, 59.

30 Dari is the Afghan version of Persian (Farsi). While there are differences, a Farsi speaker can function perfectly well in Afghanistan. However, with so many years of broken relations with Iran, only a few Farsi linguists had received training.

31 Author interview with David Sedney, then deputy chief of mission and later deputy assistant secretary of defense, April 21, 2014. Seth G. Jones also notes that Secretary Colin Powell, Ambassador James Dobbins, and others in State argued for more forces to stabilize Afghanistan, but they were successfully opposed by Secretary of Defense Donald Rumsfeld. See Seth G. Jones, *In the Graveyard of Empires: America's War in Afghanistan* (New York: W. W. Norton, 2010), 91.

32 Bradley Graham, *By His Own Rules: The Ambitions, Successes, and Ultimate Failures of Donald Rumsfeld* (Washington, DC: Public Affairs, 2009), 315.

33 Ballard, Lamm, and Wood, *From Kabul to Baghdad and Back*, 171.

34 Zakheim, *Vulcan's Tale*, 174; Ballard, Lamm, and Wood, *From Kabul to Baghdad and Back*, 299.

35 I describe the struggle for funding in detail in *The Other War: Winning and Losing in Afghanistan* (Washington, DC: Potomac Books, 2009), 40–49.

36 SIGAR, *Quarterly Report to the United States Congress* (Washington, DC, January 30, 2014), 204–5. See also Rohde and Sanger, "How a Good War in Afghanistan Went Bad."

37 Ballard, Lamm, and Wood, *From Kabul to Baghdad and Back*, 186.

38 SIGAR, *Quarterly Report* (January 30, 2014), 187.

39 For a comparison of State to DOD spending, see Amy Belasco, *The Cost of Iraq, Afghanistan, and Other Global War on Terrorism Operations since 9/11*, CRS Report RL 33110 (Washington, DC, December 8, 2014), 19. On how overspending encouraged corruption, see chapters 3, 5, and 6 in this volume.

40 George F. Kennan, *American Diplomacy* (Chicago: University of Chicago Press, 1951), 59.

41 Barack Obama, "Remarks by the President on a New Strategy for Afghanistan and Pakistan," March 27, 2009, available at www.whitehouse.gov (accessed October 11, 2014).

42 Barack Obama, "Remarks by the President in Address to the Nation on the Way Forward in Afghanistan and Pakistan," December 1, 2009, available at www.whitehouse.gov (accessed October 11, 2014).

43 Anthony H. Cordesman, *The US Cost of the Afghan War: FY2002–FY2013* (Washington, DC: Center for Strategic and International Studies, May 14, 2012), 4.

44 Bob Woodward notes the president pressed advisors on whether the strategy could be accomplished in the time allotted, but his account only addresses the military timeline and ignores the civilian aspects of the plan. See Woodward, *Obama's Wars*, 291. General Casey also noted that the Joint Chiefs of Staff estimated that building the Afghan security forces would take five years, but he did not recall whether the civilian timeline was ever subjected to searching discussion. Author interview with General George Casey, US Army (ret'd), May 1, 2014.

45 Eric Schmitt, "U.S. Envoy's Cables Show Worries on Afghan Plans," *New York Times*, January 25, 2010, A1.

46 GAO, *Afghanistan's Security Requirements*, GAO Report 10-613R (Washington, DC, May 5, 2010), 5. See also Ian S. Livingston and Michael O'Hanlon, figure 1.12, "U.S. Government Civilians in Afghanistan, 2008–2011," in *Afghanistan Index* (Washington, DC: Brookings Institution, November 30, 2013), 9.

47 Happily, the frictions eased by 2011 with personnel changes on both sides.

48 For an expanded discussion of US relations with Karzai, see Ronald E. Neumann, *Failed Relations between Hamid Karzai and the US: What Can We Learn?* (Washington, DC: US Institute of Peace, May 20, 2015).

49 For one representative example, see Judith Miller, "Is Karzai Crazy or Crazy like a Fox?," Fox News, October 28, 2010, available at www.foxnews.com (accessed September 21, 2014). See also Woodward, *Obama's Wars*, 128.

50 President Obama's memo is reproduced in Woodward, *Obama's Wars*, 386.

51 For more detail, see Neumann, *The Other War*, 152.

52 Woodward, *Obama's Wars*, 67–70. A participant at the dinner told me that Biden went on and on in a fashion that was deemed by the Afghans as deeply insulting.

53 Gates, *Duty*, 341

54 Author's discussions with President Karzai, 2010 and 2011.

55 Author's meetings with President Karzai in 2012 and 2013 in Kabul and in Doha, Qatar.

56 One such example was ISAF's decision to designate Kam Air, a private Afghan airline with connections to the Afghan government, as unsuitable for travel by Americans. Even though ISAF had tried to understand the political dynamics of its action in advance, the effort failed because the US military expected an embassy official to investigate the potential political implications of the airline designation and this was not done. The result was yet another crisis, because of Kam Air's political connections, made worse by the fact that the Afghans never believed the Americans' missteps were due to poor communication inside the ISAF coalition and the State Department. This summary is based on private discussion with US officials in Kabul shortly after the event.

57 Sharif Hassanyar, "Karzai Criticizes U.S. Definition of 'Terrorism,'" TOLOnews, December 22, 2013, available at www.TOLOnews.com (accessed October 11, 2014). I have heard the same view from senior NSC officials, Afghan ministers, confidants of Karzai, and President Karzai himself. For the

American view of Karzai's refusal to sign the BSA, see Ved Singh, "Behind Karzai's Stubbornness," *Foreign Policy in Focus*, March 6, 2014.

58 Karzai was praised by Afghans for rejecting the invitation. See "Bagram," *Khaama Press*, May 28, 2014; and Nathan Hodge, "Afghans Praise Karzai for Skipping Obama Meeting—Update," *Wall Street Journal*, May 27, 2014.

59 Barack Obama, "Statement by the President on Afghanistan," May 27, 2014, White House Press Office, available at www.whitehouse.gov (accessed October 11, 2014).

60 Frud Bezhan, "Afghans Dismayed at Future without Foreign Forces," Radio Free Europe / Radio Liberty, May 30, 2014, accessed October 11, 2014, http://www.rferl.org/content/afghans-us-karzai-future-without-foreign-forces/25404559.html.

Chapter Two

The views in this chapter do not reflect the policies of the US Naval War College, the Department of the Navy, or the Department of Defense. I would like to thank Karl Jackson, Austin Long, John Stark, and Gian Gentile for their careful reading and thoughtful suggestions on this chapter.

1 Leslie Gelb and Richard Betts, *The Irony of Vietnam: The System Worked* (Washington, DC: Brookings Institution, 1979), 247; Astri Suhkre, *When More Is Less: The International Project in Afghanistan* (New York: Columbia University Press, 2011), 4.

2 Helmut von Moltke, *Moltke on the Art of War: Selected Writings*, ed. Daniel Hughes (New York: Presidio Press, 1993), 45–47.

3 Douglas Feith, *War and Decision: Inside the Pentagon at the Dawn of the War on Terrorism* (New York: Harper, 2008), 6; Donald Rumsfeld, *Known and Unknown: A Memoir* (New York: Sentinel, 2011), 367–68.

4 Gary Schroen, *First In: An Insider's Account of How the CIA Spearheaded the War on Terror in Afghanistan* (New York: Ballantine Books, 2005), 15–16, 88, 90, 359; Henry Crumpton, *The Art of Intelligence: Lessons from a Life in the CIA's Clandestine Service* (New York: Penguin Press, 2012), 177–79; Feith, *War and Decision*, 16–17.

5 Schroen, *First In*, 98–100, 147, 189; Rumsfeld, *Known and Unknown*, 371, 376; Feith, *War and Decision*, 78.

6 Schroen, *First In*, 301.

7 Steve Call, *Danger Close: Tactical Air Controllers in Afghanistan and Iraq* (College Station: Texas A&M University Press, 2007).

8 Charles Briscoe, Richard Kiper, James Schroder, and Kalev Sepp, *Weapon of Choice: Army Special Forces in Afghanistan* (Carlisle Barracks, PA: Combat Studies Institute Press, 2003), 96–98; Tommy Franks, *American Soldier* (New York: Harper-Collins, 2004), 296–99.

9 Briscoe et al., *Weapon of Choice*, 102; Schroen, *First In*, 209.

10 Benjamin Lambeth, *Air Power against Terror: America's Conduct of Operation Enduring Freedom* (Santa Monica, CA: RAND, 2005), 79–84, 106, 121, 125–28; Schroen, *First In*, 154–55, 161, 185, 304–5; Crumpton, *Art of Intelligence*, 217–19.

11 Gary Berntsen and Ralph Pezzullo, *Jawbreaker: The Attacks on Bin Laden and Al-Qaeda* (New York: Crown Publishers, 2005), 90–91, 164–68; Feith, *War and Decision*, 96–98, 104–5.

12 Donald Wright, James Bird, Steven Clay, Peter Connors, LTC Scott Farquhar, Lynne Garcia, and Dennis Van Wey, *A Different Kind of War: The United States Army in Operation Enduring Freedom, October 2001–September 2005* (Fort Leavenworth, KS: Combat Studies Institute, 2010), 93–94; Berntsen and Pezzullo, *Jawbreaker*, 167–69.

13 Crumpton, *Art of Intelligence*, 177–78, 195–97.

14 Wright et al., *Different Kind of War*, 99–113.

15 Michael O'Hanlon, "A Flawed Masterpiece," *Foreign Affairs*, May–June 2002, 54–55; Berntsen and Pezzullo, *Jawbreaker*, 308–9; Crumpton, *Art of Intelligence*, 261; Bob Woodward, *Bush at War* (New York: Simon & Schuster, 2002), 314–17; John Greshman, "Outcomes and Consequences—Special Operations Forces and Operation Enduring Freedom," part 9 in "Operation Enduring Freedom: The First 49 Days," Defense Media Network, October 2, 2011, accessed May 10, 2014, http://www.defensemedianetwork.com/stories/operation-enduring-freedom-the-first-49-days-9/.

16 Berntsen and Pezzullo, *Jawbreaker*, 274–80, 290, 298–99, 306; Peter Krause, "The Last Good Chance: A Reassessment of U.S. Operations at Tora Bora," *Security Studies* 17 (2008): 644–84; Wright et al., *Different Kind of War*, 113–20.

17 Sean Naylor, *Not a Good Day to Die: The Untold Story of Operation Anaconda* (New York: Berkley Books, 2005); Wright et al., *Different Kind of War*, 127–74.

18 Thomas Barfield, *Afghanistan: A Cultural and Political History* (Princeton, NJ: Princeton University Press, 2010), 290; James Dobbins, *After the Taliban: Nation-Building in Afghanistan* (Washington, DC: Potomac Books, 2008), 77–97.

19 United Nations, "Agreement on Provisional Arrangements in Afghanistan Pending the Re-establishment of Permanent Government Institutions," December 5, 2001, accessed August 20, 2015, http://peacemaker.un.org/sites/peacemaker.un.org/files/AF_011205_AgreementProvisionalArrangementsinAfghanistan%28en%29.pdf.

20 Dobbins, *After the Taliban*, 85.

21 Sean M. Maloney, "Afghanistan: From Here to Eternity?," *Parameters* 34 (Spring 2004): 8; Sean M. Maloney, "The International Security Assistance Force: The Origins of a Stabilization Force," *Canadian Military Journal*, Summer 2003: 6–9; Feith, *War and Decision*, 105, 153–55.

22 Barfield, *Afghanistan*, 298, 302–3.

23 Dipali Mukhopadhyay, *Warlords, Strongman Governors, and the State of Afghanistan* (New York: Cambridge University Press, 2014), 2; Caroline Hartzell, *Missed Opportunities: The Impact of DDR on SSR in Afghanistan* (Washington, DC: US Institute of Peace, April 2011), 4.

24 Carter Malkasian, "Victory into Defeat," chap. 5 in *War Comes to Garmser: Thirty Years of Conflict on the Afghan Frontier* (New York: Oxford University Press, 2013).

25 Antonio Giustozzi, *Koran, Kalashnikov, and Laptop: The Neo-Taliban Insurgency in Afghanistan* (New York: Columbia University Press, 2008), 166–73; Wright et al., *Different Kind of War*, 231.

26 Feith, *War and Decision*, 156–58; Maloney, "International Security Assistance Force," 6–7.

27 This account oversimplifies the process of the expansion of ISAF and its growing integration with US forces. For a more detailed account, consult the NATO ISAF website: www.nato.int/cps/en/natohq/topics_69366.htm (accessed April 7, 2015).

28 Lieutenant General David Barno, "Fighting 'The Other War': Counterinsurgency Strategy in Afghanistan, 2003–2005," *Military Review*, September–October 2007, 37–41.

29 Ibid., 39.

30 Ibid., 33.

31 Tellingly, the Afghan government had initially pressed for an Afghan National Army (ANA) of 200,000 only to have this request dismissed by US and UK planners as needlessly large and unsustainable. See Wright et al., *Different Kind of War*, 201, 230.

32 Giustozzi, *Koran, Kalashnikov, and Laptop*, 185.

33 Antonio Giustozzi and Mohammed Isaqzadeh, *Policing Afghanistan: The Politics of the Lame Leviathan* (New York: Columbia University Press, 2012), 48–50.

34 This theory of armed development is not unique to Afghanistan. For a comparative treatment, see Colin Jackson, "Government in a Box? Counterinsurgency, State Building, and the Technocratic Conceit," in *The New Counter-Insurgency Era in Critical Perspective*, ed. Celeste Gventer-Ward, David Martin Jones, and M. L. R. Smith (New York: Palgrave Macmillan, 2014).

35 Robert Perito, *The U.S. Experience with Provincial Reconstruction Teams in Afghanistan*, Special Report 152 (Washington, DC: US Institute of Peace, October 2005).

36 Barno, "Fighting 'The Other War,'" 33. See also Christopher Koontz, ed., *Enduring Voices: Oral Histories of the U.S. Army Experience in Afghanistan, 2003–2005* (Washington, DC: Center for Military History, 2008), 29.

37 Paul Fishtein and Andrew Wilder, *Winning Hearts and Minds? Examining the Relationship between Aid and Security in Afghanistan* (Medford, MA: Feinstein International Center, Tufts University, January 2012), 3–6.

38 Wright et al., *Different Kind of War*, 226; "Karzai Vows to Prevent Corruption," *Toronto Star*, January 28, 2002, A10; Hamid Karzai, "Address to the Munich Security Conference," August 2, 2009, accessed December 23, 2015, https://www.securityconference.de/veranstaltungen/munich-security-conference/msc-2009/reden/hamid-karzai/.

39 Barno, "Fighting 'The Other War,'" 42; Koontz, *Enduring Voices*, 30–31.

40 Giustozzi, *Koran, Kalashnikov, and Laptop*, 101–15.

41 Dobbins, *After the Taliban*, 145–46, 151–52; Ronald Neumann, *The Other War: Winning and Losing in Afghanistan* (Washington, DC: Potomac Books, 2009), 204–6.

42 Mukhopadhyay, *Warlords*, 38–48; Barfield, *Afghanistan*, 304.

43 Malkasian, *War Comes to Garmser*, 98–102; Barfield, *Afghanistan*, 305–11.

44 International Crisis Group, *Disarmament and Reintegration in Afghanistan*, ICG Asia Report No. 65 (Kabul/Brussels: ICG, September 30, 2003), 1.

45 Carlotta Gall, *The Wrong Enemy: America in Afghanistan, 2001–2014* (New York, Houghton-Mifflin, 2014), 119–24.

46 Ahmed Rashid, *Descent into Chaos: The United States and the Failure of Nation Building in Pakistan, Afghanistan, and Central Asia* (New York: Viking, 2008), 240–41; Gall, *Wrong Enemy*, 61–63.

47 Mark Mazetti, "Pakistan Aids Insurgency in Afghanistan, Reports Assert," *New York Times*, July 25, 2010; Vahid Brown and Don Rassler, *Fountainhead of Jihad: The Haqqani Nexus, 1973–2012* (Oxford: Oxford University Press, 2013), 151–52.

48 Gall, *Wrong Enemy*, 131; Mark Mazetti, *The Way of the Knife: The CIA, a Secret Army, and a War at the Ends of the Earth* (New York: The Penguin Press, 2013), 111–12.

49 Rashid, *Descent into Chaos*, 250.

50 Gretchen Peters, *Haqqani Network Financing: The Evolution of an Industry* (West Point, NY: Combating Terrorism Center, 2012), 21–24, 35–38.

51 Carter Malkasian, *The War in Southern Afghanistan, 2001–2008* (Arlington, VA: Center for Naval Analysis, July 2009), 21–22.

52 Robert Gates, *Duty: Memoirs of a Secretary at War* (New York: Knopf, 2014), 199.

53 Neumann, *The Other War*, 114, 166; Malkasian, *War in Southern Afghanistan*, 22.

54 George W. Bush, *Decision Points* (New York: Crown Publishers, 2010), 212; Gates, *Duty*, 199; Neumann, *The Other War*, 124–28.

55 Neumann, *The Other War*, 145, 159, 205; Gates, *Duty*, 200.

56 Gates, *Duty*, 341.

57 Ibid., 338, 218.

58 Bob Woodward, *Obama's Wars* (New York: Simon & Schuster, 2010), 42–43; General Stanley McChrystal, *My Share of the Task: A Memoir* (New York: Penguin, 2013), 283; Gates, *Duty*, 222–23.

59 Woodward, *Obama's Wars*, 88–89.

60 "Press Briefing by Bruce Riedel, Ambassador Richard Holbrooke, and Michele Flournoy on the New Strategy for Afghanistan and Pakistan," The White House, March 27, 2009, accessed April 7, 2015, http://www.whitehouse.gov/the-press-office/press-briefing-bruce-riedel-ambassador-richard-holbrooke-and-michelle-flournoy-new-; "White Paper of the Interagency Policy Group's Report on U.S. Policy toward Afghanistan and Pakistan," unveiled in a presidential speech on March 27, 2009, accessed April 7, 2015, https://www.whitehouse.gov/assets/documents/Afghanistan-Pakistan_White_Paper.pdf.

61 "Remarks by the President on a New Strategy for Afghanistan and Pakistan," The White House, March 27, 2009, accessed April 7, 2015, http://www.whitehouse.gov/the-press-office/remarks-president-a-new-strategy-afghanistan-and-pakistan.

62 Gates, *Duty*, 345–46; Woodward, *Obama's Wars*, 199.

63 McChrystal, *My Share of the Task*, 92–96; Mazetti, *Way of the Knife*, 129–31.

64 Gates, *Duty*, 348–50; McChrystal, *My Share of the Task*, 294, 317.

65 McChrystal, *My Share of the Task*, 317, 321, 329, 335.

66 Woodward, *Obama's Wars*, 159–60, 167–68, 236.

67 Gates, *Duty*, 374; McChrystal, *My Share of the Task*, 349–50; Woodward, *Obama's Wars*, 158, 190.

68 Woodward, *Obama's Wars*, 216–17, 329–30, 385–90; McChrystal, *My Share of the Task*, 345

69 "Remarks by the President in Address to the Nation on the Way Forward in Afghanistan and Pakistan," December 1, 2009, accessed December 22, 2015, http://www.whitehouse.gov/photos-and-video/video/president-obama-way-forward-afghanistan-and-pakistan#transcript.

70 Woodward, *Obama's Wars*, 301.

71 Gates, *Duty*, 474–75.

72 Ibid., 371, 380, 481–83.

73 Department of Defense, *Report on Progress toward Security and Stability in Afghanistan* (Washington, DC: The Pentagon, November 2009), 11–12.

74 General Stanley McChrystal, "Tactical Directive," HQ ISAF, July 9, 2009, accessed April 2, 2015, http://www.nato.int/isaf/docu/official_texts/Tactical_Directive_090706.pdf.

75 Gates, *Duty*, 340; McChrystal, *My Share of the Task*, 323–26.

76 Dexter Filkins, "Afghan Offensive Is New War Model," *New York Times*, February 12, 2010.

77 McChrystal, *My Share of the Task*, 368.

78 Jackson, "Government in a Box?"; author interview with Lt. Col. Michael Styskal, USMC, June 2014.

79 Carl Forsberg, *Counterinsurgency in Kandahar: Evaluating the 2010 Hamkari Campaign*, Afghanistan Report 7 (Washington, DC: The Institute for the Study of War, December 15, 2010), http://www.understandingwar.org/sites/default/files/Afghanistan%20Report%207_15Dec.pdf.

80 Michael Hastings, "The Runaway General," *Rolling Stone*, June 22, 2010.

81 Gates, *Duty*, 488; McChrystal, *My Share of the Task*, 387–88.

82 General David Petraeus, "General Petraeus Assumes Command of ISAF," July 4, 2010, accessed April 2, 2015, http://www.isaf.nato.int/article/news/gen.-petraeus-assumes-command-of-isaf.html.

83 General David Petraeus, House Armed Services Testimony, March 16, 2011, p. 4, accessed April 2, 2015, http://armedservices.house.gov/index.cfm/files/serve?File_id=1bbe2277-0e46-43ab-9ae5-24dd8afad749. According to the International Centre for Prison Studies at the University of Exeter, the prison population in Afghanistan grew from 5,262 in 2004 to 25,289 in 2012 (http://www.prisonstudies.org/country/afghanistan, accessed December 20, 2015).

84 Charles M. Johnson, *Afghanistan: Oversight and Accountability of U.S. Assistance*, GAO Report 14-680T (Washington, DC, June 10, 2014), 4.

85 Author interview with senior US diplomatic source, May 2014; Gates, *Duty*, 371; Ian S. Livingston and Michael O'Hanlon, *Afghanistan Index* (Washington, DC: Brookings Institution, October 29, 2014), 8.

86 Noah Coburn and Anna Larson, *Derailing Democracy in Afghanistan: Elections in an Unstable Political Landscape* (New York: Columbia University Press, 2014), 217–23.

87 This figure is only for assistance to Afghanistan. It does not include the cost of all US military operations in the country, which added almost another hundred billion dollars to the bill in 2011 alone. SIGAR, *Quarterly Report to the United States Congress* (Washington, DC, October 30, 2012), 61–63. Afghan GDP figures were drawn from the *CIA World Factbook, 2013*, accessed January 10, 2013, https://www.cia.gov/library/publications/the-world-factbook/geos/af.html; and The World Bank, "Afghanistan," accessed January 10, 2013, http://www.worldbank.org/en/country/afghanistan.

88 The World Bank, *Islamic State of Afghanistan: Pathways to Inclusive Growth* (Washington, DC: The World Bank, March 2014), 17–20, 28, http://www-wds.worldbank.org/external/default/WDSContentServer/WDSP/IB/2014/06/18/000456286_20140618113748/Rendered/PDF/ACS82280WP0v2000Box385214B00PUBLIC0.pdf.

89 Bing West, *The Wrong War: Grit, Strategy, and the Way Out of Afghanistan* (New York: Random House, 2011), 71, 250; Fishstein and Wilder, "Winning Hearts and Minds?," 41–42.

90 Astri Suhkre, *When More Is Less: The International Project in Afghanistan* (New York: Columbia University Press, 2011), 15–16; SIGAR, *Quarterly Report to the United States Congress* (Washington, DC, April 30, 2014), 4–6.

91 Barfield, *Afghanistan*, 340; Suhkre, *When More Is Less*, 152–54; Malkasian, *War Comes to Garmser*, 266–68; Antonio Giustozzi, *Empires of Mud: Wars and Warlords in Afghanistan* (New York: Columbia University Press, 2009,), 274–76.

92 Department of Defense, *Report on Progress toward Security and Stability in Afghanistan* (Washington, DC: The Pentagon, April 2012), 1, 104–5.

93 C. Christine Fair, "Lashkar-e-Taiba beyond Bin Laden: Enduring Challenges for the Region and the International Community," testimony prepared for the US Senate, Foreign Relations Committee hearing on Al Qaeda, the Taliban, and other extremist groups in Afghanistan and Pakistan, May 24, 2011, pp. 2–3, accessed June 24, 2016, http://www.foreign.senate.gov/imo/media/doc/Fair_Testimony.pdf.

94 Gall, *Wrong Enemy*, 62–63, 98–99, 161–62; Ashley Tellis, "Beradar, Pakistan, and the Afghan Taliban: What Gives?" *Carnegie Endowment for International Peace Policy Outlook*, March 2010, 1, 3, 5, 10: Thomas Ruttig, "The Taliban Arrest Wave: Reasserting Strategic Depth?" *Combating Terrorism Center (CTC) Sentinel* 3, no. 3 (March 2010): 5–7; Robert L. Grenier, *88 Days to Kandahar: A CIA Diary* (New York: Simon & Schuster, 2015), 318, 362–63, 413.

95 Gates, *Duty*, 557.

96 Ibid., 561–65.

97 Woodward, *Obama's Wars*, 327.

98 James Willbanks, *Abandoning Vietnam: How America Left and South Vietnam Lost Its War* (Lawrence: University Press of Kansas, 2004), 9–19, 26–31.

99 DOD, *Report on Progress* (April 2012), 50.

100 Department of Defense, *Report on Progress toward Security and Stability in Afghanistan* (Washington, DC: The Pentagon, April 2014), 10–11.

101 International Crisis Group, *Afghanistan's Insurgency after the Transition*, Asia Report No. 256 (Kabul/Brussels: ICG, May 12, 2014), i; Azam Ahmed, "Taliban Making Gains in Afghanistan," *New York Times*, July 26, 2014.

102 UNAMA, *Afghanistan: Protection of Civilians in Armed Conflict, Annual Report 2014* (Kabul: UNAMA, February 2015).

103 World Bank, *Islamic State of Afghanistan*, 6–8.

104 SIGAR, *Quarterly Report to the United States Congress* (Washington, DC, January 30, 2014), 11.

105 President Obama, "Statement by the President on Afghanistan," The White House, October 15, 2015, accessed October 20, 2015, https://www.whitehouse.gov/the-press-office/2015/10/15/statement-president-afghanistan.

106 Michael Schear and Julie Hirschfeld Davis, "U.S. Agrees to Slow Pullout of Troops from Afghanistan," *New York Times*, March 25, 2015.

107 SIGAR, *Quarterly Report* (April 30, 2014), 92.

108 US Senate, Committee on Armed Services, "Nomination of Gen. Joseph F. Dunford, Jr., USMC, for Reappointment to the Grade of General and to be Commandant of the Marine Corps," July 17, 2014, accessed December 19, 2015, http://www.armed-services.senate.gov/imo/media/doc/14-64%20-%207-17-14.pdf.

109 Rodric Braithwaite, *Afghantsy: The Russians in Afghanistan, 1979–1989* (London: Profile Books, 2011), 299.

110 For an overview of post-2011 funding of the Iraqi regime and armed forces, see Kenneth Katzman, *Iraq: Politics, Governance, and Human Rights*, CRS Report 7-5700 (Washington, DC, July 2, 2014), http://fas.org/sgp/crs/mideast/RS21968.pdf.

111 General Joseph Dunford Jr., "Hearing to Receive Testimony on the Situation in Afghanistan, Wednesday, March 12, 2014," US Senate, Committee on Armed Services, Washington, DC, pp. 5, 8, accessed December 28, 2015, http://www.armed-services.senate.gov/imo/media/doc/14-19%20-%203-12-14.pdf.

112 C. Christine Fair, *Fighting to the End: The Pakistan Army's Way of War* (New York: Oxford University Press, 2014), 133–34; Brown and Rassler, *Fountainhead of Jihad*, 242–43; Gall, *Wrong Enemy*, 283–86.

113 Barfield, *Afghanistan*, 3–7, 166.

114 This observation is consistent with the judgment of other pessimists of democratization as a strategy. See Edward Mansfield and Jack Snyder, "Pathways to War in Democratic Transitions," *International Organization* 63 (Spring 2009): 381–90; and Samuel Huntington, *Political Order in Changing Societies* (New Haven, CT: Yale University Press, 1968).

115 LTC Christopher Lowe, USA, conversation with the author, 2011.

Chapter Three

The views expressed in this chapter belong solely to the authors and do not necessarily reflect the official policy of the United States Naval Academy, the Air War College, the Department of Defense, or the US government.

1 LTG William B. Caldwell IV, commander, NTM-A, 2009–2012, quoted in Nick Hopkins, "Afghanistan: Advances Made, but Country Stands at Perilous Crossroads," *The Guardian*, May 10, 2011, http://www.theguardian.com/world/2011/may/10/afghanistan-crossroads-taliban-military.

2 For just a few examples, see Thomas H. Johnson and M. Chris Mason, "No Sign until the Burst of Fire: Understanding the Pakistan-Afghanistan Frontier," *International Security* 32, no. 4 (2008): 41–77; Thomas Barfield, *Afghanistan: A Political and Cultural History* (Princeton, NJ: Princeton University Press, 2010); and Lester W. Grau, *The Bear Went over the Mountain: Soviet Combat Tactics in Afghanistan* (Washington, DC: National Defense University Press, 2013).

3 United Nations, "Agreement on Provisional Arrangements in Afghanistan Pending the Re-establishment of Permanent Government Institutions," December 2001, para. V, sec. (1), available at www.un.org (accessed May 5, 2014).

4 Ali A. Jalali, "Rebuilding Afghanistan's National Army," *Parameters*, Autumn 2002, 72.

5 Early efforts are covered in GAO, *Afghanistan Security: Efforts to Establish Army and Police Have Made Progress, but Future Plans Need to Be Better Defined*, GAO Report 05-575 (Washington, DC, June 2005); the quotation is from page 1.

6 United Front spokesperson Younis Qanooni, cited in Sean M. Maloney, "The International Security Assistance Force: The Origins of a Stabilization Force," *Canadian Military Journal*, Summer 2003, 5.

7 Peter Tomsen, *The Wars of Afghanistan* (New York: PublicAffairs, 2011), 639.

8 GAO, *Afghanistan Security*, 6–9.

9 On fuel, see SIGAR, *ANSF: Limited Visibility over Fuel Imports Increases the Risk That US Funded Fuel Purchases Could Violate U.S. Economic Sanctions against Iran*, SIGAR SP-13-2 (Washington, DC, January 2013), http://www.sigar.mil/pdf/alerts/2013-01-30-alert-sp-13-2.pdf.

10 Adrian Lewis, *The American Culture of War: The History of U.S. Military Force from World War II to Operation Iraqi Freedom* (New York: Routledge, 2007), 389.

11 Matt Waldman, "System Failure: The Underlying Causes of U.S. Policy-Making Errors in Afghanistan," *International Affairs*, July 2013, 827.

12 In 2002, early recruiting efforts struggled because attrition was as high as 50 percent. By mid-2003, it had stabilized around 30 percent. See Antonio Giustozzi, "Rebuilding the Afghan Army" (paper presented at the State Reconstruction and International Engagement in Afghanistan Conference, London School of Economics, June 1, 2003), 26n29. See also GAO, *Afghanistan Reconstruction: Deteriorating Security and Limited Resources Have Impeded Progress; Improvements in U.S. Strategy Needed*, GAO Report 04-403 (Washington, DC, June 2004), 43.

13 Pamela Constable, "An Army in Progress: Building of Afghan Force Proves Difficult," *Washington Post*, October 7, 2003, A01.

14 "First Battalion of Afghanistan Army to Be Deployed," Voice of America, July 22, 2002, accessed December 15, 2011, http://www.voanews.com/english/news/a-13-a-2002-07-22-29-First-66500992.html.

15 Anja Manuel and P. W. Singer, "A New Model Afghan Army," *Foreign Affairs*, December 1, 2002, http://www.foreignaffairs.com/articles/64208/anja-manuel-and-p-w-singer/a-new-model-afghan-army.

16 GAO, *Afghanistan Security*, 12–13, 15.

17 In 2004, attrition in the army was a manageable 12 percent, but it rose steadily thereafter. See GAO, *Afghanistan: Key Oversight Issues for Congress*, GAO Report 13-218SP (Washington, DC, February 2013), 11.

18 GAO, *Afghanistan Security*, 14.

19 The problems with the army and police in 2008 are detailed in GAO, *Report to Congressional Committees: Further Congressional Action May Be Needed to Ensure Completion of a Detailed Plan to Develop and Sustain Capable Afghan National Security Forces*, GAO Report 08-661 (Washington, DC, June 2008); and Charles Michael Johnson Jr., *U.S. Efforts to Develop Capable Afghan Police Forces Face Challenges*, GAO Report 08-883T (Washington, DC, June 18, 2008).

20 GAO, *Afghan Army Growing, but Additional Trainers Needed; Long-Term Costs Not Determined*, GAO Report 11-66 (Washington, DC, January 2011). See also GAO, *Report to Congressional Committees*, 18–30.

21 Attrition data comes from Ian S. Livingston and Michael O'Hanlon, figure 1.7, "Attrition Rates among Select ANSF," in *Afghanistan Index* (Washington, DC: Brookings Institution, March 31, 2014), 7.

22 Seth G. Jones and Arturo Muñoz, *Afghanistan's Local War: Building Local Defense Forces* (Santa Monica, CA: RAND, 2010), 48.

23 GAO, *Report to Congressional Committees*, 24, 25.

24 These problems are detailed in ibid., 11–12, 18–30.

25 Seth G. Jones, *In the Graveyard of Empires: America's War in Afghanistan* (New York: W. W. Norton, 2010), 168.

26 GAO, *Afghanistan Security*, 22–24.

27 Anthony Cordesman, *Afghanistan and the Uncertain Metrics of Progress, Part Five: Building Effective Afghan Forces* (Washington, DC: Center for Strategic and International Studies, March 2011), 7. For the statistic above on the number of German advisors in the Ministry of Interior in 2003, see Robert Perito, *Afghanistan's Police: The Weak Link in Security Sector Reform*, Special Report 227 (Washington, DC: US Institute of Peace, August 2009), 3.

28 Gootnick et al., *Afghanistan Security*, 22 (quotation), 26.

29 Kim Barker, *The Taliban Shuffle: Strange Days in Afghanistan and Pakistan* (New York: Doubleday, 2011), 53–54.

30 GAO, *Afghanistan Security*, 26.

31 Perito, *Afghanistan's Police*, 4.

32 Ibid., 170.

33 GAO, *Report to Congressional Committees*, 31–42.

34 Johnson, *U.S. Efforts*, 8; GAO, *Report to Congressional Committees*, 4.

35 GAO, *Report to Congressional Committees*, 40.

36 Ben Anderson, *No Worse Enemy: The Inside Story of the Chaotic Struggle for Afghanistan* (Oxford: Oneworld Press, 2011), 15.

37 The comparative casualty rates of ANA and ANP personnel come from Livingston and O'Hanlon, figure 1.22, "ANA and ANP Personnel Casualties 2007–2012," in *Afghanistan Index*, 14.

38 Perito, *Afghanistan's Police*, 1.

39 GAO, *Afghanistan: Key Issues for Congressional Oversight*, GAO Report 09-473SP (Washington, DC, April 2009), 28.

40 SIGAR, *Afghan Police Vehicle Maintenance Contract: Actions Needed to Prevent Millions of Dollars from Being Wasted*, SIGAR Audit 13-3 (Washington, DC, January 2013), https://www.sigar.mil/pdf/audits/2013-01-17audit-13-3.pdf.

41 Michael E. O'Hanlon and Hassina Sherjan. *Toughing It Out in Afghanistan* (Washington, DC: Brookings Institution, 2010), 2.

42 Department of Defense, *Report on Progress toward Security and Stability in Afghanistan* (Washington, DC: The Pentagon, October 2009), 29.

43 Robert Johnson, *The Afghan Way of War: How and Why They Fight* (Oxford: Oxford University Press, 2011), 276.

44 Thomas H. Johnson and M. Chris Mason, "Refighting the Last War: Afghanistan and the Vietnam Template," *Military Review*, November–December 2009, 6.

45 NATO, "NATO Training Mission-Afghanistan," April 4, 2009, accessed October 4, 2014, http://www.nato.int/cps/en/natolive/news_52802.htm.

46 Department of Defense, *Report on Progress toward Security and Stability in Afghanistan* (Washington, DC: The Pentagon, April 2010), 15.

47 Associated Press, "US Finds Problems with Training Afghans," Military.com, October 8, 2009, accessed 26 December 2010, http://www.military.com/news/article/us-finds-problems-with-training-afghans.html?ESRC=eb.nl.

48 *ANP Basic Patrolman Course: Curriculum for the Initial Education of the Patrolman*, 13. A copy of this training document is in the authors' possession.

49 Rajiv Chandrasekaran, *Little America: The War within the War for Afghanistan* (New York: Vintage, 2013), 142.

50 "Primary Drivers of ANA Attrition and Mitigating Actions," n.d., unclassified NTM-A/CSTC-A information paper; "AWOL/Attrition Items from GFC CSM," March 16, 2011, unclassified e-mail from BG William O'Neill, IJC. Copies of both are in the authors' possession.

51 DOD, *Report on Progress* (April 2010), 17.

52 By August, the ANP was still 217 Police Operational Mentor Liaison Teams short, with 88 priority districts left uncovered. By contrast, the IJC was partnered with 173 of 180 ANA units. "ANSF Monthly Progress Report, February 2011." A copy is in the authors' possession.

53 Dr. Loicano's notes from NTM-A/CSTC-A DCOM huddle, March 13, 2010.

54 Waldman, "System Failure," 829.

55 Dr. Loicano's notes from meeting between Minster of Interior Hanif Atmar and Brigadier General Anne MacDonald, MOI, March 17, 2010.

56 Stanley A. McChrystal, *My Share of the Task: A Memoir* (New York: Penguin, 2014), 300.

57 Waldman, "System Failure," 829.

58 "November ANSF Progress Overview," November 14, 2011, unclassified NTM-A report; "Infrastructure Facts and Assumptions," July 27, 2011, unclassified NTM-A PowerPoint slide. Copies of both are in the authors' possession.

59 SIGAR, *Quarterly Report to the United States Congress* (Washington, DC, January 30, 2016), 186–87, 147, 186–87.

60 Kenneth Katzman, *Afghanistan: Post-Taliban Governance, Security, and U.S. Policy* (Washington, DC: Congressional Research Service, 2016), 32, https://www.fas.org/sgp/crs/row/RL30588.pdf.

61 Testimony of Max Boot, in *Expert Assessments on the Afghan National Security Forces: Resources, Strategy, and Timetable for Security Lead Transition, Hearing before the Committee on Armed Services* (Washington, DC: GPO, June 29, 2012), 3.

62 Anderson, *No Worse Enemy*, 13–14.

63 Jones and Muñoz, *Afghanistan's Local War*, 2.

64 Fernando Gentilini, *Afghan Lessons: Culture, Diplomacy, and Counterinsurgency* (Washington, DC: Brookings Institution, 2011), 62.

65 T. E. Lawrence, "Twenty-Seven Articles," *Arab Bulletin*, August 20, 1917. The full text is available online at http://telawrence.net/telawrencenet/works/articles_essays/1917_twenty-seven_articles.htm (accessed August 10, 2011).

66 US House of Representatives, Committee on Armed Services, *Developments in Afghanistan* (Washington, DC: GPO, June 16, 2010), 1.

67 Mark Sedra, "Security Sector Reform and State Building in Afghanistan," in *Afghanistan Transition under Threat*, ed. Geoffrey Hayes and Mark Sedra (Ontario: Wilfrid Laurier University Press, 2008), 196.

68 James William Gibson, *The Perfect War: Technowar in Vietnam* (Boston: The Atlantic Monthly Press, 1986), 23.

69 Greg Jaffe and Joshua Partlow, "With Afghan Drawdown Looming, U.S. Scales Back Ambitions," *Washington Post*, October 6, 2011, http://articles.washingtonpost.com/2011-10-06/world/35278072_1_haqqani-network-commanders-high-profile-attacks; David S. Cloud, "Pentagon to Drastically Cut Spending on Afghan Forces," *Los Angeles Times*, September 12, 2011, http://articles.latimes.com/2011/sep/12/world/la-fg-us-afghan-police-20110913.

Chapter Four

1 Sarah Chayes, *The Punishment of Virtue: Inside Afghanistan after the Taliban* (New York: Penguin Group, 2006).

2 David H. Bayley, "Police Function, Structure, and Control in Western Europe and North America: Comparative and Historical Studies," *Crime and Justice* 1 (1979): 109–43.

3 Donald N. Wilber, *Afghanistan* (New Haven, CT: Human Relations Area Files, 1956), 77.

4 Martin Ewans, *Afghanistan: A Short History of Its People and Politics* (New York: Harper Perennial, 2002), 102.

5 The early history of Afghan policing is summarized in Ali A. Jalali, "Rebuilding Afghanistan's National Army," *Parameters* (Autumn 2002): 72–86.

6 Olga Oliker, *Building Afghanistan's Security Forces in Wartime: The Soviet Experience* (Santa Monica, CA: RAND, 2011), 3.

7 Amnesty International, *Afghanistan: Police Reconstruction Essential for the Protection of Human Rights*, ASA 11/003/2003 (Amnesty International, March 2003), 3–4.

8 International Crisis Group, *Reforming Afghanistan's Police*, Asia Report No. 138 (Kabul/Brussels: ICG, February 18, 2008), 2.

9 Willem Vogelsang, *The Afghans* (New York: Wiley Blackwell, 2002), 308.

10 Fred Halliday and Zahir Tanin, "The Communist Regime in Afghanistan," *Europe-Asia Studies* 50, no. 8 (1998): 1366.

11 Ibid.

12 Robert Perito, *Afghanistan's Police: The Weak Link in Security Sector Reform*, Special Report 227 (Washington, DC: US Institute of Peace, August 2009), 3.

13 Kabul Khan Tadbeer, personal interview, Kabul, January 1, 2014.

14 Oliker, *Building Afghanistan's Security Forces*, 25.

15 Abdul Samad (pseud.) was a Mujahideen commander and was arrested in his home in the north of Kandahar Province. He was put in jail for seven months in 1982 and released with the help of a relative who guaranteed for the government that he wouldn't join the Mujahideen again. Personal interview, January 8, 2014.

16 Ahmad Wali (pseud.), personal interview, Kandahar, December 28, 2013.

17 Abdul Khaliq (pseud.), personal interview, Kabul, January 12, 2014.

18 Tonita Murray, "Police Building in Afghanistan: A Case Study of Civil Security Reform," *International Peacekeeping*, vol. 14, no. 1 (2007): 108–26.

19 Abdul Manan (pseud.), 55, is from Parwan Province. He is a former Mujahideen commander who was jailed by the Taliban several times under suspicion of possessing arms (he never did). They tortured him so badly that he could not walk for months after his release. Personal interview, February 13, 2014.

20 Ralph Magnus and Eden Naby, *Afghanistan: Mullah, Marx, and Mujahid* (New York: Basic Books, 2002), 208.

21 Hajar Hussaini, personal interview, May 20, 2014.

22 This point is discussed at length in Thomas Barfield, *Afghanistan: A Cultural and Political History* (Princeton, NJ: Princeton University Press, 2010).

23 "National Police Force Sought in Afghanistan; Recruits Would Hail From All Provinces," *Washington Post*, February 5, 2002, A08.

24 Perito, *Afghanistan's Police*, 3.

25 Hamid Ahmad (pseud.), personal interview, Kandahar, December 13, 2013.

26 Ibid.

27 Perito, *Afghanistan's Police*, 5.

28 Ibid.

29 Ibid.

30 EUPOL Afghanistan, "About EUPOL: What Is EUPOL Afghanistan?," accessed December 21, 2015, http://www.eupol-afg.eu/node/2. A copy is in the author's possession.

31 House of Lords, European Union Committee, *The EU's Afghan Police Mission: Report with Evidence* (London: The Stationary Office, Limited, 2011), 9–10.

32 Perito, *Afghanistan's Police*, 10.

33 Ibid.

34 House of Lords, European Union Committee, *Afghan Police Mission*, 9, 5, 14.

35 Juma Khan (pseud.), personal interview, Kabul, May 17, 2014.

36 Ian S. Livingston and Michael O'Hanlon, figure 1.4, "Size of Afghan National Security Forces on Duty, 2003–2013," in *Afghanistan Index* (Washington, DC: Brookings Institution, November 30, 2013), 6.

37 Cornelius Friesendorf and Jorg Krempel, *Militarized versus Civil Policing: Problems of Reforming the Afghan National Police*, trans. Lynn Benstead (Frankfurt am Main: Peace Research Institute Frankfurt, 2011), 12.

38 Niaz Muhammad (pseud.), personal interview, Kabul, November 9, 2013.

39 Interim head of EUPOL Afghanistan Nigel Thomas, cited in Kim Sengupta, "Afghan Police Corruption Hits NATO Pullout," *The Independent*, November 21, 2010, http://www.independent.co.uk/news/world/politics/afghan-police-corruption-hits-nato-pullout-2139883.html.

40 Cornilius Friesendorf and Jorg Krempel, *Militarized versus Civil Policing: Problems of Reforming the Afghan National Police*, Peace Research Institute Frankfurt Report No. 102 (Frankfurt: PRIF, 2011), 1.

41 Livingston and O'Hanlon, figure 1.21, "ANA and ANP Personnel Fatalities, 2007–2013," in *Afghanistan Index*, 14.

42 Zaman Shah (pseud.), district police chief, personal interview, June 27, 2010.

43 House of Lords, European Union Committee, *Afghan Police Mission*, 19.

44 Author's observations, February 2010.

45 Gen. Niamatullah Wahid (pseud.), personal interview, May 17, 2014.

46 Gulam Farooq (pseud.), personal interview, Kandahar, November 15, 2013.

47 Sabir Ahmad (pseud.), personal interview, January 12, 2014.

48 These statistics are detailed in Department of Defense, *Report on Progress toward Security and Stability in Afghanistan* (Washington, DC: The Pentagon, April 2014), 48–53.

49 Amrullah Saleh, "Ending the Politicization of Afghan Security Forces," Aljazeera, April 19, 2012, accessed December 28, 2015, http://www.aljazeera.com/indepth/opinion/2012/04/2012418858435 40832.html.

50 Won-Huyk Im, personal interview, Parwan, July 23, 2011.

51 Personal interview with an Afghan police officer (name withheld), Kandahar, June 29, 2010.

52 "Afghan Vote-Rigging Videos Emerge," Aljazeera, September 26, 2010, accessed May 1, 2012, http://www.aljazeera.com/news/asia/2010/09/2010926 14267602479.html2.

53 This quotation comes from a Kandahar citizen who was personally familiar with the CID. Personal interview, Kandahar, March 15, 2010.

54 Abdul Karim (pseud.) is an Afghan CID official. He did not want to disclose his identity because of the delicacy of the matter. Personal interview, Kandahar, March 30, 2010.

55 Asadullah Zerasawand, accessed May 12, 2014, http://www.larawbar.net/40298.html.

Chapter Five

1 The "Agreement on Provisional Arrangements in Afghanistan Pending the Re-establishment of Permanent Government Institutions" (Bonn Agreement) was concluded on December 5, 2001.

2 Paul Collier et al., *Breaking the Conflict Trap: Civil War and Development Policy* (Oxford: Oxford University Press, 2003), 83.

3 President George W. Bush, "Remarks at the Virginia Military Institute," April 17, 2002, reprinted in *New York Times*, April 18, 2002, http://www.nytimes.com/2002/04/18/international/18FULL-PTEXT.html?pagewanted=all.

4 UN News Centre, "Afghanistan & the United Nations," UN News Service, accessed August 5, 2014, http://www.un.org/news/dh/latest/afghan/un-afghan-history.shtml.

5 "Co-chairs' Summary of Conclusions, the International Conference on Reconstruction Assistance to Afghanistan" (Tokyo conference), January 21–22, 2002.

6 This includes $1.1 billion of foreign military financing and international military education and training, which is controlled by the State Department but administered by the Department of Defense.

7 SIGAR, *Quarterly Report to the United States Congress* (Washington, DC, January 30, 2016), 186–87, 147, 186–87.

8 Charles Michael Johnson Jr., *Afghanistan Reconstruction*, GAO Report 08-689 (Washington, DC, 2008), 5.

9 These statistics are discussed in detail in Aaron B. O'Connell, "The Lessons and Legacies of the War in Afghanistan," in *Understanding the U.S. Wars in Iraq and Afghanistan*, ed. Beth Bailey and Richard H. Immerman (New York: New York University Press, 2015), 466–502.

10 William J. Durch, "Restoring and Maintaining Peace: What We Know So far," in *Twenty-First Century Peace Operations*, ed. William J. Durch (Washington, DC: US Institute of Peace, 2006), 1–48; Roland Paris and Timothy Sisk, eds., *The Dilemmas of State Building: Confronting the Contradictions of Postwar Peace Operations* (New York: Routledge, 2009), 1–20.

11 "Co-chair's Summary of Conclusions," para 8.

12 UN Security Council Resolution 1401, S/RES/1401, March 28, 2002.

13 United Nations, "The International Conference on Afghanistan: The Afghanistan Compact," January 31–February 1, 2006, "Annex I: Benchmarks and Timelines," accessed August 5, 2014, www.nato.int/isaf/docu/epub/pdf/afghanistan_compact.pdf.

14 Islamic Republic of Afghanistan, *Afghanistan National Development Strategy 2008–2013* (Kabul: General Directorate of Policy and Result Based Monitoring, Ministry of Economy, Islamic Republic of Afghanistan, June 2014), http://mfa.gov.af/Content/files/EXECUTIVE%20SUMMARY%20English%20A5.pdf (accessed August 5, 2014).

15 UN Resolution 1808, S/RES/1808, March 20, 2008.

16 Rhoda Margesson, *United Nations Assistance Mission in Afghanistan: Background and Policy Issues* (Washington, DC: Congressional Research Service, July 30, 2009), 4.

17 The various components of UNAMA's mission are detailed at http://unama.unmissions.org (accessed September 13, 2014).

18 See International Crisis Group, *Aid and Conflict in Afghanistan*, Asia Report no. 210 (Kabul/Brussels: ICG, August 2011), 11–13.

19 The JCMB was set up in 2006 at the London conference to oversee the implementation of the Afghanistan Compact. See http://www.newmof.org/index.php/jcmb/background (accessed July 12, 2014).

20 Department of Defense, *Report on Progress toward Security and Stability in Afghanistan* (Washington, DC: The Pentagon, April 2014), 92.

21 United States Embassy, Kabul, "USAID's Major Accomplishments since 2001," accessed June 9, 2014, http://kabul.usembassy.gov/usaidd50.html.

22 DOD, *Report on Progress* (April 2014), 86, 89.

23 USAID, "Survey of Afghan Women's Access to Mobile Technology," May 2013, accessed August, 5, 2014, http://www.usaid.gov/where-we-work/afghanistan-and-pakistan/afghanistan/survey-mobile-technology.

24 According to UN statistics, the percentage of seats in single or lower chamber legislatures occupied by women in 2010 was 22 percent in Pakistan and the UK and 19 percent in France. See UN, "Statistics and Indicators on Women and Men," accessed August 22, 2014, http://unstats.un.org/unsd/demographic/products/indwm/tab6a.htm.

25 Mohammed Abid Amiri, "Road Construction in Post-Conflict Afghanistan: A Cure or a Curse?," *International Affairs Review* 22, no. 2 (Spring 2013): 6. See also Qayoom Suroush, "Going in Circles: The Never-Ending Story of Afghanistan's Unfinished Ring Road," January 16, 2015, Afghanistan Analysts Network, accessed December 29, 2015, https://www.afghanistan-analysts.org/going-in-circles-the-never-ending-story-of-afghanistans-unfinished-ring-road/.

26 SIGAR John F. Sopko to USAID mission director for Afghanistan Mr. William Hammink, June 6, 2014, cited in Suroush, "Going in Circles," 5.

27 GAO, *Afghanistan Reconstruction: Despite Some Progress, Deteriorating Security and Other Obstacles Continue to Threaten Achievement of US Goals*, GAO 05-742 (Washington, DC, July 2005), 36.

28 World Bank, *Afghanistan: Country Snapshot* (Washington, DC: The World Bank, March 1, 2014), 1.

29 Suroush, "Going in Circles," 4–8. See also Amiri, "Road Construction," 8–12.

30 Kevin Sieff, "After Billions in U.S. Investment, Afghan Roads Are Falling Apart," *Washington Post*, January 30, 2014.

31 USAID, "Diesel Thermal Power Plants Operations and Maintenance" (fact sheet), December 2010.

32 Rainer Gonzales, "Social & Strategic Infrastructure," *Civil-Military Fusion Center's Afghanistan Review*, Week 3, January 15, 2013, 4.

33 Cid Standifer, "US Hopes to Complete Ill-Fated Afghan Dam Project as Pullout Nears," *Stars and Stripes*, March 19, 2014, accessed September 15, 2014, http://www.stripes.com/news/us-hopes-to-complete-ill-fated-afghan-dam-project-as-pullout-nears-1.273500.

34 Jean MacKenzie, "Watershed of Waste: Afghanistan's Kajaki Dam and USAID," *Global Post*, October 11, 2011, accessed September 15, 2014, http://www.globalpost.com/dispatch/news/regions/asia-pacific/afghanistan/111007/watershed-waste-afghanistan%E2%80%99s-kajaki-dam-and-u.

35 SIGAR-14-40-SP, "Inquiry Letter: Kajaki Unit 2 Project," Office of the SIGAR, March 11, 2014, accessed September 15, 2014, http://www.sigar.mil/pdf/special%20projects/SIGAR-14-40-SP.pdf.

36 SIGAR, *Quarterly Report to the United States Congress* (Washington, DC, April 30, 2016), 183. See also Shashank Bengali, "US Hands Troubled Dam to Afghans," *Los Angeles Times*, May 5, 2013.

37 SIGAR, *Quarterly Report to the United States Congress* (Washington, DC, July 30, 2015), 179.

38 USAID, "Powering Up Afghanistan," *Frontlines Energy/Infrastructure*, January/February 2014, http://www.usaid.gov/news-information/frontlines/energy-infrastructure/powering-afghanistan.

39 SIGAR, *Quarterly Report to the United States Congress* (Washington, DC, July 30, 2014), 173, 179.

40 Robert M. Perito, *The U.S. Experience with Provincial Reconstruction Teams in Afghanistan: Lessons Identified*, Special Report 152 (Washington, DC: US Institute of Peace, October 2005), 6.

41 GAO, *Provincial Reconstruction Teams in Iraq and Afghanistan*, GAO Report 08-905R (Washington, DC, October 1, 2008), 1.

42 In 2008, the United States contributed a total of 1,055 personnel toward PRTs in Afghanistan, of which 1,021 were military personnel and 34 were civilians from the State Department, USAID, and USDA. GAO, *Provincial Reconstruction Teams*, 2. See also Donald Rumsfeld, *Known and Unknown: A Memoir* (New York: Sentinel, 2011), 687.

43 GAO, *Provincial Reconstruction Teams*, 2.

44 Perito, *U.S. Experience*, 3.

45 UNAMA, International Conference in Support of Afghanistan, set of fact sheets, Paris, May 24, June 4, June 12, 2008, compiled from Rhoda Margesson, *United Nations Assistance Mission in Afghanistan: Background and Policy Issues* (Washington, DC: Congressional Research Service, December 27, 2010), appendix H.

46 United Nations Development Programme, *2007/2008 Human Development Index* (New York: Palgrave Macmillan, 2007), 233.

47 USAID, "FACT SHEET: USAID Assistance to Afghanistan 2002–2008," press release, March 27, 2008.

48 NATO, "Progress in Afghanistan: Bucharest Summit, 2–4 April 2008," accessed August 5, 2014, http://www.isaf.nato.int/pdf/progress_afghanistan_2008.pdf.

49 GAO, *Actions Needed to Improve Oversight and Interagency Coordination for the Commander's Emergency Response Program in Afghanistan*, GAO Report 09-615 (Washington, DC, May 18, 2009), 1.

50 SIGAR, "Alert 13-2," June 27, 2013, p. 3, accessed August 5, 2014, http://www.sigar.mil/pdf/alerts/SIGAR%20Alert%2013-2%20S-RAD.pdf. See also Anna Schector, "Report: Millions Wasted on Disappearing Tractors, Solar Panels in Afghanistan," NBC News, June 27, 2013, accessed December 29, 2015, http://investigations.nbcnews.com/_news/2013/06/26/19157126-report-millions-wasted-on-disappearing-tractors-solar-panels-in-afghanistan?lite.

51 Schector, "Millions Wasted."

52 Joel Brinkley, "Money Pit: The Monstrous Failure of U.S. Aid to Afghanistan," *World Affairs*, January/February 2013.

53 Sieff, "After Billions."

54 Department of Defense, *Enhancing Security and Stability in Afghanistan* (Washington, DC: The Pentagon, December 2015), 154, 186.

55 UN General Assembly and Security Council, *The Situation in Afghanistan and Its Implications for International Peace and Security*, A/64/364-S/2009/475 (New York: United Nations, September 22, 2009), 13.

56 Amiri, "Road Construction," 9; Sieff, "After Billions."

57 The Asia Foundation, *Afghanistan in 2008: A Survey of Afghan People* (San Francisco: CA: The Asia Foundation, 2008), 7, http://asiafoundation.org/resources/pdfs/Afghanistanin2008.pdf.

58 Headquarters ISAF, "COMISAF's Initial Assessment" (unclassified), August 30, 2009, reprinted by *Washington Post*, accessed August 5, 2014, http://media.washingtonpost.com/wp-srv/politics/documents/Assessment_Redacted_092109.pdf.

59 Sarah Sewell, "A Radical Field Manual," introduction to *The U.S. Army/Marine Corps Counterinsurgency Field Manual* (Chicago: The University of Chicago Press, 2007), xxxi.

60 See National Security Presidential Directive 44, "Management of Interagency Efforts Concerning Reconstruction and Stabilization," December 7, 2005. See also Department of the Army, *The U.S. Army Stability Operations Field Manual* (Ann Arbor: The University of Michigan Press, 2009).

61 District Delivery Program Secretariat, IDLG, *Support to the District Delivery Program* (Kabul: Islamic Republic of Afghanistan, April 2010), 3, https://info.publicintelligence.net/AfghanDistrictDeliveryPlanSecretariat.pdf (accessed August 5, 2014).

62 GAO, *Actions Needed to Improve Accountability of U.S. Assistance in Afghanistan*, GAO Report 11–710 (Washington, DC, July 2011), 8.

63 Rajiv Chandrasekaran, Alicia Parlapiano, Gene Thorp, and Laura Stanton, "Afghanistan: Measuring Strategy's Effects" (interactive graphic), *Washington Post*, December 11, 2010, accessed September 13, 2014, http://www.washingtonpost.com/wp-srv/special/nation/state-of-afghanistan-2010/index.html.

64 Curt Tarnoff, *Afghanistan: U.S. Foreign Assistance*, CRS R40699 (Washington, DC, August 12, 2010), 14.

65 Ibid. See also Rajiv Chandrasekaran, "Nawa Turns into Proving Ground for U.S. Strategy in Afghan War," *Washington Post*, December 12, 2010.

66 Chandrasekaran, "Nawa Turns into Proving Ground."

67 Dion Nissenbaum, "For Marines, Marjah Market Is Battleground for Afghans' Trust," *New York Times*, March, 1, 2010.

68 Rajiv Chandrasekaran, "'Still a Long Way to Go' for U.S. Operation in Marja, Afghanistan," *Washington Post*, June 10, 2010, A01.

69 General Stanley McChrystal, quoted in "Key Kandahar Offensive Faces Delays: US Commander," *Agence France Press*, June 10, 2010.

70 Ian S. Livingston and Michael O'Hanlon, figure 1.13, "U.S. Government Civilians in Afghanistan, August 2008–2011" in *Afghanistan Index* (Washington, DC: Brookings Institution, February 28, 2013), 9.

71 Frank Ruggiero, "The Meaning of Marjah: Developments in Security and Stability in Afghanistan," testimony before the Senate Foreign Relations Committee, May 6, 2010.

72 Carl W. Forsberg, *Counterinsurgency in Kandahar: Evaluating the 2010 Hamkari Campaign*, Afghanistan Report 7 (Washington, DC: Institute for the Study of War, 2010), 42.

73 Jeffrey Dressler, *Marjah's Lessons for Kandahar* (Washington, DC: Institute for the Study of War, July 9, 2010).

74 "Performance Evaluation: District Delivery Program," (a report commissioned by USAID and prepared by Checci and Company Consulting for USAID's SUPPORT project, April 9, 2012), pp. 21, 20, http://pdf.usaid.gov/pdf_docs/pdact900.pdf (accessed December 29, 2015).

75 On USAID, see ibid., annex J. For the UN's National Area-Based Development Program (NADP), see http://mrrd.gov.af/Content/Media/Documents/ToRforImpactAssessmentandConflictmapping112201021140125.pdf (accessed June 27, 2016). For the World Bank's National Solidarity Program, see http://www.nspafghanistan.org/ (accessed December 21, 2015).

76 The two ministries responsible for strengthening subnational governance are the Ministry for the Rural Rehabilitation of Afghanistan (MRRD) and the IDLG.

77 Matt Millham, "Despite Lingering Reliance on U.S. Aid, Afghanistan's Nawa District a Model of Transition," *Stars and Stripes*, May 28, 2011.

78 Scott Dempsey, "The Fallacy of COIN: One Officer's Frustration," *Small Wars Journal*, March 13, 2011, http://smallwarsjournal.com/blog/journal/docs-temp/702-dempsey3.pdf.

79 Chandrasekaran, "Nawa Turns into Proving Ground."

80 The World Bank managed the Afghanistan Reconstruction Trust Fund (ARTF), and the Asia Development Bank managed the Afghanistan Infrastructure Trust Fund (AITF). These were the mechanisms to funnel reconstruction funding beyond 2014.

81 US Department of State, "U.S. Support for the New Silk Road," accessed August 5, 2014, http://www.state.gov/p/sca/ci/af/newsilkroad/.

82 Marcherita Stancati and Nathan Hodge, "Kabul's Economic Bubble Bursts," *Wall Street Journal*, June 12, 2014.

83 Eugene Imas, "U.S. Post-2014 Development Plans for Central Asia Are Worth It, but at Risk for Strategic Failure," *The Diplomat*, December 18, 2013, http://thediplomat.com/2013/12/the-new-silk-road-to-nowhere/.

84 SIGAR, *Fiscal Year 2011 Afghanistan Infrastructure Fund Projects Are Behind Schedule and Lack Adequate Sustainment Plans*, SIGAR Audit-12-12, (Washington, DC, July 30, 2012), 1, https://www.sigar.mil/pdf/audits/2012-07-30audit-12-12Revised.pdf (accessed June 27, 2016).

85 "MISTI Stabilization Trends and Impact Evaluation Survey Analytical Report Wave 5: Sep 28–Nov 4, 2014" (a report commissioned by USAID and prepared by Management Systems International, April 28, 2015), pp. 2–14, http://www.d3systems.com/wp-content/uploads/2015/10/MISTI-Wave-5-Analytical-Report-FINAL_USAID.pdf (accessed June 27, 2016).

86 James Risen, "Some Afghans View the Taliban as Key to Aid, Study Finds," *New York Times*, December 16, 2015, A10.

87 SIGAR, *Quarterly Report* (January 30, 2016), 49.

88 Amy Belasco, *The Cost of Iraq, Afghanistan, and Other Global War on Terror Operations since 9/11*, CRS Report RL 33110 (Washington, DC, December 8, 2014), 14.

89 US Institute of Peace analyst Andrew Wilder, cited in James Risen, "Some Afghans," A10.

Chapter Six

The views expressed here are the authors' own and do not necessarily reflect the policies of the US Department of the Army or the Department of Defense.

1 United States Senate, Committee on Foreign Relations, "Senate Foreign Relations Subcommittee on Near Eastern and South and Central Asia Affairs Holds Hearing on Afghanistan," April 30, 2014, accessed December 21, 2015, http://www.foreign.senate.gov/hearings/a-transformation-afghanistan-beyond-2014.

2 Rod Norland, "After Rancor, Afghans Agree to Share Power," *New York Times*, September 21, 2014, A1.

3 United Nations Security Council, *Report of the Secretary General: The Rule of Law and Transitional Justice in Conflict and Post-Conflict Societies*, S/2004/616 (New York: United Nations, August 23, 2004), 3; Francis Fukuyama, *State-Building: Governance and World Order in the 21st Century* (Ithaca, NY: Cornell University Press, 2004); Chester A. Crocket, Fen Osler Hampson, and Pamela Aall, eds., *Leashing the Dogs of War: Conflict Management in a Divided World* (Washington, DC: US Institute of Peace, 2007); Fareed Zakaria, "The Rise of Illiberal Democracies," *Foreign Affairs* 76, no. 6 (November/December 1997): 22–43. On Afghanistan, see Whit Mason, ed., *The Rule of Law in Afghanistan: Missing in Action* (Cambridge: Cambridge University Press, 2011).

4 UN Security Council, *Rule of Law*, 4.

5 Neil J. Kritz, "The Rule of Law in Conflict Management," in Crocket, Hampson, and Aall, *Leashing the Dogs of War*, 401–24; William Maley, "The Rule of Law and the Weight of Politics," in Mason, *Rule of Law in Afghanistan*, 61–72.

6 Rachel Kleinfeld, "Competing Definitions of the Rule of Law," in *Promoting the Rule of Law Abroad: In Search of Knowledge*, ed. Thomas Corothers (Washington, DC: Carnegie Institute for Peace, 2006), 31, 35. See also US Army Judge Advocate General, *Rule of Law Handbook: A Practitioner's Guide for Judge Advocates* (Charlottesville, VA: Center for Law and Military Operations, 2011), 2.

7 Amanullah's plight is discussed in Martin Ewans, *Afghanistan: A Short History of Its People and Politics* (New York: Harper Collins, 2002), 118–36.

8 Hamid Khan, "Clarifying the Role of Islamic Law in Afghanistan's Justice System," June 12, 2002, US Institute of Peace, Washington, DC, accessed December 26, 2014, http://www.usip.org/publications/clarifying-the-role-islamic-law-in-afghanistans-justice-system-0.

9 A useful discussion of how Pashtuns resolve grievances at local levels is in Thomas H. Johnson and M. Chris Mason, "No Sign until the Burst of Fire: Understanding the Pakistan-Afghanistan Frontier," *International Security* 32, no. 4 (Spring 2008): 41–77.

10 The Asia Foundation, "Afghanistan in 2013: A Survey of the Afghan People," 2013, accessed December 2, 2015, http://afghansurvey.asiafoundation.org; Transparency International, "Corruption Perceptions Index 2013," accessed December 26, 2014, http://www.transparency.org/country#AFG_PublicOpinion.

11 Hatem Elliesie, "Rule of Law in Afghanistan," Rule of Law Wiki, Frei Universitat Berlin, last modified July 11, 2011, accessed December 26, 2014, http://wikis.fu-berlin.de/display/SBprojectrol/Afghanistan.

12 United Nations Security Council, "Agreement on Provisional Arrangements in Afghanistan Pending the Re-establishment of Permanent Government Institutions," Security Council Resolution 1383, S/2001/1154, December 5, 2001.

13 United Nations, *Report of the Secretary-General: The Situation in Afghanistan and Its Implications for International Peace and Security*, S/2003/333 (New York: United Nations, March 18, 2003), 10.

14 International Crisis Group, *Reforming Afghanistan's Broken Judiciary*, Asia Report no. 195 (Kabul/Brussels: ICG, November 17, 2010), 7, 10, 21.

15 US Institute of Peace, *Establishing the Rule of Law in Afghanistan*, Special Report 117 (Washington, DC: USIP, 2004), 6–10; Ali Wardak, "State and Non-State Justice Systems in Afghanistan: The Need for Synergy," *University of Pennsylvania Journal of International Law* 32, no. 5 (2014): 1305–24.

16 USIP, *Establishing the Rule of Law*, 8.

17 ICG, *Reforming Afghanistan's Broken Judiciary*, 2; USIP, *Establishing the Rule of Law*, 4–6.

18 USIP, *Establishing the Rule of Law*, 4–10; GAO, *Afghanistan: Key Issues for Congressional Oversight*, GAO Report 09-473SP (Washington, DC, April 21, 2009), 4; Liana Sun Wyler and Kenneth Katzman, *Afghanistan: U.S. Rule* *of Law and Justice Sector Assistance*, CRS Report R41484 (Washington, DC, November 9, 2010), 27.

19 US Department of State and the Broadcasting Board of Governors Office of the Inspector General, *Report of Inspection: Rule of Law Programs in Afghanistan*, OIG Report Number ISP-I-08-09 (Washington, DC, January 2008), 8.

20 The Asia Foundation, *Afghanistan in 2007: A Survey of the Afghan People* (Kabul: The Asia Foundation, 2007), 8.

21 The Asia Foundation, *Afghanistan in 2006: A Survey of the Afghan People* (Kabul: The Asia Foundation, 2006), 29, 59.

22 Kenneth Katzman, *Afghanistan: Post-War Governance, Security, and U.S. Policy*, CRS Report RL 30588, (Washington, DC, November 3, 2006), 15.

23 As characterized by Francesc Vendrell in Graeme Smith, "No Justice, No Peace: Kandahar 2005–2009," in Mason, *Rule of Law in Afghanistan*, 304.

24 Ministry of Justice in cooperation with the Justice Sector Consultative Group, *Justice for All: A Comprehensive Needs Analysis for Justice in Afghanistan* (Kabul: Islamic Republic of Afghanistan, May 2005), 2–4, http://www.rolafghanistan.esteri.it/NR/rdonlyres/B0DB53D0-A1F9-468E-8DF0-3F485F1959A7/0/JusticeforAll.pdf.

25 Islamic Republic of Afghanistan, *The Afghanistan National Development Strategy: An Interim Strategy for Security, Governance, Economic Growth and Poverty Reduction*, vol. 1 (Kabul: Islamic Republic of Afghanistan, December 19, 2005), http://reliefweb.int/sites/reliefweb.int/files/resources/AFA4970B33A0505E492571070008 11C6-unama-afg-30jan2.pdf (accessed June 26, 2016).

26 Wyler and Katzman, *Afghanistan*, 15, 27.

27 Huqooq officers are the lowest level of the formal MOJ system; they're usually located at the provincial level and sometimes the district level. Although not trained lawyers, they provide mediation services to resolve disputes in commercial law, land ownership, and family law, execute other administrative functions, and may refer cases to a local customary or informal practice. See Susanne Schmeidl, "Engaging Traditional Justice Mechanisms in Afghanistan: State Building Opportunity or Dangerous Liaison?," in Mason, *Rule of Law in Afghanistan*, 152–53, 164–69.

28 Chapter 7, Article 124 states that officials and administrative personnel of the judiciary are subject to laws related to civil servants, and that the Supreme Court "shall regulate their appointment, dismissal, promotion, retirement, rewards and punishments." ICG, *Reforming Afghanistan's Broken Judiciary*, 15.

29 SIGAR, *Support for Afghanistan's Justice Sector: State Department Programs Need Better Management and Stronger Oversight* (Washington, DC, January 2014), 4–5, http://www.sigar.mil/pdf/audits/SIGAR_14-26-AR.pdf.

30 Wyler and Katzman, *Afghanistan*, 24.

31 Ibid., 20–21. See also SIGAR, *Support for Afghanistan's Justice Sector*,18.

32 Several entities engaged in Afghan strategy assessments including the Obama transition team, the National Security Council staff, the chairman of the Joint Chiefs (CJCS) Admiral Michael Mullen, and an assessment team for General David Petraeus, who was then the CENTCOM commander. See Bob Woodward, *Obama's Wars* (New York: Simon & Schuster, 2010), 76–81. One of the authors, Colonel Linnington, served on the US Central Command (CENTCOM) Assessment Team and met regularly with assessment teams at the NSC and CJCS. The CENTCOM assessment included analysis of rule of law challenges across the Middle East and detailed recommendations such as the need for a civil-military campaign plan with rule of law as one of its pillars, a plan for transitioning detention operations to Afghan control, and the importance of linking security sector reform (such as police training) with other justice sector efforts.

33 General Stanley A. McChrystal, "Commander's Initial Assessment" (unclassified), August 30, 2009, 1-2, 2-1, 2-4, annex F, 2-5, 2–10, reprinted by *Washington Post*, September 21, 2009, accessed August 31, 2014, http://www.washingtonpost.com/wp-dyn/content/article/2009/09/21/AR2009092100110.html.

34 US Government, "Integrated Civilian-Military Campaign Plan for Support to Afghanistan [ICMCP]," August 10, 2009, accessed January 22, 2016, http://www.comw.org/qdr/fulltext/0908eikenberryandmcchrystal.pdf.

35 Several NATO countries were initially reluctant to endorse US calls for an expanded counterinsurgency campaign. See Sten Rynning, *NATO in Afghanistan: The Liberal Disconnect* (Stanford, CA: Stanford Security Studies, 2012), 62–64.

36 Maley, "Rule of Law," 75–78; Sabrina Tavernise and Abdul Waheed Wafa, "U.N. Official Acknowledges 'Widespread Fraud' in Afghan Election," *New York Times*, October 11, 2009, A10.

37 Ambassador Klemm held this position from July 2010 until January 2012.

38 For example, USAID's Rule of Law Stabilization Program, restarted in 2010, has trained 700 judges to date. See Kenneth Katzman, *Afghanistan: Politics, Elections, and Government Performance* (Washington, DC: Congressional Research Service, May 12, 2014), 13.

39 SIGAR, *Quarterly Report to the United States Congress* (Washington, DC, April 30, 2014), 228–29.

40 US Government, "Integrated Civilian-Military Campaign Plan," 15; Wyler and Katzman, *Afghanistan*, 24.

41 Amy Belasco, *Troop Levels in the Afghan and Iraq Wars, FY2001–FY2012: Cost and Other Potential Issues* (Washington, DC: Congressional Research Service, July 2, 2009), 6, 9, 29–34.

42 McChrystal, "Commander's Initial Assessment," annex F-2 and F-4.

43 In September 2011, JTF-435 was renamed Combined Joint Interagency Task

Force–435 in recognition of the participation of other US departments and agencies as well as several partner nations in the task force's initiatives.

44 From the date of its creation in early 2011 to November 2013, the JCIP prosecuted "over 3,100 detainees with a 71 percent conviction rate. In total, the JCIP has tried over 5,000 primary and appellate cases." See Department of Defense, *Report on Progress toward Security and Stability in Afghanistan* (Washington, DC: The Pentagon, November 2013), 90. See also INL Executive Director James A. Walsh to SIGAR Ms. Elizabeth A. Field, October 10, 2013, in SIGAR, *Justice Center in Parwan Courthouse: Poor Oversight Contributed to Failed Project*, SIGAR Inspection Report 14-7 (Washington, DC, October 2013), available at https://www.sigar.mil (accessed December 22, 2015).

45 DOD, *Report on Progress* (November 2013), 89–90; Associated Press, "US Military Transfers Parwan Detention Centre to Afghan Government Control," *The Guardian*, March 25, 2013.

46 The Asia Foundation, *Afghanistan in 2009: A Survey of the Afghan People* (Kabul: The Asia Foundation, 2009), 70–71, 85–97.

47 John Wendle, "The Bank Bust That Nearly Took Down Afghanistan," *Time*, November 30, 2012.

48 Kenneth Katzman, *Afghanistan: Politics, Elections, and Government Performance* (Washington, DC: Congressional Research Service, May 12, 2014), 37–48.

49 Yaroslav Trofimov "Karzai and U.S. Clash Over Corruption: Afghan President Orders Probe of Task Force After Aide's Arrest for Bribery; Pakistan Leader Says Coalition Has 'Lost,'" *Wall Street Journal*, August 3, 2010.

50 Katzman, *Afghanistan*, 40–44; Ron Nordland and Mark Mazzetti, "Graft Dispute in Afghanistan Is Test for U.S.," *New York Times*, August 24, 2010; Donald J. Planty and Robert M. Perito, *Police Transition in Afghanistan*, Special Report 322 (Washington, DC: US Institute of Peace, February 2013).

51 Katzman, *Afghanistan*, 42.

52 T. S. Allen, "Addressing an Ignored Imperative: Rural Corruption in Afghanistan," *Small Wars Journal*, February 19, 2013, accessed September 27, 2014, www.smallwarsjournal.org.

53 Critical sources include ICG, *Reforming Afghanistan's Broken Judiciary*; and Torunn Wimpelmann, "Nexuses of Knowledge and Power in Afghanistan: The Rise and Fall of the Informal Justice Assemblage," *Central Asian Survey* 32, no. 3 (October 2013): 418. For a supportive assessment of program expansion, see Department of State and the Broadcasting Board of Governors, *Rule of Law Programs*, 16.

54 Department of State and the Broadcasting Board of Governors, *Rule of Law Programs*, 16.

55 NATO Media Backgrounder, "NATO Rule of Law Field Support Mission (NROLFSM)," June 2011, accessed August 20, 2015, http://www.nato.int

/nato_static/assets/pdf/pdf_2011_06/20110609-Backgrounder-Rule_of_Law-en.pdf.

56 Brigadier General Mark Martins, "Remarks at Change of Command, NATO Rule of Law Field Support Mission and Rule of Law Field Force," September 14, 2011, accessed June 26, 2016, https://lawfare.s3-us-west-2.amazonaws.com/staging/s3fs-public/uploads/2011/09/Martins_Remarks_at_Change_of_Command-English.pdf.

57 Martins, "Remarks at Change of Command"; US Central Command, "Combined Joint Interagency Task Force-435 Fact Sheet," April 2013; NATO Media Backgrounder, "NATO Rule of Law Field Support Mission." All in authors' possession.

58 McChrystal, "Commander's Initial Assessment," 2–18.

59 See, for example, Linda Robinson, *One Hundred Victories: Special Ops and the Future of American Warfare* (New York: Public Affairs, 2013), 101–3 and 283n8, on both internal and external pressures to conduct kill-and-capture operations at the expense of supporting stability. As observed by Colonel Linnington in 2010–2011, military commanders routinely faced tough choices between allocating forces to conduct combat operations and providing forces for a host of activities related to rule of law and governance such as support for PRTs and district support teams, mentoring of local police units and border police, reconciliation programs, detainee review boards, evidence-based operations, and biometric data collection.

60 Army Judge Advocate General, *Rule of Law Handbook*, 214.

61 Thomas B. Nachbar, "Counterinsurgency, Legitimacy, and the Rule of Law North Atlantic Treaty Organization," *Parameters*, Spring 2012, 27–38; and NATO Media Backgrounder, "NATO Rule of Law Field Support Mission." In 2011, with the support of Dutch and Danish partners, NATO/ISAF endorsed the ROLFF-A as part of the command structure. In the fall of 2013, however, the NATO/ISAF command reverted back to the United States.

62 For example, congressional funding for Department of State rule of law and counternarcotics efforts (through the INCLE fund) fluctuated from a high of $709 million in 2005 to about $570 million in 2013 and $225 million in 2014. By comparison, the Department of Defense funding for security programs (through the ASFF) rose from $995 million in 2005 to a high of $10.6 billion in 2011 and then dropped to about $4.7 billion in 2014. See Curt Tarnoff, *Afghanistan: U.S. Foreign Assistance*, CRS R40699 (Washington, DC, August 12, 2010); and SIGAR, *Quarterly Report* (April 30, 2014), 228–29.

63 Islamic Republic of Afghanistan, *Afghanistan National Development Strategy*, 4.

64 The Asia Foundation, "Afghanistan in 2013," 5, 69. See also Office of the President of the Islamic Republic of Afghanistan, "Decree on the Execution of Content of the Historical Speech of June 21, 2012 in the Special Session of National Assembly, 19 July 2012," accessed June 26, 2016, www.afghanistan

-un.org; Jane Perlez, "$16 Billion in Civilian Aid Pledged to Afghanistan, with Conditions," *New York Times*, July 8, 2012; and Transparency International, "Corruption Perceptions Index 2013."

65 "Billions Down the Afghan Hole," Transparency International, July 9, 2012, accessed October 19, 2014, http://www.transparency.org/news/feature/billions_down_the_afghan_hole. See also Kai Elde, *Power Struggle over Afghanistan: An Inside Look at What Went Wrong—and What Can We Do to Repair the Damage* (New York: Skyhorse Publishing, 2013).

66 For one example, see US House of Representatives, H.R. 2107, "No More Ghost Money Act," introduced May 22, 2013, accessed June 26, 2016, https://www.congress.gov/bill/113th-congress/house-bill/2107. See also Joel Brinkley, "Money Pit: The Monstrous Failure of US Aid to Afghanistan," *World Affairs*, January/February 2013, http://www.worldaffairsjournal.org/article/money-pit-monstrous-failure-us-aid-afghanistan.

67 Whit Mason, "Axioms and Unknowns," in Mason, *Rule of Law in Afghanistan*, 319.

68 Thomas J. Barfield, "Culture and Custom in Nation-Building: Law in Afghanistan," *Maine Law Review* 60 (2008): 347–73.

69 Huma Ahmed Gosh, "A History of Women in Afghanistan: Lessons Learnt for the Future or Yesterdays and Tomorrow: Women in Afghanistan," *Journal of International Women's Studies* 4, no. 3 (May 2003): 1.

Chapter Seven

1 Robert W. Komer, *Bureaucracy Does Its Thing: Institutional Constraints on U.S.-GVN Performance in Vietnam* (Santa Monica, CA: RAND, 1972), iii–xiii.

2 Ernest Gellner, *Plough, Sword and Book* (Chicago: University of Chicago Press, 1988), 11.

3 Niccolo Machiavelli, *The Prince*, trans. W. K. Marriott (Plano, TX: Verroglyphic, 2009), 79.

4 Francis Fukuyama, *The End of History and the Last Man* (New York: Free Press, 2006).

5 "Remarks by President George W. Bush at the 20th Anniversary of the National Endowment for Democracy," October 6, 2005, accessed August 14, 2015, http://www.ned.org/remarks-by-president-george-w-bush-at-the-20th-anniversary.

6 See especially Philip Carl Salzman, *Conflict and Culture in the Middle East* (Amherst, NY: Prometheus, 2008), 11–13, 95–97.

7 See Thomas Johnson and M. Chris Mason, "No Sign until the Burst of Fire: Understanding the Pakistan-Afghanistan Frontier," *International Security* 32, no. 4 (2008): 55.

8 Salzman, *Conflict and Culture*, 59–63. See also Thomas Barfield, *Afghani-*

stan: A Cultural and Political History (Princeton, NJ: Princeton University, 2010), 67–71.

9 Barfield, *Afghanistan*, 68.

10 On violence metrics and civilian casualties, see Ian S. Livingston and Michael O'Hanlon, figures 1.12 and 1.21, in *Afghanistan Index* (Washington, DC: Brookings Institution, July 31, 2015), 9, 13.

11 The statistics on Afghan perceptions come from Nancy Hopkins, ed., *Afghanistan in 2014: A Survey of the Afghan People* (San Francisco CA: The Asia Foundation, 2014), 7–8.

12 United Nations Development Program, *Police Perception Survey: 2011* (Kabul: Aina Media, 2011), 25.

13 On corruption, see Hopkins, *Afghanistan in 2014*, 10–11, 91–92, 95.

14 Patricia Crone, *Pre-industrial Societies* (Oxford: Oneworld,1989), 42.

15 Hopkins, *Afghanistan in 2014*, 10–11.

16 Salzman, *Conflict and Culture*, 31.

17 The full text of the Afghan Constitution is at http://www.afghanembassy.com.pl/afg/images/pliki/TheConstitution.pdf (accessed August 14, 2015).

18 US Commission on International Religious Freedom, *Annual Report 2013* (Washington, DC, 2013), http://www.uscirf.gov/reports-briefs/annual-report/2013-annual-report.

19 Hopkins, *Afghanistan in 2014*, 106

20 For the rates of violence from 2003 to 2009, see GAO, *Afghanistan's Security Environment*, GAO Report 10-178R (Washington, DC, November 5, 2009).

21 *The U.S. Army/Marine Corps Counterinsurgency Field Manual* (Chicago: University of Chicago Press, 2007), 37.

22 Johann Jones to author, "Minutes of Haji Zahir Meeting in Southern Marja," April 30, 2010. Copy in author's possession.

23 Todd Pitman "Marines in Marjah Face Full Blown Insurgency," *Navy Times*, October 8, 2010.

24 *The Battle For Marjah* (HBO Films, 2010), 1:07:30–1:13:30.

25 House of Representatives, House Armed Services Committee, *Developments in Afghanistan*, March 16, 2011, 112th Cong., HASC Rep. No. 112-24 (2011), 9.

26 A good account of the early days of the ALP initiative can be found in Ann Scott Tyson, *American Spartan* (New York, NY: HarperCollins, 2014).

27 Capt. Carl-Werner Scott, USMC, e-mail to author, January 30, 2014.

28 Kathy Gannon, "Afghanistan Taliban's Popularity in Helmand Grows Despite U.S. Military Efforts," *Associated Press*, December 10, 2012, available at www.huffingtonpost.com (accessed August 14, 2015).

29 Max Weber, "Politics as Vocation," accessed August 20, 2015, http://www.ucc.ie/archive/hdsp/Weber_Politics_as_Vocation.htm.

30 Thucydides, *The History of the Peloponnesian War*, trans. Richard Crawley, book 5, verse 89, accessed August 20, 2015, http://classics.mit.edu/Thucydides/pelopwar.mb.txt.

31 On this point, see Leo Strauss, *Natural Right and History* (Chicago: University of Chicago Press, 1965), 139–40.

Chapter Eight

The views expressed in this chapter are the author's own and do not necessarily reflect the position or policies of the US Department of Defense, the US Department of State, or the US government.

1 Linda Robinson, *Masters of Chaos: The Secret History of the Special Forces* (New York: Public Affairs, 2005), 153–90.

2 Tony Schwalm, *The Guerrilla Factory: The Making of Special Forces Officers, The Green Berets* (New York: Free Press, 2012), 3.

3 Mark Bowden, *Black Hawk Down: A Story of Modern War* (New York: Grove Press, 1999); Sean Naylor, *Not a Good Day to Die: The Untold Story of Operation Anaconda* (New York: Berkley Caliber Books, 2005); Pete Blaber, *The Mission, the Men, and Me* (New York: Berkley Caliber Books, 2008); Eric Blehm, *The Only Thing Worth Dying For: How Eleven Green Berets Fought for a New Afghanistan* (New York: Harper Collins, 2010).

4 United States Special Operations Command, *Doctrine for Special Operations*, USSOCOM Publication 1 (Tampa, FL: MacDill Air Force Base, 2011), 23–24; Robinson, *Masters of Chaos*, xiii.

5 USSOCOM, *Doctrine for Special Operations*, 22.

6 Dick Couch, *Chosen Soldier: The Making of a Special Forces Warrior* (New York: Three Rivers Press, 2007); Robinson, *Masters of Chaos*, xv (quotation).

7 USSOCOM, *Doctrine for Special Operations*, 24–28.

8 Blehm, *Only Thing Worth Dying For*; Rusty Bradley and Kevin Maurier, *Lions of Kandahar: The Story of a Fight against All Odds* (Bantam Press: New York, 2011), 1–280.

9 Blehm, *Only Thing Worth Dying For*.

10 Doug Stanton, *Horse Soldiers: The Extraordinary Story of a Band of US Soldiers Who Rode to Victory in Afghanistan* (New York: Scribner's & Sons, 2010).

11 Bernard B. Fall, *Street without Joy* (Mechanicsburg, PA: Stackpole Books, 1961), 375.

12 Scott Mann, "The Shaping Coalition Forces' Strategic Narrative in Support of Village Stability Operations,"*Small Wars Journal*, March 31, 2001, accessed March 31, 2011, www.smallwarsjournal.com.

13 Michael G. Waltz, *Warrior Diplomat: A Green Beret's Battles from Washington to Afghanistan* (Dulles, VA: Potomac Books, 2014), 345.

14 Ronald Fry, *Hammerhead Six: How Green Berets Waged an Unconventional War against the Taliban to Win in Afghanistan's Deadly Pech Valley* (New York: Hachette Books, 2016).

15 Stanley A. McChrystal, "It Takes a Network,"*Foreign Policy*, March/April 2011, 66–70.

16 Matthew B. Arnold and Anthony Vinci, "The Need for Local, People-Centric Information Does Not End in Afghanistan,"*Small Wars Journal*, July 6, 2010, accessed January 4, 2016, www.smallwarsjournal.com.

17 Eric Blehm, *Fearless: The Undaunted Courage and Ultimate Sacrifice of Navy SEAL Team SIX Operator Adam Brown* (Colorado Springs, CO: Waterbrook Press, 2012).

18 Jim Gant and William McCallister, "Tribal Engagement: The Jirga and the Shura,"*Small Wars Journal*, June 6, 2010, accessed January 4, 2016, www.smallwarsjournal.com.

19 Rory Hanlin, "One Team's Approach to Village Stability Operations," *Small Wars Journal*, September 11, 2011, accessed January 4, 2016, www.smallwarsjournal.com.

20 Jim Gant, "One Tribe at a Time: A Strategy for Success in Afghanistan," (Los Angeles: Nine Sisters Imports, 2009).

21 Bradley and Maurer, *Lions of Kandahar*.

22 Daniel R. Green, *The Valley's Edge: A Year with the Pashtuns in the Heartland of the Taliban* (Dulles, VA: Potomac Books, 2011).

23 Daniel R. Green, "Defeating the Taliban's Political Program," *Armed Forces Journal*, November 2009, 18–21, 36–37.

24 *Pashtunwali* means "the way of the Pashtuns" and is a tribal honor code that has governed the Pashtun way of life for centuries.

25 Lutz Rzehak, *Doing Pashto: Pashtunwali as the Ideal of Honourable Behavior and Tribal Life among the Pashtuns* (Kabul: Afghan Analysts Network, 2011), 1–22.

26 Brian Petit, "The Fight for the Village, Southern Afghanistan, 2010,"*Military Review*, May–June 2011, 25–32.

27 William Doyle, *A Soldier's Dream: Captain Travis Patriquin and the Awakening of Iraq* (New York: NAL Caliber, 2011); Daniel R. Green, "The Fallujah Awakening: A Case Study in Counter-Insurgency," *Small Wars and Insurgencies* 21, no. 4 (2010): 591–609; Daniel R. Green, "Glubb's Guide to the Arab Tribes," *Small Wars Journal*, November 2, 2007, accessed January 4, 2016, smallwarsjournal.com; Michael Eisenstadt, "Iraq: Tribal Engagement Lessons Learned," *Military Review*, September–October 2007, 16–31.

28 Taliban 2009 rules and regulations booklet seized by coalition forces on July 15, 2009. Copy in author's possession.

29 Linda Robinson, *One Hundred Victories: Special Ops and the Future of American Warfare* (New York: Public Affairs, 2013), 12.

30 Lisa Saum-Manning, "VSO/ALP: Comparing Past and Current Challenges to Afghan Local Defense" (RAND Working Paper, December 2012), 3–4, https://www.rand.org/content/dam/rand/pubs/working_papers/2012/RAND_WR936.pdf.

31 Matthew Lefevre, "Local Defence in Afghanistan: A Review of Government-Backed Initiatives," Afghanistan Analysts Network, May 27, 2010, accessed January 4, 2016, https://www.afghanistan-analysts.org/publication/aan-papers/local-defence-in-afghanistan-a-review-of-government-backed-initiatives.

32 Saum-Manning, "VSO/ALP," 4.

33 Joseph A. L'Etoile, "Transforming the Conflict in Afghanistan," *PRISM* 2, no. 4 (September 2011): 3–16; Andrew Wilder, *Cops and Robbers? The Struggle to Reform the Afghan National Police*, Issues Paper Series (Kabul: Afghanistan Research and Evaluation Unit [AREU], July 2007); "Afghanistan New Militias: Self-Defence, a Victory of Hope over Experience?" *The Economist*, April 8, 2009.

34 Robinson, *One Hundred Victories*, 14–16.

35 Dan Madden, *The Evolution of Precision Counterinsurgency: A History of Village Stability Operations and the Afghan Local Police* (Santa Monica, CA: RAND, 2011).

36 Lefevre, "Local Defence in Afghanistan"; Saum-Manning, "VSO/ALP," 6–7.

37 Robinson, *One Hundred Victories*, 13.

38 Ibid., 25.

39 Robert Hulsander and Jake Spivey, "Village Stability Operations and Afghan Local Police," *PRISM* 3, no. 3 (June 2012): 125–38.

40 Madden, *Evolution of Precision Counterinsurgency*, 5.

41 Robinson, *One Hundred Victories*, 25.

42 Daniel R. Green, "Defeating the Taliban's Shadow Government: Winning the Population through Synchronized Governance, Development and Security Efforts,"*Australian Army Journal* 8, no. 1 (2011): 9–21.

43 Robinson, *One Hundred Victories*, 28.

44 Jonathan Goodhand and Aziz Hakimi, *Counterinsurgency, Local Militias, and Statebuilding in Afghanistan* (Washington, DC: US Institute of Peace, 2014), 11.

45 Seth G. Jones and Arturo Muñoz, *Afghanistan's Local War: Building Local Defense Forces* (Santa Monica, CA: RAND, 2010).

46 Daniel R. Green, "It Takes a Village to Raze an Insurgency,"*Foreign Policy*, May 29, 2013, accessed January 4, 2016, www.foreignpolicy.com; Stephen N. Rust, "The Nuts and Bolts of Village Stability Operations,"*Special Warfare Magazine*, July/September 2011, 28–31.

47 Joshua Thiel and Douglas A. Borer, "Withdraw and Win: Go for Victory in Afghanistan," *Small Wars Journal*, February 25, 2013, accessed January 4, 2016, www.smallwarsjournal.com.

48 Green, "It Takes a Village."

49 Robert M. Perito, *Afghanistan's Police: The Weak Link in Security Sector Reform* (Washington, DC: US Institute of Peace, 2009), 1–16.

50 Ibid.

51 Ty Connett and Bob Cassidy, "VSO: More than Village Defense,"*Special Warfare Magazine*, July–September 2011, 22–27.

52 Daniel R. Green, "A Tale of Two Districts: Beating the Taliban at Their Own Game,"*Military Review*, January–February 2014, 26–31; Linda Robinson, *One Hundred Victories*; Ann Scott Tyson, *American Spartan: The Promise, the Mission, and the Betrayal of Special Forces Major Jim Gant* (New York: William Morrow, 2014).

53 Saum-Manning, "VSO/ALP,"15.

54 Green, "Tale of Two Districts."

55 Ibid. See also Department of Defense, *Report on Progress toward Security and Stability in Afghanistan* (Washington, DC: The Pentagon, December 2012), 81.

56 Goodhand and Hakimi, *Counterinsurgency*,13, 14–15; Waltz, *Warrior Diplomat*, 346.

57 Mark Moyar, *Village Stability Operations and the Afghan Local Police*, JSOU Report 14-7 (Tampa, FL: Joint Special Operations University, MacDill AFB, 2014), 54, 57–58.

58 Afghanistan Independent Human Rights Commission, *From Arbaki to Local Police: Today's Challenges and Tomorrow's Concerns* (Kabul: AIHRC, 2012), http://www.aihrc.org.af/en/research-reports/1073/from-arbaki-to-local-police-today's-challenges-and-tomorrow's-concerns.html.

59 Moyar, *Village Stability Operations*, 67–68, 81.

60 Joseph Goldstein, "Afghan Militia Leaders, Empowered by U.S. to Fight Taliban, Inspire Fear in Villages,"*New York Times*, March 17, 2015.

61 "Generation Kill: A Conversation with Stanley McChrystal,"*Foreign Affairs*, March/April 2013, 2–8.

62 Waltz, *Warrior Diplomat*, 344–45.

63 Ibid., 346.

Chapter Nine

1 Dan Lamothe, "This New Graphic Shows the State of the U.S. War in Afghanistan," *Washington Post*, January 6, 2015. See also "NATO Led Resolute Support Mission in Afghanistan," January 30, 2015, accessed January 31, 2015, http://www.nato.int/cps/en/natohq/topics_113694.htm.

2 "Military Technical Agreement between the International Security Assistance Force and the Interim Administration of Afghanistan," pp. 4–6, Stockholm International Peace Research Institute (SIRPI) Library and Documentation Catalog, accessed August 24, 2014, http://catalogue.sipri.org/cgi-bin/koha/opac-detail.pl?biblionumber=25061#.

3 Ian S. Livingston and Michael O'Hanlon, figure 1.2, "Other Foreign Troops Deployed to Afghanistan," in *Afghanistan Index* (Washington, DC: Brookings Institution, March 31, 2016), 5. For American troops in country, see Amy Belasco, *Troop Levels in the Afghanistan and Iraq Wars, 2001–2009* (Washington, DC: Congressional Research Service, July 2, 2009).

4 "Military Technical Agreement," 2–4.

5 President Barack Obama, "Remarks by the President in Address to the Nation on the Way Forward in Afghanistan and Pakistan," The White House, December 1, 2009, accessed November 15, 2014, http://www.whitehouse.gov/the-press-office/remarks-president-address-nation-way-forward-afghanistan-and-pakistan.

6 UNAMA, "Kabul Conference Communiqué," July 20, 2010, p. 1, accessed June 28, 2016, https://www.unodc.org/documents/afghanistan//Kabul_Conference/FINAL_Kabul_Conference_Communique.pdf.

7 Kai Eide, *Power Struggle over Afghanistan: An Inside Look at What Went Wrong—and What We Can Do to Fix It* (New York: Skyhorse Publishing, 2012), 229.

8 UNAMA, "Kabul Conference Communiqué," 7.

9 Phil Stewart, "U.S. Says Not Considering NATO Afghan Troop Request," Reuters, September 7, 2010, accessed December 26, 2015, http://www.reuters.com/article/us-afghanistan-usa-nato-idUSTRE6864LC20100908.

10 NATO, "Lisbon Summit Declaration, Issued by the Heads of State and Government Participating in the North Atlantic Council in Lisbon," November 20, 2010, p. 2, accessed August 16, 2014, http://www.nato.int/cps/en/natolive/official_texts_68828.htm.

11 The composition of the JCMB was described on the Kabul Process website: http://www.thekabulprocess.gov.af/index.php/jcmb/background/12-jcmb-background (accessed August 1, 2014). This web site is no longer in existence, but the JCMB terms-of-reference document can be found here: http://mfa.gov.af/Content/files/JCMB_TOR_-_English.pdf (accessed June 28, 2016).

12 Ahmad Rashid. *Decent into Chaos: The U.S. and the Disaster in Pakistan, Afghanistan, and Central Asia.* (New York: Penguin Books, 2009), 103.

13 For more information on the Kabul Bank scandal, see Dexter Filkins, "The Afghan Bank Heist," *New Yorker*, February 14, 2011, accessed February 14, 2011, http://www.newyorker.com/magazine/2011/02/14/the-afghan-bank-heist. This article forced the coalition and the United States to put more pressure on the Afghan government to prosecute those accused of the massive theft and graft.

14 Robert M. Gates, *Duty: Memoirs of a Secretary at War* (New York: Knopf, 2014), 488, 496, 499. 557, 586.

15 Benjamin F. Jones, "Leaving Afghanistan: Transition, Trust, and Definitions" (paper presented at the Society of Military History Annual Meeting, Ottawa, Canada, April 14, 2016), 9, available at https://www.researchgate.net/publication/301348209_Leaving_Afghanistan_Transition_Trust_and_Definitions (accessed October 19, 2016).

16 Ibid., Ivo Daalder, e-mail to author, December 25, 2015.

17 Gates, *Duty*, 556–57.

18 Author's notes from Afghanistan, 2011–2012.

19 US House of Representatives, Committee on Armed Services, "Statement of General David H. Petraeus before the House Armed Services Committee," March 16, 2011, 9–10. See also Thom Shanker, "Petraeus Finishes Rules for Afghanistan Transition," *New York Times*, August 30, 2010, A7.

20 President Karzai, Nowruz address, March 21, 2011, accessed September 4, 2014, http://www.afghanistan-un.org/2011/03/remarks-to-the-nation-by-his-excellency-hamid-karzai-president-of-the-islamic-republic-of-afghanistan-on-the-occasion-of-the-new-afghan-year-1390/.

21 Author's notes from Afghanistan, September 3, 2011.

22 Author's notes from Afghanistan, April 27, 2011.

23 Gates, *Duty*, 564–65. This request stunned some of the ISAF staff, whom General Petraeus had assured the surge recovery would occur slowly, leaving substantial combat power available for two more years.

24 The day before General Petraeus turned his command over to General Allen and left Kabul, he asked the briefer, LTC Bret Van Poppel, whether it was time to consider the Taliban more and more disabled. Van Poppel told him, "We're past that time, sir." Petraeus replied, "Whew—in the nick of time!" Author's notes from Afghanistan, July 2011.

25 Senator Carl Levin (D-MI), "The Way Forward in Afghanistan," Council on Foreign Relations, Washington, DC, October 1, 2010, accessed November 15, 2014, http://www.cfr.org/afghanistan/sen-carl-levin-way-forward-afghanistan/p23075.

26 Jones, "Leaving Afghanistan," 9.

27 Ibid.

28 Lt. Col. Joseph Blevins, e-mail to author, April 8, 2012. See also Ministry of Defense, "Transition in Afghanistan Explained," April 3, 2012, accessed December 12, 2015, https://www.gov.uk/government/news/transition-in-afghanistan-explained.

29 HQ ISAF, "COMISAF's Letter to the Troops," July 18, 2011, accessed October 20, 2014, http://www.isaf.nato.int/article/focus/comisafs-letter-to-the-troops.html.

30 Troop numbers, by country, are listed in NATO, "ISAF: Key Facts and Figures" (also known as the "NATO Placemat"), accessed December 26, 2014, http://www.nato.int/cps/en/natolive/107995.htm.

31 The transition timeline and troop withdrawal numbers are listed in Kenneth Katzman, *Afghanistan: Post-Taliban Governance, Security, and U.S. Policy*, CRS Report RL30588 (Washington, DC, December 2, 2014), 21–22.

32 CERP allowed military commanders to pay Afghans for small, quick-impact projects such as ditch digging, canal cleaning, and low-grade construction.

Meant to gain community buy-in for the coalition presence, the practice was really just one step away from paying young men not to fight the foreigners.

33 The tranche 2 provinces were Herat, Balkh, Samangan, Sar-e Pul, and Nimroz. The tranche also included specific districts in Helmand, Ghazni, Daykundi, Jowzjan, Ghor, Badakshan, Parwan, Wardak, Laghman, Kapisa, and Nangahar.

34 Louisa Brooke-Holland and Claire Taylor, "Afghanistan: The Timetable for Security Transition," Parliament of the United Kingdom, House of Commons Library, Standard Note IA/5851, p. 10.

35 Troop numbers are discussed in Katzman, *Post-Taliban Governance*, 21. Casualties are listed in Livingston and O'Hanlon, figure 1.15, "Causes of Death, by Year," in *Afghanistan Index* (March 31, 2016), 10.

36 Livingston and O'Hanlon, figure 1.12, "Number of Insurgent Attacks, 2008–2013," in *Afghanistan Index* (March 31, 2016), 9.

37 Liana Rosen and Kenneth Katzman *Afghanistan: Drug Trafficking and the 2014 Transition* CRS Report R43540, (Washington, DC, May 9, 2014), 21.

38 Michael Johnson, *Afghanistan: Oversight and Accountability of U.S. Assistance*, GAO Report 14-680T (Washington, DC, June 10, 2014), 4.

39 Casualties are detailed in UNAMA, *Protection of Civilians in Armed Conflict, Annual Report 2012* (Kabul: UNAMA, February 2013), 1.

40 Livingston and O'Hanlon, figure 1.25, "Number of Afghan Asylum Applications, 2001–2013," in *Afghanistan Index* (March 31, 2016), 13.

41 US House of Representatives, House Armed Services Committee, "Statement of General John Allen, Commander US Forces Afghanistan on Developments in Afghanistan," March 20, 2012, 2.

42 Livingston and O'Hanlon, figure 1.13, "Attacks by Afghan Security Forces against Allied Troops," in *Afghanistan Index* (March 31, 2016), 8.

43 Kirk Johnson, "Guilty Plea by Sergeant in Killing of Civilians," *New York Times*, June 5, 2013.

44 International Crisis Group, *Afghanistan's Security after the Transition*, ICG Program Report 256 (Kabul/Brussels: ICG, May 12, 2014), 4.

45 Livingston and O'Hanlon, figure 4.4, "Polling and Public Opinion," in *Afghanistan Index* (March 31, 2016), 22.

46 This description of security in Paktia Province draws heavily from ICG, *Afghanistan's Security after the Transition*, 25–30, 49.

47 Ibid.,18–23, 48. The quotation appears on page 18.

48 Ibid., 35, 38, 37.

49 Department of Defense, *Report on Progress toward Security and Stability in Afghanistan* (Washington, DC: The Pentagon, April 2014), 11, 14.

50 The elections are covered in Department of Defense, *Report on Progress toward Security and Stability in Afghanistan* (Washington, DC: The Pentagon, October 2014), 22. For the details of the 96 meetings, see Rod Norland,

"Afghan Presidential Rivals Finally Agree on Power-Sharing Deal," *New York Times*, September 20, 2014.

51 Sudarsan Raghavan, "Two Americans among 21 Dead in Attacks in Kabul, Other Parts of Afghanistan," *Washington Post*, December 13, 2014.

52 Major General Payenda, e-mail to author, May 11, 2014.

53 Nadar Yama, e-mail to author, April 29, 2014.

54 Robert Ross, former US Central Command, ISAF, and IJC plans officer, e-mail to author, August 16, 2014.

55 These statistics and the quotation from Chief Executive Abdullah are in Sudarsan Raghavan, "A Year of Taliban Gains Shows We Haven't Delivered Top Afghan Official Says," *Washington Post*, December 27, 2015, A10. See also Harleen Gambhir, "ISIS in Afghanistan," *Backgrounder*, December 3, 2015, p. 3, Institute for the Study of War, accessed December 29, 2015, http://www.understandingwar.org/backgrounder/isis-afghanistan-december-3-2015.

56 Gates, *Duty*, 557.

57 Department of Defense, *Report on Progress toward Security and Stability in Afghanistan* (Washington, DC: The Pentagon, October 2014), 26. Various surveys done by ISAF, the Asia Foundation, and others consistently found that the large majority of Afghans did not wish the Taliban to return to power.

58 Adam Gabbit. "G8 Summit at Camp David and NATO Protests in Chicago," *The Guardian*, May 19, 2012, http://www.theguardian.com/world/us-news-blog/2012/may/19/g8-summit-camp-david-nato-chicago.

59 NATO, "Chicago Summit Declaration on Afghanistan," May 21, 2012, accessed October 24 2014, http://www.nato.int/cps/en/natohq/official_texts_87595.htm?.

Conclusion

The views in this chapter are the author's own and do not reflect the policies of the Department of Defense or the United States Government.

1 General John F. Campbell, "ISAF-Resolute Support Transitions Ceremony Address," December 28, 2014, Kabul, Afghanistan, accessed November 20, 2015, http://www.americanrhetoric.com/speeches/johncampbellresolutesupportceremony.htm.

2 Pamela Constable, "NATO Flag Lowered in Afghanistan as Combat Mission Ends," *Washington Post*, December 28, 2015.

3 Department of Defense, *Enhancing Security and Stability in Afghanistan* (Washington, DC: The Pentagon, December 2015), 16–19; Sudarsan Raghavan, "A Year of Taliban Gains Shows We Haven't Delivered Top Afghan Official Says," *Washington Post*, December 27, 2015, A10.

4 DOD, *Enhancing Security*, 18.

5 In 2015, 3,545 Afghan civilians were killed and another 7,457 were wounded—a 4 percent increase over the figures from 2014. See UNAMA, *Afghanistan 2015: Annual Report on Protection of Civilians in Armed Conflict* (Kabul: UNAMA, 2015), 1–3.

6 UNAMA, *Afghanistan 2015*, 23.

7 The UN reports that antigovernment forces caused 62 percent of casualties. Pro-government forces caused another 17 percent, of which 2 percent were caused by international military forces. Another 17 percent were not attributable to any group, and 4 percent were caused by unexploded remnants of war. UNAMA, *Afghanistan 2015*, 4.

8 DOD, *Enhancing Security*, 17–18; Zachary Warren and Nancy Hopkins, eds., *A Survey of the Afghan People: Afghanistan in 2015* (San Francisco: CA: The Asia Foundation, 2015), 7.

9 DOD, *Enhancing Security*, 21.

10 Ibid., 27–28, 70–76.

11 Ibid., 49, 57.

12 Ibid., 12, 36.

13 Ibid., 66, 73.

14 SIGAR, *Quarterly Report to the United States Congress* (Washington, DC, October 2015), 99.

15 Alissa J. Rubin, "For Afghans in Kunduz, Taliban Assault Is Just the Latest Affront," *New York Times*, October 7, 2015, A8.

16 SIGAR, *Afghan Local Police: A Critical Rural Security Initiative Lacks Adequate Logistics Support, Oversight, and Direction*, SIGAR 16-3 Audit Report (Washington, DC, October 2015), 1–8.

17 SIGAR, *Quarterly Report* (October 2015), 178–80; Kenneth Katzman, *Afghanistan: Post-Taliban Governance, Security and U.S. Policy*, CRS Report RL 30588 (Washington, DC, December 22, 2015), 60–61.

18 SIGAR *Quarterly Report* (October 2015), 183.

19 Ibid., 154, 186.

20 Warren and Hopkins, *Afghanistan in 2015*, 11.

21 Ibid., 99–100 (quotation on p. 100).

22 The only countries listed with more corruption in 2014 were North Korea, Somalia, and Sudan. Transparency International, "Corruption Perceptions Index 2014: Results," accessed December 30, 2015, http://www.transparency.org/cpi2014/results.

23 Katzman, *Post-Taliban Governance*, 58, 67. See also Ian S. Livingston and Michael O'Hanlon, figure 3.8, "Health Metrics," in *Afghanistan Index* (Washington, DC: Brookings Institution, November 30, 2015), 23.

24 The direct spending is discussed in Amy Belasco, *The Cost of Iraq, Afghanistan, and Other Global War on Terror Operations since 9/11*, CRS Report RL3310 (Washington, DC, December 8, 2014), 71. For the indirect costs, see

the work of Linda J. Bilmes, cited in Aaron B. O'Connell, "The Lessons and Legacies of the War in Afghanistan," in *Understanding the U.S. Wars in Iraq and Afghanistan*, ed. Beth Bailey and Richard H. Immerman (New York: New York University Press, 2015), 314–15.

25 With 15,865 killed or wounded, the US Army accounted for 71 percent of all casualties in the Afghan War. The Marine Corps' 5,404 casualties compose another 24 percent. Demographic data on casualties are on the Department of Defense's Defense Casualty Analysis System website: http://www.defense.gov/casualty.pdf (accessed January 2, 2016). The military deaths do not include the 1,616 private contractors employed by the US government who were killed in Afghanistan between 2001 and 2015. See Livingston and O'Hanlon, figure 1.19, "Private Contractor Deaths," in *Afghanistan Index* (November 30, 2015), 23.

26 Sir Michael Howard, "The Lessons of History," *The History Teacher* 15, no. 4 (August 1982): 491–92.

27 Ibid., 494–501.

28 President George W. Bush, "Joint Statement by President George W. Bush and Chairman Hamid Karzai on a New Partnership between the United States and Afghanistan," January 28, 2002, accessed August 10, 2015, http://avalon.law.yale.edu/sept11/joint_014.asp.

29 President Obama's war goals are contained in "Remarks by the President in Address to the Nation on the Way Forward in Afghanistan and Pakistan," The White House, December 1, 2009, accessed January 4, 2016, https://www.whitehouse.gov/the-press-office/remarks-president-address-nation-way-forward-afghanistan-and-pakistan. See also Bob Woodward, *Obama's Wars* (New York: Simon & Schuster, 2010), 386.

30 Barnett R. Rubin, *Afghanistan from the Cold War through the War on Terror* (New York: Oxford University Press, 2013), 21.

31 President George W. Bush, remarks at the Virginia Military Institute, April 17, 2002, accessed December 22, 2015, http://transcripts.cnn.com/TRANSCRIPTS/0204/17/se.02.html.

32 Ibid.

33 For Vietnam spending, see "Vietnam Statistics—War Costs: Complete Picture Impossible," *CQ Almanac 1975*, 31st ed. (Washington, DC: Congressional Quarterly, 1976), 301–5. For Afghanistan spending, see Belasco, *Cost of Iraq*, 19. For casualty statistics by year, see the Defense Department's Defense Casualty Analysis System webpage: https://www.dmdc.osd.mil/dcas/pages/casualties.xhtml (accessed December 18, 2015).

34 See David H. Petraeus, "The American Military and the Lessons of Vietnam: A Study of Military Influence and the Use of Force in the Post-Vietnam Era," (PhD diss., Princeton University, 1987); John A. Nagl, *Learning to Eat Soup with a Knife: Counterinsurgency Lessons from Malaya and Vietnam* (Chicago: University of Chicago Press, 2002); Conrad C. Crane, *Avoiding Viet-*

nam: The U.S. Army's Response to Defeat in Southeast Asia (Carlisle, PA: US Army Strategic Studies Institute, 2002).

35 This is a partial list of key scholars cited in the dissertations, articles, and books of General David Petraeus, Conrad C. Crane, and John A. Nagl.

36 *The Pentagon Papers*, IV.A.V, 4.1, cited in Robert W. Komer, *Bureaucracy Does Its Thing: Institutional Constraints on U.S.-GVN Performance in Vietnam* (Santa Monica, CA: RAND, 1972), 43; *The U.S. Army/Marine Corps Counterinsurgency Field Manual* (Chicago: University of Chicago Press, 2006), 298–99.

37 David H. Petraeus, "Lessons of History and Lessons of Vietnam," *Parameters*, August 1986, 54–55; Petraeus, "American Military and the Lessons of Vietnam," 110–33.

38 *Counterinsurgency Field Manual*, 39, 52–77 (quotations from 73).

39 *Counterinsurgency Field Manual*, 51 (quotation), 202–3, 215–17, 270 (quotation).

40 *Counterinsurgency Field Manual*, 67–68 (quotations from 68).

41 Howard, "Lessons of History," 501.

42 This is a major theme in Woodward, *Obama's Wars*.

43 Senator Barack H. Obama, quoted in "Obama Calls Situation in Afghanistan Urgent," CNN, July 21, 2008, accessed December 18, 2015, http://www.cnn.com/2008/POLITICS/07/20/obama.afghanistan.

44 Robert M. Gates, *Duty: Memoirs of a Secretary at War* (New York: Alfred A. Knopf, 2014), 200; Sarah Chayes, *The Punishment of Virtue: Inside Afghanistan after the Taliban* (New York: Penguin Books, 2006), 155. See also Secretary of Defense Donald Rumsfeld's comments to National Security Advisor Stephen Hadley in Hal Brands, *What Good Is Grand Strategy: Power and Purpose in American Statecraft from Harry S. Truman to George W. Bush* (Ithaca, NY: Cornell University Press, 2014), 173. For a rebuttal of the claim that Iraq distracted the Bush administration from Afghanistan, see Donald Rumsfeld, *Known and Unknown: A Memoir* (New York: Sentinel Books, 2011), 681–91.

45 On overspending in Vietnam, see Defense Technical Information Center, *A Study of Strategic Lessons Learned in Vietnam: Omnibus Executive Summary* (Maclean, VA: BDM Corporation, 1980), II-11. On overspending in the First Anglo-Afghan War, see Martin Ewans, *Afghanistan: A Short History of Its People and Politics* (New York: Harper Collins, 2002), 66.

46 Samuel P. Huntington "No More Vietnams," 111, cited in Komer, *Bureaucracy Does Its Thing*, 67.

47 *Counterinsurgency Field Manual*, 270.

About the Contributors

Dr. Aaron B. O'Connell is a lieutenant colonel in the US Marine Corps Reserve and served in Afghanistan from 2010 to 2011 as a special advisor to General David H. Petraeus. He holds a PhD in history from Yale University and is the author of *Underdogs: The Making of the Modern Marine Corps* (Harvard University Press, 2012). A former associate professor of American history at the US Naval Academy in Annapolis, Maryland, he has written articles on military culture for the *New York Times*, the *Chronicle of Higher Education*, and numerous other journals and publications.

Ambassador Ronald E. Neumann served as the US ambassador to Afghanistan from 2005 to 2007, a position his father, Robert G. Neumann, also held from 1966 to 1973. A career foreign service officer, Ambassador Neumann also served as the deputy assistant secretary of state for Near Eastern Affairs and as ambassador to Bahrain and to Algeria. A veteran of the Vietnam War, he is now the president of the American Academy of Diplomacy in Washington, DC, and is the author of *The Other War: Winning and Losing in Afghanistan* (Potomac Books, 2009).

Dr. Colin Jackson is a lieutenant colonel in the US Army Reserve and an associate professor of strategy and policy at the US Naval War College in Newport, Rhode Island. He holds a PhD in political science from the Massachusetts Institute of Technology and other advanced degrees from the University of Pennsylvania and the Johns Hopkins School of Advanced International Studies. In July 2009, Dr. Jackson served as a senior civilian advisor to Task Force Mountain Warrior in Jalalabad, Afghanistan, and in 2011, he served in uniform in Afghanistan as the executive officer for policy planning for the ISAF deputy chief of staff of operations.

Dr. Martin Loicano is chief of the Historical Office at Supreme Headquarters Allied Powers Europe and was previously associate professor in the Department of Strategy at the Air War College. He holds a PhD in history from Cornell University, and from 2010 to 2012, he served in the NATO Training Mission-Afghanistan. He is the coauthor (with Captain Craig C. Felker) of *No Moment of Victory, the NATO Training Mission in Afghanistan*, which is forthcoming from Texas A&M University Press.

Dr. Craig C. Felker is the former chair of the History Department at the US Naval Academy in Annapolis, Maryland, and a retired US Navy captain. He holds a PhD in history from Duke University and is the author of *Testing American Sea Power: U.S. Navy Exercises, 1923–1940* (Texas A&M, 2006). From 2010 to 2011, he served as command historian for the NATO Training Mission-Afghanistan in Kabul, Afghanistan.

Pashtoon Atif was born and raised in Kandahar, Afghanistan. A former captain in the Afghan National Police, he has also worked for the United Nations Development Program in Afghanistan and Sudan. He holds a BA in international relations from Tufts University and is currently a graduate student at the Blavatnik School of Government at the University of Oxford.

Jamie Lynn De Coster is a lieutenant commander in the US Naval Reserve and a PhD candidate at Tufts University's Fletcher School of Law and Diplomacy. From 2010 to 2011, she served as a special advisor to General David H. Petraeus in Afghanistan, primarily on matters of governance and development. An adjunct professor at American University School of International Service, she has written for the *New York Times*, *World Politics Review*, and the *Fletcher Forum of World Affairs*.

Dr. Abigail T. Linnington is a colonel in the United States Army. She holds a master's degree and a PhD in international relations from Tufts University's Fletcher School of Law and Diplomacy and an undergraduate degree in international relations from the United States Military Academy. From 2010 to 2011, she served as an advisor to the commander of Combined Joint Interagency Task Force-435 (Rule of Law) in Afghanistan.

Dr. Rebecca D. Patterson is a lieutenant colonel in the United States Army, a military advisor in the International Organizations Bureau at the US Department of State, and an adjunct professor at the Elliott School of International Affairs at George Washington University. She holds a PhD in national security policy from George Washington University and an undergraduate degree in economics from the United States Military Academy. She is the author of *The Challenge of Nation-Building: Implementing Effective Innovation in the U.S. Army from World War II to the Iraq War* (Rowman and Littlefield, 2014). From 2011 to 2012, she served as a strategic advisor to the ISAF commander in Kabul, Afghanistan.

Aaron MacLean holds a master's degree in medieval Arabic thought from the University of Oxford and a BA in philosophy and the history of math and science from St. Johns College in Annapolis, Maryland.

A Marshall Scholar, he worked as a journalist in Cairo, Egypt, before joining the Marine Corps in 2007. He was awarded the Bronze Star with valor device for his actions in the 2010 Battle of Marjah and left active duty as a captain in 2014. He is now the managing editor of the *Washington Free Beacon.*

Dr. Daniel R. Green is a lieutenant commander in the US Naval Reserve and a Defense Fellow at the Washington Institute for Near East Policy. He holds a PhD in political science from George Washington University and has deployed several times to Iraq and Afghanistan as both a civilian and a mobilized military reservist. Dr. Green is the author of *The Valley's Edge: A Year with the Pashtuns in the Heartland of the Taliban* (Potomac Books, 2011) and the coauthor, with Brigadier General William F. Mullen III, USMC, of *Fallujah Redux: The Anbar Awakening and the Struggle with Al Qaeda* (Naval Institute Press, 2014). His next book, *In the Warlord's Shadow: Special Operations Forces, the Afghans, and Their Fight with the Taliban,* will be published in July 2017 by the Naval Institute Press.

Dr. Benjamin F. Jones is the dean of the College of Arts and Sciences at Dakota State University and a lieutenant colonel (retired) in the United States Air Force. During his 23-year career in the Air Force, Lieutenant Colonel Jones served in Afghanistan twice, first as an advisor at the National Military Academy of Afghanistan in 2009, and later as a member of the Strategic Transition and Assessment Group from 2011 to 2012. Dr. Jones holds a PhD in history from the University of Kansas, and his book, *Eisenhower's Guerrillas: The Jedburghs, the Maquis, and the Liberation of France,* was published in 2016 by Oxford University Press.